This book comes with access to more content online.
Quiz yourself, take sample tests, and score high on test day!

Register your book or ebook at
www.dummies.com/go/getaccess.

Select your product, and then follow the prompts to validate your purchase.

You'll receive an email with your PIN and instructions.

ACT® Prep 2026/2027

by Lisa Zimmer Hatch, MA and
Scott A. Hatch, JD

ACT® Prep 2026/2027 For Dummies®

Published by: **John Wiley & Sons, Inc.**, 111 River Street, Hoboken, NJ 07030-5774, www.wiley.com

Copyright © 2025 by John Wiley & Sons, Inc. All rights reserved, including rights for text and data mining and training of artificial technologies or similar technologies.

Media and software compilation copyright © 2025 by John Wiley & Sons, Inc. All rights reserved, including rights for text and data mining and training of artificial technologies or similar technologies.

Published simultaneously in Canada

No part of this publication may be reproduced, stored in a retrieval system or transmitted in any form or by any means, electronic, mechanical, photocopying, recording, scanning or otherwise, except as permitted under Sections 107 or 108 of the 1976 United States Copyright Act, without the prior written permission of the Publisher or authorization through payment of the appropriate per-copy fee to the Copyright Clearance Center, Inc., 222 Rosewood Drive, Danvers, MA 01923, (978) 750-8400, fax (978) 750-4470, or on the web at www.copyright.com. Requests to the Publisher for permission should be addressed to the Permissions Department, John Wiley & Sons, Inc., 111 River Street, Hoboken, NJ 07030, (201) 748-6011, fax (201) 748-6008, or online at http://www.wiley.com/go/permissions.

The manufacturer's authorized representative according to the EU General Product Safety Regulation is Wiley-VCH GmbH, Boschstr. 12, 69469 Weinheim, Germany, e-mail: Product_Safety@wiley.com.

Trademarks: Wiley, For Dummies, the Dummies Man logo, Dummies.com, Making Everything Easier, and related trade dress are trademarks or registered trademarks of John Wiley & Sons, Inc. and may not be used without written permission. ACT is a registered trademark of ACT Education Corp. All other trademarks are the property of their respective owners. John Wiley & Sons, Inc. is not associated with any product or vendor mentioned in this book.

LIMIT OF LIABILITY/DISCLAIMER OF WARRANTY: THE PUBLISHER AND THE AUTHORS MAKE NO REPRESENTATIONS OR WARRANTIES WITH RESPECT TO THE ACCURACY OR COMPLETENESS OF THE CONTENTS OF THIS WORK AND SPECIFICALLY DISCLAIM ALL WARRANTIES, INCLUDING WITHOUT LIMITATION WARRANTIES OF FITNESS FOR A PARTICULAR PURPOSE. NO WARRANTY MAY BE CREATED OR EXTENDED BY SALES OR PROMOTIONAL MATERIALS. THE ADVICE AND STRATEGIES CONTAINED HEREIN MAY NOT BE SUITABLE FOR EVERY SITUATION. THIS WORK IS SOLD WITH THE UNDERSTANDING THAT THE PUBLISHER IS NOT ENGAGED IN RENDERING LEGAL, ACCOUNTING, OR OTHER PROFESSIONAL SERVICES. IF PROFESSIONAL ASSISTANCE IS REQUIRED, THE SERVICES OF A COMPETENT PROFESSIONAL PERSON SHOULD BE SOUGHT. NEITHER THE PUBLISHER NOR THE AUTHORS SHALL BE LIABLE FOR DAMAGES ARISING HEREFROM. THE FACT THAT AN ORGANIZATION OR WEBSITE IS REFERRED TO IN THIS WORK AS A CITATION AND/OR A POTENTIAL SOURCE OF FURTHER INFORMATION DOES NOT MEAN THAT THE AUTHOR OR THE PUBLISHER ENDORSES THE INFORMATION THE ORGANIZATION OR WEBSITE MAY PROVIDE OR RECOMMENDATIONS IT MAY MAKE. FURTHER, READERS SHOULD BE AWARE THAT INTERNET WEBSITES LISTED IN THIS WORK MAY HAVE CHANGED OR DISAPPEARED BETWEEN WHEN

For general information on our other products and services, please contact our Customer Care Department within the U.S. at 877-762-2974, outside the U.S. at 317-572-3993, or fax 317-572-4002. For technical support, please visit https://hub.wiley.com/community/support/dummies.

Wiley publishes in a variety of print and electronic formats and by print-on-demand. Some material included with standard print versions of this book may not be included in e-books or in print-on-demand. If this book refers to media that is not included in the version you purchased, you may download this material at http://booksupport.wiley.com. For more information about Wiley products, visit www.wiley.com.

Library of Congress Control Number: 2025940161

ISBN 978-1-394-35134-3 (pbk); ISBN 978-1-394-35136-7 (ebk); ISBN 978-1-394-35135-0 (ebk)

SKY10120018_063025

Contents at a Glance

Introduction 1

Part 1: Coming to Terms with Reality: An Overview of the ACT 7
CHAPTER 1: Getting Your ACT Together: ACT 101 9
CHAPTER 2: Succeeding on the ACT 17
CHAPTER 3: Forming an ACT Study Plan 21

Part 2: Serving Your "Sentence": The English Test 27
CHAPTER 4: Mastering the English Test 29
CHAPTER 5: Getting a Grip on Grammar and Usage 35
CHAPTER 6: Spotting Usage Errors and Ripping through Rhetorical Questions 45
CHAPTER 7: It's Not What You Say but How You Say It: English Practice Questions ... 61

Part 3: Don't Count Yourself Out: The Math Test 69
CHAPTER 8: Numbers Nuts and Bolts 71
CHAPTER 9: Getting into Shapes: Geometry and Trig Review 95
CHAPTER 10: Algebra and Other Sleeping Aids 123
CHAPTER 11: Numb and Number: Acing the Mathematics Test 149
CHAPTER 12: More Fun than a Root Canal: Mathematics Practice Questions 159

Part 4: Time to Read the Riot ACT: The Reading Test 167
CHAPTER 13: This, Too, Shall Pass(age): Sailing through the Reading Test 169
CHAPTER 14: Where Are SparkNotes When You Need Them? Reading Practice Questions ... 179

Part 5: Studying Brain Defects in Laboratory Rats: The (Optional) Science Test ... 185
CHAPTER 15: From Frankenstein to Einstein: Excelling on the Optional Science Test ... 187
CHAPTER 16: Faking Atomic Ache Won't Get You out of This: Science Practice Questions ... 209

Part 6: Writing Rightly: The Optional Writing Test 219
CHAPTER 17: Excelling on Your Essay: The Writing Test Review 221
CHAPTER 18: Practicing Promptly with Practice Prompts: Essay Practice Questions ... 239

Part 7: Putting It All Together with a Full-Length Practice ACT 243
CHAPTER 19: Practice Exam 245
CHAPTER 20: Practice Exam: Answers and Explanations 287

Part 8: The Part of Tens 321
CHAPTER 21: Ten Wrong Rumors about the ACT 323
CHAPTER 22: Ten (or So) Ways You Can Help Your Child Succeed on the ACT 327

Index 329

Table of Contents

INTRODUCTION 1
    About This Book 1
    Foolish Assumptions 2
    Icons Used in This Book 3
    Beyond the Book 3
    Where to Go from Here 4
    Figuring Out How Long All This Studying Will Take 5

PART 1: COMING TO TERMS WITH REALITY: AN OVERVIEW OF THE ACT 7

CHAPTER 1: Getting Your ACT Together: ACT 101 9
    What to Take to the ACT 10
    What Not to Take to the ACT 11
    What to Do If You Have Special Circumstances 11
    Guessing for Points to Maximize Your Score 12
    Your Number's Up: Scoring on the ACT 12
    What the ACT Expects You to Know 13
    Repeating the Test for a Better Score 14

CHAPTER 2: Succeeding on the ACT 17
    Surviving the ACT with Four Stress-Busters 17
        Inhaling deeply 17
        Stretching a little 18
        Thinking positive thoughts 18
        Practicing POE 18
    Avoiding a Few Dumb Mistakes That Can Mess Up Your ACT 18
        Losing concentration 19
        Panicking over time 19
        Messing up on the paper test answer grid 19
        Rubbernecking 19
        Cheating 20
        Worrying about previous sections 20
        Worrying about the hard problems 20
        Forgetting to double-check 20

CHAPTER 3: Forming an ACT Study Plan 21
    When to Take the ACT 21
    Planning Your Study Time for Maximum Success 22
        If you have six months to prepare 23
        If you have six weeks to prepare 24
        If you have three weeks to prepare 25

PART 2: SERVING YOUR "SENTENCE": THE ENGLISH TEST.........27

CHAPTER 4: Mastering the English Test..........29
Figuring Out What the English Questions Want You to Know...........29
Seeing Is Believing: The Test's Format..........30
    The passages..........30
    The question types..........30
Their Pain, Your Gain: Looking Out for Traps That Others Fall into..........32

CHAPTER 5: Getting a Grip on Grammar and Usage..........35
Reviewing the Parts of Speech..........36
    Getting in the action with verbs..........36
    Identifying the culprit with nouns..........37
    Avoiding repeating yourself with pronouns..........37
    Defining nouns with adjectives..........37
    Clarifying the questions with adverbs..........37
    Joining together with conjunctions and prepositions..........38
Piecing Together the Parts of a Sentence..........38
    Subjects and predicates..........38
    Phrases and clauses..........39
Keeping Track of Punctuation Rules for Every Occasion..........39
    Periods and question marks..........39
    Semicolons..........40
    Colons..........40
    Commas..........40
    Dashes..........42
    Apostrophes..........43

CHAPTER 6: Spotting Usage Errors and Ripping through Rhetorical Questions..........45
Spotting Questions That Test Standard English (Grammar) Conventions..........45
    Properly placing punctuation marks..........45
    Picking up on pronoun errors..........49
    Forming possessives..........50
    Evaluating verbs..........51
    Calling out sentence fragments..........52
    Identifying problems with parallelism..........52
    Recognizing misplaced modifiers..........52
Checking for Proper Production of Writing..........53
    Eliminating superfluous words..........54
    Completing the mission..........54
    Determining the function of a deletion..........55
    Pondering an addition..........55
    Creating smooth transitions..........56
    Organizing and positioning elements..........57
    Seeing the big picture..........57
    Sticking to appropriate vocabulary and standard expressions..........57

CHAPTER 7: It's Not What You Say but How You Say It: English Practice Questions..........61

PART 3: DON'T COUNT YOURSELF OUT: THE MATH TEST 69

CHAPTER 8: Numbers Nuts and Bolts 71
The Wonderful World of Numbers 71
    Keeping it real: Types of numbers 72
    Lining things up along the number line 73
    Understanding absolute value 73
    Getting familiar with prime numbers and factorization 73

Minor Surgery: Basic Math Operations 75
    Adding and subtracting 75
    Multiplying and dividing 75
    Working with odds/evens and positives/negatives 75

Focusing on Fractions, Decimals, and Percentages 76
    Converting fractions, decimals, and percentages 76
    Working with fractions 77
    Pondering percentages 79

Eyeing Ratios and Proportions 80
    Ratios 80
    Proportions 81

Covering Your Bases: Exponents 82
Smooth Operator: Order of Operations 83
Dealing with Average, Median, Mode, and More 84
    Doing better than average on averages 84
    Weighing in on weighted averages 85
    Mastering medians 85
    Managing modes 85
    Getting ready for range 86

Abracadabra: Elementary Algebra 86
    Variables 101 86
    Solving simple equations 87
    Adding and subtracting expressions 88
    Multiplying and dividing expressions 88
    Curses! FOILed again 89
    Extracting by factoring 90
    Solving a system of equations 91

CHAPTER 9: Getting into Shapes: Geometry and Trig Review 95
Toeing the Line 95
Analyzing Angles 96
Triangle Trauma 99
    Classifying triangles 99
    Sizing up triangles 99
    Zeroing in on similar triangles 100
    Figuring out area and perimeter 101
    Taking the shortcut: Pythagorean triples and other common side ratios 102

Thanks 4 Nothing: A Quick Look at Quadrilaterals 104
Missing Parrots and Other Polly-Gones (Or Should We Say "Polygons"?) 107
    Measuring up polygons 107
    Solving for volume 108

Running Around in Circles 109

Trying Your Hand at Trigonometry..115
    Introducing trigonometric functions.......................................115
    Circumventing the unit circle..117
    Measuring in radians..118
    Graphing trig functions on a coordinate plane....................119
    Applying the Law of Sines and Law of Cosines...................121

CHAPTER 10: Algebra and Other Sleeping Aids..............................123

Suffering Inequalities..123
Using Your Imagination: Complex Numbers..............................125
Too Hip to Be Square: Roots and Radicals..................................126
    Adding and subtracting radicals..126
    Multiplying and dividing radicals...127
Thinking Exponentially: Logarithms...128
    Log rules...128
    Natural logarithms...128
Barely Functioning with Functions...129
Taking a Flight on the Coordinate Plane....................................130
    Defining the coordinate plane...130
    Knowing which formulas you need to guide your flight.....131
    Graphing more functions..133
    Evaluating graphs of functions..137
Picking Your Way through Percent Increase, Probability, Permutations, and Combinations..139
    Managing the ups and downs...139
    Practicing probability..140
    Calculating outcomes and orderings..................................142
Setting Up Sequences...145
Managing Matrices...146

CHAPTER 11: Numb and Number: Acing the Mathematics Test..............149

What You See Is What You Get: The Format and Breakdown of the Math Test.....149
Absence Makes the Heart Grow Fonder: What Isn't on the Math Test............150
Getting into the Grind: The Approach..150
Translating English into Math...152
Time Flies When You're Having Fun: Timing Tips.......................153
    Skim for your favorite questions...153
    Backsolve when the answers are actual values..................154
    Plug in values for variables..155
    Kindly refrain from showing off everything you know......156
    Put aside two minutes to fill in the remaining ovals..........156
Do's, Don'ts, and Darns: What to Do and Not Do on the Math Test............156
    Do get the lead out..156
    Don't start working until you've read the entire problem...157
    Do reread the problem with your answer inserted............157
    Don't strike out over a difficult question early on..............157

CHAPTER 12: More Fun than a Root Canal: Mathematics Practice Questions..............159

PART 4: TIME TO READ THE RIOT ACT: THE READING TEST 167

CHAPTER 13: This, Too, Shall Pass(age): Sailing through the Reading Test 169
Facing 36 Questions: The Reading Test 169
  Timing 170
  Scoring 170
Getting Prepared: Reading Test Strategies 170
  Approach passages efficiently 170
  Skim the passage effectively 172
  Skip a passage if necessary 173
Identifying Reading Question Types and Formats 174
  Find key ideas and details 174
  Determine craft and structure 176
  Integrate knowledge and ideas 177
Approaching Comparative Passages 178

CHAPTER 14: Where Are SparkNotes When You Need Them? Reading Practice Questions 179

PART 5: STUDYING BRAIN DEFECTS IN LABORATORY RATS: THE (OPTIONAL) SCIENCE TEST 185

CHAPTER 15: From Frankenstein to Einstein: Excelling on the Optional Science Test 187
Examining the Science Test's Format 188
Classifying Passage Format 188
  Data-representation passages 189
  Research summaries 189
  Conflicting viewpoints 191
Analyzing Tables, Graphs, and Diagrams 193
  Tackling tables 193
  Grappling with graphs 194
  Dissecting diagrams 194
Examining Experimental Procedures 195
  Independent and dependent variables 196
  The control 196
Immersing Yourself in Answer Choices 197
Considering Question Types 198
  Questions about results 199
  Questions about procedure 202
  Questions about viewpoints 206

CHAPTER 16: Faking Atomic Ache Won't Get You out of This: Science Practice Questions 209
Passage 210
Initial Analysis 211
Questions 211

Table of Contents **xi**

PART 6: WRITING RIGHTLY: THE OPTIONAL WRITING TEST 219

CHAPTER 17: Excelling on Your Essay: The Writing Test Review 221
What to Expect From the ACT Writing Test 221
Making the Grade: How the ACT Folks Score Your Essay 222
Examining the Prompt and Creating a Thesis...222
Putting Up Your Dukes: Defending Your Perspective 224
Throwing a Good First Punch: The Hook 224
The Proof Is in the Pudding: Defending Yourself 225
    Using specific examples..225
    Mixing things up with a variety of examples......................................226
    Forming logical arguments..226
Hamburger Writing: Organizing Your Essay 228
    The top bun: Introduction 228
    The three meats: Example paragraphs 228
    The lettuce, tomato, and special sauce: Transitions.......................229
    The bottom bun: Conclusion 230
Wielding the Red Pen: Editing and Proofing 230
    Using the touch method to look for spelling mistakes and ghost words 230
    Calling all action verbs: Be descriptive 230
    Avoiding problems with punk-tu-a-tion: Punctuate properly 231
    Handwriting check: Write legibly...231
Writing Don'ts...231
    Writing before you think..231
    Panicking about time..231
    Referring to the perspectives by number 232
    Sticking to the status quo...232
    Using words you don't know 232
    Being overly critical of yourself 233
    Writing like you speak..233
    Repeating yourself over and over again..233
    Failing to edit your essay 233
Reviewing Some Example Essays and Their Scores 233
    1 — 1 is the loneliest number: How not to be a 1.............................234
    2 — 2 little 2 late: Steering clear of coming in second 234
    3 — Still finding yourself on the wrong side of the tracks.............234
    4 — Reaching 4 a better score..235
    5 — Shining brightly: A 5-star winner 236
    6 — Unlocking the code to a perfect score 237

CHAPTER 18: Practicing Promptly with Practice Prompts: Essay Practice Questions 239
Writing Prompt 1..239
Writing Prompt 2..241

PART 7: PUTTING IT ALL TOGETHER WITH A FULL-LENGTH PRACTICE ACT 243

CHAPTER 19: Practice Exam 245
Answer Sheet..246
English Test..248
Mathematics Test...257
Reading Test..264
Science Test (Optional)...273
Writing Test..285

CHAPTER 20: Practice Exam: Answers and Explanations 287
    English Test. 287
    Mathematics Test 295
    Reading Test. 305
    Science Test 311
    Writing Test. 317
        Sample response 317
    Score One for Your Side: Evaluating Your Test Results 318

PART 8: THE PART OF TENS 321

CHAPTER 21: Ten Wrong Rumors about the ACT 323
    You Can't Study for the ACT 323
    Different States Have Different ACTs 323
    The ACT Has a Passing Score 324
    The ACT Tests IQ 324
    You Should Never Guess on the ACT 324
    The ACT Is Adaptive Like the SAT 324
    The ACT Is Easier Than the SAT 325
    Selective Colleges Prefer the SAT to the ACT. 325
    You Have to Write an Essay 325
    You Have to Know A Lot about Science for the ACT 325

CHAPTER 22: Ten (or So) Ways You Can Help Your Child Succeed on the ACT 327
    Give Awesome Test-Prep Materials 327
    Encourage Studying. 327
    Supply a Good Study Environment 327
    Take Practice Tests Together 328
    Model Good Grammar 328
    Help Memorize Math Formulas. 328
    Encourage Reading 328
    Explore Colleges Together 328
    Arrive at the Test Site on Time. 328

INDEX 329

Introduction

Welcome to *ACT Prep 2026/2027 For Dummies*. This is a nondiscriminatory, equal-opportunity book. You're welcome to participate whether you're a genius or (like us) you need a recipe to make ice. Besides, the book's title is not a slam at you. You're not the dummy; the test is (and we've heard it called worse, believe us — especially on the Friday night before the exam).

The goal of this book is to show you exactly how to survive the ridiculous situation called the ACT. No matter how excellent your high school teachers are (or were), they've prepared you for the real world, a world that, alas, has very little connection to the ACT. High school teachers can give you a good foundation in grammar, reading, math, science, and writing skills (the areas tested on the ACT), but you may want to think of them as the friendly old GPs, the general practitioners whose job it is to keep you well and handle the little day-to-day problems. What do you do when you have a crisis, like the ACT, that's making you really sick? We like to think of *ACT Prep 2026/2027 For Dummies*, as a loony but gifted specialist you can call when your situation becomes desperate.

No one wants to deal with the eccentric specialist for too terribly long. The goal of this book, just like the goal of the expert, is to come in with the Code Blue crash cart, deal with the situation, and then leave rapidly with as few lives destroyed as possible. This book has one goal: to prepare you for the ACT — period. We're not here to teach you every grammar rule ever created or every math formula that Einstein knew. We don't include any extra "filler" material to make this book look fat and impressive on bookstore shelves. If you want a thick book to use as a booster seat for the vertically challenged, go find *War and Peace*. If you're looking for something that you can use to prepare you for the ACT as quickly and painlessly as possible, again, we say to you, welcome to *ACT Prep 2026/2027 For Dummies*.

About This Book

You likely have to at least consider taking the ACT. Many colleges expect (but don't require) you to take an entrance exam as a component of your application. Virtually every college accepts scores from either the ACT or the SAT. (Wiley just so happens to publish *Digital SAT Prep For Dummies* as well, should you choose to take that exam.) Many students decide to take both tests to see which one results in a better score. Is that a good idea? Absolutely. Even better, take practice tests for both (you can download a free full-length ACT from www.act.org and access six complete SATs from www.collegeboard.org) to see which one suits you best and then concentrate on just that test.

Many colleges emphasize ACT scores to compensate for grade inflation. That is, some high schools may give you an A for doing the same level of work that would gain you a C at other high schools. Because the ACT is the same for everyone (students all over the world take the exact same exam), colleges can use the scores to get inside your head and see what's really there. Think of this test as an opportunity, not a crisis: A good ACT score may help offset a low GPA. In just a few hours, one fine Saturday morning, you can make up a little for a few mishaps in school.

In *ACT Prep 2026/2027 For Dummies*, you find out what types of questions are on the exam, which questions you should work on carefully, and which ones you're better off guessing at quickly. (Good news: The ACT has no penalty for wrong answers, so guess on absolutely every question you don't know.) We also help you figure out which approach to use for each type of question, and, perhaps most importantly, we show you some traps that are built into each question style. We've been test-prep tutors for many years and have developed a list of the "gotchas" that have trapped thousands of students over the years. We show you how to avoid being trapped, too.

This book is also full of the substantive information that you need to know, including grammar rules, geometry, algebra, and arithmetic formulas. And this edition has been updated to reflect the recent enhancements to the ACT. We add information throughout about the scoring changes and other modifications to the ACT as of April 2025, and the practice tests match the multiple-choice sections' new formats and timing. Occasionally, we include some truly sick humor on the principle that, as you're groaning at our jokes, you won't notice that you're suffering from the questions. (Hey, as the mushroom said to his friends, "Of course, everyone likes me. I'm a fun-gi!")

Note to nontraditional students: The days of high school may be just a fading memory for you (along with your thin waistline and full head of hair). We recognize that not everyone taking the ACT is a high school junior or senior. Maybe you took a few years off to build your career or to nurture a family (or to pay your debt to society) and are now having to go back and review what you thought you had left behind years ago. It can be totally frustrating to have to deal with proper punctuation or quadratic equations all over again. Postpone your nervous breakdown. Things aren't as dismal as they look. You'll probably be surprised how quickly material comes back to you as you go through this book.

Foolish Assumptions

Although you could've picked up this book just because you have an insatiable love for English, math, reading, and science, we're betting you picked it up because you need to take the ACT. (Isn't it good to know at the outset that your authors have a remarkable grasp of the obvious?) And because we weren't born yesterday, we figure that you're taking the ACT in anticipation of applying to college. How exciting for you!

Because we've rarely met a person who actually looks forward to taking standardized entrance exams, we're lumping you into the category of "readers who are going into the ACT kicking and screaming." Okay, maybe we're being overly dramatic, but we've got a hunch that you're not especially excited about the prospect of spending four hours of precious sleeping-in time sitting in a stark classroom, darkening endless ovals on a bubble sheet under the watchful eye of a heartless proctor who continues to yell "Time!" before you've finished the section. Call us crazy!

Nevertheless, you picked up this book, so we assume that getting the best ACT score you can is important to you and that you care enough to sacrifice some of your free time to achieve that goal. Good for you!

Here are the other assumptions we've made about you while writing this book:

>> You're a high school student, and, like most high school students, you carry a full course load, participate in a number of extracurricular activities, may even have a job, and prefer to carry on a social life. Or you may have already graduated from high school and may hold down a career and tend to a family. Either way, you don't want us to waste your time with a bunch of stuff that isn't on the ACT. For instance, as much as we enjoy creating vocabulary flashcards,

we don't share those with you in this book because you don't need to memorize word meanings to ace the ACT.

» You're not all work and no play. We want to make studying for the ACT as painless as possible, so we've tried to lighten things up a bit with a few jokes. Forgive us, please. Some are really lame.

» Because you're college-bound, you've spent some years engaged in a college-prep curriculum that includes algebra, geometry, and likely a little algebra II and trigonometry. We're pretty sure you've had your fair share of English, social studies, and science classes, and you've written an essay or two. Therefore, we don't bore you too much with the elementary stuff. (We do, however, cover the basic math and grammar concepts that you may have forgotten.)

Icons Used in This Book

Some information in this book is really, really important. We flag it by using an icon. Here's a list of the icons we use and details about what they mean:

TIP

Follow the arrow to score a bull's-eye by using the tips we highlight with this icon.

REMEMBER

Burn this stuff into your brain or carve it into your heart; it's the really important material. If you skip or ignore the Remember icons, you won't get your money's worth out of this book.

EXAMPLE

This icon marks sample problems.

WARNING

Pay heed to this advice and avoid the potential pitfall.

Beyond the Book

In addition to what you're reading right now, this book comes with a free access-anywhere Cheat Sheet that includes tips to help you prepare for the ACT. To get this Cheat Sheet, simply go to www.dummies.com and type **"ACT For Dummies Cheat Sheet"** in the Search box.

You also get access to all the full-length online practice tests, more than 100 math and science flashcards, and extra resources for understanding your scores for the test (including the essay!). To gain access to the online practice, all you have to do is register. Just follow these simple steps:

1. **Register your book or e-book at** Dummies.com **to get your pin.**

   Go to www.dummies.com/go/getaccess.

2. **Select your product from the dropdown list on that page.**

Introduction 3

3. **Follow the prompts to validate your product, and then check your email for a confirmation message that includes your PIN and log-in instructions.**

    If you don't receive this email within two hours, check your spam folder before contacting us through our Technical Support website at http://support.wiley.com or by phone at 877-762-2974.

Now you're ready to go! You can come back to the practice material as often as you want — simply log on with the username and password you created during your initial login. No need to enter the access code a second time.

Your registration is good for one year from the day you activate your PIN.

Where to Go from Here

You've probably heard the joke about the student who was debating whether to buy a book at the bookstore. The sales clerk, eager to make his commission, proclaims, "Buy this book — it'll do half the work for you!" The student brightens up and exclaims, "Great! I'll take two!"

As much as we wish we could simply transfer test-taking material into your brain in one dump, we realize that learning it takes effort on your part. Meet us halfway. We've done our job by showing you what to study and how to go about it; now it's your turn. We suggest two ways to use this book:

- **Fine-tune your skills.** Maybe you're already a math whiz and just need help with the English grammar. Go right to the English review we provide in Part 2. If, on the other hand, you're a grammar guru who wouldn't know a nonagon if you met one in a dark alley, turn to the math review we offer in Part 3.

- **Start from scratch.** Grab a sack of food and some sharpened pencils, lock yourself in your room, and go through this book word for word. Don't worry; it's not as bad as it seems. Actually, starting from scratch is the preferred method. Many students make what we call the "mediocre mistake": They're good at one section, mediocre at a second, and dismal at another. They spend all their time in their worst section and barely look at the sections that they're mediocre or good in. Big mistake! If you spend two hours studying something that's totally incomprehensible to you, you may improve your score a few points. If you spend two hours studying your mediocre material, you may improve your score by one or two points. A couple of points that you gain in your mediocre section are just as valuable as — and a heck of a lot easier to get than — the same number of points you gain in your weakest section. Humor us and read the book from cover to cover. You'll pick up some great material.

Regardless of whether you hunt and peck your way through the chapters or approach the first six parts consecutively, absolutely take the practice test in Part 7. How you choose to use the full-length practice test is entirely up to you. However, may we suggest two tried-and-true methods?

- **Diagnostic:** Take the first practice exam to see how you score. Then, devour the subject reviews and advice we provide in the first six parts of the book. Finish by taking the online practice tests to see how much your score has improved.

- **Pure practice:** Devour the reviews and advice first and use the full-length exams (in the book and online) to practice and reinforce what you've learned in the rest of the book.

Either way, you should also get your hands on the current edition of *The Official ACT Prep Guide* (John Wiley & Sons, Inc.) and visit act.org, the ACT's official website, for more resources. The official exams in the book give you ample opportunity to practice what you discover in *ACT Prep 2026/2027 For Dummies* so that you can walk into the test site with the test questions fresh in your brain, and the website contains free practice questions for the online format, a practice test booklet to download to study for the paper test, and loads of other information about the ACT and how to prepare for it.

After you've covered the information in this book, you may discover that you need more in-depth English or math review. Or maybe you just can't get enough of this stuff! Several Wiley publications are available to accommodate you; just search for the most recent editions. Dig more deeply into the rules of Standard English in the latest editions of *English Grammar For Dummies* and find tons of grammar practice in the *English Grammar Workbook For Dummies*, both by Geraldine Woods. Those of you who are math challenged will find the latest editions of these books helpful: *ACT Math Prep For Dummies* and *Digital SAT Math Prep For Dummies* by Mark Zegarelli; *Algebra I For Dummies* and *Algebra II For Dummies* by Mary Jane Sterling; and *Geometry For Dummies* by Mark Ryan (all by John Wiley & Sons, Inc.).

Figuring Out How Long All This Studying Will Take

In the real world, you have classes, family obligations, community service projects, sports practices, work, and, if you're lucky, a social life. How on earth are you going to fit reviewing this book and studying for the ACT into your schedule? The answer is that you have to commit to this project and make it a priority. How many hours should you carve out of your schedule? Here's what we suggest.

Reading the ACT overview in the first three chapters shouldn't cut out too much of your free time, no more than 30 minutes. Other parts require more of an investment.

The five parts of the book that review English, math, writing, reading, and science contain one or more chapters that explain how to approach the subject at hand and one short chapter full of practice questions. Soaking up the information in the explanations and taking the short practice tests should take you about an hour or two per test subject.

Additionally, the English Test part features a very important grammar review that we strongly suggest you spend at least an hour or two studying. Even if you're good at grammar, this section features all sorts of persnickety grammar rules, just the type that (with your luck) you'd get caught on during the ACT. Finally, the Math Test part features a pretty comprehensive math review — number basics, geometry, algebra, coordinate geometry, and trigonometry — that should take you about three hours to fully absorb.

And don't forget the full-length practice tests, of course — one in this book and more online. Each of the tests takes about 2 hours to complete (40 minutes longer for the optional Science Test and another 40 minutes for the optional Writing Test), not including breaks. Give yourself about an hour to review the answer explanations for each exam. That should be enough time for you to review the answer explanations to every question and to take advantage of the opportunity to see shortcuts you may not have noticed or traps you luckily avoided. So, taking and reviewing each exam should take you about 3 or 4 hours. Here's the final timetable:

Activity	Time
Reading the ACT overview	30 minutes
Reviewing the approaches to the five test topics and working through the practice questions at 1.5 hours per topic	7.5 hours
Absorbing the three math review chapters at 1 hour per chapter	3 hours
Engrossing yourself in the grammar review chapter at 2 hours	2 hours
Enjoying the full-length practice exams at 3-4 hours per exam	12–16 hours
Groaning in pain at the authors' lame jokes	15 minutes
Firing off letter complaining about authors' lame jokes (or sending along better ones!)	15 minutes
TOTAL TIME	26-30 hours

Fear not: You don't have to do it all in one sitting. The last thing we advocate is sleep deprivation! This book is designed so that you can start any part at any time. You don't have to have finished the general math chapter, for example, before you go through the general reading chapter.

Okay, are you ready? Are you quivering with anticipation, living for the moment when you can pick up your yellow No. 2 pencil and hold on for the thrill of a lifetime? (Or are you thinking, "These authors need to get a life!"?) Listen, you're going to take the ACT anyway, so you may as well have a good time learning how to do so. Laughing while learning is the whole purpose of this book. Take a deep breath, rev up the brain cells, and go for it! Good luck. Just remember that for you, ACT can come to stand for Ace Conquers Test!

1
Coming to Terms with Reality: An Overview of the ACT

IN THIS PART . . .

Get cozy with the format and content of the ACT and develop a checklist of the items to take with you to the exam (and leave home).

Find out how your efforts will be scored and when it's a good idea to take the ACT for a second, or even third, time.

Develop a plan to beat stress during the test and discover other ways to avoid messing up your performance so that you can achieve your best possible score.

Create an effective study plan based on the amount of time you have to study for the next ACT test.

IN THIS CHAPTER

» Figuring out what — and what not — to take to the ACT

» Dealing with unusual circumstances

» Taking a chance with dumb-luck guessing

» Knowing what to expect on the ACT and understanding how the test's scoring works

» Repeating the ACT if necessary

Chapter 1
Getting Your ACT Together: ACT 101

Are you the type of person who jumps into the cold water all at once instead of dipping your toe in a little at a time? If so, do we have a table for you! Table 1-1 gives you an overview of the ACT and shocks you with the entire kit and caboodle all at once.

If you add up the numbers, with the three required sections of English, Math, and Reading under regular timing, you have 131 multiple-choice questions to answer in 125, or just a little more than 2 hours. If you elect to take the optional Science Test, you add 40 questions and 40 minutes to your test for a total of 171 questions in 2 hours and 45 minutes. If you choose not to take the optional Writing Test, you get to walk out right after that.

TABLE 1-1 ACT Breakdown by Section

Test	Number of Questions	Time Allotted
English	50	35 minutes
Mathematics	45	50 minutes
Reading	36	40 minutes
Science (optional)	40	40 minutes
Writing (optional)	1	40 minutes

To test questions for future tests, the ACT incorporates into each of the four multiple-choice sections what the ACT calls *field test* questions. The questions don't count toward your score, but you won't be able to distinguish between field and actual questions when you're taking the test. About 20 percent of the English and math questions and 15 percent of the reading and science questions are field questions.

You have two ACT formats to choose from: paper-based and digital. The two formats are exactly the same; just the deliveries are different. If you feel more comfortable with a test you can hold and write on with your number 2 pencil, you can opt for the paper version. If screens are your thing, the digital version provides handy tools that allow you to approach it in much the same way you would for the paper test:

- **Highlighter and line reader:** Use these tools to focus on important data and sentences.
- **Answer eliminator and masker:** Use these tools to help you mark out wrong answers.
- **Magnifier:** This tool allows you to read the fine print for charts and graphs in the science questions.

You also have a timer to keep track of your time, built-in graphing calculator, and the ability to move between questions and mark them for later review.

What to Take to the ACT

If you can't borrow the brain of that whiz kid in your calculus class for the day, you're stuck using your own. To compensate, be sure that you have the following with you before you leave for the ACT test center:

- **Admission ticket:** You receive your ticket when you register online. Be sure to print it out so you have it for test day.
- **Pencils:** Take a bunch of sharpened No. 2 pencils with you. You may also want to take good erasers (nothing personal — everyone makes mistakes). Mechanical pencils aren't allowed. You use pencils to mark answers and keep notes on the paper test and to make notes on the scratch paper with the digital version.
- **Map or directions:** Go to the test center a few days before the actual exam to scope out your driving route and parking area. Often, the ACT is given at high schools or colleges that have parking lots far, far away from the test rooms. Drive to the location a few days in advance, park your car, and see just how long it takes you to get to the room. You don't need the stress of having to run to the test room at the last minute on test day.
- **Clothing:** Schools that host the ACT may turn off the heat for the weekend (the ACT is usually offered on a Saturday), and the test room can be freezing cold. Alternately, in the summer, schools may turn off the air conditioning, making the room boiling hot. Dress in layers and be prepared for anything.
- **Photo ID:** Showing the birthmark your boyfriend or girlfriend thinks is so cute isn't going to cut it with the test proctor. You need to upload a photo when you register for the test and bring a photo ID (student ID, driver's license, passport, military ID, FBI Most Wanted mug shot, whatever) to the exam. If you don't have a photo ID, you can bring a letter of identification. The form is available on the official ACT website (act.org).

- » **Eyeglasses:** Students taking the ACT frequently forget their reading glasses at home and then squint for the four long hours of the test. The ACT is enough of a headache on its own; you don't need eyestrain, as well. If you wear contacts, be sure to bring cleaning/wetting solution in case you have to take the lenses out and reinsert them during the break. (Hey, all those tears can really mess up your lenses!)

- » **Watch:** For the paper test, keeping track of time on your own timepiece may be more efficient than wasting precious seconds seeking out the clock on the testing site wall. Place your watch on the desk where you can refer to it easily throughout the exam. Digital watches may not be allowed. Stick with ones that have faces and hands. Your watch can't make any sounds, either. If the proctor hears so much as a beep from your watch, they will not-so-politely request that you leave the building and cancel your test.

- » **Calculator:** The ACT gurus allow you to use a graphing calculator on the Mathematics Test of the paper test. Although the ACT information bulletin has an entire quarter page detailing which calculators you can and cannot use on the paper test, generally, you can use any calculator as long as it doesn't make a noise or have a computer algebra system. Make sure the one you bring has at least a square root function and, ideally, basic trigonometry functions. The digital version has an integrated calculator for your use during the math questions.

What Not to Take to the ACT

Do not, we repeat, *do not*, take any of the following items with you to the ACT test room:

- » **Cell phones and other electronic devices:** Leave your cell phone in the car. You aren't allowed to bring it into the test room. One student we know was dismissed from the test because he accidentally left his cell phone in his pocket, and it rang during the exam. The same goes for other electronics, such as iPads, PC tablets, or anything else that can access the Internet or make a sound. Currently, you can't use your own device to take the digital ACT.

- » **Books and notes:** Take it from us: Last-minute studying doesn't do much good. So leave all your books at home; you aren't allowed to take them into the test room with you. (Just be sure to fill your parents in on this rule. We once had a student whose mother drove all the way to the test center with her daughter's ACT prep book, thinking the girl needed it for the test. The mom actually pulled the girl out of the test to give her the book, resulting in the girl's nearly being disqualified from the test.)

- » **Scratch paper:** You may not bring your own scratch paper to the paper test. Fortunately, the exam booklet has plenty of blank space on which you can do your calculations. The test center supplies scratch paper or whiteboards for digital version test takers to use during the exam.

What to Do If You Have Special Circumstances

Not everyone takes the ACT under the same conditions. You may have a special circumstance that can allow you to change the date of the ACT or the way you take your exam. Here are a few of the special circumstances that may affect how you take the ACT:

- » **Learning differences:** If you have a diagnosed learning disability (LD), you may be able to get special accommodations, such as more time to take the test. However, you must specifically request such accommodations way in advance. Prepare your requests for fall tests by the prior

June and for spring tests by the prior September. Please note that in order to be eligible for special testing on the ACT, your LD must have been diagnosed by a professional, and you should have a current individualized education plan (IEP) at school that includes extended test time. Talk to your counselor for more information. Note that you can only request special accommodations in conjunction with a test registration.

» **Physical disabilities:** If you have a physical disability, you may be able to take a test in a special format — in Braille, large print, or on audio. Go to the official ACT website (act.org) for complete information about special testing.

» **Religious obligations:** If your religion prohibits you from taking a test on a Saturday, you may test on an alternate date. The ACT registration website specifies dates and locations in each state.

» **Military duty:** If you're an active military person, you don't complete the normal ACT registration form. Instead, ask your Educational Services Officer about testing through DANTES (Defense Activity for Nontraditional Educational Support).

Guessing for Points to Maximize Your Score

Scoring on the ACT is very straightforward:

» You get one point for every answer you get right.

» You get zero points for every answer you omit.

» You get zero points for every answer you get wrong.

REMEMBER

The ACT doesn't penalize you for wrong answers. Therefore, guessing on the ACT obviously works to your advantage. Never leave any question blank. We suggest that you save a couple of seconds at the end of each section just to go through the test and make sure that you've filled in an answer for every single question.

Your Number's Up: Scoring on the ACT

We once had a frustrated student tell us that the scores on the ACT looked a lot like measurements to him: 34, 29, 36. However, the ACT has several scores, which makes for a very strange set of measurements! The ACT scores are nothing like high school scores based on percentages. They're not even like the familiar SAT scores that range from 200 to 800. Instead, they range from 1 to 36. Scoring on the ACT works like this:

» **Scaled score:** Each multiple-choice test (English, Mathematics, Reading, and Science) receives a *scaled score* between 1 (low) and 36 (high) that appears on your score report.

» **Composite score:** The *composite score* is the average of the three required test-scaled scores. The ACT uses customary rounding to determine the composite, so if your composite average is 26.67, your composite score will be 27. If your average is 26.33, your composite score will be 26.

» **STEM score:** A *STEM score* is the average of your scaled Mathematics Test score and your scaled Science Test score. If you take the optional Science Test, you receive a separate score

12 PART 1 Coming to Terms with Reality: An Overview of the ACT

for that section that isn't averaged into the composite score. You also receive a separate STEM score.

» **Writing Test score:** If you take the ACT with the optional Writing Test, you receive a Writing score that ranges from 2 (low) to 12 (high). The writing score is the sum of the average of each of the four subscores you receive from each of the two people who grade your essay. The Writing Test score is completely separate from your composite ACT score.

» **English Language Arts (ELA) score:** If you take the Writing Test, the ACT will convert that score to a 1–36 scale and use it in combination with your English Test and Reading Test scores to give you a separate ELA score. The ELA score is only provided if you take the ACT with Writing.

» **Percentile score:** A *percentile score* tells you where your scores rank in your state and nationwide.

Look at the percentiles. Just knowing that you got a 26 doesn't tell you much. You need to know whether a 26 is in the 50th percentile, the 75th percentile, or the 99th percentile. If you get a 36, you have documented lifetime bragging rights because that's a perfect score!

» **Additional scores:** You may see additional readiness scores:

- The Progress Toward Career Readiness Indicator measures your progress toward career readiness for a variety of careers.

- The Understanding Complex Tests indicator tells you whether you sufficiently understand text material for college and career-level reading.

Colleges will see these scores, but they aren't combined in any way with your ACT composite.

The ACT website (act.org) provides a sample score report and scoring information that shows you what all these scores look like when you and your colleges of choice receive them.

What the ACT Expects You to Know

The ACT tests the following subjects:

» **English:** The ACT expects you to know the fundamentals of grammar, usage, punctuation, diction, and rhetorical skills. For example, you must understand sentence construction — what makes a run-on and what makes a fragment. You need to know how to distinguish between commonly confused words, like *affect* and *effect* or *principal* and *principle*. You must be able to use the proper forms of words, distinguishing between an adjective and an adverb, and you must know the difference between a comma and a semicolon. Part 2 addresses the English portion of the test.

» **Mathematics:** The ACT requires basic skills in arithmetic, geometry, and algebra. If you've had two semesters of algebra, two semesters of geometry, and a general math background, you have the math you need to answer about 90 percent of the questions. The ACT also tests algebra II and trigonometry. Oh, and you don't have to know calculus. The ACT has no calculus questions. Happy day! Refer to Part 3 for more.

» **Reading:** The ACT expects you to be able to read a passage in a relatively short amount of time and answer questions based on it. Your reading skills are probably pretty set by now. However, this fact doesn't mean you can't improve your ACT Reading score. Chapter 13 shows you a few tricks you can use to improve your speed and tells you how to recognize and avoid traps built into the questions.

>> **Science (optional):** You don't have to have much specific science background to ace the Science Test. The passages may test chemistry, biology, botany, physics, or any other science, but you don't have to have had those courses. The test gives you all the information you need to answer most of the science questions in the passages, diagrams, charts, and tables.

WARNING

Although the Science Test is optional, some colleges may require it for admissions. Be sure to check each college's testing policies before your make the decision to skip the science questions. Head to Part 5 for more about the Science Test.

>> **Writing (optional):** The ACT folks added this optional section to test your writing ability. Don't worry! You've been writing for years, and the ACT people know that you can't possibly write a perfect essay in a measly 40 minutes. They're not focusing on perfection; instead, they're looking at your thesis, organization, and ability to support your thoughts. The ACT doesn't require you to write the essay, and few colleges require or even recommend the essay. Part 6 gives you the lowdown on the Writing portion of the ACT.

Repeating the Test for a Better Score

Are you allowed to repeat the ACT? Yes. Should you repeat the ACT? Probably. Other than the additional cost (both financial and emotional) required to test again, there is no real downside to retesting. Decide whether you want to repeat the ACT based on your answers to the following questions:

>> **What errors did I make the first time around?** If your mistakes were from a lack of knowledge, that is, you just plain didn't know a grammar rule or a math formula, you can easily correct those mistakes by studying.

>> **Why do I want to repeat the test?** Is your ego destroyed because your best friend got a better score than you did? That's probably not a good enough reason to retake the ACT. Do retake the exam if you're trying to get a minimum qualifying score to enable you to get into a college or earn a scholarship.

>> **Can I go through this all over again?** How seriously did you take studying the first time around? If you gave it all you had, you may be too burned out to go through the whole process again. On the other hand, if you just zoomed through the test booklet and didn't spend much time preparing for the test, you may want a second chance to show your stuff.

>> **Were my mistakes caused by factors that were not my fault?** Maybe you were in a fender-bender on your way to the exam, or perhaps you stayed up late the night before in an argument with your parents or your best friend. If you just weren't up to par when you took the exam, definitely take it again, and this time, be sure to get a good night's sleep the night before.

TIP

If you take the ACT in a certain national administration (usually April, June, or December), you may be able to pay to see a digital copy of your full ACT test and the questions you missed. This handy resource gives you valuable information to study for a future test. The cost for My Answer Key is $30 when you register for the test, and access to the test questions is available as soon as you receive your scores for that ACT test date. You can order My Answer Key after you receive your scores, but it'll cost you $40. This service is only available on certain test dates in the United States and isn't offered for international administrations of the test.

The ACT doesn't automatically send colleges the scores for every time you take the test. It gives you the option of deciding which set of scores you want colleges to see. If you don't want to report the results of all your tests, keep these issues in mind:

» **The ACT automatically sends scores to the colleges you list on your test registration form.** If you want to wait until after you see your report to decide whether certain colleges can see your scores for a particular test administration, don't list those colleges with your ACT registration.

» **Many colleges figure your ACT composite score by averaging the highest scores you get in each section across all administrations of the test.** They refer to this practice as *superscoring* the ACT. If you get a 24 in English, a 22 in Math, and a 23 in Reading the first time you take the ACT and a 25, 20, and 24, respectively, the second time, these colleges will figure your composite score by averaging your higher 25 English score, 22 Math score, and 24 Reading score. Your composite score for each administration would be 23, but the composite score the colleges calculate would be 24 (23.67 rounded to 24). Therefore, you may want the colleges to get reports from all the times you take the ACT so that they can superscore your highest section scores. When the ACT institutes section retesting and the superscore report, your highest section scores will appear on one report, and (if colleges allow), you'll only have to send (and pay for) one report.

» **A handful of colleges require you to report your scores from every test date.** Check with the admissions committee at the colleges to which you're applying to make sure they allow you to withhold score reports from particular test dates.

REMEMBER

A growing number of colleges allow you to self-report your ACT scores. Those colleges consider the ACT scores you list on your college applications or report within the college's online portal on a separate form, depending on the policies of the individual school, to make admissions decisions. You only send an official score report after you've been admitted and have decided to attend that particular college. Self-reporting allows you to save the money you'd have spent to send official score reports to every college on your application list. If you're able to take advantage of the self-reporting option, be sure to follow the college's procedures exactly and report your scores accurately. A discrepancy between the scores you report on your application and the scores that appear on your official report could be grounds for rescinding your college acceptance.

> **IN THIS CHAPTER**
>
> » Mellowing, chilling, and relaxing before and during the ACT
>
> » Identifying and sidestepping some easy ways to mess up your score

Chapter 2
Succeeding on the ACT

On the wall of our office, we have a padded cushion that's imprinted with the words, "BANG HEAD HERE!" We've found that most of our students use it either to reduce stress (we guess one headache can replace another!) or — much more commonly — to express their exasperation over unnecessary, careless (we're trying not to say it, but okay — dumb!) mistakes. Going through the material in this chapter about how to relax before and during the ACT and how to recognize and avoid common mistakes can prevent you from becoming a head-banger later.

Surviving the ACT with Four Stress-Busters

Most people are tense before a test and often feel butterflies dancing in their stomachs. The key is to use relaxation techniques that keep your mind on your test and not on your tummy. To avoid becoming paralyzed by a frustrating question during the test, we suggest that you develop and practice a relaxation plan (perhaps one that includes the techniques we describe in the following sections). At the first sign of panic, take a quick timeout. You'll either calm down enough to handle the question or get enough perspective to realize that it's just one little test question and not worth your anguish. Mark your best guess and move on. If you have time, you can revisit the question later.

TIP

Practice a quick relaxation routine in the days before the exam so that you know what to do when you feel panicky on test day.

Inhaling deeply

Stressing out causes you to tighten up and take quick breaths, which doesn't do much for your oxygen intake. Restore the steady flow of oxygen to your brain by inhaling deeply. Feel the air go all the way down to your toes. Hold it, and then let it all out slowly. Repeat this process several times.

CHAPTER 2 Succeeding on the ACT   17

Stretching a little

Anxiety causes your muscles to get all tied up in knots. Combat its evil effects by focusing on reducing your muscle tension while breathing deeply. If you feel stress in your neck and shoulders, also do a few stretches in these areas to get the blood flowing. You can shrug your shoulders toward your ears, roll your head slowly in a circle, stretch your arms over your head, or even open your mouth wide as if to say, "Ahhh." (But don't actually say it out loud.)

Thinking positive thoughts

Any time you feel yourself starting to panic or thinking negative thoughts, make a conscious effort to say to yourself, "Stop! Keep positive." For example, suppose you catch yourself thinking, "Why didn't I study this math more? I saw that formula a hundred times but can't remember it now!" Change the script to, "I got most of this math right; if I leave my subconscious to work on that formula, maybe I'll get it, too. No sense worrying now. Overall, I think I'm doing great!"

The ACT isn't the end-all, be-all of your life. Cut yourself some slack on test day. You probably won't feel comfortable about every question, so don't beat yourself up when you feel confused. If you've tried other relaxation efforts and you still feel frustrated about a particular question, fill in your best guess and mark it in your test booklet in case you have time to review it at the end, but don't think about it until then. Put your full effort into answering the remaining questions. Focus on the positive, congratulate yourself for the answers you feel confident about, and force yourself to leave the others behind.

Practicing POE

You may think that acing the ACT requires that you find correct answers to the questions, and essentially, you're right. But facing the challenge of staring down a set of four answer choices in the hope that the correct one will reveal itself can be daunting. Change your perspective. Instead of searching for the one correct answer in the bunch, focus on the wrong answers. You'll usually have an easier time finding something wrong with an answer. The key to a successful process of elimination (POE) lies in making sure you're rejecting choices based on careful analysis rather than a gut feeling.

Usually, two of the four answer choices will be relatively easy to identify as wrong. They will obviously be off-topic or contain specific information that the passages or questions don't address. When you're deliberating between the two remaining options, look for problems with one of the answers. Sometimes, just one word will make the answer incorrect. The correct answer is the one left standing after you've found problems with the others.

Tap your pencil (or your mouse pointer if you're taking the digital version) on every word as you read through an answer choice to make sure you carefully consider all components before you eliminate or select that answer choice.

Avoiding a Few Dumb Mistakes That Can Mess Up Your ACT

Throughout this book, you discover techniques for doing your best on the ACT. We're sorry to say, however, that there are just as many techniques for messing up big-time on this test. Take a few minutes to read through these techniques in the following sections to see what dumb things people do to blow the exam totally. By being aware of these catastrophes, you may prevent them from happening to you. And no — the student who makes the greatest number of these mistakes doesn't receive any booby prize.

Losing concentration

When you're in the middle of an excruciatingly boring reading passage, the worst thing you can do is let your mind drift off to a more pleasant time (last night's date, last weekend's soccer game, the time that you stole your rival school's mascot and set it on the john in the principal's private bathroom — you get the point). Although visualization (picturing yourself doing something relaxing or fun) is a good stress-reduction technique to practice *before* the exam, it stinks when it comes to helping your ACT score during the test. Even if you have to pinch yourself to keep from falling asleep or flaking out, stay focused. Taking the ACT requires only a few hours of your life. You've probably had horrible blind dates that lasted longer than the test, and you managed to survive them. This, too, shall pass.

Panicking over time

Every section on the ACT begins with directions and a line that tells you exactly how many questions are in the section and, therefore, how many minutes you have per question. The ACT is no big mystery. You can waste a lot of time and drive yourself crazy if you keep flipping pages and counting how many more questions you have to answer. You can do what you can do; that's all. Looking ahead and panicking are counterproductive and waste time.

Messing up on the paper test answer grid

Suppose you take the paper test and decide to postpone doing Question 11, hoping that inspiration will strike later. But now you accidentally put the answer to Question 12 in the blank for Question 11 . . . and mess up all the numbers from that point on. After you answer Question 40, you suddenly realize that you just filled in Bubble Number 39 and have one bubble left — *aaargh!* Stroke City! It's easy to say, "Don't panic," but chances are that your blood pressure will go sky-high, especially when you eyeball the clock and see that only one minute remains.

If you have a good eraser with you (and you should), the wrong answers on the answer grid should take only a few seconds to erase. But how on earth are you going to re-solve all those problems and reread and reanswer all the questions? You're not; you will thank your lucky stars for buying this book and taking the following advice: When you choose an answer, *circle that answer in your test booklet first* and *then* fill in the answer on the answer grid. Doing so takes you a mere nanosecond and helps you not only in this panic situation but also as you go back and double-check your work.

Rubbernecking

Rubbernecking is craning your neck around to see how everyone else is doing. Forget those bozos. You have too much to do on your own to waste precious seconds checking out anyone else. You don't want to psych yourself out by noticing that the guy in front of you is done with his section and is leaning back whistling while you're still sweating away. Maybe the guy in front of you is a complete moron and didn't notice that the booklet has yet another page of problems. After you have the exam booklet in front of you, don't look at anything but it and your watch until time is called.

Cheating

Dumb, dumb, *dumb!* Cheating on the ACT is a loser's game — it's just plain stupid. Apart from the legal, moral, and ethical questions, you can't predict what types of grammatical mistakes will show up in the questions; what are you going to do, copy a textbook on the palm of your hand? All the math formulas that you need can't fit onto the bottom of your shoe.

Worrying about previous sections

Think of the ACT as three or four separate lifetimes. You're reborn each time, so you get several more chances to "do it right." Every time the proctor says, "Your time is up. Please turn to the next test and begin," you get a fresh start. The ACT rules are very strict: You can't go back to a previous section and finish work there or change some of your answers. If you try to do so, the proctor will catch you, and you'll be in a world of hurt.

Worrying about the hard problems

The ACT contains a few incredibly hard questions. Forget about 'em. Almost no one gets them right, anyway. Every year, a ridiculously small number of students receive a score of 36, and if you get into the 30s, you're in a superelite club of only a few percent of the thousands and thousands of students who take the ACT annually. Just accept the fact that you either won't get to or can't answer a few of the hard questions and learn to live with your imperfection. If you do go quickly enough to get to the hard questions, don't waste too much time on them. See if you can use common sense to eliminate any answers. Then, mark your best guess from the remaining choices. Keep reminding yourself that every question counts the same in a section, whether that question is a simple 1 + 1 = 2 or some deadly word problem that may as well be written in Lithuanian.

Forgetting to double-check

Mark questions on the digital test or in your paper test booklet when you're unsure about the answers. If you finish a test early, go back and double-check the *easy* and *medium* marked questions first. Don't spend more time trying to do the hard questions. If a question was too time-consuming for you five minutes ago, it's probably still not worth your time. If you made a totally careless or dumb mistake on an easy question, however, going back over the problem gives you a chance to catch and correct your error. You're more likely to gain points by double-checking easy questions than by staring open-mouthed at the hard ones.

REMEMBER

Every question counts the same. A point you save by catching a careless mistake is just as valuable as a point you earn, grunting and sweating, by solving a mondo-hard problem.

IN THIS CHAPTER

» Deciding when to take the ACT

» Developing an ACT study plan

Chapter 3
Forming an ACT Study Plan

You're taking the ACT either by choice or because your high school requires it. Now what? Studying for a comprehensive, multiple-choice test may seem daunting, and you may be wondering where to start. First, you need to determine when to take the test. Then, you need to create a study plan. This chapter helps you do both.

When to Take the ACT

Currently, the ACT is offered at testing sites nationwide and internationally on weekends every February, April, June, July, September, October, and December. Additionally, some school districts offer the ACT during the school day in March, April, October, and November, depending on the high school. If you live in a district that offers one of these schoolday tests, your test date is set for you, but all other options allow for a little freedom of choice.

The best time to take the ACT is not a one-size-fits-all consideration. You may want to wait to take the test until you feel most prepared, but you also need to give yourself plenty of time to retake the test before you apply to college. Most colleges don't require you to send the scores every time you take the ACT, so you don't necessarily have to be completely prepared before you take your first official test. Also, many colleges allow you to *superscore* your ACT scores, which means they'll consider only your highest English, math, and reading scores from all the times you take the ACT. In fact, the ACT even creates a superscore score report if you take the test more than once. Therefore, there's not a major downside to taking the test sooner rather than later.

REMEMBER

If you take the ACT in a national administration in April, June, or December, you may be able to pay to see a digital copy of your full ACT and the questions you missed. This handy resource called My Answer Key gives you valuable information to study for a future test. For more information about My Answer Key, see Chapter 1.

Generally, if you've taken algebra II and trigonometry during your sophomore year, we suggest that you consider taking your first ACT in the first semester of your junior year in either September, October, or December. (If you're taking algebra II and trig during your junior year, you may want to wait until February or April of your junior year to take the first test.) The beauty of testing in the fall of your junior year is that you can devote the summer before to extensive ACT study.

CHAPTER 3 Forming an ACT Study Plan   21

If you take the test in the fall, you have plenty of options to retake the ACT in the spring and summer to achieve your top score. You can even get some extra summer study time in during the summer before your senior year and take the September ACT. Your scores from this test should be available in plenty of time before the earliest application deadlines in October and November. If you postpone taking your first ACT until April or June of your junior year, you may not have enough retakes to optimize your score.

Planning Your Study Time for Maximum Success

After you've chosen your testing start date, begin studying. The best way to avoid freaking out on exam day is to be fully prepared. So, make sure you have a strategy that fits your preparation timeline. You have many resources available to help you. Of course, this copy of *ACT Prep 2026/2027 For Dummies* is a great place to start. I also recommend that you access the Free ACT Practice Test and Resources from the ACT website (go to https://tinyurl.com/5hsrexpm and get your hands on the most current edition of *The Official ACT Prep Guide* (John Wiley & Sons, Inc.) for access to a bunch of official full ACTs. You can also supplement these books with the series of official guides to each of the four ACT sections: *The Official ACT English Guide*, *The Official ACT Mathematics Guide*, *The Official ACT Reading Guide*, and *The Official ACT Science Guide* (all published by John Wiley & Sons, Inc.). The ACT also offers an online self-study course.

Table 3-1 references suggested resources to include in your study plan based on your schedule.

TABLE 3-1   Following an ACT Preparation Schedule

Resource	Around 6 Months	Around 6 weeks	Around 3 weeks
ACT Prep 2026/2027 For Dummies Chapter 19 timed practice test and online tests	X	X	X
The Free ACT Practice Test and Resources available from the ACT website	X	X	X
Focused study in *ACT Prep 2026/2027 For Dummies* Parts 2–6 based on evaluation of pretest results	X	X	X
Extensive practice question quizzes in the online material accompanying *ACT Prep 2026/2027 For Dummies*	X	X	
Practice questions from the current edition of *The Official ACT Prep Guide* (John Wiley & Sons, Inc.)	X	X	
Practice questions from editions of The Official ACT English Guide, The Official ACT Guide Mathematics Guide, The Official ACT Reading Guide, and The Official ACT Science Guide	X		

Regardless of how much study time you have, stick to your practice schedule. Create space in your calendar four or more times a week for at least 30 minutes to an hour of ACT practice. Regular practice will reinforce the concepts in *ACT Prep 2026/2027 For Dummies* and familiarize you with the ACT questions to help increase your test-taking efficiency.

If you have six months to prepare

If you're a high school sophomore planning to test in the fall of your junior year or a high school junior prepping for the upcoming spring, summer, or fall ACT test dates, you likely have about six months to get ready. Here are the steps to follow when you have a pretty hefty chunk of time before you officially sharpen your no. 2 pencils for test day:

1. **Month 1: Grasp a general understanding of the ACT.**
   - Read Chapters 1 and 2 of this book to get an overview of the test format and scoring considerations.
   - Access the Free ACT Practice Test and Resources available from the ACT website and take a practice test. Read the ACT overview and instructions for taking a practice test. Set aside two to three hours (depending on whether you're taking the optional Science Test) to take and score the full ACT included in these resources.

2. **Month 2: Take a stab at the English questions.**
   - Read Chapters 4, 5, and 6 of this book and answer the practice questions in Chapter 7.
   - Use the online test bank included with your purchase of this book to practice English questions. Check your answers and read through the explanations.
   - If you need more practice, work through *The Official ACT English Guide.*

3. **Month 3: Master the math questions.**
   - Read Chapters 8, 9, 10, and 11 of this book and answer the practice questions in Chapter 12.
   - Use the online test bank included with your purchase of this book to practice math questions. Check your answers and read through the explanations.
   - If you need more practice, work through *The Official ACT Mathematics Guide.*

4. **Month 4: Run through the reading questions.**
   - Read Chapter 13 of this book and answer the sample questions in Chapter 14.
   - Use the online test bank included with your purchase of this book to practice reading questions. Check your answers and read through the explanations.
   - If you need more practice, work through *The Official ACT Reading Guide.*

5. **Month 5: If you're taking the optional Science Test, run through the science questions.**
   - Read Chapter 15 of this book and work through the sample questions in Chapter 16.
   - Use the online test bank included with your purchase of this book to practice science questions. Check your answers and read through the explanations.
   - If you need more practice, work through *The Official ACT Science Guide.*

6. **Month 6: Practice, practice, practice.**
   - Take the practice test in Chapter 19 of this book. Read the answer explanations in Chapter 20.
   - Take the three online practice tests that come with this book (see the Introduction to discover how to access those tests).
   - Take more timed practice tests in *The Official ACT Prep Guide.* Score yourself and read through the explanations provided for each test.

- Work through more practice questions in the online test bank that accompanies this book.
- Try to incorporate at least 40 minutes of ACT practice at least four to five days a week during the last two weeks before the test.
- If you're taking the ACT Writing Test, read Chapters 17 and 18 of this book and write a practice essay using one of the prompts in the practice test chapters of this book.

If you have six weeks to prepare

If you have six weeks before the big day, follow this plan:

1. **Week 1: Grasp a general understanding of the ACT.**
   - Read Chapters 1 and 2 of this book to get an overview of the test format and scoring considerations.
   - Access the Free ACT Practice Test and Resources available from the ACT website and take a practice test. Read the ACT overview and instructions for taking a practice test. Set aside two to three hours (depending on whether you're taking the optional Science Test) to take and score the full ACT included in these resources

2. **Week 2: Take a stab at the English questions.**
   - Read Chapters 4, 5, and 6 of this book and answer the practice questions in Chapter 7.
   - Use the online test bank included with your purchase of this book to practice English questions. Check your answers and read through the explanations.

3. **Week 3: Master the math questions.**
   - Read Chapters 8, 9, 10, and 11 of this book and answer the practice questions in Chapter 12.
   - Use the online test bank included with your purchase of this book to practice math questions. Check your answers and read through the explanations.

4. **Week 4: Run through the reading questions.**
   - Read Chapter 13 of this book and answer the sample questions in Chapter 14.
   - Use the online test bank included with your purchase of this book to practice reading questions. Check your answers and read through the explanations.

5. **Week 5: If you're taking the optional Science Test, run through the science questions.**
   - Read Chapter 15 of this book and work through the sample questions in Chapter 16.
   - Use the online test bank included with your purchase of this book to practice the science questions. Check your answers and read through the explanations.

6. **Week 6: Practice and more practice.**
   - Try the practice test in Chapter 19 of this book. Read the answer explanations in Chapter 20 to incorporate at least 40 minutes of ACT practice at least four to five days a week during the week or two before the test.
   - Work through more practice questions in the online test bank that accompanies this book.
   - Take a timed practice test in *The Official ACT Prep Guide*. Score yourself and read through the explanations provided for each test.
   - If you're taking the ACT Writing Test, read Chapters 17 and 18 of this book and write a practice essay using one of the prompts in the practice test chapters of this book.

If you have three weeks to prepare

If you've completely procrastinated (not recommended!), it's not too late. Here's what to do if you have just a few weeks to prepare:

1. **Week 1: Grasp a general understanding of the ACT and practice the English questions.**
   - Read Chapters 1 and 2 of this book to get an overview of the test format and scoring considerations.
   - Read Chapters 4, 5, and 6 of this book and answer the practice questions in Chapter 7.
   - Use the online test bank included with your purchase of this book to practice English questions. Check your answers and read through the explanations.

2. **Week 2: Master the math and reading questions.**
   - Read Chapters 8, 9, 10, and 11 of this book and answer the practice questions in Chapter 12.
   - Read Chapter 13 of this book and answer the sample question in Chapter 14.
   - Use the online test bank included with your purchase of this book to practice math and reading questions. Check your answers and read through the explanations.

3. **Week 3: Take some timed practice tests.**
   - Use the practice tests in Chapter 19 of this book. Read the answer explanations in Chapter 20 to incorporate at least 40 minutes of ACT practice at least four to five days a week during the week or two before the test.
   - Work through more practice questions in the online test bank that accompanies this book.
   - Access the Free ACT Practice Test and Resources available from the ACT website and take a practice test. Read the ACT overview and instructions for taking a practice test. Set aside about two hours to take and score the full ACT included in these resources

2
Serving Your "Sentence": The English Test

IN THIS PART . . .

Introduce yourself to the types of questions you'll encounter on the ACT English Test and collect tips for handling each question format.

Review important punctuation rules, define parts of speech, and structure sentences to help you pick up on punctuation, pronoun, and possessive formatting errors and find out how to approach questions that test your knowledge of what makes for good writing.

Strut your stuff on a two-passage quick quiz that tests your knowledge of grammar, usage, and effective writing skills.

IN THIS CHAPTER

» Knowing what skills the English Test requires

» Understanding the way the ACT presents English questions

» Avoiding falling for the ACT traps . . . or creating your own

Chapter 4
Mastering the English Test

When you open your ACT booklet, the first thing you see is the English Test. Your still-half-asleep brain and bleary eyes encounter 6 passages and 50 questions. Somehow, you're to read all the passages and answer all the questions within 35 minutes. That may seem like a lot of questions in a little bit of time, but the English questions really aren't super time-consuming. You'll be fine. Just take a deep breath and read on to discover everything you need to know to succeed on the English Test.

Figuring Out What the English Questions Want You to Know

The questions on the English Test fall into the following three categories:

» **Conventions of Standard English (CSE):** These questions cover the ever-popular English topics of usage and mechanics. They include sentence structure (whether a sentence maintains parallel structure and properly positions the descriptive words and phrases), grammar and usage (just about everything most people think of as English, such as pronoun use, verb tense, subject/verb agreement, possessive form, and so on), and punctuation (don't worry — this isn't super hard once you've mastered the few commonly tested rules). In Chapter 5, we review the foundational concepts you need to know to master usage and mechanics questions.

» **Knowledge of Language (KLA):** The questions that ask you to eliminate unnecessary or redundant expressions comprise a good chunk of the English Test. With practice, you'll spot repetitive language almost instinctively.

» **Power of Writing (POW):** These questions test writing skills, such as organization and relevance (reordering the sentences or adding sentences to the passage), style (which expression, slang or formal, is appropriate within the passage, or which transition properly joins two thoughts), and strategy, ("Which answer most specifically conveys what Grandpa likes to eat for supper?")

Chapter 6 provides the tips and techniques you need to identify and ace all question types.

Some questions are much more doable than others. For example, most students would agree that a simple grammar question asking about a pronoun reference or verb tense is easier to answer than an organization question expecting you to reposition a paragraph within the entire passage.

Seeing Is Believing: The Test's Format

The ACT English Test passages look like standard reading-comprehension passages — you know, the kind you've seen on tests for years. The difference is that these passages have many underlined portions. An underlined portion can be an entire sentence, a phrase, or even just one word. (You may want to take a quick look right now at the practice passage and questions in Chapter 7 to get an idea of what an English Test passage looks like. We'll wait.)

Okay, you're back. Here are the details about what information you get on the English Test and what you're expected to do with it.

The passages

The passages cover a variety of topics. You may get a fun story that's a personal anecdote — someone talking about getting a car for his 16th birthday, for example. Or you may encounter a somewhat formal scientific passage about the way items are carbon-dated. Some passages discuss history; some, philosophy; others, cultural differences among nations. One type of passage is not necessarily more difficult than another. You don't need to use specific reading techniques for these passages (as you do with standard reading-comprehension passages). In fact, you won't spend much time reading the passages at all. Just be prepared to answer the questions that accompany the passages (see the next section for details).

Although these English passages aren't reading-comprehension passages per se, you do need to pay at least a little attention to the content instead of just focusing on the underlined portions. Why bother? Because a few of the questions are reading-comprehension–type questions that ask you about the purpose of the passage or what a possible conclusion may be. These questions usually appear at the end of the passage, and you'll likely have a pretty good idea of the passage content by then. More about those appears in Chapter 6.

The question types

You won't see anything like "Which of the following is an adjective?" or "The purpose of the subjunctive is to do which of these?" Instead, questions ask you to analyze underlined portions of passages and choose the answer that presents the underlined words in the best way possible. Thrown into the mix are several questions that ask you for the best writing strategy or the best way to organize sentences or paragraphs.

Analyzing answer choices

Most of the test is about examining answer choices and then choosing which answer fits best in the place occupied by underlined words in a sentence. The questions indicate what type of error you're supposed to focus on. Your job is to determine which of the choices provides the correct expression. Consider that the underlined answer is no more correct or incorrect than any of the other three alternate answer choices. On the paper test, the answer choices are (A), (B), (C), and (D) for the odd-numbered questions and (F), (G), (H), and (J) for the even-numbered questions. Choices (A) and (F) are often *NO CHANGE*. You select that choice if the original is the best of the versions offered. Occasionally, the last answer (Choice (D) or (J) on the paper test) says, *DELETE the underlined portion*. Choose that answer when you want to dump the whole underlined portion and forget that you ever saw it. (And no, you can't do that with the entire test!)

Approach these types of questions methodically:

1. **Read the question stem clues to the type of error the question tests.**

   Chapter 6 summarizes the kinds of errors to look for, such as pronoun or punctuation problems, word choice issues, redundancy, and subject/verb agreement mistakes.

2. **Eliminate answer choices that contain errors.**

   Chapter 6 shows you which choices to examine first, depending on the tested error type.

3. **Reread the sentence with the answer you've chosen inserted.**

   Don't skip this step. You may overlook a problem with your answer until you see how it works in the complete sentence.

Here's an example to demonstrate how to use this approach.

A full case of juice boxes, when opened by a horde of thirsty athletes who have been running laps, <u>don't go</u> very far.

EXAMPLE Which choice makes the sentence most grammatically acceptable?

(A) NO CHANGE

(B) do not go

(C) doesn't go

(D) doesn't get to go

The answer choices contain a verb. Problems with verbs usually involve tense or subject/verb agreement. All the answers are in present tense, so the issue is probably subject/verb agreement. Find the subject that goes with "don't go." When you sift through the clauses and prepositional phrases, you see that the subject is *case*. Because *case* is singular, it requires the singular verb *doesn't*. Eliminate Choices (A) and (B) immediately because they don't contain singular verbs. Choices (C) and (D) correct the verb problem, but Choice (D) adds unnecessary words and makes the sentence seem silly. So Choice (C) is correct.

Did you see the trap in this sentence? Some students think that *boxes*, *athletes*, or *laps* — each of which is plural — is the subject of the sentence. (*Laps* is especially tricky because it's right next to the verb.) In that case, they think the verb has to be plural, too, and choose Choice (A). You didn't fall for that cheap trick, did you?

TIP

Dealing with "yes, yes, no, no" questions

A few of the questions in the English Test ask you to strategize about content, style, and organization. The best way to approach these questions is by eliminating answer choices that can't be right.

Sometimes, the answer to a question is a simple yes or no. Two of the answer choices provide the yes option; the other two give you the no option. First, you decide whether the answer to the question is yes or no. Then, you choose the answer that provides the best reason for the yes or no answer.

Here's an example. Say that this question appears in an excerpt from a stuffy scientific journal article. Most of the passage is written in third person, but one paragraph suddenly switches to first person.

EXAMPLE

Given the topic and the tone of the passage, was the author's use of the pronoun *I* in this paragraph proper?

(F) Yes, because the only way to express an opinion is by using first person.

(G) Yes, because they were projecting their personal feelings onto the topic.

(H) No, because the use of *I* is inconsistent with the rest of the passage.

(J) No, because using *I* prevents the readers from becoming involved with the topic.

In this case, you're expected to get a feel for the tone of the passage as a whole. You may think the best way to approach this question is to determine whether the answer is yes or no, but it may be easier to eliminate answers based on the "because" statements. Get rid of any choices that are outright false. Usually two of them are obviously wrong. In this case, Choices (F) and (J) can't be right; it's simply not true that using first person is the only way to express an opinion and that using first person prevents readers from getting involved.

Now you have a 50 percent chance of answering the question correctly. Examine the statements in Choices (G) and (H). Because most of the passage is in third person, the one paragraph in first person probably isn't right. So the answer to the question is most likely no. Thus, the correct answer is (H).

Their Pain, Your Gain: Looking Out for Traps That Others Fall into

We've taught the ACT for a couple of decades now. By this point, we've seen students fall for every trap the test makers have thought of — and some they probably never considered! Watch out for these most commonly tumbled-into traps:

> » **Forgetting the NO CHANGE option:** Because the first answer choice — Choice (A) for odd-numbered questions, Choice (F) for even-numbered questions — may be NO CHANGE, students tend to gloss over it. Don't forget that the answer in the passage has the same potential to be right as the other three options.
>
> » **Automatically choosing DELETE each time it shows up:** Although you may be tempted to shorten this section by screaming, "Dump it! Just dump the whole stupid thing!" every chance you get, don't fall into that habit. When you see the DELETE answer — usually either Choice (D) or Choice (J) — realize that it has the same one-in-four chance of being right as the other answers have. Consider it, but don't make it a no-brainer choice.

- **Automatically selecting the answer with a word or grammar rule you don't know well:** When you see *who* in a sentence, you're often tempted to change it immediately to *whom* simply because you aren't sure how to use *whom*. (Don't worry. We tell you how in Chapter 6.) Apply the process of elimination and employ the knowledge you gain in Chapters 5 and 6, and you'll be fine.

- **Wasting time on the time-consuming questions:** Some questions, like the mission ones ("Which answer most specifically conveys the type of snacks Jimbo prefers?"), can be quite simple. But others, such as the ones that ask you to reposition sentences, can seem incredibly time-wasting and frustrating. You may have to read and reread a paragraph, changing and rearranging the sentences again and again. You may be able to get the question right, but at what price? How much time do you chew up? How many more of the easy questions could you have gotten right in that time?

- **Ignoring the big picture:** Some questions are style questions. A style question expects you to sense the overall picture, to know whether the tone of the passage is friendly so that you can appropriately use a slang expression (for example, *totally lame*), or whether you need to be a bit more formal (*useless* rather than *totally lame*). If you focus on only the underlined portions and don't consider the passage as a whole, you can easily miss this type of question.

TIP

Even if a question doesn't seem to expect you to understand the entire passage, you may need to read a few sentences ahead of the question. For example, whether you add a new sentence to the passage may depend on the topic of the entire paragraph.

> **IN THIS CHAPTER**
> » Picking apart the parts of speech
> » Putting together the pieces of a sentence
> » Reviewing the proper placement of commas, semicolons, colons, and other punctuation marks

Chapter 5
Getting a Grip on Grammar and Usage

The ACT English Test tests Standard written English. In the real world, you can use slang and casual English and still communicate perfectly well with your buddies, but on the ACT, you have to use the formal English that you learned in school. When you knock on a friend's door, for example, you call out, "It's me!" Right? Well, on the ACT, you have to say, "It is I." The ACT English Test focuses on two types of questions: those that test grammar and usage and those that require you to make decisions about the best way to construct sentences. Chapter 6 gives you the skinny on how to recognize and efficiently answer both types of questions.

This chapter gives you a basic grammar review that brings back those thrilling days of yesteryear when you learned the various uses for commas or perhaps filled in the gaps for English stuff you never actually covered in class. The review starts off with the really easy stuff, but don't get too bored and drop out. The harder, picky stuff comes later, and chances are that's the stuff you really need to review.

REMEMBER

Only teachers care about the technical names for all this grammar stuff. All you need to know is how to use the right rules, so don't worry about what to call things. We're very careful to use technical terms sparingly throughout this material.

The rules of grammar are really pretty logical. After you understand the basic rules regarding the parts of speech and the elements of a sentence, you have the hang of it. The following sections cover what you need to know to do well on grammar and usage questions. Bear with us as we run through the grammar basics. We promise to get through them as quickly as possible and highlight the concepts that are most important to acing the ACT English Test.

TIP

If you're a grammar guru, you may be able to skim or skip this chapter and focus on Chapter 6. If you encounter any confusing concepts or terms when you get there, come back to this chapter for some explanation.

CHAPTER 5 Getting a Grip on Grammar and Usage   35

Reviewing the Parts of Speech

Most of the English Test questions ask you to evaluate sentences. Every word in a sentence has a purpose, known as its *part of speech.* The parts of speech you should know for the ACT are verbs, nouns, pronouns, adjectives, adverbs, conjunctions, and prepositions. We're here to help you as we explain them in these chapters.

Getting in the action with verbs

A sentence must have a *verb* to be complete. For the ACT, make sure you know these concepts about verbs:

» **The difference between an action verb and a linking verb:** *Action verbs* state what's going on in a sentence. *Linking verbs*, such as the verb *to be*, link one part of the sentence to the other, sort of like the equals sign in an equation.

» **The distinction between a verb's infinite form, conjugated form, and participle form:**

- The *infinitive* is the basic form — to + the verb: To run or to be.

- The *conjugated* verb is the form that alters depending on its subject: He runs; they run; he is; they are; I am.

- A *participle* is the form a verb takes when it helps out other verbs as part of a verb phrase: He is running; they have run; he has been.

A verb in its participle form, such as *being* or *given*, can't work as a verb by itself. It must be paired with a helper, such as a conjugated form of "to be" or "to have" to function as a verb.

REMEMBER

» **The types of verb tenses:** The most important verb tenses to know for the test are present, past, future, present perfect, and past perfect tenses. Table 5-1 gives you a quick overview of these tenses and shows you an example of how to use them.

TABLE 5-1 Verb Tenses

Verb Tense	Purpose	Examples
Present	Shows an action or a condition that happens right now	Steve studies grammar every day. The dog is asleep.
Past	Shows an action or a condition that was completed in the past	Steve studied grammar in high school. The dog was asleep when I came in.
Future	Shows an action or a condition that hasn't happened yet but will happen	Steve will study grammar in college, too. The dog will be asleep when the guests arrive.
Present perfect	Shows an action or a condition that's already started and may continue, or that happened at an undefined time	Steve has studied grammar for the exam. The dog has been sleeping for several hours.
Past perfect	Shows an action or a condition that happened before another one did	Steve had studied grammar for many weeks before he took the exam. The dog had been sleeping for several hours when the cat awakened him.

36   PART 2 Serving Your "Sentence": The English Test

Identifying the culprit with nouns

You've undoubtedly heard *nouns* defined as persons, places, things, or ideas. They provide information about what's going on in a sentence and who or what is performing or receiving the action, such as the italicized nouns in this sentence: The social studies *teacher* gave the *students* five *pages* of *homework* regarding *countries* in *Europe* and asked them to write an *essay* on the political *consequences* of *joining* the *European Union*. Nouns can be subjects (teacher), direct objects (pages, essay, European Union), indirect objects (students), objects of prepositions (homework, countries, Europe, consequences, joining), and predicate nouns.

Avoiding repeating yourself with pronouns

Pronouns rename nouns and provide a way to avoid too much repetition of nouns in a sentence or paragraph. To answer English Test questions on the ACT, get familiar with these types of pronouns:

>> **Personal pronouns rename specific nouns.** They take several forms: subjective, objective, possessive, and reflexive.

- The *subjective pronouns* are *I, you, he, she, it, we, you* (plural), and *they*, and (surprise, surprise) you use them as subjects in the sentence.
- The *objective personal pronouns* are *me, you, him, her, it, us,* and *them.* You use them as objects in a sentence.
- The *possessive pronouns* are *my, mine, your, yours, his, her, hers, its, our, ours, their,* and *theirs*. None of the personal pronouns form their possessives with an apostrophe.
- The *reflexive pronouns* are *myself, yourself, himself, herself, itself, ourselves, yourselves,* and *themselves*.

>> **Demonstrative pronouns point to nouns.** Words like *some, many, both, that, this, those,* and *these,* when not paired with a noun, can also serve as pronouns. (*That* is my favorite book.)

>> **Relative pronouns connect descriptions to nouns.** Relative pronouns include *that, which,* and *who* (the subjective form), *whom* (the objective form), and *whose* (the possessive form). These pronouns are the subjects of descriptive clauses; *who* is the subject of clauses that describe persons, and *which* and *that* refer to entities that aren't people. Clauses that start with *which* are always nonessential (and therefore are set off with commas), and clauses that start with *that* are essential.

Defining nouns with adjectives

Adjectives describe and clarify nouns. In the sentence "The putrid odor in the lab resulted in a bunch of sick students," *putrid* defines the kind of odor, and *sick* describes the condition of the students. Without the adjectives, the sentence takes on a different and ridiculous meaning: The odor in the lab resulted in a bunch of students.

TIP

When you check a sentence on the exam for errors, make sure the adjectives are in the correct places so that each adjective describes the word it's supposed to.

Clarifying the questions with adverbs

Adverbs give extra information about action verbs, adjectives, and other adverbs. They include all words and groups of words (called *adverb phrases*) that answer the questions where, when, how,

how much, and why. In the sentence, "The chemistry students gradually recovered from smelling the very putrid odor," *gradually* explains how the students recovered.

Many adverbs end in *ly*, but not all of them do. You know a word is an adverb if it answers the question where, when, how, how much, or why in the sentence.

You may see a question that asks for the best placement of an adverb. The most logical position for an adverb in the sentence is cozied up to the action verb it describes.

Joining together with conjunctions and prepositions

Conjunctions and *prepositions* link the main elements of a sentence. These often seemingly inconsequential words can play a major role in English Test questions. Here is what you need to remember:

» **Conjunctions join words, phrases, and clauses.** The three types of conjunctions are *coordinating, correlative,* and *subordinating*. Don't worry about memorizing these terms; just know that they exist.

- The seven coordinating conjunctions — *for, and, nor, but, or, yet,* and *so* — are the ones you probably think of when you think of conjunctions. Some English teachers refer to these by their mnemonic — FANBOYS.

- Correlative conjunctions always appear in pairs: *either/or, neither/nor,* and *not only/but also*.

- Subordinating conjunctions introduce dependent clauses and connect them to independent clauses. *Although, as, because, before, if, since, unless, when,* and *while* are common examples of subordinating conjunctions. (For more on clauses, see the later section, "Phrases and clauses.")

» **Prepositions join nouns to the rest of the sentence.** We'd need several pages to list all the prepositions, but common examples are *about, above, by, for, over,* and *with*. Prepositions always appear in prepositional phrases, which also include nouns. Prepositional phrases usually describe a noun (the students *in the band*) or a verb (the football player ran *down the field*).

Piecing Together the Parts of a Sentence

The parts of speech we describe in the preceding section work together to form sentences. Every sentence has at least a subject and a verb, but most add a little bit (or a lot) more information.

Subjects and predicates

Every sentence and clause has two parts: the subject and the predicate. The subject is the main actor in the sentence; it's the noun that's doing the action in the sentence or whose condition the sentence describes. The predicate is the verb and pretty much everything else in the main idea of the sentence that isn't part of the subject. The part of the predicate that isn't the verb is called the *complement*. The complement can be an adjective, predicate noun, direct object, or indirect object.

38 PART 2 Serving Your "Sentence": The English Test

Phrases and clauses

A sentence usually contains single words, phrases, or clauses that convey more information about the sentence's main message. *Phrases* and *clauses* are groups of words that work together to form a single part of speech, like an adverb or adjective. The difference between phrases and clauses is that clauses contain their own subjects and verbs; phrases don't.

The two types of clauses are independent and dependent:

> » **Independent clauses express complete thoughts and can stand as sentences by themselves.** The sentence "Jeff opened the door, and the cat slipped out" contains two independent clauses.
>
> » **Dependent clauses express incomplete thoughts and are, therefore, sentence fragments if left by themselves.** "Although the cat slipped out" is an example of a dependent clause. To convert any dependent clause into a complete sentence, you must add an independent clause, as in "Although the cat slipped out, Jeff caught it before it could run away."

REMEMBER

Here's how to distinguish between a phrase and a clause and between an independent and a dependent clause:

> » If a group of words has a subject and a verb, it's a clause, not a phrase.
>
> » If a group of words has a subject and a verb and doesn't begin with a subordinating conjunction (see the section, "Joining together with conjunctions and prepositions," for examples of subordinating conjunctions), then it's an independent clause, not a dependent clause.

Understanding the difference between independent and dependent clauses helps you recognize a bunch of errors, such as sentence fragments, reference issues, and punctuation problems. (To understand how to spot these errors, see Chapter 6.)

Keeping Track of Punctuation Rules for Every Occasion

You use periods, commas, semicolons, and other forms of punctuation all the time when you write. But are you using them correctly? The ACT English Test gives you questions to make sure you know how to do it. Punctuation rules are pretty straightforward. After you have them down, you can be sure you're practicing proper punctuation.

Periods and question marks

The ACT rarely tests marks that end the sentence, but just in case, here's what you need to know about periods and question marks. Periods end sentences that aren't questions (like this one). Periods also follow initials, as in *J. K. Rowling*, and abbreviations, such as *etc*. But you don't use periods for initials in agency names, such as *ROTC* and *YMCA*, or for commonly used shortened forms, such as *ad* or *memo*, but the ACT rarely tests these rules.

Question marks end direct questions, like "When will dinner be ready?" However, you never put a question mark at the end of indirect questions, such as "Pam asked me when dinner would be ready."

CHAPTER 5 **Getting a Grip on Grammar and Usage** 39

Semicolons

The semicolon links two independent clauses in one sentence. Using semicolons is appropriate in the following instances:

> » **To join two independent yet closely related clauses without a conjunction:** For example, the sentence "It's almost the weekend; I can finally relax" has two independent clauses that are closely related, so they appear together in the same sentence separated by a semicolon.
>
> » **To begin a second clause with a conjunctive adverb:** Clauses that begin with conjunctive adverbs (such as *accordingly, also, besides, consequently, furthermore, hence, however, indeed, likewise, moreover, nevertheless, otherwise, similarly, so, still, therefore,* and *thus*) use a semicolon to separate them from another clause. Here's an example: "I should relax this weekend; otherwise, I'll be tired all week." Note that a comma comes after the conjunctive adverb.
>
> » **To provide clarity in complex sentences:** Semicolons appear in sentences that have a numbered series or when using commas would be confusing. See what we mean in this sentence: "The secretary's duties include (1) creating, sending, and filing documents; (2) making and organizing appointments; and (3) scheduling and planning meetings." The ACT rarely tests this use for semicolons.

Colons

Colons have several functions. You can use them in place of periods to separate two independent clauses (although semicolons usually fill this role). You can also use them to relate the introductory clause in a sentence to a relevant list of specifics, a long appositive or explanation, or a quotation. Here's an example: "Megan will be finished with her homework when she completes these three tasks: a rough outline for an essay, a worksheet of math problems, and the final draft of her chemistry report." For the ACT, the only rule you need to consider when evaluating colons is that they must be preceded by a complete independent clause.

REMEMBER

If the words before the colon don't form a complete sentence, then you've used the colon incorrectly, as in this wrong construction: "Megan will be finished with her homework when she completes: a rough outline for an essay, a worksheet of math problems, and the final draft of her chemistry report." Deleting the colon fixes the problem.

Commas

The comma is perhaps the most misused punctuation mark in the English language. Whenever you see an underlined comma in the English Test, evaluate its purpose. Here are a couple of important general rules to keep in mind when you encounter commas on the ACT:

> » **Don't put a comma in a sentence just because you think it needs a pause.** Pausing is subjective; comma rules for the ACT aren't. You may pause between *cow* and *on* in this sentence to emphasize just how whacky the image is: *I saw a cow, on a bike!* But the ACT wouldn't agree with you. That comma is wrong. Use the rules that follow in this section (not your ears) to justify whether a comma is placed properly.
>
> » **Remember that a single comma *never* separates a subject from its verb or a verb from the rest of the predicate.** A comma never comes between a prepositional phrase and the noun it describes. You may see *a pair* of commas between the subject and verb, but not a lone comma without a comma buddy.

40   PART 2 Serving Your "Sentence": The English Test

Remember these comma uses to take the guesswork out of placing commas:

- » **Series:** In a series of three or more expressions joined by one conjunction, put a comma after each expression except the last one, as in the sentence "Rachel, Bryan, and Tyler bought sandwiches, fruit, and doughnuts for the picnic." Notice that no comma comes after *Tyler,* and no comma comes before *doughnuts*.

  The ACT won't test whether you put a comma before the *and* in a series because there isn't a firm rule about that.

- » **Omitted *and*:** Use a comma to replace an omitted *and* from a sentence in certain circumstances.

  - The comma stands in for the omitted *and* that joins coordinate adjectives (those that precede and describe the same noun): Henry adores his slick, speedy bike. If there isn't an omitted *and* joining the adjectives, don't stick a comma between them: Henry adores his shiny red bike.

  - The comma replaces an omitted *and* that joins two like phrases: I studied with Jerry yesterday, with Pam today.

- » **Separation of clauses:** Use commas to join together clauses in these situations:

  - Put a comma before a coordinating conjunction that joins two independent clauses. Here's an example: The polka-dot suit was Sammie's favorite, but she didn't wear it when she was feeling shy.

  - Use a comma to set apart a beginning dependent clause from the rest of a sentence, as in "When Sammie feels shy, she doesn't wear her polka-dot suit." But don't put in a comma when the dependent clause comes after the independent clause: Sammie doesn't wear her polka-dot suit when she feels shy.

- » A run-on sentence happens when a sentence with two or more independent clauses has improper punctuation. Here's an example: I had a college interview yesterday morning and I'm pretty sure I knocked the interviewer's socks off.

- » "I had a college interview yesterday morning" and "I'm pretty sure I knocked the interviewer's socks off" are independent clauses because both have subjects (I) and verbs (*had* and *am*) and neither begins with a subordinating conjunction such as *while* or *although*. You can't just stick a conjunction or comma between these two independent clauses to make a sentence. However, you have other options:

  - Put a comma before the *and*: I had a college interview yesterday morning, and I'm pretty sure I knocked the interviewer's socks off.

  - Replace *and* with a semicolon: I had a college interview yesterday morning; I'm pretty sure I knocked the interviewer's socks off.

  - Create two separate sentences by putting a period after *morning* and taking out the *and*: I had a college interview yesterday morning. I'm pretty sure I knocked the interviewer's socks off.

  - Change one of the clauses so it's no longer independent: During my college interview yesterday morning, I'm pretty sure I knocked the interviewer's socks off.

CHAPTER 5 **Getting a Grip on Grammar and Usage** 41

- » **Nonessentials:** When a sentence includes information that's important but not crucial to the meaning of the sentence, you set off that information with commas on both sides (unless the nonessential info begins or ends a sentence — then you just use one comma). Sometimes determining whether an expression is essential is difficult, but following these guidelines can help:

  - *Asides* consist of words such as *however, in my opinion,* and *for example* and are set apart from the rest of the sentence. Here's an example: In my opinion, Sammie looks smashing in her polka-dot suit.

  - *Appositives* provide additional information about a noun that isn't critical to understanding the main idea of the sentence: The polka-dot swimsuit, the one that Sammie wears only when she isn't feeling shy, contains pink dots on a black background. In the sentence "The science teacher, Ms. Paul, scheduled a meeting with her top students," *Ms. Paul* lets you know the science teacher's name. Yet, without that information, the sentence still retains its meaning. When a name is part of a title, as in the sentence "Professor Paul requested a meeting" or "Science teacher Ms. Paul won an award," don't use commas.

  - *Titles and distinctions* that follow a name are enclosed in commas. Case in point: Georgia White, RN, is the first speaker for career day.

  - *Abbreviations,* such as *etc., e.g.,* and *i.e.,* are enclosed in commas. Here's an example: Tyler pulled out the sandwiches, drinks, doughnuts, etc., from the picnic basket.

  - *Dates and place names* contain what can be considered nonessential information and are, therefore, punctuated with commas. For example, "Mike attended school in Boulder, Colorado, from September 1, 2008, to May 23, 2011." Notice that commas appear on both sides of the state name and both sides of the year in the date.

  - *Nonrestrictive clauses* are by definition nonessential. Because nonrestrictive clauses always provide information that doesn't affect the meaning of a sentence, commas always set them apart from the rest of the sentence. The second clause in the sentence "The meeting took place in Ms. Paul's classroom, which is just down the hall from the library" provides important information, but the meaning of the sentence wouldn't change if that information were left out.

  - A *restrictive* clause provides essential descriptive information, so commas don't separate it from the rest of the sentence: The meeting took place in the classroom that is just down the hall from the library.

REMEMBER

    You begin nonrestrictive clauses with *which*, restrictive clauses with *that*. (Notice in that last sentence we used a comma to replace the omitted *and* that joined the two similarly-constructed phrases.) If a clause describes a person, begin it with *who* regardless of whether it's restrictive or nonrestrictive.

Dashes

Dashes work like colons to introduce long appositives or like commas to designate nonessential information. They can separate a beginning series from the rest of a sentence and signal abrupt breaks in the continuity of a sentence. Here's an example: A state championship, a college scholarship, and a Super Bowl ring — such were the dreams of the high school quarterback.

Apostrophes

Apostrophes have two purposes — creating contractions and forming possessives. The apostrophe takes the place of the missing letter or letters in a contraction. Think *they're* (they are), *can't* (cannot), *here's* (here is), and so on.

To show ownership of one noun by another, use an apostrophe. For example, a dog owned by a girl is "the girl's dog" and an opinion of a judge is "a judge's opinion." Here are some rules for forming possessives:

> » **Most possessives are formed by adding 's to the end of a singular noun or a plural noun that doesn't end in s.** Here are three examples: "Betty's car," "children's teacher," and "the committee's decision."
>
> » **If the possessive noun is plural and ends in s, only add the apostrophe.** Some examples include "the four boys' bikes" and "the neighbors' front porch."

TIP

Whenever you see one noun immediately followed by another, you're almost certainly dealing with the possessive form. The first noun possesses the other, so you format it appropriately.

REMEMBER

None of the possessive pronouns contain an apostrophe. (*It's* is a contraction of *it is*, not the possessive form of *it*.) But indefinite pronouns do contain apostrophes, as in the sentence "Somebody's dog chewed my carpet."

IN THIS CHAPTER

» Recognizing English Test errors and discovering how to correct them

» Finding the best way to add, delete, or position elements of paragraphs and passages

Chapter 6
Spotting Usage Errors and Ripping through Rhetorical Questions

Almost half of the ACT English Test questions test what most people lump together in the general category they call English: punctuation, sentence structure, and basic grammar, including subject/verb agreement, verb tense, pronoun use, and so on. That's the stuff you probably forget (or intentionally purge from your brain) ten minutes after being tested on it. The other half covers rhetorical skills, which test general writing style and organization — in other words, the stuff you use every time you construct a sentence. Chapter 5 provides the foundation for the grammar and structure basics you need to know to do well on the English Test. In this chapter, we identify the errors and concepts that continually crop up on the ACT and show you exactly what to focus on to deal with them.

Spotting Questions That Test Standard English (Grammar) Conventions

The ACT tests a bunch of writing errors. You can spot these grammar questions because they're proceeded by this prompt: "Which choice makes the sentence most grammatically acceptable?" This section highlights some of the usage errors that appear most frequently so that you're prepared to conquer them without breaking a sweat.

Properly placing punctuation marks

A preponderance (or huge number) of English Test questions require you to evaluate the proper way to punctuate one sentence or more. This section reviews the types of punctuation errors the ACT tests the most and pinpoints the clues to look for when you're choosing the best mark for the job.

When you're tasked with making a sentence grammatically acceptable, consider the underlined (and highlighted in the digital format) portion of an English passage and first look for a comma, semicolon, or other punctuation. Chances are the underlined punctuation mark is the focus of the question, especially if you glance at the answer options, and all contain similar words with different punctuation options. Choose the best answer based on your keen knowledge of the rules (see Chapter 5) rather than a subjective feeling.

Semicolons and periods

Underlined semicolons and periods are easy to evaluate. The two marks essentially have the same purpose: they separate independent clauses. Periods punctuate sentences, and the primary job of a semicolon is to join independent clauses in the same sentence. So just follow these steps when you see a period or semicolon in a potential answer choice:

1. **Read the words that come before the period or semicolon.**

    If the group of words doesn't contain a subject and a verb or does but begins with a subordinating conjunction or relative pronoun, it isn't an independent clause, and the period or semicolon can't be right. If the words have a subject and verb and don't begin with a subordinating conjunction, the clause is independent, and the period or semicolon may be proper. Check Step 2.

2. **Read the words after the period or semicolon.**

    If they don't create an independent clause, the period or semicolon doesn't work. If they do make an independent clause, however, the period or semicolon is probably appropriate. If an answer follows a semicolon with a coordinating conjunction such as *and*, *but*, or *or*, that answer is incorrect. It's never appropriate to place a semicolon before a clause that begins with a coordinating conjunction.

If your answer choices include an option with a period and another option with a semicolon, and everything else in the two answers is exactly the same (except for the capitalized word after the period), then you can likely eliminate both answers. Because both punctuation marks serve a similar function and you can't have two right answers, both options must be wrong.

Try the steps on a sample sentence:

Which choice makes the sentence most grammatically acceptable?

<u>The pond dried up after the year-long drought; the wildlife that</u> previously fed on the fish and insects had to find resources elsewhere.

(A) NO CHANGE

(B) The pond dried up after the year-long drought; and the wildlife that

(C) The pond dried up after the year-long drought, the wildlife that

(D) When the pond dried up after the year-long drought; the wildlife that

The underlined part contains a semicolon, so check first for punctuation. If the semicolon joins two independent clauses, the answer is likely Choice (A). The words to the left of the semicolon make up an independent clause. They contain a main subject *pond* and verb *dried* and don't begin with a subordinating conjunction. So far, so good. The stuff that comes after the semicolon is also an independent clause. There's a main subject *wildlife* and verb *had* and no beginning subordinating conjunction. The semicolon in Choice (A) is likely the correct answer. (For more on how to approach English Test questions, see Chapter 4.)

Choice (B) places a conjunction after the semicolon, which makes the semicolon wrong. Choice (C) creates the dreaded comma splice. It's never proper to join independent clauses with a comma and no coordinating conjunction. Choice (D) sticks the subordinating conjunction *when* ahead of the first clause, making it dependent instead of independent. You separate a beginning dependent clause with a comma instead of a semicolon. The sentence is right the way it is.

Colons

When the underlined part or possible answer choices contain a colon, concentrate on the words that come before the colon. If they create an independent clause that doesn't continue after the colon, the colon is likely okay. If the beginning is a phrase or dependent clause, the colon can't be right.

Although the colon has to be preceded by an independent clause, any format (a list, phrase, or clause) can come after it as long as it elaborates on the information in the beginning independent clause before the colon.

Dashes

To figure out whether a single dash is proper, determine whether it could be replaced by a colon. When you see two dashes in a sentence, ask yourself whether they could be exchanged with two commas designating nonessential information. If the answer is "yes" in either situation, the dashes work just fine.

Commas

The ACT mainly tests the use of the comma for designating nonessential information and separating phrases and clauses. If a question gives you four choices with the same wording but different comma positions, you're likely applying the rules for separating out nonessential stuff. A pair of commas (or a comma paired with a period) work together to designate nonessential information, such as asides and descriptive clauses that begin with *which*. See Chapter 5 for the types of detail that aren't essential and information about the rules. Basically, if the main idea doesn't change when you take out the words between the commas, then that information is likely nonessential.

Here's an example of what these questions look like:

Which choice makes the sentence most grammatically acceptable?

The <u>concert, which was held outdoors, attracted</u> thousands of music lovers from all over the country.

(A) NO CHANGE

(B) concert which, was held outdoors, attracted

(C) concert which was held outdoors, attracted

(D) concert, which was held outdoors attracted,

Notice that all answers are exactly the same except for the comma placement. This is your clue that the question likely tests the proper punctuation of a nonessential element. To answer this question, examine the information between the commas in the sentence and answer choices. The phrase "which was held outdoors" provides extra information about the concert that isn't essential to the core meaning of the sentence. Choice (A) is looking good. The commas in Choice (B) suggest that "was held outdoors" is expendable, but if you remove those words, you're left with "The concert which attracted thousands of music lovers from all over the country," which isn't

CHAPTER 6 **Spotting Usage Errors and Ripping through Rhetorical Questions** 47 even a complete sentence. Choice (C) indicates that all the words after "outdoors" are nonessential; removing them leaves you with "The concert which was held outdoors," another incomplete sentence. Choice (D) is also incorrect because it includes "attracted" in the nonessential element. Without "attracted," the sentence has no verb. Choice (A) is the only choice that properly punctuates the nonessential information in the sentence.

Other comma questions likely concern the rules for separating phrases and clauses. Eliminating wrong answers for both situations requires you to perform a little detective work. Don your tweed cape, Sherlock style, and answer these questions to solve the Case of the Perfectly Placed Comma:

» **Does a single comma appear anywhere between the subject and verb?** If the answer is "yes," the comma isn't perfectly placed. So you know that the comma in this sentence doesn't work because it appears by itself between the subject *pond* and the verb *provided*: The pond that dried up last year, formerly provided a viable habitat for local wildlife.

» **Does a single comma come between the verb and the rest of the predicate?** If so, the comma isn't placed perfectly. This comma is wrong because it separates the verb *provided* from its object *what*: The little pond provided, what many would consider to be a viable habitat for the local wildlife.

» **Does a single comma separate a prepositional phrase from the noun it describes?** If so, the comma isn't correct. This faulty comma comes between the prepositional phrase *for the local wildlife* and the noun it describes *habitat*: The pond provides a viable habitat, for the local wildlife.

» **Does the comma separate two independent clauses without the help of a conjunction?** If it does, the comma isn't correctly placed. Check the words that precede the comma to see whether they make up an independent clause (which has a main subject and verb and no beginning subordinating conjunction). Then check the words that come after the comma. If they also create an independent clause, the comma is wrong. The comma in this example is improper because it joins two independent clauses: The pond that dried up last year provided a viable habitat for local waterfowl, now those birds must find another resource.

The options to correct this comma splice vary. Here are some of the options the ACT may provide:

- **Add a coordinating conjunction.** The pond that dried up last year provided a viable habitat for local waterfowl, but now those birds must find another resource.

- **Replace with a semicolon.** The pond that dried up last year provided a viable habitat for local waterfowl; now those birds must find another resource.

- **Create two sentences.** The pond that dried up last year provided a viable habitat for local waterfowl. Now those birds must find another resource.

- **Change one of the clauses so that it's no longer independent.** The pond that dried up last year provided a viable habitat for local waterfowl, birds that now must find another resource.

TIP

Although the ACT expects you to know that commas separate items in a series, it doesn't contain questions that directly test this rule. Take heart. Although ACT passages always includes a comma before *and* in any series, you will never encounter an English question that asks you to pick a side in the intense grammar controversy regarding whether a comma belongs before *and* in a series. If you need to review the general rule regarding serial commas, see Chapter 5.

REMEMBER

Notice that the questions don't include "Does the sentence need a pause?" Pauses are subjective, so evaluate commas based on the rules rather than whether you think the sentence could use a break.

48 PART 2 Serving Your "Sentence": The English Test

Picking up on pronoun errors

If you see a pronoun in the underlined part of a sentence for a grammar question, you're likely being tested on issues with the pronoun reference (the noun the pronoun refers to) or using the proper form. Here are some tips on what to look for when you see a pronoun in the underlined part:

» **An underlined *this*, *that*, *which*, *these*, *those*, *it*, or *they*, may indicate a faulty reference.** Whenever you see one of these pronouns in the underlined part, check the sentence or prior sentence for the noun the pronoun renames. If the noun is plural, the pronoun must be plural; if it's singular, the pronoun must be singular.

The pronoun reference in this sentence is faulty: You can determine the ripeness of citrus by handling them and noting their color. *Citrus* is a singular noun, so using a plural pronoun such as *them* to refer to it is wrong. To correct this sentence, change it to this: You can determine the ripeness of citrus by handling it and noting its color.

» **An underlined *this*, *that*, *some*, *which*, *these*, *those*, *it*, or *they*, or other personal, relative, and demonstrative pronouns may indicate an unclear reference problem.** If you can't easily find the noun a pronoun renames (we mean actually be able to point your finger to it) the reference is unclear and must be clarified. Usually you correct these problems by replacing the pronoun with a specific noun. Look for a noun in the answer choices.

This sentence contains an unclear reference: Smart growers make sure they supply the ripest fruits possible so they will buy again. The second *they* in the sentence has an ambiguous reference. The only nouns the pronoun could rename are *growers* and *fruits*. Neither of these would buy from growers again. To correct the problem, replace the second *they* with the actual noun that designates the buyer: Smart growers make sure they supply the ripest fruits possible so consumers will buy again.

» **An underlined *who* or *whom* is likely testing proper form.** You use *who* as a subject and *whom* as an object. So it's "the man who gives the gift" and "the man to whom the gift is given."

To figure out whether *who* or *whom* is better, substitute *he* and *him*. If *him* works better, choose *whom*; if *he* is a better substitute, choose *who*: He gives the gift, but the gift is given to him. Usually *whom* is only proper when the pronoun follows a preposition.

The next time your grammar teacher asks you to name two pronouns, you can be a smart aleck and shout out, "Who, me?"

» **Evaluate whether an underlined reflexive pronoun is proper.** The ACT hardly ever tests you on whether you use the subjective or objective forms of personal pronouns other than who, but it may test you on when the reflexive form is proper.

Use reflexive pronouns only when the receiver and the doer of an action are the same. The sentence "Please return the forms to the secretary and myself" is wrong because you aren't the doer of the action of returning the forms; you're telling someone else to give the forms to you and your secretary. The correct version of this sentence is "Please return the forms to the secretary and me." Note that a sentence such as "He came up with the idea all by himself" is accurate because the doer and the receiver of the action are the same person.

» **An underlined *its*, *it's*, *they*, or *they're* usually indicates a question that tests you on the possessive form of personal pronouns.** No personal pronoun uses an apostrophe to form the possessive, so *it's* and *they're* are contractions of "it is" and "they are" rather than the possessives of *it* and *they*. This sentence demonstrates the proper use of both forms: It's an indication of happiness when a dog wags its tail.

To test whether *it's* or *its* is proper, replace the pronoun with "it is." If "it is" sounds right, the proper form is *it's*; if "it is" doesn't work, the proper form is *its*.

CHAPTER 6 Spotting Usage Errors and Ripping through Rhetorical Questions 49

REMEMBER

The form of *its'* doesn't exist in the English language, so an answer that includes *its'* is never correct.

» **Underlined relative pronouns may test whether you know what pronoun goes with what kinds of nouns.** Use *who* to refer to people. On the ACT, *which* and *that* refer to animals and things. So it's better to say, "There's the police officer who pulled me over yesterday" than "There's the police officer that pulled me over yesterday." Though we can't think of a time when we would be happy to make either statement!

TIP

The ACT won't ask you to choose the correct third-person pronouns to refer to people. You won't encounter English questions that ask you choose whether to refer to a person as "he," "she," or "they" because these designations depend on a person's pronoun preferences rather than adherence to any set of pronoun rules.

Forming possessives

Whenever you see an underlined part that includes two nouns smack dab next to each other, you're likely dealing with the possessive form of the first noun, especially if the answer choices show you a variety of formats with apostrophes. These questions require you to determine whether the possessive form is necessary, and then if it is, to apply it correctly. Here's an example question to show you how:

EXAMPLE

Which choice makes the sentence most grammatically acceptable?

The parents made sure that their bags included several of the <u>babies colorful toys</u> to amuse the twins during the car trip.

(A) NO CHANGE

(B) babies' colorful toys

(C) baby's colorful toys

(D) babies fully colored toys

To answer this question, first check the answers. Notice that two of the four contain apostrophes — a good clue that you're dealing with possessive form. Check to see whether you have two nouns right next to each other. Almost always, seeing two nouns together indicates that the first should be in possessive form. The rule is true even when an adjective that describes the second noun comes between the two nouns. The noun *babies* precedes *colorful*, an adjective. But that adjective describes the noun *toys* right after it, so the simplified form would be "babies toys." Because *babies* is a noun and *toys* is a noun, you must put *babies* in the proper possessive form.

TIP

You can double-check by flipping the nouns and adding an "of the" like this: "toys of the babies." If the "of the" test works, you can be absolutely sure you're dealing with the possessive form.

So eliminate Choices (A) and (D) because neither is in possessive form. (The *fully colored* is just there in Choice (D) to try to distract you from the real error.) The remaining two choices provide either the singular possessive or the plural possessive. Figuring out which is correct on the ACT is usually easy. Look for clues in the sentence. The toys are supposed to amuse the twins, and *twins* is plural, so the correct answer is the plural possessive in Choice (B) where the apostrophe follows the ending *s*. For more on how to form possessives, check out Chapter 5. To review the possessive forms of personal pronouns, see "Picking up on pronoun errors" earlier in this chapter.

50   PART 2 **Serving Your "Sentence": The English Test**

Evaluating verbs

When you see an underlined verb, check for two potential errors in this order:

1. **Make sure the verb agrees in number (plural or singular) with its subject.**

   Okay, so subjects and verbs don't actually fight, but they do sometimes disagree. To bring peace to the situation, you must pair plural subjects with plural verbs and singular subjects with singular verbs. If you see a verb in the underlined portion of the English Test, find the subject it goes with and make sure they agree.

   When the subject isn't simple or obvious, finding it may be difficult. Just take a look at this sentence: Terry's continual quest to embellish his truck with a ton of amenities make it hard for him to stick to a budget. The subject is *quest* (a singular noun), but the interjection of "to embellish his truck with a ton of amenities" between the subject and verb may confuse you into thinking that *amenities* (a plural noun) is the subject. However, *amenities* can't be the subject of the sentence because it's the object of a preposition, and a noun can't be an object and a subject at the same time.

   To spot subject/verb agreement errors in a complex sentence, focus on the main elements of the sentence by crossing out nouns that function as objects (especially those in prepositional phrases). Then check the subjects and verbs to make sure they agree. When you remove all the objective noun forms from the sentence "Terry's continual quest to embellish his truck with a ton of amenities make it hard for him to stick to a budget," you get "Terry's quest make it hard." Now the problem is obvious! The singular noun *quest* requires the singular verb *makes*.

   You don't need to check for subject/verb agreement when the verb in question is a past tense action verb. Action verbs in the past tense don't have a plural and singular form.

2. **Check for proper verb tense.**

   After you've made sure that the verb agrees with the subject, check the tenses of underlined verbs. Verb forms must be in the proper tense for a sentence to make sense. Review the purpose for each verb tense in Chapter 5 to help you spot incorrect tenses. For example, you know that using future perfect tense in "Yesterday, I will have read 300 pages" is incorrect because *yesterday* is in the past, and you don't use future tense to refer to past events.

   The other verbs in the same sentence and usually the same paragraph give you clues to what tense a particular verb should be in. Generally, all verbs in a sentence should be in the same tense. For example, the sentence "I had read 300 pages in the book when my friends invite me to see a movie" must be incorrect because *had read* is past perfect tense and *invite* is present tense. You can correct the sentence by changing *invite* from present tense to past tense *(invited)*.

   In recent tests, the ACT has included at least one question that gives you the option to choose one of these tenses: *must of, may of, might of, could of, should of, would of,* and so on. These questions are easy to answer correctly because *of* **isn't a verb.** It's a preposition. The proper constructions are *must have, may have, might have, could have, should have,* and *would have* or their contractions, for example, *would've*. There will never ever be a time when one of these verb + *of* constructions will be the right answer. You just added a point to your raw score by reading this chapter!

   Whenever you see a verb in a grammar question, check subject/verb agreement first. The ACT will often throw a bunch of different tenses in the answer choice options to distract you from the real issue of subject/verb agreement.

Calling out sentence fragments

Sentence fragments are incomplete sentences. They usually show up on the ACT either as dependent clauses that pretend to convey complete thoughts or as a bunch of words with something that looks like a verb but doesn't act like one.

Always keep the following in mind:

>> **Dependent clauses by themselves are fragments because they don't provide complete thoughts.** "Although the stairs are steep . . ." is far from a complete thought.

>> **Phrases that contain verb participles (one part of a verb phrase such as a word that ends in *ing* or *ed*) don't express complete thoughts even though the participles look like verbs.** The ACT most commonly offends with the participle *being*. *Being* all by itself isn't a verb. So this phrase isn't a sentence: "The project being quite complicated." To correct the problem, look for an answer choice that converts the *ing* word to its conjugated form. For the sample sentence, you'd look for an *is* or a *was* to replace *being*.

Whenever you see *being* in the underlined part or the answer choices, run from it like the plague. An answer that contains *being* is almost always wrong.

Identifying problems with parallelism

All phrases joined by conjunctions should be constructed in the same way. For example, the following sentence has a problem with parallelism: "Ann spent the morning taking practice tests, studying word lists, and she read a chapter in a novel." Not all the elements joined by the *and* in this sentence are constructed in the same way. The first two elements are phrases that begin with a gerund (or *ing* form); the last element is a clause. Changing *read* to a gerund and dropping *she* solves the problem: "Ann spent the morning taking practice tests, studying word lists, and reading a chapter in a novel."

When you see a sentence with a list of any sort, check for a lack of parallelism. Items in a series may be nouns, verbs, adjectives, or entire clauses. However, nonparallel verbs are the items that most commonly have errors. When a clause contains more than one verb, watch out for this particular error.

Recognizing misplaced modifiers

The ACT will surely test how well you can spot errors in modification. *Modifier* is a fancy term for words or phrases, such as adjectives and adverbs, that give more information about other words, usually nouns and verbs. Errors occur when modifiers are too far away from the words they modify and when what they're modifying is unclear.

Keep the following guidelines in mind whenever you're dealing with modifiers:

>> **Modifiers must be as close to the words they modify as possible.** The sentence "Sam set down the speech he wrote on the desk" is incorrect because of a misplaced modifier. It sounds like Sam wrote the speech on the desk! The sentence "Sam set down his speech on the desk" is much better. The ACT tests adjectives and adverbs in two general ways:

- **The English Test may give you four constructions and ask you to pick the one that pairs the proper parts of speech.** So you need to be able to recognize the best construction of paired words such as these:

    (A) blind admiration

    (B) blindly admiration

    (C) blind admire

    (D) blind admiringly

    The first pair is correct because it has an adjective *blind* describe a noun *admiration*. The other three are wrong because they incorrectly have an adverb *blindly* describe a noun *admiration*, an adjective *blind* describe a verb *admire*, and an adjective *blind* describe an adverb *admiringly*.

- **It may ask you to position an underlined part of speech — usually an adverb.** Whenever a question asks you to position an underlined portion in a sentence, first determine the part of speech of the underlined part. Underlined adverbs or adverb phrases should be near a verb. Underlined adjectives or adjective phrases or clauses should go next to the noun they describe.

» **Beginning participle phrases must have a clear reference.** A beginning participle phrase in a sentence always modifies the subject of the sentence, so the sentence has to be constructed in a way that relates the phrase to the subject. If it doesn't, the sentence contains a dangling participle. For a definition of a participle, read "Calling out sentence fragments" earlier in this chapter.

Consider this sentence: "Driving down the road, a deer darted in front of me." If you read this sentence literally, you may believe the *deer* drove down the road because the beginning phrase "driving down the road" refers to the subject of the sentence, which is *deer*. To make it clear that the driver — not the deer — drove down the road, you need to change this phrase to a clause: "As I was driving down the road, a deer darted in front of me." Alternatively, you may need to rewrite the sentence to change the subject: "Driving down the road, I spotted a deer darting out in front of me."

TIP

Because the test makers tend to focus on modification errors involving beginning phrases, be sure to check for this error every time you see a sentence with a beginning phrase.

» **Place *not only* and *but also* in parallel positions within a sentence.** People often place *not only* and *but also* incorrectly. Here's an example of a wrong way to use these expressions: "Angelique *not only* was exasperated *but also* frightened when she locked herself out of the house."

See the problem? The phrase *not only* comes before the verb was, but the phrase *but also* comes before the adjective frightened. Correct it so that both elements come before adjectives: "Angelique was *not only* exasperated *but also* frightened when she locked herself out of the house."

Checking for Proper Production of Writing

The other types of English Test questions deal with general writing and language skills, which is a fancy way of saying they test the best way to structure and word a piece of writing. For these questions, you generally seek answers that reflect the clearest, most precise constructions. The question prompts for these types vary.

Eliminating superfluous words

Sentences that say the same idea twice or that use more words than necessary may be grammatically correct but still need fixing. The ACT wants you to notice and get rid of superfluous language. For example, saying, "The custodian added an additional row of desks that were brown" is silly. The construction of "added an additional" is needlessly repetitive, and the desks can be described more efficiently. The sentence reads better as "The custodian added a row of brown desks."

The good news is that the ACT lets you know when you've come upon a redundancy question. It simply asks you to determine "Which choice is least redundant in context?" Here are some tips for approaching redundancy questions:

> » **When the answer choices say roughly the same thing, choose the one that contains the fewest words.** The extra stuff in the other answer choices usually restates information that's already conveyed elsewhere. Here's an example of a redundant construction: The essay contains numerous redundancies that create lots of repetition. The definition of redundancy is that it creates repetition, so you should eliminate the ending relative clause, "that create lots of repetition." So "story's moral" is better than "the moral of the story" (sorry Aesop), and "flawed reasoning" is more succinct than "reasoning that is fallacious."

WARNING

> Don't automatically choose the shortest answer for redundancy questions. Always read the short answers in the context of the whole sentence to make sure they don't produce an error.

> » **Check the answers for an omit option.** If a redundancy question contains an option to omit the underlined portion, check the sentence and surrounding sentences to see whether the underlined part repeats an idea or is irrelevant. If it does or is, choose the answer that gets rid of the underlined part altogether.

> » **Check for adjectives and adverbs that have the same meaning as the words they describe or two or more describing words that mean the same.** Describing someone as an "intelligent genius" or as an "able, capable leader" doesn't add new information because geniuses are by their nature intelligent and *able* and *capable* have pretty much the same meaning. Find the answer that eliminates the repetition.

> » **If you're given a choice between active voice and passive voice, choose active voice.** Passive voice isn't wrong, but it's weak and vague. It beats around the bush to make a point. The passive voice in the following sentence hides who's doing the action: "The speech was heard by most of the students." The sentence isn't technically incorrect, but it's better said this way: "Most of the students heard the speech." Notice also that the sentence in active voice uses fewer words.

Completing the mission

We call questions that ask you for an answer that accomplishes a certain goal *mission questions*. The mission question gives you a task, and your job is to find the choice that best completes this task. The task could be to find an answer that matches the author's style or tone or effectively accomplish an author's goal. For example, you may see something like this: "The author wishes to convey a high level of urgency in extricating the clown from the packed Volkswagen. Which of the following choices best accomplishes this goal?"

REMEMBER

The key to finding the correct answer to a mission question is to remember what you aren't looking for. You aren't evaluating whether the answer choices contain grammar errors or sentence structure problems; you aren't choosing the best-constructed answer. Your only focus is on the answer that fulfills the mission.

Here are some tips for answering mission questions:

>> Read the question carefully to find the one or two qualifications the correct answer must fulfill. In the clown car example, you're looking for great urgency and getting the clowns out.

>> Highlight the qualifications in the question so you can find them easily as you read through the answer choices.

>> Eliminate answers that don't meet the qualifications.

>> From the remaining, choose the most specific correct answer — the one that provides the most vivid images. So an answer such as "carnival workers rushed to wrench the terrified clowns from the flaming car" is better than "carnival workers urgently pulled the clowns out of the car." The second option tries to entice you with its inclusion of *urgently*, but its language isn't as powerful as the words in the first.

Determining the function of a deletion

The ACT may underline or otherwise designate a word, phrase, or clause and then ask you what would happen to the text if the indicated part were deleted. These questions are easier to answer if you concentrate on the role the proposed deletion serves in the sentence before you look at the answer choices.

So you may be asked what this sentence would lose if its underlined part were deleted: "The floral arrangement contained a variety of blooms of vivid oranges, brilliant blues, and sunny yellows." The underlined part gives you specific details. Without it, you wouldn't know the flowers' colors. You then check the answer choices for one that clarifies that the sentence would lose visual details. Eliminate answers that are beyond the scope of the underlined information, such as that the sentence would lose information that conveyed a list of the florist's favorite colors.

Often a deletion question provides you with an answer option that suggests the underlined part contains irrelevant information. That answer is hardly ever correct. Although the ACT frequently tests you on whether details are necessary, it doesn't usually use deletion questions for this task.

Pondering an addition

To test relevance (and sometimes redundancy), the ACT presents you with phrases and clauses and asks you whether they should be added to the paragraph. The overwhelming consideration is whether the information is relevant. Skim the entire paragraph that would contain the proposed addition to answer these two questions:

>> **What is the paragraph's topic?** If the addition relates to that topic, it's likely relevant and should be included. If the addition's topic is unrelated, it shouldn't be inserted.

>> **Does the paragraph already state the information in the addition?** Even if the proposed addition is relevant, it shouldn't be added if it repeats information that's already there.

Addition questions are usually formatted as "yes, yes, no, no." (See Chapter 4 for details on this question format.) If the answer to the first question is *yes* and the second question is *no*, choose between the two *yes* answer options based on which provides the best justification for the *yes*. If the answer to the first question is *no* or the answer to the second question is *no*, choose between the two *no* options. Usually the two *no* options will give you a "no because it's irrelevant" or a "no because it's redundant." Choose the one that fits.

Creating smooth transitions

There are two types of transition questions: one that asks you to choose the best transition word or phrase to introduce a clause and one that asks you for the best first or last sentence of a paragraph. In both cases, check for clues in the elements that precede and follow the transition.

Transition words

The first type asks you this: "Which transition word or phrase is most logical in context?" The transition is underlined in the sentence, and your answers give you a NO CHANGE and three possible replacements. To figure out the best answer, examine the events in the sentence, or sentences, that come before the transition and the sentence that contains the transition. Then choose the word or words that best relate the two events.

Transitions show three main relationships between events:

> » **Similarity:** If the events are similar, choose transitions such as *likewise, additionally, similarly,* and so on, or choose no transition at all.
>
> » **Contrast:** If the events oppose each other, choose transitions such as *however, in contrast, on the contrary,* and so on.
>
> » **Cause and effect:** If one event causes the other, choose transitions such as *therefore, because, as a result,* and so on.

Whenever you see two answer choices that provide the same transition type (for example, *in contrast*, and *on the other hand*), you can eliminate both of them. They can't both be right, so they must both be wrong.

Transition sentences

Questions that seek the best transition sentences may resemble mission questions, something like "Which of the following sentences would best conclude this paragraph and introduce the next one?" or "Which of the following sentences would best introduce the topic of this paragraph?" Or they may simply underline the first sentence of a paragraph and ask you to choose the best option. In all cases, you're looking for an answer that relates the topic of the second paragraph to elements of the preceding paragraph. Attack them in two steps:

1. **Eliminate answers that don't relate to the second paragraph — the one that comes after if you're dealing with a concluding sentence or the one that contains a first sentence.**

    Read the entire paragraph to determine its main topic. If an answer doesn't somehow set up that topic, it's likely wrong.

2. **From the remaining answers, choose the one that harkens back to an element in the first paragraph — the one that contains a concluding sentence or precedes an introductory sentence.**

An answer choice that provides the option to include *no* transition is almost always the correct answer. Read the two sentences without the transition. If it doesn't sound wrong without it, you don't need a transition.

Transition questions can be tricky if you try to answer them too quickly. Take the time to carefully examine the stuff that precedes and follows the transition, and the correct answer will become clear.

Organizing and positioning elements

The ACT will ask you to position words, sentences, and even whole paragraphs. Questions that require placing words in a sentence are usage questions. We discuss these in an earlier section "Recognizing misplaced modifiers." In this section, we cover what to do with the sentences and paragraphs. Positioning questions are easy to spot because the answer choices are usually just a list of numbers that refer to numbered sentences or paragraphs.

TIP

Some students get overwhelmed by positioning questions and the time it takes to answer them. Remember, though, the ACT must supply obvious clues to the correct position because it has to be able to justify its correct answers, so these questions really aren't that time-consuming. Here are some tips to help you spot the clues and become a star at perfectly proper placement:

- » **Before you examine the paragraphs and passages for clues, check the answer options.** The digital format highlights the position choices, but if you're taking a paper test, put a pencil mark on your booklet to indicate the four possible placements for yourself. So if an answer gives you "before Sentence 3," find Sentence 3 in the paragraph and put a pencil dot or check before it. Do the same for the other three choices. Then you don't have to keep checking the answer choices to see your options. And you won't waste time considering positions that aren't included in the answer choices.

- » **When you place sentences in paragraphs, look for pronouns in the sentence you're placing or in the paragraph it fits into.** Almost always, there'll be one. Remember that pronouns refer back to the nouns they rename, so you'll position the sentence so the pronoun comes in after the noun it refers to.

- » **Check the paragraphs you position for key, but sometimes subtle, clues.** For example, it's customary in essays and articles to introduce people by their first and last names and after that, refer to them by just their last names. So don't put a paragraph that calls a person by last name before a paragraph that contains both the first and last name.

- » **When you place a sentence or paragraph, determine whether it contains mostly details or mostly general information.** Details generally follow general information. Also, note the transition words that initiate sentences and paragraphs. They'll tip you off. For example, a sentence or paragraph that begins with *finally* will conclude others in a list.

Seeing the big picture

Questions that ask you about the passage as a whole come in several varieties. The most common are really just mission questions. They ask you whether the passage fulfills a particular goal. The answers are presented in "yes, yes, no, no" format. Often, the easiest way to determine the main purpose of a passage is to read its title. Compare the title to the answer choices; if you find a similarity, you've likely found the answer. If you're still not sure whether the answer is *yes* or *no*, read the reasons given by each answer choice. Usually, you can eliminate two choices because the reasons they give are so off-base. Examine the remaining answers carefully to choose the most true and relevant reason.

Sticking to appropriate vocabulary and standard expressions

The ACT includes questions that ask "Which choice is clearest and most precise in context?" Usually that means picking an answer that most specifically conveys the sentence's intended meaning and tone. Most of the time, you'll be familiar with the options, and finding the correct answer is as simple as reading each choice within the context of the sentence to determine which sounds right.

Don't despair if an answer isn't part of your *lexicon* (fancy vocab word for vocabulary), though. You can use the words you do know to help you eliminate or choose a vocab word you've never seen before. For instance, if none of the familiar words in the answers work in the sentence, the answer you don't know is probably correct. If one of the answers works nicely in the sentence, it's likely correct, and you can ignore the unfamiliar answer.

Don't pick an unfamiliar word in the choices just because you don't know it and think difficult words equal correct answers. Often, words you do know offer the clearest, most precise construction.

You may have to determine the best choice of words for a particular context or tone, or you may need to recognize proper idiomatic expressions. English speakers use certain words in certain ways for no particular reason other than because that's the way it is. It's called proper diction. But sometimes, even native English speakers fail to use idiomatic expressions correctly. It's common to hear people use *further* instead of *farther* when they mean distance or *less* instead of *fewer* when they refer to the number of countable items. Memorizing all of the standard forms is impossible, but thankfully, you'll be able to figure out the answers to most of the diction questions by using your ear. Check out Table 6-1 to see a few of the expressions that may be less obvious.

The ACT often contains diction questions that involve prepositions. When you see an underlined preposition in a question, make sure the preposition works with the elements it joins. For example, "we drove *across* the country" is correct, while "we drove *on* the country" is incorrect.

TABLE 6-1 Commonly Tested Words and Expressions

Word or Expression	Rule	Correct Use
among/between	Use among for comparing three or more things or persons and between for comparing two things or persons.	Between the two of us there are few problems, but among the four of us there is much discord.
amount/number	Use amount to describe singular nouns and number to describe plural nouns.	I can't count the number of times I've miscalculated the amount of money I've spent on groceries.
as . . . as	When you use as in a comparison, use the construction as . . . as.	The dog is as wide as he is tall.
better/best worse/worst	Use better and worse to compare two things; use best and worst to compare more than two things.	Of the two products, the first is better known, but this product is the best known of all 20 on the market.
different from	Use different from rather than different than.	This plan is different from the one we implemented last year. (Not this: This plan is different than last year's.)
effect/affect	Generally, use effect as a noun and affect as a verb.	No one could know how the effect of the presentation would affect the client's choice.
either/or neither/nor	Use or with either and nor with neither.	Neither Nellie nor Isaac wanted to go to either the party or the concert.
er/est	Use the er form (called the comparative form) to compare exactly two items; use the est form (called the superlative form) to compare more than two items.	I am taller than my brother Beau, but Darren is the tallest member of our family.

PART 2 Serving Your "Sentence": The English Test

Word or Expression	Rule	Correct Use
farther/further	Use farther to refer to distance and further to refer to time or quantity.	Carol walked farther today than she did yesterday, and she vows to further study the benefits of walking.
good/well	Good is an adjective that modifies a noun. Well is an adverb that usually answers the question how.	It's a good thing that you're feeling so well after your bout of the flu.
if/whether	If introduces a condition. Whether compares alternatives.	If I crack a book this summer, it will be to determine whether I need to study more math for the ACT.
imply/infer	To imply means to suggest indirectly. To infer means to conclude or deduce.	I didn't mean to imply that your dress is ugly. You merely inferred that's what I meant when I asked you whether you bought it at an upholstery store.
less/fewer	Use less to refer to a quantity (something that can't be counted) and few to refer to number (things that can be counted).	That office building is less noticeable because it has fewer floors. That glass has less water and fewer ice cubes.
less/least	Use less to compare two things and least to compare more than two things.	He is less educated than his brother is, but he isn't the least educated of his entire family.
like/as	Use like before nouns and pronouns; use as before phrases and clauses.	Like Ruth, Steve wanted the school's uniform policy to be just as it had always been.
many/much	Use many to refer to number and much to refer to quantity.	Many days I woke up feeling much anxiety, but I'm better now that I'm reading Catholic High School Entrance Exams For Dummies.
more/most	Use more to compare two things and most to compare more than two things.	Of the two girls, the older is more generous, and she is the most generous person in her family.

The ACT may apply what we call the "least/not" format to test many diction questions. These questions ask for the "least appropriate" or "not appropriate" answer. Consider these to be a game of "one of these things is not like the other." Here is how to approach these questions:

> » **Circle the LEAST or NOT in the question so you remember you're looking for the answer that doesn't work.** The words will be capitalized, but you'd be surprised how many students still miss them.
>
> » **Compare each answer choice to another.** Ask yourself whether the two have similar meanings. If they do, lightly cross out both answers with your pencil. Then compare one of the remaining two answers with the ones you just penciled through. If the answer has a similar meaning, cross it out too and choose the other.

Least/not questions almost always test word meanings, but every once in a while, the ACT uses them to test usage errors. Generally, though, when you see this format, think diction.

The "least/not" format may become one of your favorites. Questions asked in this manner are easy to answer once you master the approach and remind yourself to pay attention to the capitalized words.

CHAPTER 6 Spotting Usage Errors and Ripping through Rhetorical Questions   59

Chapter 7
It's Not What You Say but How You Say It: English Practice Questions

IN THIS CHAPTER

» Putting your grammar skills to the test with a practice English passage

» Practicing questions that test sentence structure concerns

» Seeing the English Test questions in context

You didn't think that we crammed those grammar, punctuation, and sentence structure rules into your head just so you could lord your perfect speech over your friends, did you? Here, we show you just how knowing the stimulating rules we cover in Chapters 5 and 6 comes in handy for the ACT. This practice chapter has one longer passage with 10 questions and one shorter passage with 5 questions. The real ACT English Test has two shorter passages with five questions each and four longer passages with ten questions each. After you complete each question, you can review your answer by reading the explanation that follows.

Directions: Following are four paragraphs containing underlined portions. Alternate ways of stating the underlined portions follow the paragraphs. Choose the best alternative. If the original is the best way of stating the underlined portion, choose NO CHANGE. You also see questions that refer to the passage or ask you to reorder the sentences within the passage. These questions are identified by a number in a box on the paper test or an asterisk on the digital version. Choose the best answer.

Questions 1–10 are based on the following passage.

Marian Anderson: Groundbreaking Singer and Friend of First Ladies

[1] Marian Anderson possibly has had the greatest influence opening doors and gaining
                                              1
well-deserved opportunities for other African American singers than anyone else to date. [2] Anderson, born in Philadelphia, Pennsylvania, had an early interest in music. [3] She learned to play the piano and was singing in the church at the age of six. [4] She gave her first concert at age eight, when she was still a young child.
    2

[5] In 1925, Anderson won a concert hosted by the New York Philharmonic, beating out no less than 300 singers. [6] It launched her career but, America was not quite ready for her fantastic voice, personality, or racial heritage.
                                                                3   4

In 1936, the White House asked her to give a performance. She confessed that this occasion was different from other concerts because she was very nervous. She and Eleanor Roosevelt had been close friends, but this friendship between she and the First Lady became even more
              5   6
evident when Anderson was snubbed by the Daughters of the American Revolution (DAR). The DAR refused to let Anderson perform in Constitution Hall in 1939, the White House made
                                                                                7
arrangements for Ms. Anderson to sing on the steps of the Lincoln Memorial instead. [8]

In 1977, First Lady Rosalynn Carter presented Marian Anderson with a Congressional Gold Medal, making Ms. Anderson the first African American to receive such an honor. Later she was
                9
inducted into the Women's Hall of Fame in Seneca Falls, New York. [10]

1. Which choice makes the sentence most grammatically acceptable?

   (F) NO CHANGE
   (G) a greater
   (H) one of the greatest
   (I) a great

You need to read the entire sentence before deciding on an answer. If you read "the greatest influence" all by itself, it sounds correct. However, if you continue to read the sentence, you find the comparative *than*. You cannot say "the greatest influence than" but rather "a greater influence than." The correct answer is (G).

Be very careful to read the entire sentence. You may save a few seconds by reading only the underlined portion, but you'll sacrifice a lot of points.

REMEMBER

2. Which choice is least redundant in context?

   (A) NO CHANGE
   (B) at age eight, still a young child
   (C) at age eight, still young
   (D) at age eight

A person who is eight is still a young child. The underlined portion is superfluous, unnecessary. Eliminate it. The correct answer is (D).

3. Which choice is clearest and most precise in context?

   (F) NO CHANGE
   (G) less than
   (H) fewer than
   (J) no fewer than

62   PART 2 Serving Your "Sentence": The English Test

Use *fewer* to describe plural nouns, as in fewer brain cells, for example. Use *less* to describe singular nouns, like less intelligence. Because *singers* is a plural noun, use *fewer* rather than *less*. The correct answer is (J).

REMEMBER

If you picked Choice (H), you fell for the trap. You forgot to reread the sentence with your answer inserted. The meaning of the whole sentence changes with the phrase "fewer than 300 singers." In that case, you're diminishing the winner's accomplishment. The tone of the passage is one of respect. The author is impressed that Ms. Anderson beat out "no fewer than 300 singers." Keep in mind that you must make your answers fit the overall tone or attitude of the passage. If a passage is complimentary, be sure that your answers are, too.

4. Which choice makes the sentence most grammatically acceptable?

   (A) NO CHANGE
   (B) Launching her career,
   (C) The win launched her career, but
   (D) Upon launching it,

TIP

Be very suspicious of that two-letter rascal *it*. Always double-check *it* out because *it* is so often misused and abused. It must refer to one specific noun: "Where is the book? Here it is." In Question 7, *it* doesn't have a clear reference. It could mean that winning the concert launched her career, or it may seem that the New York Philharmonic launched her career. Another problem with Choice (A) is that pesky comma. It belongs before *but*, not after *it*. Choices (B) and (D) sound as if America launched Ms. Anderson's career: "Upon launching it . . . America was not quite ready . . . ." A beginning phrase always describes the sentence's subject. Be sure to go back and reread the entire sentence with your answer inserted. Because Choice (C) clarifies exactly what launched Anderson's career, it is the correct answer.

5. Which choice makes the sentence most grammatically acceptable?

   (F) NO CHANGE
   (G) close friends, and
   (H) close friends — which
   (J) close and friendly,

The clause "but this friendship . . . became evident . . ." makes no sense in the context. Use *but* only to indicate opposition or change; use a comma and the word *and* to add to and continue a thought. The correct answer is (G).

6. Which choice makes the sentence most grammatically acceptable?

   (A) NO CHANGE
   (B) between the First Lady and she became
   (C) between her and the First Lady became
   (D) OMIT the underlined portion.

The pronoun is the problem in this question. *Between* is a preposition, which means that the pronoun and noun that come after it are objects of the preposition. Therefore, the pronoun has to be in objective form. The objective form of *she* is *her*. You can't omit the underlined words because the resulting clause has no verb. The correct answer is (C).

CHAPTER 7 It's Not What You Say but How You Say It: English Practice Questions

Many students tend to choose "OMIT the underlined portion" every time they see it, reasoning that it would not be a choice unless it were correct. Not so. If you decide to omit the underlined portion, be especially careful to reread the entire sentence. Often, omitting the underlined portion makes nonsense out of the sentence.

REMEMBER

7. Which choice makes the sentence most grammatically acceptable?

    (F) NO CHANGE

    (G) in 1939; however, the White House

    (H) in 1939 but the White House

    (J) in 1939. Although the White House

To answer this question, you must correct the comma splice in the original sentence. You can't use a comma all by itself to join two independent clauses (complete sentences) in one sentence. You could separate them by putting a period after 1939 and capitalizing *the*. The answers don't give you that option, though. Choice (J) separates the clauses with a period, but adding *although* makes the second sentence a fragment. Another way to join two independent clauses together is with a semicolon. Choice (G) changes the comma to a semicolon and adds *however* for a smooth transition to the next thought. It properly places a comma after *however*, too. Choice (H) lacks a necessary comma before *but*. The correct answer is (G).

8. The author is considering inserting a sentence that presents a short list of other venues where Marian Anderson performed during her career. Would that insertion be appropriate here?

    (A) Yes, because the primary purpose of this paragraph is to emphasize the great number of places where Marian Anderson performed.

    (B) Yes, because it's always better to include many specific examples to advance an idea.

    (C) No, because the paragraph is about the obstacles that Marian Anderson had to overcome rather than the number of concert halls she performed in.

    (D) No, because providing a list of examples is never appropriate in an essay about a person's life.

When you see one of these "yes, yes, no, no" questions on the English Test, figure out the short answer to the question. Would a list of venues be appropriate? Probably not. (Please. The test is boring enough without having to read through a list of concert venues.) Ignore the yes answers for now and focus on the no choices. The paragraph seems to focus on the racial prejudice Anderson experienced rather than the number of places she performed in. So the correct answer is (C).

You can be pretty certain that Choices (B) and (D) are wrong. Both of them contain debatable words, such as *always* and *never*, that should raise a red flag for you. If you're thinking of choosing an answer that contains one of these all-encompassing words that leaves no room for exception, first make sure that the position is justified.

REMEMBER

9. Which choice makes the sentence most grammatically acceptable?

    (F) NO CHANGE

    (G) Medal, being the first African American

    (H) Medal; the first African American

    (J) Medal, the first African American

64   PART 2 Serving Your "Sentence": The English Test

The original is okay the way it's written. The other choices make it sound like the medal was the first African American to receive such an honor. Choice (H) adds insult to injury by using a semicolon to do a comma's job. Note that the job of the semicolon is to separate two independent sentences; each sentence could stand alone. The correct answer is (F).

REMEMBER

Don't forget that the sentence doesn't have to have an error. About 20 percent of the time, the underlined portion requires NO CHANGE.

10. If the author of this passage were to add the following lines to the article, where would they be most logically placed?

It was an era of racial prejudice, a time when people were still legally excluded from jobs, housing, and even entertainment merely because of their race. Thus, the early promise of success seemed impossible until something amazing for the times happened.

(A) After Sentence 2
(B) After Sentence 6
(C) After Sentence 3
(D) After Sentence 5

You know from the answer options to look only in the first two paragraphs. Because the first sentence of the addition talks about racial prejudice, look in the beginning of the passage for something that mentions Marian Anderson's race. That topic is specifically discussed only in Sentence 6. So the correct answer is (B).

REMEMBER

Be sure to go back to the passage and reread the entire paragraph with the new lines inserted to make sure that they make sense.

TIP

If you find yourself wasting too much time on a question like this one, your best bet is to eliminate answers if you can, guess, and move on. *Remember:* The ACT doesn't penalize you for wrong answers. Marking a guess for any question that has you stumped is to your advantage.

Questions 11–15 are based on the following passage.

Is Deviant Behavior Learned?

The debate over nature versus <u>nurture, whether genetics or environment</u> plays a
                                                      11
greater role in shaping an individual—has long been discussed in psychology. One case that challenges the nurture perspective is Aleister Crowley, born on October 12, 1875. As a child, <u>his behavior displayed characteristics</u> that some might call inherently deviant. Raised in a strict
                        12
Protestant household, he rejected Christianity, <u>and his mother nicknamed him</u> "The Beast."
                                                                    13
Despite his religious upbringing, he turned to black magic, acted violently, and pursued what he believed were dark forces. His life raises the question: was Crowley shaped by <u>them</u> , or was his
                                                                                                    14
path determined by nature?

Supporters of the nurture theory argue that environment determines behavior, but Crowley's case suggests otherwise. If nurture were the deciding factor, one might expect him to follow in his father's religious footsteps. Some psychologists insist external influences shape character, yet Crowley's life challenges this notion. The nature theory, which posits that genetics play a primary role in personality, may better explain why individuals like Crowley display seemingly predetermined behaviors. It also accounts for identical twins raised apart who develop strikingly similar traits. When examining cases like Crowley's, the argument for nature over nurture becomes difficult to ignore.

11. Which choice makes the sentence most grammatically acceptable?

(F) NO CHANGE
(G) nuture—whether environment or genetics
(H) nuture, whether environment or genetics
(J) nuture whether environment or genetics

Whenever you see dashes in your answer choices, check the rest of the sentence for a dash. The dash after *individual* needs a partner dash to indicate the nonessential descriptive information explaining what *nature versus nurture* means. The only answer to provide the proper partner dash is (G).

12. Which choice makes the sentence most grammatically acceptable?

(A) NO CHANGE
(B) Crowley's behavior displayed characteristics
(C) Crowley displayed behavioral characteristics
(D) the characteristics of Crowley's behavior

The phrase "As a child" at the beginning of the sentence is an introductory phrase and must modify the subject that follows it. In the original sentence ("his behavior displayed characteristics"), the subject is "his behavior," but "behavior" can't be a child — only Crowley can. The only answer that provides Crowley as the subject of the sentence is (C).

A beginning descriptive phrase must relate to the subject of the sentence.

REMEMBER

13. If the writer were to delete the underlined text (adjusting the punctuation as needed), the paragraph would primarily lose:

(F) a detail that gives the reader clear insight into his parents' childrearing methods.
(G) an explanation of why Crowley rejected Christianity.
(H) an additional detail the supports the author's point that Crowley engaged in deviant behavior when he was young.
(J) a necessary transition that links a primary assertion in the first sentence of the paragraph to a contrasting point at the end of the paragraph.

The underlined phrase adds support to the idea that Crowley exhibited unusual or deviant behavior early in life. The nickname suggests that even his own mother saw something in him that appeared off. Removing this phrase would eliminate a key piece of evidence supporting the author's claim. Therefore, Choice (H) is best. The nickname reflects Crowley's reputation rather than his parents' specific childrearing practices, so Choice (F) is wrong. Though Crowley did reject Christianity, the phrase about his nickname does not provide a reason, so Choice (G) is out. Choice (J) is clearly wrong because the phrase is a detail rather than a transition.

14. Which choice makes the sentence most grammatically acceptable?

    (A) NO CHANGE
    (B) it
    (C) this
    (D) his environment

    The first three answers are pronouns with no clear antecedent. The previous sentence lists *black magic, violent behavior, and dark forces*, but these aren't logical influences on Crowley in the context of the nature versus nurture debate. Replacing *them* with "his environment" clarifies the external influences that shaped Crowley. (D) is correct.

15. Given that all choices are accurate, which one most accurately leads into the rest of the essay:

    (F) NO CHANGE
    (G) An examination of the life of Crowley seems to indicate that deviant behavior is closely linked to black magic and dark forces.
    (H) Crowley's case demonstrates that it is impossible to draw conclusions about whether nature or nurture is more important in determining behavior.
    (J) No one can argue that Crowley was a good person.

    The original is okay the way it's written. This choice provides the best transition because it directly connects Crowley's life, discussed in the first paragraph, to the broader nature versus nurture argument in the second paragraph. It introduces the nurture theory while immediately challenging it with Crowley's case, setting up the discussion in the second paragraph about how nature may play a more significant role. The best answer is (F).

    Choice (G) shifts the focus toward black magic rather than the nature versus nurture debate. Choice (H) contradicts the second paragraph, which argues in favor of nature over nurture rather than stating that no conclusion can be drawn. The opinion stated in Choice (J) doesn't have anything to do with the nature versus nurture discussion in the second paragraph.

3 Don't Count Yourself Out: The Math Test

IN THIS PART . . .

Review number basics, such as absolute value, the number line, and other math concepts you may not have seen since fourth grade.

Remember how to work with geometric shapes and formulas and review how to solve trigonometry problems on the ACT.

Harken back to middle school with an algebra refresher.

Refer to the table of logarithm rules and take a flight on the coordinate plane to make sure you've memorized commonly tested coordinate geometry concepts.

Move through math questions more quickly with tips on using the answer choices to focus plugging in real values for variables to solve theoretical problems.

Practice old and new math skills and approaches with 12 mini test questions. Read through the answer explanations to formulate a solid approach to the ACT Mathematics Test.

IN THIS CHAPTER

» Reviewing numbers and basic math operations

» Figuring out fractions, decimals, and percentages

» Reasoning through ratios, proportions, and exponents

» Finding order in operations and calculating the mean, median, mode, and range

» Considering units and measurements

» Exploring variables and attacking algebra

Chapter 8
Numbers Nuts and Bolts

You've seen them before. They crop up everywhere: your high school math tests, those dreaded achievement tests, and now your college entrance exam. Yes, we're talking about multiple-choice math questions. Take heart! Many of the math questions on the ACT cover the basics.

Even though you may already know most of the math that we discuss in this chapter, it never hurts to refresh your memory. After all, the questions on the ACT that ask about the basic math topics we cover here tend to be the easiest, so they offer you the best chance for getting correct answers. Brush up on your elementary and middle school math, and you're sure to improve your score on the ACT Math Test.

The Wonderful World of Numbers

You're probably not surprised to find out that the math problems on the ACT involve numbers, but you also probably haven't thought about the properties of numbers in a long time. That's why we offer you a fairly complete number review here. (You can thank us later.)

Keeping it real: Types of numbers

Numbers fall under a hierarchy of classifications (see Figure 8-1) and are defined as such:

> » **Complex:** All numbers you can think of.
>
> » **Imaginary:** Represented by the variable *i*, the value of the square root of a negative number. Every once in a while, the ACT spits out a question that deals with an imaginary number. Just keep in mind that $i^2 = -1$ and $i = \sqrt{-1}$.
>
> » **Real:** All complex numbers that aren't imaginary.
>
> » **Irrational:** Numbers that can't be written as fractions, such as π and $\sqrt{2}$.
>
> » **Rational:** All real numbers that aren't irrational and therefore include fractions and decimal numbers that either end or repeat. For example, the fraction $\frac{1}{6}$ is a rational number. It can also be expressed as $0.1\overline{6}$.
>
> » **Integers:** All the positive and negative whole numbers, plus zero. Integers aren't fractions or decimals or portions of a number, so they include –5, –4, –3, –2, –1, 0, 1, 2, 3, 4, 5, and continue infinitely on either side of zero. Integers greater than zero are called *natural numbers* or *positive integers;* integers less than zero are called *negative integers*.

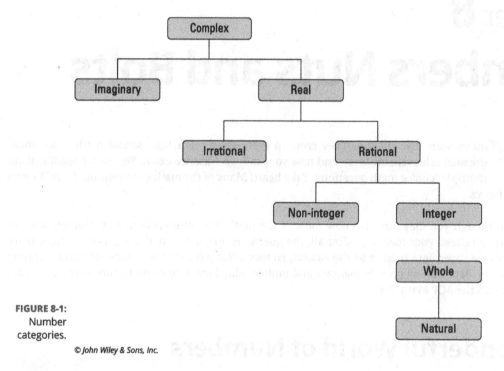

FIGURE 8-1: Number categories.

© John Wiley & Sons, Inc.

REMEMBER Carefully tread when working with zero. It's neither positive nor negative.

> » **Whole:** All the positive integers and zero.
>
> » **Natural:** All the positive integers, excluding zero.

So when a question tells you to "express your answer in real numbers," don't sweat it. That's almost no constraint at all because nearly every number you know is a real number.

Lining things up along the number line

You may have an easier time visualizing numbers if you see them on a number line. The *number line* shows all real numbers. Zero holds a place in the middle of the line. All positive numbers carry on infinitely to the right of zero, and all negative numbers extend infinitely to the left of zero, like this:

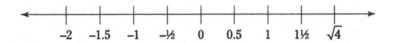

Understanding absolute value

The concept of absolute value crops up quite a bit on the ACT. The *absolute value* of any real number is that same number without a negative sign. It's the value of the distance a particular number is from zero on a number line (see the preceding section). For example, the absolute value of 1 is written mathematically as $|1|$. Because 1 sits one space from zero on the number line, $|1| = 1$. But because -1 also sits one space away from zero on the number line, $|-1| = 1$.

REMEMBER

Absolute value relates only to the value that's inside those absolute value bars. If you see a negative sign outside the bars, the value of the result is negative. For example, $-|-1| = -1$. You must always perform operations within the absolute value signs before you make the value positive: $-|-1| = -1$.

Equations with a variable inside absolute value signs usually have two solutions: the one when the value within the signs is positive and the one when the value is negative.

$$|-3 + x| = 12$$
$$-3 + x = 12$$
$$x = 15$$
$$|-3 + x| = 12$$
$$-(-3 + x) = 12$$
$$3 - x = 12$$
$$x = -9$$

Getting familiar with prime numbers and factorization

The ACT expects you to know about *prime numbers*, which are all the positive integers that can be divided only by themselves and 1. A number that can be divided by more numbers than 1 and itself is called a *composite number*. Here are some other facts you should know about prime numbers:

» 1 is neither prime nor composite.

» 2 is the smallest of the prime numbers, and it's also the only number that's both even and prime. (See the section, "Working with odds/evens and positives/negatives," for more on even numbers.)

» 0 can never be a prime number because you can divide zero by every number in existence, but it's not considered to be a composite number either.

TIP

You don't need to memorize all the prime numbers before you take the ACT (yikes!), but do keep in mind that the lowest prime numbers are 2, 3, 5, 7, 11, 13, 17, 19, 23, and 29.

CHAPTER 8 Numbers Nuts and Bolts   73

When you know how to recognize prime numbers, you can engage in *prime factorization*, which is just a fancy way of saying that you can break down a number into all the prime numbers (or *factors*) that go into it (refer to Figure 8-2). For instance, 50 factors into 2 and 25, which factors into 5 and 5, giving you 2, 5, and 5 for the prime factors of 50.

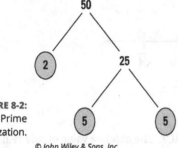

FIGURE 8-2: Prime factorization.

© John Wiley & Sons, Inc.

The ACT may test your knowledge of numbers with a question such as the following example.

EXAMPLE

If $|7(-4) + x| = 34$, what is the smallest solution for x?

(A) −10

(B) −6

(C) 6

(D) 62

When you solve questions that involve variables and absolute value, you usually have more than one solution: the one that results from the positive value within the absolute value signs and the one that results from the negative value within the absolute value signs.

$$|7(-4) + x| = 34$$
$$7(-4) + x = 34$$
$$-28 + x = 34$$
$$x = 62$$

You may be tempted to stop here and choose (D), but the question asked for the *smallest* solution. The value within the absolute value signs could also be negative:

$$|7(-4) + x| = 34$$
$$-(-28 + x) = 34$$
$$28 - x = 34$$
$$-x = 6$$
$$x = -6$$

Because −6 is a smaller value than 62, Choice (B) is the correct answer. If you chose (C), you changed −4 to positive 4 before you multiplied. You don't change individual negative values within the absolute value sign to positive before you calculate.

74 PART 3 **Don't Count Yourself Out: The Math Test**

Minor Surgery: Basic Math Operations

You don't have to be a brain surgeon to perform the basic mathematical operations of addition, subtraction, multiplication, and division, but you do have to train your brain to do these simple calculations without error. The following sections go over these basic operations, so you don't miss questions because of silly calculation mistakes.

Adding and subtracting

Addition is when you combine two or more numbers to get an end result called the *sum*.

No matter what order you add a bunch of numbers in, you always end up with the same sum: $(2+3)+4=9$ and $2+(3+4)=9$; $2+3=5$ and $3+2=5$.

When you *subtract* one number from another, you take one value away from another value and end up with the *difference* (the answer to a subtraction problem). So if $4+5=9$, then $9-5=4$.

REMEMBER

Unlike addition, order *does* matter in subtraction. You get completely different answers for $20-7-4$ based on what order you subtract them: $(20-7)-4=9$, but $20-(7-4)=17$. For another example, $2-3=-1$ doesn't give you the same answer as $3-2=1$.

Multiplying and dividing

Think of *multiplication* as repeated addition with an end result called the *product*. The multiplication problem 3×6 is the same as the addition problem $6+6+6$. Both problems equal 18.

REMEMBER

Multiplication is like addition in that the order in which you multiply the values doesn't matter: $2 \times 3 = 3 \times 2$ and $(2 \times 3) \times 4 = 2 \times (3 \times 4)$.

Another property of multiplication you need to know is the *distributive property*. You can multiply a number by a set of added or subtracted values by distributing that number through the values in the set values, like so:

$$2(3+4) =$$
$$(2 \times 3) + (2 \times 4) =$$
$$6 + 8 = 14$$

Of course, you can solve this problem by adding the numbers in parentheses ($3+4=7$) and multiplying the sum by 2 ($7 \times 2 = 14$). But when you start to add variables to the mix (see the later section, "Variables 101"), you'll be glad you know about distribution.

Division is all about dividing one value into smaller values; those smaller values, or end results, are called *quotients*. Consider division to be the reverse of multiplication:

$$2 \times 3 = 6$$
$$6 \div 3 = 2$$
$$6 \div 2 = 3$$

Working with odds/evens and positives/negatives

The ACT may ask questions that require you to know what happens when you perform operations with odd and even numbers, as well as positives and negatives. *Even numbers* are numbers that are

CHAPTER 8 **Numbers Nuts and Bolts** 75

divisible by 2 (2, 4, 6, 8, 10, and so on), and *odd numbers* are numbers that aren't divisible by 2 (1, 3, 5, 7, 9, 11, and so on). The easiest way to figure out operations with odds and evens is to try them with sample odd and even values.

To perform basic math operations with positive and negative numbers, remember these rules:

» When you multiply or divide two positive numbers, the answer is positive.

» When you multiply or divide two negative numbers, the answer is also positive.

» When you multiply or divide a negative number by a positive number, you get a negative answer.

You also have to know a thing or two (or three, actually) about adding and subtracting positive and negative numbers:

» When you add two positive numbers, your answer is positive: $3 + 5 = 8$.

» When you add two negative numbers, your answer is negative: $-3 + -5 = -8$.

» When you add a negative number to a positive number, your answer can be positive or negative: $-3 + 5 = 2$ and $3 + (-5) = -2$.

The ACT may test basic operations with a question like the following.

EXAMPLE

$(23 - 40)(-5) - (-4)$ is equal to:

(F) -89

(G) -81

(H) 81

(J) 89

Start with the operation in parentheses: $23 - 40 = -17$. Multiply that number by -5 to get the positive value of 85. When you subtract -4 from 85, you get 89, Choice (J). When you subtract a negative number, you add. If you chose Choice (H), you subtracted 4 from 85 instead of adding. The other answers result from other operation errors.

Focusing on Fractions, Decimals, and Percentages

Fractions, decimals, and percentages all represent parts of a whole. The ACT asks you to manipulate these figures in all sorts of ways.

Converting fractions, decimals, and percentages

Because fractions, decimals, and percentages are different ways of showing similar values, you can change pretty easily from one form to another. Here's what you need to know:

» To convert a fraction to a decimal, just divide: $\frac{3}{4} = 3 \div 4 = 0.75$.

» To convert a decimal back to a fraction, first count the number of digits to the right of the decimal point. Then divide the number in the decimal over a 1 followed by as many zeros as there were digits to the right of the decimal. Finally, simplify the fraction (see the section, "Simplifying fractions," for details): $0.75 = \frac{75}{100} = \frac{3}{4}$.

» To change a decimal to a percent, just move the decimal two places to the right and add a percent sign: $0.75 = 75\%$.

» To turn a percent into a decimal, move the decimal point two places to the left and get rid of the percent sign: $75\% = 0.75$.

Working with fractions

Fractions tell you what part a piece is of a whole. The *numerator* is the top number in the fraction, and it represents the piece. The *denominator* is the bottom number of the fraction, and it indicates the value of the whole. If you cut a whole apple pie into 8 pieces and eat 5 slices, you can show the amount of pie you eat as a fraction, like so: $\frac{5}{10}$.

In the following sections, we show you how to do basic math operations with fractions. As a bonus, we also explain how to simplify fractions and work with mixed numbers.

Simplifying fractions

The ACT expects all fraction answers to be in their simplest forms. To simplify a fraction, first find the largest number you can think of that goes into both the numerator and denominator (called the *greatest common factor*). Then, just divide the numerator and denominator by that number. For example, if you end up with $\frac{5}{10}$, you must simplify it further by dividing the numerator and denominator by 5: $\frac{5}{10} = \frac{1}{2}$.

Multiplying and dividing fractions

Multiplying fractions is easy. Just multiply the numerators by each other and then do the same with the denominators. Then simplify if you have to. For example:

$$\frac{3}{4} \times \frac{2}{5} = \frac{3 \times 2}{4 \times 5} = \frac{6}{20} = \frac{3}{10}$$

Always check whether you can cancel out any numbers before you begin working to avoid having to deal with big, awkward numbers and having to simplify at the end. In the preceding example, you can reduce the 4 and cancel the 2, leaving you with

$$\frac{3}{{}_2\cancel{4}} \times \frac{\cancel{2}^1}{5} = \frac{3 \times 1}{2 \times 5} = \frac{3}{10}$$

You get to the right solution either way; canceling in advance just makes the numbers smaller and easier to work with.

CHAPTER 8 Numbers Nuts and Bolts

Dividing fractions is pretty much the same as multiplying them except for one very important additional step. First, find the *reciprocal* of the second fraction in the equation (that is, turn the second fraction upside down). Then multiply (yes, you have to multiply when dividing fractions) the numerators and denominators of the resulting fractions. For example:

$$\frac{1}{3} \div \frac{2}{5} = \frac{1}{3} \times \frac{5}{2} = \frac{5}{6}$$

Adding and subtracting fractions

Adding and subtracting fractions can be a little tricky, but you'll be fine if you follow these guidelines:

» **You can add or subtract fractions only if they have the same denominator.** Add or subtract just the numerators, like so:

$$\frac{1}{3} + \frac{4}{3} = \frac{5}{3}$$

$$\frac{3}{8} - \frac{2}{8} = \frac{1}{8}$$

» **When fractions don't have the same denominator, you have to find a common denominator.** To find a common denominator, you can multiply all the denominators, but doing so often doesn't give you the lowest common denominator. As a result, you end up with some humongous, overwhelming number that you'd rather not work with.

To find the lowest (or least) common denominator, think of multiples of the highest denominator until you find the one that all denominators go into evenly. For instance, to solve $\frac{4}{15} + \frac{1}{6}$, you have to find the lowest common denominator of 15 and 6. Sure, you can multiply 15 and 6 to get 90, but that's not the lowest common denominator. Instead, count by fifteens — because 15 is the larger of the two denominators — $15 \times 1 = 15$. But 6 doesn't go into 15. Moving on, $15 \times 2 = 30$. Hey! Both 15 and 6 go into 30, so 30 is the lowest common denominator.

Here's another example. To find the lowest common denominator for 2, 4, and 5, count by fives. What about 5? No, 2 and 4 don't go into it. How about 10? No, 4 doesn't go into it. Okay, 15? No, 2 and 4 don't go into it. What about 20? Yes, all the numbers divide evenly into 20.

You can use your graphing calculator to find the lowest common denominator (also known as the least common multiple, or LCM) for two or more numbers. Apply the *lcm* function, enter the set of numbers, and press Enter.

Here's a trick for working with fractions with variables (see the later section, "Variables 101," for more about variables). Multiply the denominators to find the lowest common denominator. Then cross-multiply to find the numerators (see the later section, "Proportions," for details on cross-multiplying).

Say you're asked to solve this problem:

$$\frac{a}{b} - \frac{c}{d} = ?$$

Find the common denominator by multiplying the two denominators: $b \times d = bd$. Then cross-multiply:

$$a \times d = ad$$
$$c \times b = cb$$

78 PART 3 Don't Count Yourself Out: The Math Test

Put the difference of the results over the common denominator:

$$\frac{ad - cb}{bd}$$

Mixing things up with mixed numbers

A *mixed number* is a whole number with a fraction tagging along behind it, such as $2\frac{1}{3}$. To add, subtract, multiply, or divide with mixed numbers, you first have to convert them into *improper fractions* (fractions in which the numerator is larger than the denominator). To do so, multiply the whole number by the denominator and add that to the numerator. Put the sum over the denominator. For example:

$$2\frac{1}{3} = \frac{(2 \times 3) + 1}{3} = \frac{7}{3}$$

Pondering percentages

In terms of percentages, the ACT usually asks you to find a percentage of another number. When you get a question like "What is 30% of 60?" evaluate the language like so:

- *What* means *?* or *x* (the unknown) or what you're trying to find out.
- *Is* means = (equals).
- *Of* means × (multiply).

Your job is to convert the words into math, like so: $? = 30\% \times 60$.

To solve this problem, convert 30% to a decimal (0.30) and multiply by 60. Tada! The answer is 18. Or, if you prefer, you could convert 30% to a fraction and multiply, like so:

$$? = \frac{30}{100} \times \frac{60}{1} = \frac{180}{100} = 18$$

Sometimes a problem asks you to figure out what percent one number is of another. For example, the number 20 is what percent of 80? To solve this type of problem, just apply a little translation to the question to get a math equation you can work with.

The *number 20* is, of course, 20. You know that *is* means =. *What* gives you the unknown, or *x*, and *of* means multiply. Put it all together, and you get this expression: $20\% \times 80$. Now all you have to do is solve for *x*. Divide both sides by 80, and you get $\frac{20}{80} = x\%$, or $\frac{20}{80} = \frac{1}{4} = 0.25$. Convert 0.25 to a percent by multiplying by 100 (or moving the decimal point two places to the right), and you have your answer: $0.25 = 25\%$. (See the later section, "Solving simple equations," for more details on how to solve for *x* and other variables.)

Here's a sample question to test what you know about parts of a whole.

CHAPTER 8 **Numbers Nuts and Bolts** 79

EXAMPLE

What is 25% of $5\frac{3}{4}$?

(A) $\frac{37}{130}$

(B) $5\frac{3}{4}$

(C) $1\frac{7}{16}$

(D) $2\frac{3}{16}$

First, you don't need to do any calculations to eliminate Choice (B). Twenty-five percent of $5\frac{3}{4}$ can't be $5\frac{3}{4}$. Then notice that the answer choices are in fraction rather than decimal form, so work the problem with fractions. When you convert 25% to a fraction, you get $\frac{1}{4}$. *Of* means multiply. So your equation is $\frac{1}{4} \times 5\frac{3}{4} = ?$. Convert the second fraction and multiply: $\frac{1}{4} \times \frac{23}{4} = \frac{23}{16} = 1\frac{7}{16}$. The correct answer is (C).

TIP

Some questions ask you to find a percentage of a value and then increase or decrease that value by the percentage. You can perform each of these tasks in one step:

> » To increase a number by a particular percentage of that number, multiply the number by 1 plus the percentage. So, to find the total purchase amount of a $9.50 item with 6% tax, multiply 9.50 by 1.06: $9.50 \times 1.06 = 10.07$.
>
> » To decrease a number by a particular percentage of that number, multiply the number by the percentage you get when you subtract the original percentage from 100%. So, to find the sale price of a $9.50 item that has been discounted by 6%, multiply 9.50 by 94% (100% − 6%): $9.50 \times .94 = 8.93$.

Eyeing Ratios and Proportions

When you know the tricks we show you in this section, ratios and proportions are some of the easiest problems to answer quickly. We call them *heartbeat problems* because you can solve them in a heartbeat. Of course, if someone drop-dead gorgeous sits next to you and makes your heart beat faster, you may need two heartbeats to solve them.

Ratios

Here's what you need to know to answer ratio problems:

> » A *ratio* is written as $\frac{of}{to}$ or of:to. The ratio *of* sunflowers *to* roses = $\frac{sunflowers}{roses}$. The ratio *of* umbrellas *to* heads = umbrellas:heads.

TIP

When you see a ratio written with colons, rewrite it as a fraction. It's easier to evaluate ratios when they're written in fraction form because you can more easily set up proportions or see that you need to give ratios common denominators to compare them.

> » A *possible total* is a multiple of the sum of the numbers in the ratio. For example, you may be given a problem like this: At a party, the ratio of blondes to redheads is 4:5. Which of the following could be the total number of blondes and redheads at the party? Mega-easy. Add the

80 PART 3 **Don't Count Yourself Out: The Math Test**

numbers in the ratio: 4 + 5 = 9. The total number of blondes must be a multiple of 9, such as 9, 18, 27, 36, and so on.

>> **When a question gives you a ratio and a total and asks you to find a specific term, do the following:**

1. **Add the numbers in the ratio.**

2. **Divide that sum into the total.**

3. **Multiply that quotient by each term in the ratio.**

4. **Add the answers to double-check that their sum equals the total.**

Confused? Consider this example: Yelling at the members of their team, who had just lost 21–0, the irate coach pointed their finger at each member of the squad and called every player either a wimp or a slacker. If there were 3 wimps for every 4 slackers and every member of the 28-person squad was either a wimp or a slacker, how many wimps were there?

First, add the ratio: 3 + 4 = 7. Divide 7 into the total number of team members: $\frac{28}{7} = 4$. Multiply 4 by each term in the ratio: $4 \times 3 = 12$; $4 \times 4 = 16$. Make sure those numbers add up to the total number of team members: 12 + 16 = 28.

Now you have all the information you need to answer a variety of questions. There are 12 wimps and 16 slackers. There are 4 more slackers than wimps. The number of slackers that would have to be kicked off the team for the number of wimps and slackers to be equal is 4. The ACT's math moguls can ask all sorts of things about ratios, but if you have this information, you're ready for anything they throw at you.

REMEMBER

Be sure that you actually do Step 4 — adding the terms to double-check that they add up to the total. Doing so catches any careless mistakes that you may have made.

Proportions

The ACT may toss in a few proportion problems, too. A *proportion* is a relationship between two ratios where the ratios are equal. Just like with fractions, multiplying or dividing both numbers in the ratio by the same number doesn't change the value of the ratio. So, for example, these two ratios make up a proportion: 2:8 and 4:16, which you may also see written as $\frac{2}{8} = \frac{4}{16}$.

REMEMBER

Often, you see a couple of equal ratios with a missing term that you have to find. To solve these problems, you *cross-multiply*. In other words, you multiply the terms that are diagonal from each other and solve for *x*. For example, to solve this equation $\frac{3}{8} = \frac{6}{x}$, follow these steps:

1. **Identify the diagonal terms: 3 and *x*; 6 and 8.**

2. **Multiply each set of diagonal terms and set the products equal to each other.**

    $3 \times x = 3x$
    $6 \times 8 = 48$
    $3x = 48$

3. **Solve for *x*.**

    $x = 16$

For more on how to solve for *x*, go to the later section, "Solving simple equations."

CHAPTER 8 **Numbers Nuts and Bolts** 81

EXAMPLE

Here's a sample ratio problem for you to try.

Trying to get Willie to turn down his stereo, his mother pounds on the ceiling and shouts up to his bedroom. If she pounds seven times for every five times she shouts, which of the following could be the total number of poundings and shouts?

(F) 75

(G) 57

(H) 48

(J) 35

Add the numbers in the ratio: $7+5=12$. The total must be a multiple of 12 (which means it must be evenly divisible by 12). Here, only 48 is evenly divisible by 12, so the correct answer is (H).

Covering Your Bases: Exponents

Many ACT questions require you to know how to work with bases and exponents. Exponents represent repeated multiplication. For example, 5^3 is the same as $5 \times 5 \times 5 = 125$. When you work with exponents, make sure you know these important concepts:

» **The *base* is the big value on the bottom.** The *exponent* is the little value in the upper-right corner. In 5^3, 5 is the base, and 3 is the exponent.

» **The exponent tells you how many times to multiply the base times itself.**

» **A base to the zero power equals one.** For example, $5^0 = 1$; $x^0 = 1$.

» **A base to a negative exponent is the reciprocal of itself.**

This concept is a little more confusing. When you have a negative exponent, just put the base and exponent under a 1 and make the exponent positive again. For example, $5^{-3} = \dfrac{1}{5^3}$. Keep in mind that the resulting number is not negative. When you flip it, you get the reciprocal, and the negative just sort of fades away.

» **You can rewrite a fractional exponent as a radical.** The denominator in the exponent tells you the type of radical, the numerator is the exponent that remains with the base, and the base and exponent are placed underneath the radical sign. For example, $5^{\frac{2}{3}} = \sqrt[3]{5^2}$.

» **To multiply like bases, add the exponents.** For example, $5^4 \times 5^9 = 5^{4+9} = 5^{13}$.

REMEMBER

You can't multiply *unlike* bases. Think of it as trying to multiply dogs and cats — it doesn't work. All you end up with is a miffed meower and a damaged dog. You actually have to work out the problem: $5^2 \times 6^3 \ne 30^5$; $5^2 \times 6^3 = 5^2 \times 6^3$.

» **To divide like bases, subtract the exponents.** For example, $5^9 \div 5^3 = 5^{9-3} = 5^6$.

WARNING

Did you think that the answer was 5^3? It's easy to fall into the trap of dividing rather than subtracting, especially when you see numbers that just beg to be divided, like 9 and 3. Keep your guard up.

» **Multiply the exponents of a base inside and outside the parentheses.** That's quite a mouthful. Here's what it means: $\left(5^3\right)^2 = 5^{3 \times 2} = 5^6$.

> » **To add or subtract like bases that are variables that have like exponents, add or subtract the numerical coefficient of the bases.**
>
> The *numerical coefficient* (a great name for a rock band, don't you think?) is simply the number in front of the base. So the numerical coefficient in $5x^2$ is 5. Notice that it is *not* the little exponent in the right-hand corner but the full-sized number to the left of the base. Here are two examples of adding and subtracting bases that are variables that have like exponents:
>
> $$37x^3 + 10x^3 = 47x^3$$
> $$15y^2 - 5y^2 = 10y^2$$
>
> The numerical coefficient of any variable on its own is 1: $x = 1x$.

You can't add or subtract like bases with different exponents: $13x^3 - 9x^2 \neq 4x^3$, $4x^2$, or $4x$. The bases and exponents must be the same for you to add or subtract the terms. For more about working with variables, go to the later section, "Variables 101."

The following question demonstrates that knowing fundamental exponent rules can help you solve seemingly complex questions.

If $7^{3x+3} = 1$, what is the value of x?

(A) −1

(B) 1

(C) $\sqrt[3]{3}$

(D) Cannot be determined

Any base to a power of zero is = to 1. So, the left side of the equation is equal to 7^0. Now you know that $3x + 3 = 0$. When you solve for x, you find that $x = -1$. The answer is Choice (A).

Very rarely is "Cannot be determined" the correct answer. Don't choose it simply because you don't know how to solve the problem.

Smooth Operator: Order of Operations

When you have several operations (addition, subtraction, multiplication, division, squaring, and so on) in one problem, you must perform the operations in the following order:

1. **Parentheses.**

   Do what's inside the parentheses first.

2. **Exponent.**

   Do the squaring or the cubing (whatever the exponent is).

3. **Multiply or divide.**

   Do multiplication and division left to right. If multiplication is to the left of division, multiply first. If division is to the left of multiplication, divide first.

4. **Add or subtract.**

   Do addition and subtraction left to right. If addition is to the left of subtraction, add first. If subtraction is to the left of addition, subtract first.

CHAPTER 8 **Numbers Nuts and Bolts** 83

An easy *mnemonic* (memory device) for remembering the order of operations is *PEMDAS*: Parentheses, Exponents, Multiply, Divide, Add, Subtract.

Here's a sample problem.

EXAMPLE

$10(3-5)^2 + \left(\dfrac{30}{5}\right)^0 = ?$

(F) –39

(G) 40

(H) 41

(J) 46

First, calculate what's inside the parentheses: $3-5 = -2$ and $\dfrac{30}{5} = 6$. Next, evaluate the exponents: $-2^2 = 4$ and $6^0 = 1$. Next, multiply: $10 \times 4 = 40$. Finally, add: $40 + 1 = 41$. The answer is Choice (H). The other answers result from failing to follow the order of operations or from exponent errors.

Dealing with Average, Median, Mode, and More

Don't be surprised if the ACT asks you a few basic statistics questions (it contains more advanced probability and statistics problems, too, but we cover those in Chapter 10). Most of these questions ask about average (also known as *average mean* or just *mean*), but you may see a few that deal with other related concepts, which is where the following sections come in.

Doing better than average on averages

To perform above average on questions about averages, you need to know how to apply the following formula for finding the average value of a set of numbers:

$$\text{Average} = \dfrac{\text{Sum of the numbers in the set}}{\text{Amount of numbers in the set}}$$

For example, to find the average of 23, 25, 26, and 30, apply the formula and solve, like so:

$$\text{Average} = \dfrac{23+25+26+30}{4} = \dfrac{104}{4} = 26$$

You can use given values in the average formula to solve for the other values. In other words, if the exam gives you the average and the sum of a group of numbers, you can figure out how many numbers are in the set by using the average formula.

For example, Jeanette takes seven exams. Her scores on the first six are 91, 89, 85, 92, 90, and 88. If her average on all seven exams is 90, what did she get on the seventh exam? To solve this problem, apply the formula:

$$90 = \dfrac{Sum}{7}$$

Because you don't know the seventh term, call it *x*. Add the first six terms (which total 535) and *x*:

$$90 = \frac{535 + x}{7}$$

Cross-multiply:

$$90 \times 7 = 535 + x$$
$$630 = 535 + x$$
$$95 = x$$

The seventh exam score was 95.

Weighing in on weighted averages

In a *weighted average*, some scores count more than others. Here's an example to help you see what we mean:

Number of Students	Score
12	80
13	75
10	70

If you're asked to find the average score for the students in the class shown in the preceding table, you know that you can't simply add 80, 75, and 70 and divide by 3 because the scores weren't evenly distributed among the students. Because 12 students got an 80, multiply 12 and 80 to get 960. Do the same with the other scores and add the products:

$$13 \times 75 = 975$$
$$10 \times 70 = 700$$
$$960 + 975 + 700 = 2635$$

Divide not by 3 but by the total number of students, which is 35 ($12 + 13 + 10 = 35$):

$$\frac{2635}{35} = 75.29$$

Mastering medians

The *median* is the middle value in a list of several values or numbers. To find out the median, list the values or numbers in order, usually from low to high, and choose the value that falls exactly in the middle of the other values. If you have an odd number of values, just select the middle value. If you have an even number of values, find the two middle values and average them (see the previous section on averages). The outcome is the median.

Managing modes

The *mode* is the value that occurs most often in a set of values. For example, you may be asked what income occurs most frequently in a particular sample population. If more people in the population have an income of $45,000 than any other income amount, the mode is $45,000.

Getting ready for range

The *range* is the distance from the greatest to the smallest. In other words, just subtract the smallest term from the largest term to find the range.

WARNING

The only trap you're likely to see in these basic statistics questions is in the answer choices. The questions themselves are quite straightforward, but the answer choices may assume that some people don't know one term from another. For example, one answer choice to a median question may be the mean (the average). One answer choice to a range question may be the mode. In each question, circle the word that tells you what you're looking for to keep from falling for this trap.

Try a sample statistics problem for yourself.

EXAMPLE

Find the range of the numbers 11, 18, 29, 17, 18, −4, 0, 11, 18.

(A) 33

(B) 29

(C) 19

(D) 0

Ah, did this one fool you? True, 33 is not one of the numbers in the set. But to find the range, you subtract the smallest from the largest number: $29-(-4)=29+4=33$. So the correct answer is (A).

Abracadabra: Elementary Algebra

Algebra is the study of properties of operations carried out on sets of numbers. That definition may sound like mumbo-jumbo, but, bottom line, algebra is just arithmetic in which symbols — usually letters — stand in for numbers. You study algebra to solve equations and to find the values of variables. The ACT gives you all sorts of opportunities to "solve the equation for x," so this chapter is here to review the basics of problem-solving.

Variables 101

As you probably already know, you encounter a lot of variables in algebra problems. *Variables* are merely symbols that stand in for numbers. Usually the symbols take the form of the letters x, y, and z and represent specific numeric values. True to their name, variables' values can change depending on the equation they're in.

Constants, on the other hand, are numbers that don't change their values in a specific problem. In algebra, letters can refer to constants, but they don't change their values in an equation like variables do. To distinguish constants from variables, the ACT generally designates constants with the letters a, b, or c.

Think of variables as stand-ins for concrete things. For example, if a store charges a certain price for apples and a different price for oranges, and you buy two apples and four oranges, the clerk can't just ring up your purchase by adding $2+4$ to get 6 and then applying one price. If they did, they'd be incorrectly comparing apples and oranges! In algebra, you use variables to stand in for the price of apples and oranges, something, for instance, like a for apple and o for orange. When you include variables, the equation to figure out the total price of your order looks something like this: $2a+4o=$ total cost.

86 PART 3 **Don't Count Yourself Out: The Math Test**

The combination of a number and a variable multiplied together is called a *term*. In the case of your fruit shopping spree, 2*a* and 4*o* are both terms. The number part of the term is called the *coefficient*. When you have a collection of these terms joined by addition and/or subtraction, you've got yourself an *algebraic expression*.

Terms that have the same variable (and the same exponents on those variables), even if they have different coefficients, are called *like terms*. For example, you may see an expression that looks something like this:

$$5x + 3y - 2x + y = ?$$

5*x* and −2*x* are like terms because they both contain an *x* variable; 3*y* and *y* are also like terms because they both contain the *y* variable.

If a variable doesn't have a coefficient next to it, its coefficient is 1; so *y* really means 1*y*. To combine the like terms, add or subtract their coefficients. In this example, you combine the *x* terms by adding 5 and −2. To combine the *y* variable terms, you add the coefficients of 3 and 1. Your original expression with four terms simplifies to two: $3x + 4y$.

On the ACT, you work with variables to perform some basic algebraic procedures. We walk you through these procedures in the following sections.

Trivia Question: Where was algebra supposedly invented? *Answer:* Muslim scholars invented Algebra in Zabid, Yemen. See? You can't blame the Greeks for everything!

Solving simple equations

One of the first algebraic procedures you need to know is how to solve for *x* in an equation. To solve for *x*, follow these steps:

1. **Isolate the variable.**

    In other words, get all the *x*'s on one side, and all the non-*x*'s on the other side.

2. **Add or subtract all the *x*'s on one side; add or subtract all the non-*x*'s on the other side.**

3. **Divide both sides of the equation by the number in front of the *x*.**

Try out this procedure by solving for *x* in this equation: $3x + 7 = 9x - 5$.

1. **Isolate the variable.**

    Move the 3*x* to the right by subtracting it from both sides. In other words, *change the sign* to make it −3*x*.

    WARNING

    Forgetting to change the sign is one of the most common careless mistakes that students make. To catch this mistake on the ACT, test makers often include trap answer choices that you'd get if you forgot to change the sign.

    Move the −5 to the left, changing the sign to make it +5. You now have $7 + 5 = 9x - 3x$.

2. **Add the *x*'s on one side; subtract the non-*x*'s on the other side.**

    $12 = 6x$

3. **Divide both sides by the 6 that's next to the *x*.**

    $2 = x$

CHAPTER 8 **Numbers Nuts and Bolts** 87

TIP

If you're weak in algebra or know that you often make careless mistakes, plug the 2 back into the equation to make sure it works:

$$3(2)+7 = 9(2)-5$$
$$6+7 = 18-5$$
$$13 = 13$$

If you absolutely hate algebra, see whether you can simply plug in the answer choices. If this were a problem-solving question with multiple-choice answers, you could plug 'n' chug to get the answer.

EXAMPLE

$3x + 7 = 9x - 5$. Solve for x.

(F) 7
(G) $5\frac{1}{2}$
(H) 5
(J) 2

Don't ask for trouble. Keep life simple by starting with the simple answers first, and begin in the middle with Choice (H). That is, try plugging in 5. When it doesn't work, don't bother plugging in $5\frac{1}{2}$. That's too much work. Go right down to 2. The correct answer is (J).

TIP

If all the easy answers don't work, go back to the harder answer of $5\frac{1}{2}$, but why fuss with it unless you absolutely have to?

Adding and subtracting expressions

If a question asks you to add together two or more expressions, you can set them up vertically like you would for an addition problem in arithmetic. Just remember that you can combine only like terms this way. Here's an example:

$$\begin{array}{r}3x+4y-7z\\2x-2y+8z\\-x+3y+6z\\\hline 4x+5y+7z\end{array}$$

To subtract expressions, distribute the minus sign throughout the second expression and then combine the like terms. (To review the distributive property of multiplication, go to the earlier section, "Minor Surgery: Basic Math Operations.") Here's an example of how to subtract two expressions:

$$(2x^2 - 3xy - 6y^2) - (-4x^2 - 6xy + 2y^2) = 2x^2 - 3xy - 6y^2 + 4x^2 + 6xy - 2y^2 = 6x^2 + 3xy - 8y^2$$

WARNING

Notice that distributing the minus sign changes the signs of all the terms in the second expression. Make sure you keep the signs straight when you subtract expressions.

Multiplying and dividing expressions

When you multiply a term by a *binomial* (an expression with two terms), you have to multiply the number by each term in the binomial, like so:

$$4x(x-3) = 4x(x) - 12x = 4x^2 - 12x$$

To divide a binomial, just divide each term in the binomial by the term, like so:

$$\frac{16x^2 + 4x}{4x} = \frac{16x^2}{4x} + \frac{4x}{4x} = 4x + 1$$

An easy way to multiply *polynomials* (expressions with many terms) is by stacking the two numbers to be multiplied on top of each other. Say you're asked to multiply these expressions: $(x^2 + 2xy + y^2)(x - y)$. Don't pass out! First of all, the ACT rarely asks you to perform this task. Second, you can calculate this expression just like an old-fashioned arithmetic problem. Just remember to multiply each term in the second line by each term in the first line, like so:

$$\begin{array}{r} x^2 + 2xy + y^2 \\ x - y \\ \hline x^3 + 2x^2y + xy^2 \\ -x^2y - 2xy^2 - y^3 \\ \hline x^3 + x^2y - xy^2 - y^3 \end{array}$$

TIP

Line up your numbers during the first round of multiplication so that like terms match up before you add your first two products together.

Curses! FOILed again

When you have to multiply two binomials, use the FOIL method. *FOIL* stands for *First, Outer, Inner, Last* and refers to the order in which you multiply the variables in parentheses when you multiply two expressions. The result is a quadratic expression. You can practice FOILing by using the equation $(a + b)(a - b) = ?$ and following these steps.

1. **Multiply the *First* variables:** $a(a) = a^2$.

2. **Multiply the *Outer* variables:** $a(-b) = -ab$.

3. **Multiply the *Inner* variables:** $b(a) = ba$ (which is the same as *ab*).

   Remember that you can multiply numbers forward or backward, such that $ab = ba$.

4. **Multiply the *Last* variables:** $b(b) = b^2$.

5. **Combine like terms:** $-ab + ab = 0ab$.

   The positive and negative *ab* cancel each other out. So you're left with only $a^2 - b^2$.

Try another one: $(3a + b)(a - 2b) = ?$.

1. **Multiply the *First* terms:** $3a(a) = 3a^2$.

2. **Multiply the *Outer* terms:** $3a(-2b) = -6ab$.

3. **Multiply the *Inner* terms:** $b(a) = ba$ (which is the same as *ab*).

4. **Multiply the *Last* terms:** $b(-2b) = -2b^2$.

5. **Combine like terms:** $-6ab + ab = -5ab$.

   The final answer is $3a^2 - 5ab - 2b^2$.

CHAPTER 8 **Numbers Nuts and Bolts** 89

TIP

You need to out-and-out *memorize* the following three FOIL problems. Don't bother to work them out every time; know them by heart. Doing so saves you time, careless mistakes, and acute misery on the actual exam.

» $(a+b)^2 = a^2 + 2ab + b^2$

You can prove this equation by using FOIL to multiply $(a+b)(a+b)$.

» **Multiply the *First* terms:** $a(a) = a^2$.

» **Multiply the *Outer* terms:** $a(-b) = -ab$.

» **Multiply the *Inner* terms:** $b(a) = ba$.

» **Multiply the *Last* terms:** $b(b) = b^2$.

» **Combine like terms:** $ab + ab = 2ab$.

The final solution is $a^2 + 2ab + b^2$.

» $(a-b)^2 = a^2 - 2ab + b^2$

You can prove this equation by using FOIL to multiply $(a-b)(a-b)$.

Notice that the b^2 at the end is positive, not negative, because multiplying a negative times a negative gives you a positive.

» $(a-b)(a+b) = a^2 - b^2$

You can prove this equation by using FOIL to multiply $(a-b)(a+b)$.

Note that the middle term drops out because $+ab$ cancels out $-ab$.

Extracting by factoring

Now that you know how to do algebra forward (by distributing and FOILing), are you ready to do it backward? In this section, we show you how to switch to reverse gear and do some factoring.

Factors are the terms that make up a product. Extracting common factors can make expressions much easier to deal with. See how many common factors you can find in this expression; then extract, or *factor*, them out:

$-14x^3 - 35x^6$

First, you can pull out -7 because it goes into both -14 and -35. Doing so gives you $-7(2x^3 + 5x^6)$.

Next, you can take out the common factor of x^3 because x^3 is part of both terms. The simplified result is $-7x^3(2 + 5x^3)$.

You also need to know how to factor quadratic equations, which you accomplish by using FOIL in reverse. Say that the test gives you $x^2 + 13x + 42 = 0$ and asks you to solve for *x*. Take this problem one step at a time:

1. **Draw two sets of parentheses.**

   ( )( ) = 0

2. **To get x^2, the *First* terms have to be *x* and *x*, so fill those in first.**

   (*x*)(*x*) = 0

3. **Look at the *Outer* terms.**

   You need two numbers that multiply together to get +42. Well, you have several possibilities: 42 and 1, 21 and 2, or 6 and 7. You can even have two negative numbers: –42 and –1, –21 and –2, or –6 and –7. You can't be sure which numbers to choose yet, so go on to the next step.

4. **Look at the *Inner* terms.**

   You have to add two values to get +13. What's the first thing that springs to mind? Probably 6 + 7. Hey, that's one of the possible combinations of numbers you came up with in Step 3 for the *Outer* terms! Plug them in and multiply.

   $$(x+6)(x+7) =$$
   $$x^2 + 7x + 6x + 42 =$$
   $$x^2 + 13x + 42 =$$

5. **Solve for *x*.**

   If the whole equation equals 0, then either $(x+6) = 0$ or $(x+7) = 0$. After all, any number times 0 equals 0. Therefore, when you solve for *x* for either of these possibilities, *x* can equal –6 or –7.

The ACT tests your ability to factor quadratic equations in a variety of ways. Here's a sample problem:

EXAMPLE

Which of the following is a possible sum of the two solutions for the equation, $x^2 - 11x + 30 = 0$?

(A) –17

(B) –11

(C) –1

(D) 11

You find the solutions for a quadratic equation by finding its binomial factors and setting both equal to 0. The two values whose product is 30 and whose sum is –11 are –6 and –5: $-6 \times -5 = 30$ and $-5 + (-6) = -11$. So the binomial factors are $(x-5)$ and $(x-6)$. Set both equal to 0 and solve for *x*:

$$x - 5 = 0$$
$$x = 5$$
$$x - 6 = 0$$
$$x = 6$$

So the two solutions are 5 and 6. Their sum is 11, which is Choice (D). If you pick Choice (B), you've missed a step. You've forgotten to set the factors equal to zero and solve for *x*. The signs for the solutions to a quadratic are the opposite of those of the values within the binomial factor.

TIP

Whenever you see an ACT problem that includes a quadratic equation, you can pretty much bet you're going to have to perform some factoring. Make sure you're familiar with the steps because factoring problems crop up frequently. Or you can use your graphing calculator or the Desmos calculator in the digital version to factor quadratic equations. If your calculator doesn't already contain the program, you can find ways to add the program on the Internet.

Solving a system of equations

Suppose you have two algebraic equations with two different variables. For example, an ACT question may ask you to solve for *x* when $4x + 5y = 30$ and $y + x = 2$. You're dealing with a *system*

CHAPTER 8 **Numbers Nuts and Bolts** 91

of equations. By themselves, there could be an infinite number of values for *x* and *y*. However, when considered together, there is only one value for *x* and one value for *y* as long as the two equations aren't equal.

There are two ways to solve for a variable in simultaneous equations: substitution or elimination.

Here's how substitution works. Because you're solving for *x*, you need to get rid of the *y* variable. Find a value for *y* in one equation and substitute that value for *y* in the other equation.

For the preceding sample equations, it takes fewer steps to solve for *y* in the second equation. You get $y = 2 - x$.

All you really have to do then is substitute $2 - x$ for the value of *y* in the first equation and solve for *x*:

$$4x + 5(2 - x) = 30$$
$$4x + 10 - 5x = 30$$
$$10 - x = 30$$
$$-x = 20$$
$$x = -20$$

An easier way to solve for *x*, especially for more complex equations, may be by elimination — stacking the equations and manipulating them in a way that allows you to eliminate one variable and solve for the other.

Here's how it's done for this problem. You need to get rid of the *y* variable, which you can do if you change *y* in the second equation to $-5y$. You can accomplish this feat by multiplying every term in the second equation by -5: $(-5)y + (-5)x = (-5)2$. It's legal to change the equation as long as you perform the same operation with each of its terms. The resulting equation is $-5y - 5x = -10$. Just change the order of the first equation so the like terms match up, stack the two equations, and solve for *x*:

$$5y + 4x = 30$$
$$\underline{-5y - 5x = -10}$$
$$0 - x = 20$$
$$x = -20$$

Either method gives you the same result: $x = -20$.

TIP

You can use your graphing calculator or the Desmos calculator built into the ACT digital version to quickly solve systems of equations

If an ACT question tells you that a system of linear equations has no solutions, the lines represented by the system are parallel and have equal slopes. If the system has unlimited solutions, the two equations are equal and represent the same line. To work with a linear system of unlimited solutions, create equal equations. The ACT may give you the following equations, tell you that there are unlimited solutions for the system, and ask you to solve for *a*.

$$5y + 4x = 30$$
$$-15y - 12x = -10a$$

You just need to recognize that the second equation is the same as the first with each term multiplied by -3. Therefore, the value for *a* that would make the third term equal to 30×-3 is 9: $30 \times -3 = -10(9)$.

92 PART 3 Don't Count Yourself Out: The Math Test

So don't get discouraged if you see two equations with two similar variables. You have several tools for dealing with them. They're not as hard to work with as you think! Here's a sample question.

EXAMPLE

What is the value of a in the solution of the following system of equations?

$$4a + 8b = 52$$
$$a - 2b = -12$$

(F) 0

(G) $\frac{1}{2}$

(H) 1

(J) $\frac{25}{4}$

To solve for a, you must eliminate the b terms. You can accomplish that by multiplying each term in the bottom equation by 4 and adding the equations:

$$4a + 8b = 52$$
$$4a - 8b = -48$$
$$\overline{8a + 0 = 4}$$
$$a = \frac{4}{8} = \frac{1}{2}$$

Choice (G) is the answer. If you picked (J), you solved for b instead of a.

CHAPTER 8 Numbers Nuts and Bolts 93

IN THIS CHAPTER

» Getting to the point with lines and angles

» Identifying the ins and outs of triangles and similar figures

» Centering in on polygons and circles

» Applying SOH CAH TOA and other trigonometric identities

» Working with the unit circle

Chapter 9
Getting into Shapes: Geometry and Trig Review

Geometry may seem like one of the areas that can mess you up on the ACT. But it's easy when you take the time to memorize some rules. This chapter provides a lightning-fast review of the major points of geometry so that you can go into the test equipped to tackle the geometry questions with ease.

Toeing the Line

You don't need to memorize the following definitions for the ACT, but you do need to be familiar with them. Here are the common terms about lines that may pop up on your test:

» **Line segment:** The set of points on a line between any two points on that line. Basically, a line segment is just a piece of a line from one point to another that contains those two points and all the points in between. See line segment *CD* in Figure 9-1.

» **Midpoint:** The point halfway (an equal distance) between two endpoints on a line segment. In Figure 9-1, point *D* is the midpoint between points *A* and *B*.

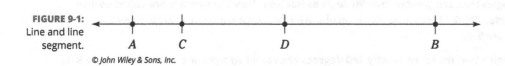

FIGURE 9-1: Line and line segment.

© John Wiley & Sons, Inc.

» **Intersect:** To cross. Two lines can intersect each other much like two streets cross each other at an intersection.

» **Vertical line:** A line that runs straight up and down. Figure 9-2 shows you an example of a vertical line as well as the following three kinds of lines.

» **Horizontal line:** A line that runs straight across from left to right (refer to Figure 9-2).

» **Parallel lines:** Lines that run in the same direction and keep the same distance apart. Parallel lines never intersect one another (refer to Figure 9-2).

» **Perpendicular lines:** Two lines that intersect to form a square corner. The intersection of two perpendicular lines forms a right, or 90-degree, angle (refer to Figure 9-2).

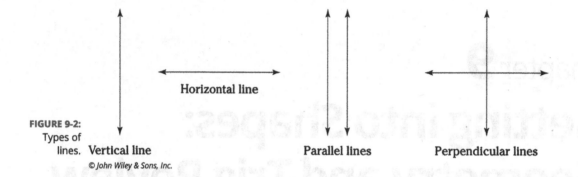

FIGURE 9-2: Types of lines. Vertical line   Horizontal line   Parallel lines   Perpendicular lines
© John Wiley & Sons, Inc.

Analyzing Angles

Angle problems make up a big part of the ACT geometry test. Fortunately, understanding angles is easy when you memorize a few basic concepts. After all, you don't have to do any proofs on the test. Finding an angle is usually a matter of simple addition or subtraction.

Here are a few things you need to know about angles to succeed on the ACT:

» **Angles that are greater than 0 but less than 90 degrees are called *acute angles*.** Think of an acute angle as being a *cute* little angle (see Figure 9-3).

» **Angles that are equal to 90 degrees are called *right angles*.** They're formed by perpendicular lines and indicated by a box in the corner of the two intersecting lines (refer to Figure 9-3).

WARNING

Don't automatically assume that angles that look like right angles are right angles. Without calculating the degree of the angle, you can't know for certain that an angle is a right angle unless one of the following is true:

- The problem directly tells you, "This is a right angle."
- You see the perpendicular symbol ⊥, indicating that the lines form a 90-degree angle.
- You see a box in the angle, like the one in Figure 9-3.

» **Angles that are greater than 90 degrees but less than 180 degrees are called *obtuse angles*.** Think of obtuse as obese; an obese (or fat) angle is an obtuse angle (refer to Figure 9-3).

» **Angles that measure exactly 180 degrees are called *straight angles*.** (Refer to Figure 9-3.)

96   PART 3 Don't Count Yourself Out: The Math Test

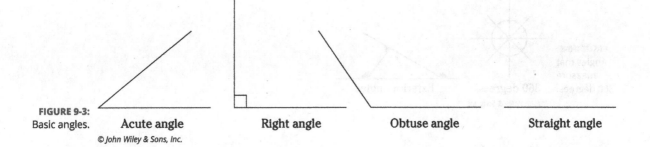

FIGURE 9-3: Basic angles.
Acute angle   Right angle   Obtuse angle   Straight angle
© John Wiley & Sons, Inc.

» **Angles that total 90 degrees are called *complementary angles*.** Think of *C* for corner (the lines form a 90-degree corner angle) and *C* for complementary (see Figure 9-4).

» **Angles that total 180 degrees are called *supplementary angles*.** Think of *S* for supplementary (or straight) angles. Be careful not to confuse complementary angles with supplementary angles. If you're likely to get them confused, just think alphabetically: *C* comes before *S* in the alphabet; 90 comes before 180 when you count (refer to Figure 9-4).

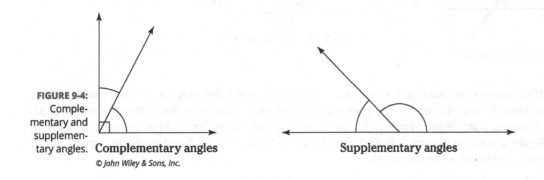

FIGURE 9-4: Complementary and supplementary angles.
Complementary angles   Supplementary angles
© John Wiley & Sons, Inc.

» **Angles that are greater than 180 degrees but less than 360 degrees are called *reflex angles*.** (See Figure 9-5 for an example.)

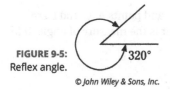

FIGURE 9-5: Reflex angle.
© John Wiley & Sons, Inc.

» **Angles around a point total 360 degrees.** (See Figure 9-6.)

» **The exterior angles of any figure are supplementary to the two opposite interior angles and always total 360 degrees.** (Refer to Figure 9-6.)

» **Angles that are opposite each other have equal measures and are called *vertical angles*.** Just remember that vertical angles are *across* from each other, whether they're up and down (vertical) or side by side (horizontal). (Figure 9-7 shows two sets of vertical angles.)

» **Angles in the same position around two parallel lines and a transversal are called *corresponding angles* and have equal measures.** (Figure 9-8 shows two sets of corresponding angles.)

CHAPTER 9 **Getting into Shapes: Geometry and Trig Review** 97

FIGURE 9-6:
Angles that measure 360 degrees.

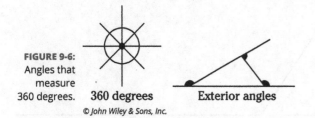

© John Wiley & Sons, Inc.

FIGURE 9-7:
Vertical angles have equal measures.

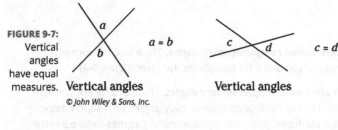

© John Wiley & Sons, Inc.

FIGURE 9-8:
Corresponding angles have equal measures.

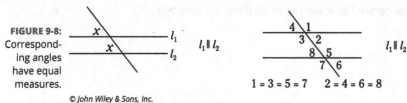

© John Wiley & Sons, Inc.

TIP

When you see two parallel lines and a *transversal* (that's the line going across the parallel lines), number the angles. Start in the upper-right corner with 1 and go clockwise. For the second batch of angles, start in the upper-right corner with 5 and go clockwise. (See the second figure in Figure 9-8 for an example.) Note that in Figure 9-8, all odd-numbered angles are equal, and all even-numbered angles are equal.

Be careful not to zigzag back and forth when numbering. If you zig when you should have zagged, you can no longer use the tip that all even-numbered angles are equal to one another and all odd-numbered angles are equal to one another.

The ACT tests your knowledge of angles in various ways. Here's an example.

EXAMPLE

In the figure, $\overline{AB}$ and $\overline{DE}$ are parallel, points B, C, and D are collinear, and points A, C, and E are collinear. Angle ABD measures 72°, and angle ACB measures 66°. What is the measure of angle AED?

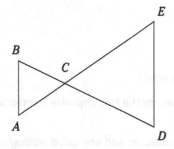

(A) 40°
(B) 42°
(C) 66°
(D) 72°

98 PART 3 Don't Count Yourself Out: The Math Test

To keep track of the details, write the provided angle measures on the figure. Then determine the measures of the other angles by applying the rules. Line *BD* is a transversal of the parallel lines *AB* and *DE*, so angles *ABD* and *BDE* are corresponding angles along a transversal and have the same measure, so angle *BDE* also measures 72°. Angles *ACB* and *DCE* are vertical angles, and vertical angles have equal measures, so *DCE* is 66°. When you know two angles of any triangle, you also know the third because the sum of the three angles is 180°. $72°+66°+AED=180°$. $180°-(72°+66°)=42°$. The answer is Choice (D).

Triangle Trauma

Many of the geometry problems on the ACT require you to know a lot about triangles. Remember the facts and rules about triangles in this section, and you're on your way to acing geometry questions.

Classifying triangles

Triangles are classified based on the measurements of their sides and angles. Here are the types of triangles you may need to know for the ACT:

- **Equilateral:** A triangle with three equal sides and three equal angles (see Figure 9-9).
- **Isosceles:** A triangle with two equal sides and two equal angles. The angles opposite equal sides in an isosceles triangle are also equal (refer to Figure 9-9).
- **Scalene:** A triangle with no equal sides and no equal angles (refer to Figure 9-9).

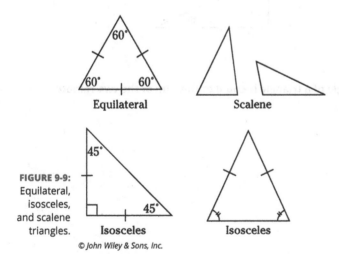

FIGURE 9-9: Equilateral, isosceles, and scalene triangles.

© John Wiley & Sons, Inc.

Sizing up triangles

When you're figuring out ACT questions that deal with triangles, you need to know these rules about the measurements of their sides and angles:

- **In any triangle, the largest angle is opposite the longest side.** (See Figure 9-10.)
- **In any triangle, the sum of the lengths of two sides must be greater than the length of the third side.**

CHAPTER 9 **Getting into Shapes: Geometry and Trig Review** 99

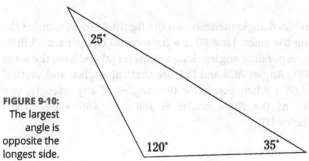

FIGURE 9-10:
The largest angle is opposite the longest side.

© John Wiley & Sons, Inc.

» **In other words, $a + b > c$, where a, b, and c are the sides of the triangle** (see Figure 9-11).

» **In any type of triangle, the sum of the interior angles is 180 degrees.** (See Figure 9-12.)

FIGURE 9-11:
The sum of the lengths of two sides of a triangle is greater than the length of the third side.

 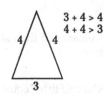 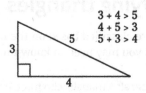

© John Wiley & Sons, Inc.

FIGURE 9-12:
The sum of the interior angles of a triangle is 180 degrees.

 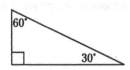

© John Wiley & Sons, Inc.

» **The measure of an exterior angle of a triangle is equal to the sum of the two remote interior angles.** (See Figure 9-13.)

FIGURE 9-13:
The measure of an exterior angle is equal to the sum of the two remote interior angles.

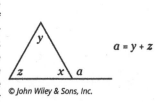

© John Wiley & Sons, Inc.

Zeroing in on similar triangles

Several ACT math questions require you to compare similar triangles. *Similar triangles* look alike but are different sizes. Here's what you need to know about similar triangles:

» Similar triangles have the same angle measures. If you can determine that two triangles contain angles that measure the same degrees, you know the triangles are similar.

» The sides of similar triangles are in proportion. For example, if the heights of two similar triangles are in a ratio of 2:3, then the bases of those triangles are also in a ratio of 2:3 (see Figure 9-14).

FIGURE 9-14: Similar triangles have proportionate sides.

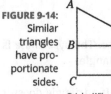 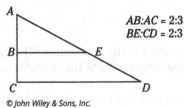

AB:AC = 2:3
BE:CD = 2:3

© John Wiley & Sons, Inc.

REMEMBER

Don't assume that triangles are similar on the ACT just because they look similar to you. The only way you know two triangles are similar is if the test tells you they are, or you can determine that their angle measures are the same.

Figuring out area and perimeter

To succeed on the Mathematics Test, you should be able to figure out the area and perimeter of triangles in your sleep. Memorize these formulas:

» **The area of a triangle is $\frac{1}{2}$ base × height.**

The height is always a line perpendicular to the base. The height may be a side of the triangle, as in a right triangle (see Figure 9-15a). But the height may also be inside the triangle. In that case, it's often represented by a dashed line and a small 90-degree box (see Figure 9-15b). The height may also be outside the triangle. You can always drop an altitude. That is, put your pencil on the tallest point of the triangle and draw a line straight from that point to where the base would be if it were extended (see Figure 9-15c).

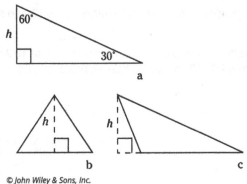

FIGURE 9-15: The height of a triangle.

© John Wiley & Sons, Inc.

» **The perimeter of a triangle is the sum of the lengths of its sides.** (See Figure 9-16.)

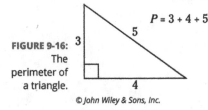

FIGURE 9-16: The perimeter of a triangle.

© John Wiley & Sons, Inc.

Taking the shortcut: Pythagorean triples and other common side ratios

In any right triangle, you can find the lengths of the sides by using the *Pythagorean theorem*, which looks like this:

$$a^2 + b^2 = c^2$$

In this formula, a and b are the sides of the triangle, and c is the hypotenuse. The *hypotenuse* is always opposite the 90-degree angle and is always the longest side of the triangle.

WARNING

Keep in mind that the Pythagorean theorem works only on right triangles. If a triangle doesn't have a right — or 90-degree — angle, you can't use any of the information in this section.

Having to work through the whole Pythagorean theorem formula every time you want to find the length of a right triangle's side is a pain in the posterior. To make your life a little easier, memorize these Pythagorean triples and other common right-triangle side ratios:

» **Ratio 3:4:5.** If one side of the triangle is 3 in this ratio, the other side is 4, and the hypotenuse is 5 (see Figure 9-17).

Because this is a ratio, the sides can be in any multiple of these numbers, such as 6:8:10 (two times 3:4:5), 9:12:15 (three times 3:4:5), or 27:36:45 (nine times 3:4:5).

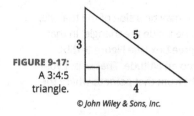

FIGURE 9-17: A 3:4:5 triangle.
© John Wiley & Sons, Inc.

» **Ratio 5:12:13.** If one side of the right triangle is 5 in this ratio, the other side is 12, and the hypotenuse is 13 (see Figure 9-18).

Because this is a ratio, the sides can be in any multiple of these numbers, such as 10:24:26 (two times 5:12:13), 15:36:39 (three times 5:12:13), or 50:120:130 (ten times 5:12:13).

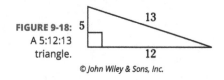

FIGURE 9-18: A 5:12:13 triangle.
© John Wiley & Sons, Inc.

» **Ratio $s : s : s\sqrt{2}$, where s stands for the side of the figure.** Because two sides are equal, this formula applies to an isosceles right triangle, also known as a 45:45:90 triangle. If one side is 2, then the other side is also 2, and the hypotenuse is $2\sqrt{2}$ (see Figure 9-19).

102 PART 3 Don't Count Yourself Out: The Math Test

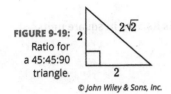

FIGURE 9-19: Ratio for a 45:45:90 triangle.

TIP

This formula is great to know for squares. If a question tells you that the side of a square is 5 and wants to know the diagonal of the square, you know immediately that it is $5\sqrt{2}$. Why? A square's diagonal cuts the square into two isosceles right triangles (*isosceles* because all sides of the square are equal; *right* because all angles in a square are right angles). What is the diagonal of a square of side 64? $64\sqrt{2}$.

You can write this ratio another way. Instead of writing $s : s : s\sqrt{2}$, write $\frac{s}{\sqrt{2}} : \frac{s}{\sqrt{2}} : s$, where s still stands for the side of the triangle, but now you've divided everything in the ratio by $\sqrt{2}$. Why do you need this complicated ratio? Suppose you're told that the diagonal of a square is 5. That's enough information to figure out the area of the square and its perimeter.

If you know the ratio $\frac{s}{\sqrt{2}} : \frac{s}{\sqrt{2}} : s$, you know that s stands for the hypotenuse of the triangle, which is also the diagonal of the square. If s = 5, then the side of the square is $\frac{5}{\sqrt{2}}$ and you can figure out the area or the perimeter. After you know the side of a square, you can figure out just about anything.

» **Ratio $s : s\sqrt{3} : 2s$.** This special formula is for the sides of a 30:60:90 triangle (see Figure 9-20).

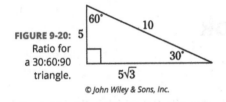

FIGURE 9-20: Ratio for a 30:60:90 triangle.

This type of triangle is a favorite of test makers. The important thing to keep in mind here is that the hypotenuse is twice the length of the side opposite the 30-degree angle. If you get a word problem that says, "Given a 30:60:90 triangle of hypotenuse 20, find the area" or "Given a 30:60:90 triangle of hypotenuse 100, find the perimeter," you can do so because you can find the lengths of the other sides (see Figure 9-21 for details).

FIGURE 9-21: Using the ratio for a 30:60:90 triangle to find the lengths of the triangle's sides.

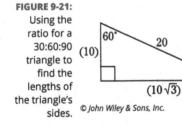 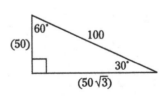

ACT triangle questions are often easier to answer when you remember the common side ratios of right triangles. Here's a sample triangle question.

EXAMPLE

Triangle *ABC* is equilateral and has a perimeter of 168 units. What is its area in square units?

(A) $28\sqrt{3}$

(B) 168

(C) 224

(D) $784\sqrt{3}$

Because triangle *ABC* is equilateral, each of its angles measures 60°, and the three side lengths are equal. If the perimeter of the triangle is 168 units, each side measures 56 units. The area of a triangle is $\frac{1}{2}bh$. You know the base is 56 units, but you need to calculate the height. The height of the triangle is the length from the base to its highest point. The height of an equilateral triangle divides the triangle into two equal 30°–60°–90° triangles with side ratios of $s : s\sqrt{3} : 2s$, where *s* is the length of the smallest side. The length of the smallest side of each right triangle is 28 units, half the length of the original base. The longer leg (the original triangle's height) is $28\sqrt{3}$.

Once you know the base and the height, you can calculate the area in square units:

$$\frac{1}{2}bh = A$$

$$\frac{1}{2}(56)(28\sqrt{3}) = A$$

$$784\sqrt{3} = A$$

The answer is Choice (D). If you pick Choice (A), you solved for the height rather than the area.

Thanks 4 Nothing: A Quick Look at Quadrilaterals

Another favorite figure of the ACT test-making folks is the *quadrilateral*, which is the fancy label mathematicians give shapes with four sides. Here's a summary of the four-sided figures you may see on the ACT:

> » **A *quadrilateral* is any four-sided figure.**
>
> The interior angles of any quadrilateral total 360 degrees. You can cut any quadrilateral into two 180-degree triangles (see Figure 9-22).

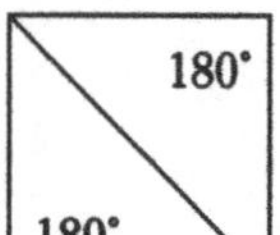

FIGURE 9-22: A quadrilateral.

© John Wiley & Sons, Inc.

> » **A *square* is a quadrilateral with four equal sides and four right angles.**
>
> The area of a square is s^2 (or base × height) or $\frac{1}{2}d^2$, where *d* stands for the *diagonal* (see Figure 9-23).

104 PART 3 Don't Count Yourself Out: The Math Test

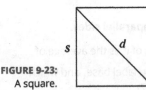

FIGURE 9-23:
A square.

© John Wiley & Sons, Inc.

REMEMBER

» **A *rhombus* is a quadrilateral with four equal sides and four angles that are not necessarily right angles.** A rhombus often looks like a drunken square, tipsy on its side and wobbly.

The area of a rhombus is $\frac{1}{2}d_1 d_2$ or $\frac{1}{2}$ diagonal$_1$ × diagonal$_2$ (see Figure 9-24).

All squares are rhombuses, but not all rhombuses are squares.

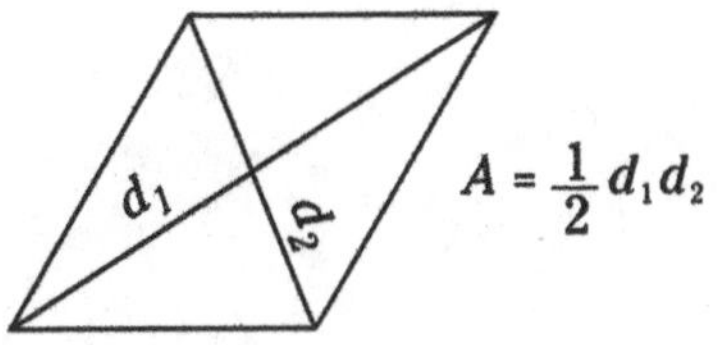

FIGURE 9-24:
A rhombus.

© John Wiley & Sons, Inc.

» **A *rectangle* is a quadrilateral with four right angles and two opposite and equal pairs of sides.** That is, the top and bottom sides are equal, and the right and left sides are equal.

The area of a rectangle is length × width, which is the same as base × height (see Figure 9-25).

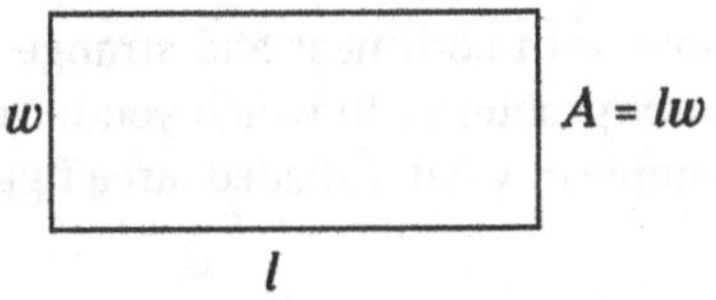

FIGURE 9-25:
A rectangle.

© John Wiley & Sons, Inc.

» **A *parallelogram* is a quadrilateral with two opposite and equal pairs of sides.** The top and bottom sides are equal, and the right and left sides are equal. Opposite angles are equal but not necessarily right (or 90 degrees).

The area of a parallelogram is base × height. Remember that the height is always a perpendicular line from the tallest point of the figure down to the base (see Figure 9-26). Diagonals of a parallelogram bisect each other.

All rectangles are parallelograms, but not all parallelograms are rectangles.

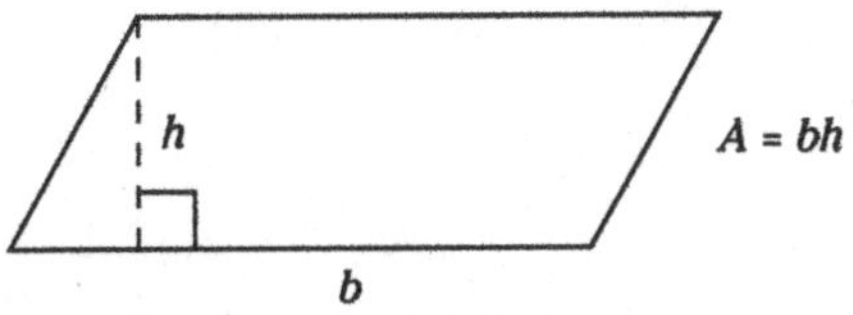

REMEMBER

FIGURE 9-26:
A parallelogram.

© John Wiley & Sons, Inc.

CHAPTER 9 Getting into Shapes: Geometry and Trig Review   105

>> A *trapezoid* is a quadrilateral with two parallel sides and two nonparallel sides.

The area of a trapezoid is $\frac{1}{2}(\text{base}_1 + \text{base}_2) \times \text{height}$. We like to think of it as the average of the two bases times the height. It makes no difference which base you label base₁ and which you label base₂, because you're adding them together (see Figure 9-27).

Keep in mind that some quadrilaterals, like the one in Figure 9-28, don't have nice, neat shapes or special names.

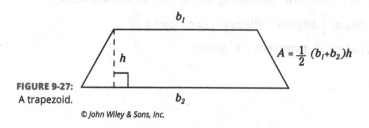

FIGURE 9-27:
A trapezoid.

© John Wiley & Sons, Inc.

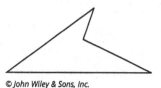

FIGURE 9-28:
Not all quadrilaterals have special names.

© John Wiley & Sons, Inc.

WARNING

If you see a strange shape, don't immediately say that you have no way of finding its area. You may be able to divide the quadrilateral in Figure 9-28 into two triangles, find the area of each triangle, and then add them together.

Knowing how to find the area of quadrilaterals (those with both neat and strange shapes) and other figures can help you solve *shaded-area* or *leftover* problems, in which you have to subtract the unshaded area from the total area. Here's an example of what a shaded-area figure may look like on the ACT:

Shaded areas can often be unusual shapes. Your first reaction may be that you can't possibly find the area of that shape. Generally, you're right, but you don't have to find the area directly. Instead, be sly, devious, and sneaky; in other words, think the ACT way! Find the area of the total figure, find the area of the unshaded portion, and subtract.

106 PART 3 Don't Count Yourself Out: The Math Test

EXAMPLE What is the area of the shaded portion of the circle inscribed in a square that follows?

(F) 64

(G) 16π

(H) $64 - 16\pi$

(J) $48 - 16\pi$

First, you have to find the area of the square. You know that the radius of the circle is 4, so the diameter of the circle, as well as the side of the square, is 8. $8 \times 8 = 64$. Therefore, the area of the square is 64. Next, find the area of the circle:

$$A = (4^2)\pi$$
$$A = 16\pi$$

Then just subtract to find the shaded area: $64 - 16\pi$. The answer is Choice (H).

Missing Parrots and Other Polly-Gones (Or Should We Say "Polygons"?)

Triangles and quadrilaterals are probably the most commonly tested polygons on the ACT. What's a polygon? A *polygon* is a closed-plane figure bounded by straight sides.

Measuring up polygons

Here's what you need to know about the side and angle measurements of polygons:

>> **A polygon with all equal sides and all equal angles is called *regular*.** For example, an equilateral triangle is a regular triangle, and a square is a regular quadrilateral.

The ACT rarely asks you to find the areas of any polygons with more than four sides.

>> **The *perimeter* of a polygon is the sum of the lengths of all the sides.**

>> **The *exterior angle measure* of any polygon, also known as the sum of its exterior angles, is 360 degrees.** (An *exterior angle* is the angle formed by any side of the polygon and the line that's created when you extend the adjacent side.)

>> **To find the *interior angle measure* of any regular polygon, also known as the sum of its interior angles, use the formula $(n-2)180°$, where *n* stands for the number of sides.** For example, to find the interior angle measure for a pentagon (a five-sided figure), just substitute 5 for *n* in the formula and solve:

$(5-2)180° = 3 \times 180 = 540°$

So the sum of the interior angles of a pentagon is 540°.

CHAPTER 9 Getting into Shapes: Geometry and Trig Review 107

Solving for volume

The volume of any polygon is area of the base × height. If you remember this formula, you don't have to memorize any of the following specific volume formulas. If you take the time to memorize specific formulas, though, you'll use fewer steps to work out volume problems and you'll save some precious time.

> **Volume of a cube** = e^3
>
> A *cube* is a three-dimensional square. All of a cube's dimensions are the same; that is, length = width = height. In a cube, these dimensions are called *edges* (see Figure 9-29).

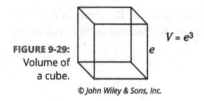

FIGURE 9-29: Volume of a cube.

© John Wiley & Sons, Inc.

> **Volume of a rectangular solid** = *lwh*
>
> A *rectangular solid* is a box. The base of a box is a rectangle, which has an area of length × width. Multiply that by the height to fit the original volume formula: Volume = (area of base) × height, or $V = lwh$ (see Figure 9-30).

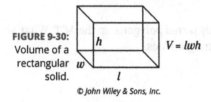

FIGURE 9-30: Volume of a rectangular solid.

© John Wiley & Sons, Inc.

> **Volume of a cylinder** = $(\pi r^2)h$
>
> Think of a *cylinder* as a can of soup. The base of a cylinder is a circle. The area of a circle is πr^2. Multiply that by the height of the cylinder to get the volume. Note that the top and bottom of a cylinder are identical circles. If you know the radius of either the top base or the bottom base, you can find the area of the circle (see Figure 9-31). (See the section, "Running Around in Circles" for more on circles.)

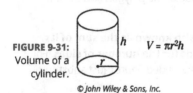

FIGURE 9-31: Volume of a cylinder.

© John Wiley & Sons, Inc.

108   PART 3 Don't Count Yourself Out: The Math Test

EXAMPLE

A circular cylinder box with a radius of 6 inches and a height of 8 inches is filled completely with sand. Which answer is closest to the volume of the sand within the cylinder?

(A) 301

(B) 368

(C) 460

(D) 904

The formula for the volume of a circular cylinder is $\pi r^2 h$. Substitute the values the question gives you for height and radius into the formula: $\pi 6^2 8$ or 288π. Use the π key on your calculator or multiply 288 by 3.14. The volume is a little over 904, Choice (D).

If you pick Choice (A), you doubled rather than squared the radius.

Running Around in Circles

Did you hear about the Rube who pulled his son out of college, claiming that the school was filling his head with nonsense? As the Rube said, "Joe Bob told me that he learned πr^2. But any fool knows that *pie* are round; *cornbread* are square!"

Circles are among the least complicated geometry concepts. To excel on circle questions, you must remember the vocabulary and be able to distinguish an arc from a sector and an inscribed angle from a central angle. Here's a quick review of the basics:

» **A circle's *radius* goes from the center of the circle to its *circumference* (or perimeter).** (See Figure 9-32.)

FIGURE 9-32: The radius of a circle.

© John Wiley & Sons, Inc.

» **A circle gets its name from its *midpoint* (or center).**

For example, the circle in Figure 9-33 is called circle *M* because its midpoint is *M*.

FIGURE 9-33: The midpoint of a circle.

 Circle *M*

© John Wiley & Sons, Inc.

» **A circle's *diameter* connects two points on the circumference of the circle, goes through the circle's center, and is equal to two radii (which is the plural of *radius*).** (See Figure 9-34.)

CHAPTER 9 **Getting into Shapes: Geometry and Trig Review** 109

FIGURE 9-34: The diameter equals two radii.

» A *chord* connects any two points on a circle. (See Figure 9-35 for two examples.) The longest chord in a circle is the diameter.

FIGURE 9-35: Two examples of a chord.

» The area of a circle is πr^2. (See Figure 9-36.)

FIGURE 9-36: Area of a circle.

» The circumference of a circle is $2\pi r$ or πd because two radii equal one diameter.

TIP

On the Math Test, you may encounter a wheel question in which you're asked how much distance a wheel covers or how many times a wheel revolves. Or you may be asked to figure out the distance that a minute hand travels around a clock. The key to solving these types of questions is knowing that one rotation of a wheel or minute hand equals one circumference of that wheel or clock.

» A *central angle* has its endpoints on the circumference of the circle and its center at the center of the circle.

The degree measure of a central angle is the same as the degree measure of its intercepted arc (see Figure 9-37). (Keep reading to find out what an arc is.)

FIGURE 9-37: A central angle.

» An *inscribed angle* has both its endpoints and its center on the circumference of the circle.

The degree measure of an inscribed angle is half the degree measure of its intercepted arc (see Figure 9-38).

FIGURE 9-38: An inscribed angle.

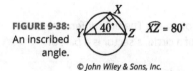

© John Wiley & Sons, Inc.

Thales's theorem tells you that the endpoints of an inscribed angle in a semicircle create a right triangle. If YZ in the figure is the diameter of the circle, ∠YXZ is a right angle, and △YXZ is a right triangle.

» **When a central angle and an inscribed angle have the same endpoints, the degree measure of the central angle is twice that of the inscribed angle.** (See Figure 9-39.)

FIGURE 9-39: Central and inscribed angles with the same endpoints.

© John Wiley & Sons, Inc.

» **The degree measure of a circle is 360.**

» **An *arc* is a portion of the circumference of a circle.**

The degree measure of an arc is the same as its central angle and twice its inscribed angle (see Figure 9-40).

FIGURE 9-40: An arc on a circle.

© John Wiley & Sons, Inc.

To find the *length* of an arc, follow these steps:

1. **Find the circumference of the entire circle.**

2. **Put the degree measure of the arc over 360 and then reduce the fraction.**

3. **Multiply the circumference by the fraction.**

4. **A *sector* is a portion of the area of a circle.**

The degree measure of a sector is the same as its central angle and twice its inscribed angle.

To find the *area* of a sector, follow these steps:

1. **Find the area of the entire circle.**

2. **Put the degree measure of the sector over 360 and then reduce the fraction.**

3. **Multiply the area by the fraction.**

CHAPTER 9 Getting into Shapes: Geometry and Trig Review

Finding the area of a sector is very similar to finding the length of an arc. The only difference is in the first step. Whereas an arc is a part of the circumference of a circle, a sector is a part of the area of a circle.

» **A *tangent line* is one that intersects (or touches) the circle at just one point.**

A tangent line is always perpendicular to the radius at the point on the circumference where the line touches the circle. (See Figure 9-41.)

A pair of lines drawn from an external point and both tangent to different points on the circumference of a circle are congruent. So, lines *BC* and *CD* in Figure 9-42 are the same length, and triangle *BCD* is isosceles. The angles formed by the lines and radii at points *B* and *D* are right angles.

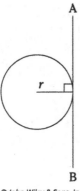

FIGURE 9-41: Tangent line.

© John Wiley & Sons, Inc.

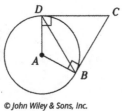

FIGURE 9-42: Two tangent lines from one external point.

© John Wiley & Sons, Inc.

Here are a few examples of how the ACT may test you about circles.

EXAMPLE

What is the area of a circle whose longest chord is 12?

(F) 144π

(G) 72π

(H) 36π

(J) Cannot be determined from the information given

The diameter of this circle is 12, which means its radius is 6 because a diameter is twice the radius. The area of a circle is πr^2, and $6^2 \pi = 36\pi$. The correct answer is Choice (H).

WARNING

Choice (J) is the trap answer. If you know only that a chord of the circle is 12, you can't solve the problem. A circle has many different chords. You need to know the length of the longest chord, or the diameter.

EXAMPLE

A child's wagon has a wheel with a radius of 6 inches. If the wagon wheel travels 100 revolutions, approximately how many feet has the wagon rolled?

(A) 325

(B) 314

(C) 255

(D) 201

One revolution is equal to one circumference: $2\pi r$, which is approximately 12(3.14) or 37.68 inches. Multiply that by 100 to get 3,768 inches. Then divide by 12 to get 314 feet. The correct answer is Choice (B).

EXAMPLE

Find the sum of $a+b+c+d+e$.

Note: Figure not drawn to scale.

(F) 65 degrees

(G) 60 degrees

(H) 55 degrees

(J) 50 degrees

Although this figure looks a lot like a string picture you made at summer camp, with all sorts of lines running every which way, answering the question that goes along with it isn't as complicated as you may think. To get started, take the time to identify the endpoints of the angles and the center point. Each angle is an inscribed angle; it has half the degree measure of the central angle, or half the degree measure of its intercepted arc. If you look carefully at the endpoints of these angles, you see that they're all the same. They're all along arc XY, which has a measure of 20 degrees. Therefore, each angle is 10 degrees, for a total of 50. The correct answer is Choice (J).

EXAMPLE

Find the length of arc *AC* in Circle B, shown here.

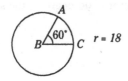

(A) 6π

(B) 12π

(C) 16π

(D) 36π

CHAPTER 9 Getting into Shapes: Geometry and Trig Review 113

Take the steps one at a time. First, find the circumference of the entire circle: $C = 2\pi = 36\pi$. Don't multiply π out; problems usually leave it in that form. Next, put the degree measure of the arc over 360 and simplify. The degree measure of the arc is the same as its central angle, which is 60 degrees.

$$\frac{60}{360} = \frac{1}{6}$$

The arc is $\frac{1}{6}$ of the circumference of the circle. Multiply the circumference by the fraction:

$$36\pi \times \frac{1}{6} = 6\pi$$

The correct answer is Choice (A).

After you get the hang of these, they're kinda fun. Right?

EXAMPLE

Find the area of sector *ABC* in Circle B, shown here.

$r = 8$

Angle *ABC* = 90°

(F) 64π
(G) 36π
(H) 16π
(J) 12π

First, find the area of the entire circle:

$$A = \pi r^2$$
$$A = 64\pi$$

Second, put the degree measure of the sector over 360. The sector is 90 degrees, the same as its central angle: $\frac{90}{360} = \frac{1}{4}$.

Third, multiply the area by the fraction:

$$64\pi \times \frac{1}{4} = 16\pi$$

The correct answer is Choice (H).

114 PART 3 Don't Count Yourself Out: The Math Test

Trying Your Hand at Trigonometry

Many of our students cringe when they hear that the ACT has trigonometry questions. If you're cringing right now, too, relax and stand tall. The ACT has only a few trig questions, and this section covers what you need to know to answer most of those few, even if you've never stepped foot in a trigonometry classroom.

Dealing with trigonometric functions is about all you need to know for most of the trig questions. A few may deal with more advanced trig concepts.

Introducing trigonometric functions

ACT trigonometry questions concern trigonometric functions. *Trigonometric functions* express the relationships between the angles and sides of a right triangle in terms of one of its angles. You can answer almost every ACT trig question if you remember the mnemonic for the three basic trigonometric functions, SOH CAH TOA.

SOH CAH TOA stands for

$$\text{Sine} = \frac{\text{opposite}}{\text{hypotenuse}}$$

$$\text{Cosine} = \frac{\text{adjacent}}{\text{hypotenuse}}$$

$$\text{Tangent} = \frac{\text{opposite}}{\text{adjacent}}$$

Are you scratching your head now and asking, "Opposite? Opposite *what*?" Take a look at this right triangle and consider the guidelines that follow it.

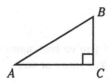

Side *AB* is the *hypotenuse* of the triangle. In relation to the angle at point *A*, side *BC* is the *opposite* side. The other side, the one that's not the hypotenuse or opposite angle *A*, is the *adjacent* side.

> » **To find sin *A* (in other words, the sine of angle *A*), all you need to do is find the length of opposite side *BC* and divide it by the length of the hypotenuse (or *AB*).**
>
> $$\sin A = \frac{\text{opposite } A}{\text{hypotenuse}}$$
>
> $$\sin A = \frac{\overline{BC}}{\overline{AB}}$$
>
> *Sine* is usually abbreviated as *sin*; the terms mean the same thing.

CHAPTER 9 Getting into Shapes: Geometry and Trig Review 115

- **To find cos A (the cosine of angle A), find the length of adjacent side AC and use the CAH part of SOH CAH TOA.**

$$\cos A = \frac{\text{adjacent } A}{\text{hypotenuse}}$$

$$\cos A = \frac{\overline{AC}}{\overline{AB}}$$

Cosine is usually abbreviated as *cos*; they mean the same thing.

- **To find tan A (the tangent of angle A), use the TOA part of SOH CAH TOA.**

$$\tan A = \frac{\text{opposite } A}{\text{adjacent } A}$$

$$\tan A = \frac{\overline{BC}}{\overline{AC}}$$

Yes, *tangent* is usually abbreviated as *tan*; they mean the same thing.

When you work with cosine and sine, keep these very simple but very important rules in mind:

- No side in a right triangle can be greater than the hypotenuse, so you can never have a sine greater than 1.
- Because the adjacent side can't be greater than the hypotenuse, you can never have a cosine greater than 1.
- The sum of sine squared and cosine squared for an angle is 1, and therefore the following equations are true:
    - $\sin^2 \theta + \cos^2 \theta = 1$
    - $\sin \theta = \sqrt{1 - \cos^2 \theta}$
    - $\cos \theta = \sqrt{1 - \sin^2 \theta}$

Additional trig functions appear less frequently on the ACT, so if you've had about all you can stand of trig, you can ignore them and still be okay on exam day. For those of you who can't get enough, review Table 9-1 for the reciprocal trig functions.

TABLE 9-1 Reciprocal Trigonometric Functions

Trig Function	Definition	Ratio
secant (sec)	reciprocal of sine: $\sec \theta = \frac{1}{\cos \theta}$	$\frac{\text{hypotenuse}}{\text{opposite}}$
cosecant (csc)	reciprocal of cosine: $\csc \theta = \frac{1}{\sin \theta}$	$\frac{\text{hypotenuse}}{\text{adjacent}}$
cotangent (cot)	reciprocal of tangent: $\cot \theta = \frac{1}{\tan \theta}$	$\frac{\text{adjacent}}{\text{opposite}}$

Occasionally, the ACT may spring inverse trig functions on you. Arcsine ($\sin^{-1}$), arcosine ($\cos^{-1}$), and arctangent (tan^{-1}) are the inverse functions of sine, cosine, and tangent, respectively. When you know the inverse of a function, you can calculate the corresponding angle measurement. So if you're told that $tan^{-1} = 1.192$, you could plug that value into your calculator to determine that the angle in question measures 50°. The likelihood of you encountering an inverse trig function question on the ACT is slim.

Here's an example of a common question that tests your knowledge of SOH CAH TOA.

A right triangle has an angle with a degree measure of 45. Find tan 45°.

(A) $\sqrt{2}$

(B) $\dfrac{\sqrt{2}}{2}$

(C) $\dfrac{1}{\sqrt{2}}$

(D) 1

First draw a 45:45:90 triangle. Remember that the ratio of the sides of this triangle is $s : s : s\sqrt{2}$, where s stands for the length of the side. (We discuss this ratio in an earlier section, "Taking the shortcut: Pythagorean triples and other common side ratios.")

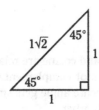

Then figure out the tan by using the TOA part of SOH CAH TOA.

$$\tan 45° = \dfrac{\text{opposite } 45°}{\text{adjacent } 45°}$$

$$\tan 45° = \dfrac{1}{1}$$

$$\tan 45° = 1$$

The answer is Choice (D). If you picked Choice (A), you tried to find the ratio of the hypotenuse to one of the other sides, which isn't one of the three main trig ratios. Choice (B) is what you'd get if you were asked to find the sine or cosine of the 45-degree angle.

You know that Choice (C) can't be correct, because you can't have a radical in the denominator. If you were asked to find the sine or cosine of the 45-degree angle, you would have to rationalize the final answer: $\dfrac{1}{\sqrt{2}} \times \dfrac{\sqrt{2}}{\sqrt{2}} = \dfrac{\sqrt{2}}{2}$.

Circumventing the unit circle

A picture is worth a thousand words, and trigonometric functions are no exception. Once you see how trigonometric functions show up on a graph, you have a far better understanding of the repeating nature of these functions. They're called repeating functions, or *periodic functions*, because they repeat themselves in cycles over and over again.

One way to visualize this periodic trait is by looking at the *unit circle*, which is simply a circle on the coordinate plane with its center at the origin, and having a radius of 1. The unit circle is a great way to define and graph the sine and cosine functions in terms of that radius. Figure 9-43 shows, to some extent, how this circle graphically displays these two functions.

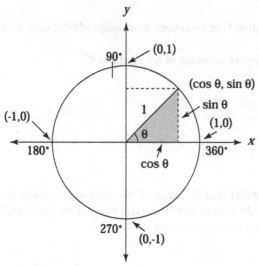

FIGURE 9-43:
The unit circle.

© John Wiley & Sons, Inc.

From the vantage point of the unit circle, you can see how the sine and cosine are related to one another. You know that these two functions are the measurements of complementary angles. When one of the acute angles in the triangle gets bigger, the other acute angle gets smaller, and vice versa. So, the sine and cosine of an angle vary directly with each other.

The sine and cosine have some important properties about their positive and negative signs when the $\angle \theta$ increases on the unit circle in a counter-clockwise manner.

» Any angle between 0° and 90° (Quadrant I) has a positive sine and a positive cosine.

» Any angle between 0° and 180° (Quadrant II) has a positive sine and a negative cosine.

» Any angle between 90° and 270° (Quadrant III) has a negative sine and a negative cosine.

» Any angle between 270° and 360° (Quadrant IV) has a negative sine and a positive cosine.

The unit circle shows the repeating nature of trig functions. The measure of the sine at 0° is equal to 0, and the cosine measures 1. If you move the angle around the circle and come back to the beginning, the measure of the angle is now 360°, but the sine and cosine have the same measurement at this new angle as they had when the angle was 0°. The angle looks the same, even though it has a difference of 360°. All that work for nothing!

Measuring in radians

You may be asked a question that tests your knowledge of *radians* instead of degrees as a way of measuring angles. The *radian measure* of an angle on the unit circle is the ratio of the length of the arc to the radius. The radian measure is unit-free — that is, it doesn't matter if you measure the radius of the circle in inches or miles; it's still simply a proportionate measure of the arc to the angle.

The circumference of a circle is equal to $2\pi r$, so the total radian measurement of a circle is 2π radians, and the radian measurement of a semicircle is π radians. You can have a little over 6 radians in a circle. Figure 9-44 compares radian and degree measurements of angles in a circle.

118   PART 3 Don't Count Yourself Out: The Math Test

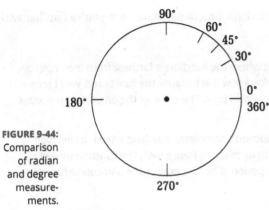
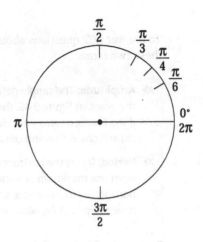

FIGURE 9-44: Comparison of radian and degree measurements.

© John Wiley & Sons, Inc.

You can see that because there is a total of 2π radians in a circle, each increment of 30° is equal to $\frac{1}{6}\pi$, or length = width = height radians. Each 90° angle is $\frac{\pi}{2}$ radians. So Quadrant I is between 0 and $\frac{\pi}{2}$ radians, Quadrant II is between $\frac{\pi}{2}$ and π radians, Quadrant III is between π and $\frac{3\pi}{2}$ radians, and Quadrant IV is between $\frac{3\pi}{2}$ and 0 radians.

TIP

When you're working in radians, keep in mind that $\pi = 180°$. You can use that information to convert from radians to degrees if you're ever confused.

Graphing trig functions on a coordinate plane

The ACT may require you to recognize the graph of a trigonometric function on a coordinate plane. The graph of a trig function on a coordinate plane looks a bit like the unit circle, but it's easier to see the repeating nature of trig functions on the coordinate plane. Typically, on the coordinate plane, the x-axis becomes a numerical measure of the angle, which is usually measured in radians.

Figure 9-45 shows the graph of $y = \cos x$ on the coordinate plane. The pattern goes on forever in both directions. Because sine and cosine vary indirectly and proportionately with each other, the graph of $y = \sin x$ looks very similar, except that for $y = \sin x$, the curve begins at $y = 0$ instead of $y = 1$ for $y = \cos x$.

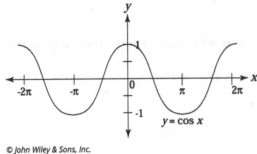

FIGURE 9-45: Graph of $y = \cos x$.

© John Wiley & Sons, Inc.

To answer ACT questions about the graphs of periodic functions, make sure you're familiar with these two terms:

> » **Amplitude:** The simple definition is the point where the function is farthest from the origin on the y-axis. In Figure 9-45, the amplitude is 1. You know this because the function is $y = (1)\cos x$. If the function were $y = 2\sin x$, the amplitude would be 2. The value of the amplitude precedes sin and cos in sine and cosine functions.
>
> » **Period:** This is the horizontal length of the function's complete cycle (also known as *interval*) from one maximum or minimum amplitude to another. In Figure 9-45, the function moves horizontally from $-\pi$ to π in one cycle, so the period is 2π. Generally, sine and cosine functions have periods of 2π, which equals 360°.

The graph of tangent functions look, different, as you can see in Figure 9-46.

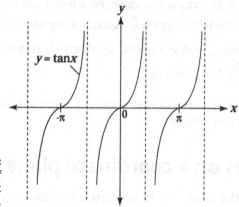

FIGURE 9-46: Graph of tangent functions.

© John Wiley & Sons, Inc.

Tangent functions are also periodic functions, but their shapes are different from sine or cosine graphs. The tangent function has a period of only π radians, because it repeats itself twice as often as the sine and cosine. Also, you'll notice that it goes on forever upward and downward, but each cycle of the tangent has a limit on the x-axis. In Figure 9-46, the dotted vertical lines are *asymptotes* — that is, they are values of x where the function does not exist. The asymptote lines represent values that the tangent function approaches but never quite touches.

TIP

The main thing to remember about these graphs is that you should be able to recognize the function when you see it on the ACT.

Here's an example of one of the more advanced trig questions that may appear on the ACT.

EXAMPLE

In right triangle ABC, $\sin x° = \frac{4}{5}$. What is $\cos(90° - x°)$?

(F) $\frac{4}{5}$

(G) $\frac{3}{5}$

(H) $\frac{3}{4}$

(J) $\frac{5}{4}$

120 PART 3 **Don't Count Yourself Out: The Math Test**

The sine of one of the non-right angles in a right triangle is the same as the cosine of the other non-right angle in the triangle. If one of those angles is $x°$, the other angle would be $x°-90°$ because the sum of those two angles is $90°$. So, $\cos(90°-x°)$ is the same as $\sin x°$. Choice (F) is the correct answer.

Applying the Law of Sines and Law of Cosines

You can also use trig functions to help you figure out measurements of sides and angles on irregular, or *oblique*, triangles. Questions on the ACT expect you to memorize the formulas for these two laws and know when and how to apply them:

» The *Law of Sines* shows that the sides of any triangle are proportional to the sines of their opposite angles. The sides are indicated by lowercase letters, and the angles by uppercase letters, as shown in Figure 9-47.

$$\frac{\sin A}{a} = \frac{\sin B}{b} = \frac{\sin C}{c}$$

» The *Law of Cosines* indicates that the square of the length of any one side of a triangle equals the sum of the squares of the lengths of the other two sides less twice the product of these two sides and the cosine of their included angle.

$$c^2 = a^2 + b^2 - 2ab\cos C$$

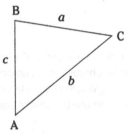

FIGURE 9-47:
Triangle demonstrating the Law of Sines and the Law of Cosines.

© John Wiley & Sons, Inc.

After you're familiar with the formulas, you'll need to know when to use them.

The Law of Sines comes in handy when you want to find out measurements of a triangle, and you already know the following:

» One side and two angles

» Two sides and an angle opposite from one of them

The Law of Cosines comes in handy when you know the following:

» Three sides of a triangle

» Two sides of a triangle and their included angle

The questions that involve these two laws are usually simple after you know how to use them.

EXAMPLE Find the equation that gives you the measure of the unknown side in $\triangle ABC$ where the shortest side of the triangle measures 8 units, the longest side measures 13 units, and the angle opposite the unknown side measures 65°.

(A) $\dfrac{\sin A}{13} = \dfrac{\sin C}{c}$

(B) $\dfrac{\sin A}{8} = \dfrac{\sin B}{13}$

(C) $c = \sqrt{8^2 + 13^2 - 2(8)(13)\cos 65°}$

(D) $c = \sqrt{8^2 - 13^2 + 2(8)(13)\cos 65°}$

Here's how to solve:

TIP

1. **Draw a picture and label the parts you know, something like this:**

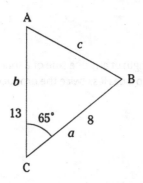

2. **Browse your answer choices.**

   Choices A and B apply the Law of Sines, and Choices C and D look like the Law of Cosines. The question doesn't indicate that the triangle contains a 90° angle, so Choice C must be wrong. That formula works for right triangles only. Because the question gives you two side lengths and the measure of the angle that includes those two sides, you can use the Law of Cosines.

3. **Eliminate Choices A and B.**

   The Law of Sines would work only if the problem also gave you information about one of the angles across from the longest and shortest sides. When you examine the remaining two rearrangements of the Law of Cosines, notice that Choice D contains the wrong operators. The proper form for the Law of Cosines is to add and then subtract ($a^2 + b^2 - 2ab\cos C$), not subtract and then add. Choice C is the answer.

122   PART 3 Don't Count Yourself Out: The Math Test

IN THIS CHAPTER

» Setting inequalities straight

» Getting familiar with symbols, roots, and radicals

» Filling your time with logarithms and functions

» Understanding the point of the coordinate plane

Chapter 10
Algebra and Other Sleeping Aids

The ACT tests your knowledge of core high school subjects, and most high schools require students to study algebra. We cover elementary algebra in Chapter 8, so this chapter reviews more advanced algebra concepts, including dealing with inequalities, radicals, functions, and even logarithms. We also outline what you need to know to work with questions that cover the coordinate plane.

Suffering Inequalities

Mathematical expressions don't always involve equal sides. You may, in fact, see a few *symbols of inequality*, or signs that mean values aren't equal to each other or that one value is greater or less than another.

Mathematics applies standard symbols to show how the two sides of an equation are related. You're probably pretty familiar with these symbols, but a little review never hurts. Table 10-1 gives you a rundown of the more commonly used algebra symbols that signify inequality. Expect to see them crop up here and there on the ACT.

When you use the greater than or less than symbols, always position the wide side of the arrow toward the bigger value, like so: 5 > 2 or 2 < 5.

TIP

Think of the greater than or less than symbols as sharks and the numbers as fish. The shark's open mouth always heads for the bigger fish, which just so happens to be the bigger value.

TABLE 10-1 Mathematical Symbols for Inequality

Symbol	Meaning
≠	Not equal to
>	Greater than
<	Less than
≥	Greater than or equal to
≤	Less than or equal to

You can solve for x in simple inequalities the same way you do in equations. Just add or subtract the same number to or from both sides of the inequality and multiply or divide both sides by the same number. Here's an example:

$$x + 6 \leq 0$$
$$x \leq -6$$

REMEMBER

When you multiply or divide both sides of an inequality by a negative number, you have to reverse the direction of the inequality symbol. For example, when you simplify $-2x < 6$ by dividing both sides by -2 to isolate x, you must switch the symbol so that the final answer is $x > -3$:

$$-2x < 6$$
$$x > -3$$

You can also use inequalities to show a range of numbers instead of just one single value. For example, the ACT may show the range of numbers between -3 and $+2$ as an inequality, like so: $-3 < x < 2$. This expression, called a *compound inequality*, means that x could be -2, -1, 0, and 1 or any number that falls between -3 and 2.

To show the range of -3 to $+2$, including -3 and $+2$, use the ≤ sign: $-3 \leq x \leq 2$. Now numbers represented by x include -3 and 2 in the possibilities.

The following example problems show you how inequalities may appear on the ACT.

EXAMPLE

If $3 > x > -1$ and x is an odd integer, what does x equal?

(A) 2
(B) 0
(C) 1
(D) −1

Use the process of elimination to narrow down your choices. The problem says that x is odd, so you know that Choices (A) and (B) are wrong; 2 and 0 aren't odd. Because x is greater than −1, it can't equal −1. Consequently, Choice (D) is also out. The answer must be Choice (C) because you know that x is between 3 and −1. Therefore, the possible integers for x are 2, 1, and 0. The only odd integer in that list is 1.

124 PART 3 Don't Count Yourself Out: The Math Test

EXAMPLE

Which of the following inequalities describes the solution set for $-4x - 7 > 2x + 3$?

(F) $x < -4$

(G) $x > -\dfrac{4}{3}$

(H) $x < -\dfrac{5}{3}$

(J) $x > -5$

Start solving this inequality as you would an equation. Add 7 to and subtract 2x from both sides:

$$-4x - 7 > 2x + 3$$
$$-6x > 10$$

Then divide both sides by –6. Remember to switch the direction of the sign because you're dividing by a negative number:

$$x < -\dfrac{10}{6}$$

Because $-\dfrac{10}{6}$ simplifies to $-\dfrac{5}{3}$, the answer is Choice (H).

Using Your Imagination: Complex Numbers

Imaginary numbers (expressed by the variable *i*) are downright difficult to imagine. In fact, they don't appear on a traditional number line. The fundamental concept to remember is that *i* represents the value that, when squared, results in –1 ($i^2 = -1$). Besides that mind-blowing equation, here are the other rules regarding imaginary numbers that you need to know for the ACT:

» $i = \sqrt{-1}$: If $i^2 = -1$, it stands to reason that $i = \sqrt{-1}$.

» **There are only four possible results for taking *i* to a power:** $\sqrt{-1}$, -1, $-\sqrt{-1}$, and 1. $i^1 = \sqrt{-1}$, $i^2 = -1$, $i^3 = -\sqrt{-1}$, $i^4 = 1$. Then it repeats: $i^5 = \sqrt{-1}$, $i^6 = -1$, and so on.

» **To add imaginary numbers, just add them as you would any other variable:**
$(3i - 4) + (5i - 6) = 8i - 10$

» **When you multiply imaginary numbers, replace i^2 with –1:**

$$(3i - 4)(5i - 6) =$$
$$15i^2 - 18i - 20i + 24 =$$
$$15i^2 - 38i + 24 =$$
$$15(-1) - 38i + 24 =$$
$$-15 - 38i + 24 =$$
$$-38i + 9$$

CHAPTER 10 Algebra and Other Sleeping Aids 125

> **Eliminate an imaginary number in the denominator:**
> - **For one complex term, multiply both the numerator and denominator by that term:**
>
> $$\frac{(3i-4)}{5i} =$$
> $$\frac{(3i-4)}{5i} \times \frac{5i}{5i} =$$
> $$\frac{15i^2 - 20i}{25i^2} =$$
> $$\frac{-15 - 20i}{-25} =$$
> $$\frac{(-3-4i)}{-5}$$
>
> - **For complex binomial terms, multiply both the numerator and denominator by the conjugate:**
>
> $$\frac{(3i-4)}{(5i-6)} =$$
> $$\frac{(3i-4)}{(5i-6)} \times \frac{(5i+6)}{(5i+6)} =$$
> $$\frac{-2i - 39}{25i^2 + 30i - 30i - 36} =$$
> $$\frac{-2i - 39}{25(-1) - 36} =$$
> $$\frac{-2i - 39}{-61} =$$

Too Hip to Be Square: Roots and Radicals

ACT math questions require you to know how to work with roots and radicals. For the purposes of the ACT, the two terms mean the same thing. The *square root* of a value is the number you multiply by itself to get that value. In other words, the square root of 9 (or $\sqrt{9}$) is 3 because you multiply 3 by itself to get 9. A cube root of a value is the number you multiply by itself 3 times to get that value. So the cube root of 27 (or $\sqrt[3]{27}$) is 3 because $3 \times 3 \times 3 = 3^3 = 27$. To simplify working with square roots or cube roots (or any other roots), think of them as variables. You work with them the same way you work with x, y, or z.

Adding and subtracting radicals

Adding and subtracting radicals is easy to do as long as you remember a couple of guidelines:

> **To add or subtract like radicals, add or subtract the number in front of the radical.**
>
> $$2\sqrt{7} + 5\sqrt{7} = 7\sqrt{7}$$
> $$9\sqrt{13} - 4\sqrt{13} = 5\sqrt{13}$$

> **You *can't* add or subtract unlike radicals (just as you cannot add or subtract unlike variables).**
>
> $$6\sqrt{5} + 4\sqrt{3} = 6\sqrt{5} + 4\sqrt{3}$$
>
> You can't add the terms and get $10\sqrt{8}$.

Don't glance at a problem, see that the radicals aren't the same, and immediately assume that you can't add the two terms. You may be able to simplify one radical to make it match the radical in the other term. For example,

$$\sqrt{52} + \sqrt{13} = ?$$

Begin by simplifying. Take out a perfect square from the term:

$$\sqrt{52} = \sqrt{4} \times \sqrt{13}$$

Because $\sqrt{4} = 2$, $\sqrt{52} = 2\sqrt{13}$.

So you can add the two original terms:

$$\sqrt{52} + \sqrt{13} = 2\sqrt{13} + \sqrt{13} = 3\sqrt{13}$$

Here's another example:

$$\sqrt{20} + \sqrt{45} = x$$
$$\left(\sqrt{4} \times \sqrt{5}\right) + \left(\sqrt{9} \times \sqrt{5}\right) = x$$
$$2\sqrt{5} + 3\sqrt{5} = x$$
$$5\sqrt{5} = x$$

Multiplying and dividing radicals

When you multiply or divide radicals, the motto is "Just do it." All you do is multiply or divide the numbers and then pop the radical sign back onto the finished product. For example,

$$\sqrt{5} \times \sqrt{6} = \sqrt{30}$$
$$\sqrt{15} \div \sqrt{5} = \sqrt{3}$$

If you have numbers in front of the radical, multiply them as well. Let everyone in on the fun. For example,

$$6\sqrt{3} \times 4\sqrt{2} = (6 \times 4)\left(\sqrt{3} \times \sqrt{2}\right) = 24\sqrt{6}$$

When you express the division of a radical as a fraction, you have to be careful. A fraction with a radical in the denominator is an irrational number (for more on irrational numbers, review Chapter 8). The ACT won't credit any answer choice with a radical in the denominator. Whenever your calculations result in a fraction with a square root in the denominator, you have to rationalize your answer. (That doesn't mean you justify to the teacher how on earth you came up with that answer; it means you get rid of the root in the denominator.) Don't worry. Rationalizing is easy. Just multiply both the top and the bottom by the square root in the denominator, like so:

$$\frac{1}{\sqrt{2}} \times \frac{\sqrt{2}}{\sqrt{2}} = \frac{\sqrt{2}}{2}$$

Find the value of $37\sqrt{5} \times 3\sqrt{6}$.

(A) $40\sqrt{11}$
(B) $40\sqrt{30}$
(C) $111\sqrt{11}$
(D) $111\sqrt{30}$

CHAPTER 10 Algebra and Other Sleeping Aids   127

This problem calls for straightforward multiplication: $37 \times 3 = 111$ and $\sqrt{5} \times \sqrt{6} = \sqrt{30}$. The correct answer is Choice (D).

Thinking Exponentially: Logarithms

The ACT may include one or two questions that present you with a *logarithm*, which is essentially the number of times you multiply the base times itself to get the big number. The definition of a logarithm can be boiled down to taking this equation, $x = a^y$, and rearranging it to become $y = \log_a x$. It's just another way of saying y is the log to the base a of x.

So $\log_4 256$ is the number of times you multiply 4 (the base) by itself to get 256 (the big number, to use the technical term). In this case, $\log_4 256 = 4$.

If the ACT asks you to find the value for x in $\log_x 16 = 4$, you know what to do. Find which base to a power of 4 equals 16. The answer is 2 because 2^4 is 16.

Log rules

The ACT may include a question that asks you to apply logarithm rules, so make sure you memorize the information in Table 10-2.

TABLE 10-2 Logarithm Rules

Logarithm Rule Name	Rule
Logarithm product rule	$\log_b(xy) = \log_b(x) + \log_b(y)$
Logarithm quotient rule	$\log_b\left(\dfrac{x}{y}\right) = \log_b(x) - \log_b(y)$
Logarithm power rule	$\log_b(x^y) = y \times \log_b(x)$
Logarithm base switch rule	$\log_b(c) = \dfrac{1}{\log_c(b)}$
Logarithm of 1 = 0	$\log_b(1) = 0$
Logarithm of the base = 1	$\log_b(b) = 1$

Natural logarithms

A certain irrational number is very useful in calculating compounded interest on savings, the natural decay of radioactive material, and other scientific measures such as atmospheric pressure at various altitudes. This versatile value is represented by e and is called a *natural logarithm*. The natural logarithm of a positive number x (written as $\ln x$ and pronounced "ell enn" x) is a logarithm to the base e of x, where $e = 2.71828\ldots$.

Natural logarithms can be expressed in several different ways:

- $\ln a = x$
- $\log_e a = x$
- $e^x = a$

Natural log problems on the ACT are usually straightforward. What's more, you can use the *ln* function on your graphing calculator to solve them. You use the *log* key for base 10 common logs.

TIP

If logarithms make your head spin, don't worry. You won't get too dizzy on the ACT because you're not likely to see more than one of them on the Mathematics Test.

Here's an example.

EXAMPLE

If $\ln x = 3$, then $x = ?$

(F) e^3

(G) e

(H) 0

(J) $3e$

This question simply asks you to express the natural log in a different format. Another way of writing $\ln a = x$ is as $e^x = a$. This problem tells you that $\ln x = 3$, so $x = e^3$, which is Choice (F). Don't let the variables confuse you. The problem uses x to indicate a in the natural log formula, so you're really finding the value of a when $x = 3$.

Barely Functioning with Functions

If you've never studied functions, don't worry. You're essentially just applying substitution. For example, you may see a problem like this one:

$$f(x) = (2x)^2$$

Solve for $f(2)$.

The function shows the relationship between x and y. $f(x) = y$, and x is the x-coordinate you plug into the function to solve for y. So, the $f(2)$ supplies the x-value (2) you input into the function. The output is the y-value that results when you input the 2 into the function and solve. In other words, just plug in the 2 where you see an x in the equation to find the corresponding value for y, or $f(x)$:

$$f(2) = (2 \times 2)^2 = 4^2 = 16$$

You may also need to find functions of variables. Treat them exactly the same way that you do actual values. So if you're given $f(x) = (2x)^2$ and asked to find $f(x + y)$, you solve by following the same steps:

1. **Substitute all the stuff in the parentheses ($x + y$) for x in the original function:**

    $$f(x + y) = [2(x + y)]^2$$

2. **Distribute the 2:**

$$f(x+y) = (2x+2y)^2$$

3. **Square the binomial expression:**

$$f(x+y) = (2x+2y)(2x+2y)$$
$$f(x+y) = 4x^2 + 4xy + 4xy + 4y^2$$
$$f(x+y) = 4x^2 + 8xy + 4y^2$$

Regardless of what's inside the parentheses of the function, you substitute that for x in the original function.

The ACT may provide seemingly more complex functions, but if you follow the rules, solving these problems is simple. Here's an example.

EXAMPLE

Find $f[(g(x))+3]$ when $f(x) = 4x-7$ and $g(x) = 3x^2$.

(A) $16x^2 + 5$

(B) $16x^2 + 3$

(C) $12x^2 + 19$

(D) $12x^2 + 5$

Work from the inside out, substituting the values within the parentheses for x in the functions. The given function is $f(x) = 4x-7$. The question asks you to replace x in the function with the provided input of $f[(g(x))+3]$.

First replace $(g(x))$ in the input with $3x^2$ because the problem tells you that $g(x) = 3x^2$. You're finding the value of $4x-7$ for $f[(3x^2)+3]$.

Then substitute $[3x^2+3]$ for x in the given function:

$$f(3x^2+3) = 4(3x^2+3)-7$$
$$f(3x^2+3) = 12x^2+12-7$$
$$f(3x^2+3) = 12x^2+5$$

The correct answer is Choice (D). The other answers incorrectly apply exponents or add improperly.

Taking a Flight on the Coordinate Plane

Quite a few questions on the ACT cover coordinate geometry, which involves working with points on a graph that's officially known as the *Cartesian coordinate plane*. This perfectly flat surface has a system that allows you to identify the position of points by using a pair of numbers. The following sections take a closer look at the coordinate plane.

Defining the coordinate plane

Here are some terms you need to know to answer the ACT's coordinate geometry questions. Figure 10-1 shows you these terms on a coordinate plane.

- » **x-axis:** The x-axis is the horizontal axis on a coordinate plane, where values or numbers start at the intersect point that has a value of 0. Numbers increase in value to the right of this point and decrease in value to the left of it. All points along the x-axis have a y-value of 0.

- » **y-axis:** The y-axis is the vertical axis on a coordinate plane, where values or numbers start at the intersect point that has a value of 0. Numbers increase in value going up from this point and decrease in value going down from it. All points along the y-axis have an x-value of 0.

- » **Origin:** The origin is the point (0, 0) on the coordinate plane; it's where the x- and y-axes intersect.

- » **Quadrant:** The intersection of the x- and y-axes forms four quadrants on the coordinate plane, which just so happen to be named Quadrants I, II, III, and IV, as shown in Figure 10-1.

- » **Ordered pair:** An ordered pair is made up of two coordinates, which describe the location of a point in relation to the origin. The horizontal (x) coordinate is always listed first, and the vertical (y) coordinate is always listed second. Point A in Figure 10-1 designates (2, 3).

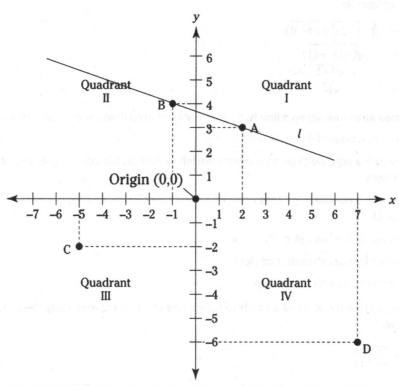

FIGURE 10-1: The coordinate plane.

© John Wiley & Sons, Inc.

Knowing which formulas you need to guide your flight

When working with elements on the coordinate plane, keep these rules in mind:

- » A line connecting points with the same x- and y-coordinates — (1, 1), (2, 2), and (3, 3), for example — forms a 45-degree angle (see Figure 10-2).

- » To locate the middle point of a line, use the *midpoint formula*:

$$M = \left(\frac{x_1 + x_2}{2}, \frac{y_1 + y_2}{2}\right)$$

CHAPTER 10 **Algebra and Other Sleeping Aids** 131

For example, to figure out the midpoint of a line that ends at points A (2, 3) and B (–1, 4) in Figure 10-1, use the formula:

$$M = \left(\frac{2+(-1)}{2}, \frac{3+4}{2}\right)$$
$$M = \left(\frac{1}{2}, \frac{7}{2}\right)$$
$$M = \left(\frac{1}{2}, 3\frac{1}{2}\right)$$

To help you remember the midpoint formula, think of it as the average of the two x-coordinates and the average of the two y-coordinates.

» **To find the distance between two points, use the *distance formula*:**

$$\sqrt{(x_2 - x_1)^2 + (y_2 - y_1)^2}$$

For example, you can figure the distance between points A (2, 3) and B (–1, 4) in Figure 10-1 by using this formula:

$$D = \sqrt{(-1-2)^2 + (4-3)^2}$$
$$D = \sqrt{(-3)^2 + (1)^2}$$
$$D = \sqrt{9+1}$$
$$D = \sqrt{10}$$

» ***Slope* measures how steep a line is.** It's commonly referred to as *rise over run*. Think of slope as a fraction. A slope of 4 is really a slope of $\frac{4}{1}$.

  • A line with a negative slope goes down from left to right (its left side is higher than its right side).
  • A line with a positive slope goes down from right to left (its right side is higher than its left side).
  • A horizontal line has a slope of 0.
  • A vertical line has an undefined slope.
  • Parallel lines have the same slope.

» **One way to find the slope of a line is to locate two of its points and apply the formula for slope:**

$$Slope = \frac{y_2 - y_1}{x_2 - x_1}$$

You can calculate the slope of line *l* in Figure 10-1 using Points A and B, like so:

$$\frac{4-3}{-1-2} = \frac{1}{-3} = -\frac{1}{3}$$

» **The *equation of a line* (or slope-intercept form) is** $y = mx + b$. The *m* is the slope of the line, and the *b* is where the line crosses the *y*-axis (called the *y*-intercept). So a line with an equation of $y = 4x + 1$ has a slope of $\frac{4}{1}$ and a *y*-intercept of 1.

You can draw a line on the plane if you know its equation. Find the *y*-intercept on the *y*-axis. Then use the slope to create the line. Go up by the slope's numerator and across by the slope's denominator.

132   PART 3 Don't Count Yourself Out: The Math Test

TIP

Whenever you get an equation for a line that doesn't fit neatly into the slope-intercept form, go ahead and play with the equation a little bit (sounds fun, doesn't it?) to get it into the $y = mx + b$ format. That way, you can either solve the problem or get a visual idea of the graph of the line. For instance, if you see the equation $\frac{1}{3}y - 3 = x$, all you have to do is manipulate both sides of the equation until it looks like the slope-intercept form that you know and love:

$$\frac{1}{3}y = x + 3$$
$$y = 3x + 9$$

» *Voilà!* You now know the slope of the line (3) as well as the y-intercept (9) by using some basic algebra. Pretty tricky!

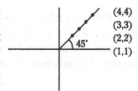

FIGURE 10-2: A line connecting points with the same x- and y-coordinates.

© John Wiley & Sons, Inc.

EXAMPLE

Here's a sample question that tests your knowledge of the equation of a line.

What is the equation of a line with a slope $-\frac{2}{3}$ and a y-intercept of 7?

(F) $3x + 2y = 21$

(G) $-2x + 3y = 14$

(H) $2x - 3y = 21$

(J) $2x + 3y = 14$

When you look at the answer choices, you see that they all have the same format: $ax + by = c$.

You need to convert the equation to that format as well. Because the equation of a line is $y = mx + b$, you know that m is the slope and b is the y-intercept. So what are you waiting for? Plug in the values:

$$y = \left(-\frac{2}{3}\right)x + 7$$
$$3y = -2 + 21$$
$$2x + 3y = 21$$

The correct answer is (K).

Graphing more functions

Occasionally, the ACT may ask you more complex questions about the coordinate plane. While not every ACT includes the following concepts, there are definite possibilities for test questions, so make sure you're familiar with them.

» **Graphing a linear inequality is almost exactly the same as graphing the equation for a line, except a linear inequality covers a lot more ground on the coordinate plane.** While the graph of an equation for a line simply shows the actual line on the coordinate plane, the

CHAPTER 10 **Algebra and Other Sleeping Aids** 133

graph of a linear inequality shows everything either above or below the line on the plane. The graph appears as a shaded area to one side of the line. Figure 10-3 shows the graphs of several inequalities.

» **When you graph a quadratic equation, it appears as a** *parabola*, **a curve shape that opens either upward or downward.** A parabola is a figure on a plane where every point on the figure is the same distance from a fixed point called the *focus* and a fixed line called a *directrix*. Following are some important properties of parabolas.

- **The axis of symmetry:** This is the vertical line that bisects the parabola so that each side is a mirror image of the other.

- **The vertex:** This is the rounded end of the parabola, which is the lowest point on a curve that opens upward and the highest point on a curve that opens downward. It's where the parabola crosses the axis of symmetry.

» **The** *standard form* **equation of a parabola is** $y = a(x-h)^2 + k$ **(where** $a \neq 0$**).** The coordinate point (h, k) is the vertex. The vertical line $x = h$ is the axis of symmetry. If a is a positive number, the parabola opens upward. If a is negative, the parabola opens downward. When a is less than 1 but greater than –1, the curve widens; when a is greater than 1 or less than –1, the curve narrows.

» **The** *general form* **equation is** $y = ax^2 + bx + c$ **(where** $a \neq 0$**).** When $y = 0$, the solutions for x tell you where the parabola crosses the x-axis. The coordinate point (0, c) represents the y-intercept of the parabola. The axis of symmetry is the line $x = -\frac{b}{2a}$, and the x-coordinate of the vertex is $-\frac{b}{2a}$. When you apply the *discriminant* ($-b^2 - 4ac$) to the general form, you find out the following:

- If the value of the discriminant is 0, the parabola touches the x-axis at only one point, which means that the vertex is on the x-axis.

- If the value of the discriminant is positive, the parabola intersects the x-axis at two points.

- If the value of the discriminant is negative, the parabola doesn't intersect the x-axis at any point.

Figure 10-4 shows the graph of several parabolas and their formulas. In the graph of $y = x^2$, the values for h and k are 0, so the vertex is at the origin. The parabola opens upward because a is 1, a positive number. A change in the constant h moves the parabola sideways along the x-axis. No h in the equation (that is, if h = 0) indicates that the vertex lies on the y-axis. The constant k determines whether the vertex of the parabola moves up or down in relation to the y-axis. No k in the equation (that is, if k = 0) means the vertex of the parabola is on the x-axis.

» **The equation of a circle is** $(x-h)^2 + (y-k)^2 = r^2$, **where the center of the circle is point (h, k) and r is the circle's radius.** If the origin is the center of the circle, the equation will be $x^2 + y^2 = r^2$.

» **An** *ellipse* **contains all points on a plane that are located the same distance from the sum of two points called** *foci*. The long distance across the ellipse is called the *major axis*. The short distance across the ellipse is called the *minor axis*. The *center* of the ellipse is the midpoint of the two foci, and the *vertices* are the two points farthest from the center, the points on the ellipse that intersect with the major axis. Figure 10-5 shows an ellipse and its components. The formula for the area of an ellipse is πab, and the standard equation of an ellipse is

$$\frac{(x-h)^2}{a^2} + \frac{(y-k)^2}{b^2} = 1$$

The value of a in the formula is equal to half the length of the horizontal axis, and the value of b is half the length of the vertical axis. Points h and k refer to the coordinates at the center of the ellipse.

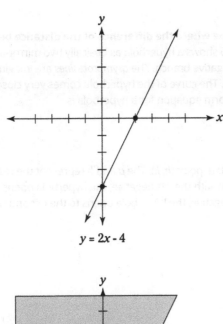
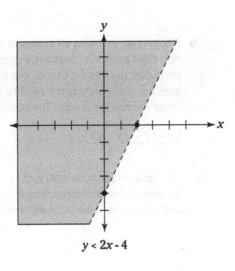
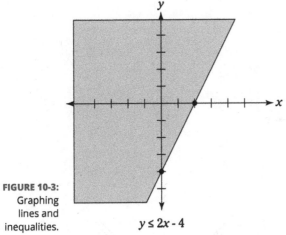
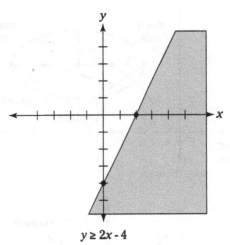

FIGURE 10-3: Graphing lines and inequalities.
© John Wiley & Sons, Inc.

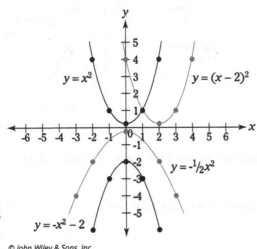

FIGURE 10-4: Graphs of parabolas.
© John Wiley & Sons, Inc.

CHAPTER 10 **Algebra and Other Sleeping Aids** 135

» **A *hyperbola* contains all points in a plane where the difference of the distance between two fixed points is constant.** Figure 10-6 shows a hyperbola as basically two mirror-image parabolas: the positive branch and the negative branch. The *asymptote lines* are imaginary lines that run alongside the two branches. The curve of the hyperbola comes very close to but never touches these lines. The standard form equation for a hyperbola is

$$\frac{(x-h)^2}{a^2} - \frac{(y-k)^2}{b^2} = 1$$

The center of the hyperbola is the coordinate point (*h*, *k*). The *a* and *b* represent the respective distances from the fixed points. If the term with the *x* is negative, the hyperbola opens upward and downward. If the term with the *y* is negative, the hyperbola opens to the left and right.

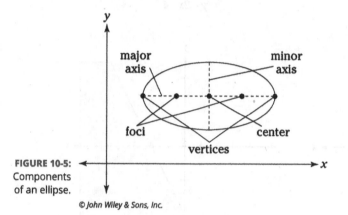

FIGURE 10-5: Components of an ellipse.

© John Wiley & Sons, Inc.

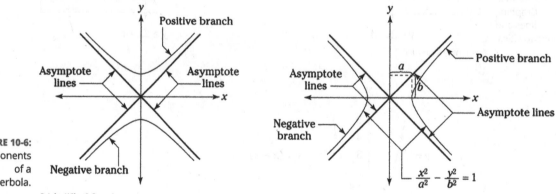

FIGURE 10-6: Components of a hyperbola.

© John Wiley & Sons, Inc.

You can try a couple of practice questions to see how some of these concepts may appear on the ACT.

EXAMPLE

What is the vertex of the graph of the equation $y = -2(x-3)^2 + 4$?

(A) (−3, −4)

(B) (3, 4)

(C) (3, −4)

(D) (−3, 4)

Remember the equation of a parabola: $y = a(x-h)^2 + k$. The vertex of the parabola is (*h*, *k*). The *h* value in the equation is 3, and the *k* value is 4. So the vertex of the graph of the equation in the question is (3, 4). The correct answer is Choice (B).

Choice (D) is a trap answer. Note that the value of h is 3 and not -3. The only way that the value of h could be -3 is if the original equation were $y = -2[x-(-3)]^2 + 4$. Then you'd have to switch the sign to put the equation into the correct form for the equation of a parabola.

EXAMPLE

What is the equation of a circle with the coordinate point (5, −1) as its center and a radius of 6?

(F) $(x-5)^2 + (y+1)^2 = 6$
(G) $(x-5)^2 + (y-1)^2 = 36$
(H) $(x-5)^2 + (y+1)^2 = 36$
(J) $(x+5)^2 + (y-1)^2 = 12$

The answer choices look so similar that you definitely need to know the details of the formula for a circle if you have any hope of getting this one right: $(x-h)^2 + (y-k)^2 = r^2$.

Because you know the radius is 6, you also know the radius squared is 36, which means you can easily eliminate Choices (F) and (J). Choice (K) is obviously incorrect because you know that you have to add the two terms together in the formula for the circle; Choice (K) subtracts the two terms. That leaves you with Choices (G) and (H). Choice (G) would be okay if the center had the coordinate point of (5, 1), but in your question, the y-coordinate of the center is negative. So you switch the sign around when you plug it into the equation. The correct answer is (H).

Evaluating graphs of functions

Every function has a distinct y-value for every x-value. So any graph on the coordinate plane that meets these criteria (think straight lines, circles, parabolas and hyperbolas, and ellipses) is the graph of a function. The ACT may ask you to evaluate more functions on the coordinate plane. Here are a few preliminary considerations for accomplishing this:

> » The function's input is the x-coordinate of a point on the plane.
>
> » The output — the value that results when you input the value and solve — is the y-coordinate of that point on the plane.
>
> » Using the x- and y-coordinates indicated by the function, you can plot the function's points on the coordinate plane.

Say a test question tells you to find $f(3)$ on the coordinate plane when $f(x) = 2x^2 + 7$. The input (or x-coordinate) is 3. Plug 3 into the function to find the output (or y-coordinate):

$f(3) = 2(3)^2 + 7$
$f(3) = (2 \times 9) + 7$
$f(3) = 18 + 7$
$f(3) = 25$

In graphing terms, you know the x-coordinate is 3 (because the question tells you so), and the y-coordinate is 25. If you were to graph this point on a coordinate plane, the ordered pair would be (3, 25). It's that simple.

Here are some more concepts to remember when you encounter function questions:

> » The *domain* of a function is the set of all possible numbers for the input (x) of the function, usually all real numbers. An imaginary x-value or one that would create a zero denominator wouldn't be included in the domain for that function.

CHAPTER 10 **Algebra and Other Sleeping Aids** 137

- » The *range* of a function is the set of possible numbers for an output (y) of the function.

- » The *root* of a function is the solution you get when the equation equals 0, a point where the graph of the equation or function intersects with the x-axis. In other words, the roots are the x-values when y = 0.

- » The *degree* of a function is the highest power (exponent) of any variable or term that occurs in the function. The degree of the function indicates the highest possible number of roots for that function. These roots may be distinct or the same. To have distinct roots, the polynomial function needs to have separate and distinct solutions to the function. The polynomial function $g(x) = x^3 - 4x^2 - 3x + 18$ has three roots (its highest power) but only two distinct roots or solutions (x = 3 and x = -2) because its factors are $(x-3)^2(x+2)$.

The degree can also indicate the shape of the function:

- A first-degree function has no exponents and is a straight line.

- A second-degree function has a highest power of 2, as in a quadratic formula, which forms a parabola. Second-degree functions have a low point or high point, also known as the *extremum*. In a parabola, the extremum is the vertex.

- A third-degree function has a highest power of 3, and no more than two extrema, a fourth-degree function has a highest power of 4 and no more than three extrema, and so on. The extrema for these functions are called *local minimums* and *local maximums*. You can get information about the degree of a function from its graph. Figure 10-7 illustrates what could be at least a fourth-degree function because it has three extreme values: two local minimums and a local maximum. It also has four distinct zeroes (four points where the function crosses the x-axis, indicating that it likely has four distinct solutions.)

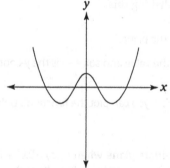

FIGURE 10-7: Fourth-degree function.

© John Wiley & Sons, Inc.

Occasionally, the test makers may ask you to find a *piecewise function*, which is a function that's broken into pieces, or different rules. It's not much different from a "normal" function. You determine the function depending on how you define the possible values of the domain. Here's an example:

$$f(x) = \begin{cases} 2x - 1, & x \leq 1 \\ x + 4, & x > 1 \end{cases}$$

Notice that the function is split into pieces. The value of x determines the value of y just as it does in normal functions, but the y-value of a piecewise function follows a different pattern depending on which of the two rules x falls under.

So, if $x = 0$ in the preceding function, it's less than 1, which means the first rule applies. Plug in 0 for x: $2(0) - 1 = -1$. The point on the coordinate plane would be $(0, -1)$. If $x = 1$, $y = 2(1) - 1$, or 1, and the point would be $(1, 1)$. You can graph these points on the coordinate plane and draw the line between them. Just remember that the line is limited to x-values that are equal to or less than 1.

If $x = 2$, then the second rule governs, and the corresponding y-coordinate is $2 + 4$, or 6. When $x = 3$, y is $3 + 4$, or 7. The points are $(2, 6)$ and $(3, 7)$. You can draw this line on the plane, too. A picture of these two functions on the coordinate plane would look something like this:

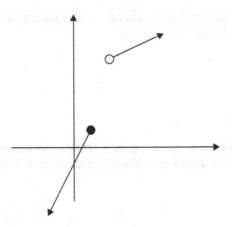

Picking Your Way through Percent Increase, Probability, Permutations, and Combinations

In addition to traditional algebra and arithmetic, the ACT may also test your knowledge of how to deal with percent increase/decrease, probability, and more advanced statistics. Plan to see several of these question types on your Mathematics Test.

Managing the ups and downs

You may see a problem that asks you what percent increase or decrease occurred in the number of games a team won or the amount of commission a person earned.

To find a percent increase or decrease, use this formula:

$$\% \text{ increase or decrease} = \frac{\text{number increase or decrease}}{\text{original whole}}$$

In basic English, to find the percentage by which something has increased or decreased, you take two simple steps:

1. **Find the number (amount) by which the thing has increased or decreased.**

   For example, if a team won 25 games last year and 30 games this year, the number increase was 5. If a salesperson earned $10,000 last year and $8,000 this year, the number decrease was $2,000. Make that number the numerator (the top part) of the fraction.

CHAPTER 10 **Algebra and Other Sleeping Aids** 139

2. Find the original whole.

This figure is what you started out with before you increased or decreased. If a team won 25 games last year and won 30 games this year, the original number was 25. If the salesperson earned $10,000 last year and $8,000 this year, the original number was $10,000. Make the number you started out with the denominator (the bottom part) of the fraction.

You now have a complete fraction. Divide the fraction to convert to a decimal and multiply by 100 to make it a percentage.

EXAMPLE

In 2020, Coach Denges won 20 prizes at the county fair by tossing a basketball into a bushel basket. In 2011, he won 25 prizes. What was his percent increase?

(A) 100%

(B) 30%

(C) 25%

(D) 20%

The number by which his prizes increased, from 20 to 25, is 5. That's the numerator. The original whole, or what he began with, is 20. That's the denominator. So your fraction looks like this:

$$\frac{5}{20} = \frac{25}{100} = 25\%$$

The correct answer is Choice (C).

Practicing probability

Probability questions are usually word problems. They may look intimidating, with so many words that make you lose sight of where to begin, but they aren't impossible to solve. In fact, by using the two simple rules we explain in the following sections, you can solve the simple probability problems the ACT tosses at you.

TIP

No matter what kind of probability problems you face, remember that probability can only be 0, 1, or a number in between 0 and 1. You can't have a negative probability, and you can't have a probability greater than 1, or 100 percent.

Finding the probability of one event

To find a probability, use this formula to set up a fraction:

$$P = \frac{\text{Number of possible desired outcomes}}{\text{Number of total possible outcomes}}$$

The denominator is the easier of the two parts to begin with because it's the total possible number of outcomes. For example, when you're flipping a coin, you have two possible outcomes, giving you a denominator of 2. When you're tossing a die (one of a pair of dice), you have six possible outcomes, giving you a denominator of 6. When you're pulling a card out of a deck of cards, you have 52 possible outcomes (a deck of cards contains 52 cards), giving you a denominator of 52. When 25 marbles are in a jar, and you're going to pull out one of them, you have 25 possibilities, giving you a denominator of 25. Very simply, the denominator is the whole shebang — everything possible.

The numerator is the total number of the outcomes you want. If you want to see heads when you toss a coin, you have exactly one desired outcome because the coin has only one head side, giving you a numerator of 1. Your chance of tossing heads, therefore, is $\frac{1}{2}$ — one possible heads and two possible outcomes altogether. If you want to roll a 5 when you toss a die, the numerator is 1 because the die has exactly one 5 on it. The probability of tossing a 5 is $\frac{1}{6}$ — one possible 5 out of six possible outcomes altogether.

If you want to draw a jack from a deck of cards, you have four chances because the deck contains four jacks: hearts, diamonds, clubs, and spades. Therefore, the numerator is 4. The probability of drawing a jack out of a deck of cards is $\frac{4}{52}$ (which reduces to $\frac{1}{13}$). If you want to draw a jack of hearts, the probability is $\frac{1}{52}$ because the deck contains only one jack of hearts.

EXAMPLE

A jar of marbles has 8 yellow marbles, 6 black marbles, and 12 white marbles. What is the probability of drawing out a black marble?

(F) $\frac{1}{6}$

(G) $\frac{3}{13}$

(H) $\frac{4}{13}$

(J) $\frac{6}{13}$

Use the formula. Begin with the denominator, which is all the possible outcomes: $8 + 6 + 12 = 26$. The numerator is how many outcomes result in what you want: 6 black marbles. The probability is $\frac{6}{26}$, which you can reduce to $\frac{3}{13}$, which is Choice (G).

If you came up with Choice (H) or (J), you figured out the probability of choosing a yellow or white marble, respectively. You know that Choice (K) can't be right. A probability of 1 means that there's a 100 percent chance that you'll pick a black marble.

Finding the probability of multiple events

You can find the probability of multiple events by following several rules. Table 10-3 lists and describes each rule, shows the corresponding formula, and provides an example of when you'd use it.

EXAMPLE

A candy machine contains gumballs: three blue, two red, seven yellow, and one purple. The machine distributes one gumball for each dime. A child has exactly two dimes with which she will purchase two gumballs. What is the chance that the child will get two red gumballs?

(A) $\frac{2}{169}$

(B) $\frac{1}{13}$

(C) $\frac{2}{13}$

(D) $\frac{1}{78}$

CHAPTER 10 Algebra and Other Sleeping Aids   141

TABLE 10-3 Finding the Probability of the Occurrence of Multiple Events

Rule	Circumstance	Formula	Example
Special Rule of Addition	The probability of the occurrence of either of two possible events that are mutually exclusive	$P(A \text{ or } B) = P(A) + P(B)$	The probability of rolling a 5 or 6 on one roll of one die
General Rule of Addition	The probability of the occurrence of either of two possible events that can happen together	$P(A \text{ or } B) = P(A) + P(B) - P(A \text{ and } B)$	The probability of drawing a playing card that displays a club or a queen
Special Rule of Multiplication	The probability of the occurrence of two events at the same time when the two events are independent of each other	$P(A \text{ and } B) = P(A) \times P(B)$	The probability of rolling a 5 and a 6 on one roll of two dice
General Rule of Multiplication	The probability of the occurrence of two events when the occurrence of the first event affects the outcome of the second event	$P(A \text{ and } B) = P(A) \times P(B/A)$ (The line between the B and A stands for "B given A"; it doesn't mean divide.)	The probability of first drawing the queen of clubs from a pack of 52 cards, keeping the queen of clubs out of the pack, and then drawing the jack of diamonds on the next try

TIP

You need to treat getting the two red gumballs as two events. The occurrence of the first event affects the probability of the second event because after the child extracts the first red gumball, the machine has one fewer gumballs. So you apply the general rule of multiplication.

The chance of getting a red gumball with the first dime is 2 (the number of red gumballs) divided by 13 (the total number of gumballs in the machine), or $\frac{2}{13}$. If the child tries to get the second gumball, the first red gumball is already gone, which leaves only 1 red gumball and 12 total gumballs in the machine, so the chance of getting the second red gumball is $\frac{1}{12}$. The probability of both events happening is the product of the probability of the occurrence of each event:

$$P(A \text{ and } B) = P(A) \times P(B/A)$$
$$P(A \text{ and } B) = \frac{2}{13} \times \frac{1}{12}$$
$$P(A \text{ and } B) = \frac{2}{156}$$
$$P(A \text{ and } B) = \frac{1}{78}$$

Choice (D) is the correct answer. Choice (A) is $\frac{2}{13} \times \frac{1}{13}$, which would look right if you didn't subtract the withdrawn red gumball from the total number on the second draw. Choice (B) is the chance of drawing one red gumball from a machine with 13 gumballs and only one red gumball. In this problem, $\frac{1}{13}$ is also the chance of drawing the purple gumball. If you picked Choice (C), you found the chance of drawing the first red gumball.

Calculating outcomes and orderings

A few questions in each Mathematics Test will ask for the possible number of outcomes, either combinations or orderings for particular events. Some of these problems are easy; you just need to apply the *counting principle*. Others may require you to dust off the chapter on factorials from math classes past.

142 PART 3 Don't Count Yourself Out: The Math Test

Combinations

When a question asks for the total possible outcomes given two or more events and order isn't an issue, you're dealing with a *combination*. Apply the counting principle. The counting principle just means that you multiply the number of possibilities for one event by the number of possibilities for the other event. Say you go to an ice cream social that offers three flavors of ice cream, five kinds of toppings, and four different-patterned bowls to put them in. To determine the number of different combinations you could pick for one ice cream flavor, one topping, and one bowl, you just multiply $3 \times 4 \times 5$. That's 60 different combinations to choose from!

Calculations become a little more complex when you must create combinations with a smaller number of members than the original pool. For example, say you want to know how many possible five-number lock combinations you can create from the ten possible 1-digit numbers when the order of the lock combination doesn't matter and no number is repeated. Here's where factorials come into the picture.

The *factorial function* designates the product of descending whole numbers. Its symbol is the exclamation point, !. So $4! = 4 \times 3 \times 2 \times 1$. The formula for finding the number of possible combinations of fewer elements drawn from a greater pool is this:

$$\frac{n!}{r!(n-r)!}$$

The n signifies the total number of options to draw from, and the r stands for the number in the groups you're putting together.

So for the lock scenario, you set up the formula like this:

$$\frac{10!}{5!(10-5)!}$$

In the formula, n is 10 because there are ten digits to choose from (0, 1, 2, 3, 4, 5, 6, 7, 8, 9); r is 5 because you seek to create five-number combinations from the ten total digits.

To calculate the number of combinations, expand the formula:

$$\frac{10 \times 9 \times 8 \times 7 \times 6 \times 5 \times 4 \times 3 \times 2 \times 1}{5 \times 4 \times 3 \times 2 \times 1 (5!)} = C$$

The $5 \times 4 \times 3 \times 2 \times 1$ in the numerator and denominator cancel to give you this:

$$\frac{10 \times 9 \times 8 \times 7 \times 6}{(5)!} = C$$

You can then calculate the answer like this:

$$\frac{10 \times 9 \times 8 \times 7 \times 6}{(5)!} = C$$
$$\frac{10 \times 9 \times 8 \times 7 \times 6}{5 \times 4 \times 3 \times 2 \times 1} = C$$
$$\frac{30,240}{120} = C$$
$$252 = C$$

There are 252 possible five-number lock combinations from all ten digits when order doesn't matter and no digits are repeated.

Permutations

Permutation problems ask you to determine how many arrangements of numbers are possible given a specific set of numbers and a particular order for the arrangements. For example, figuring out the number of possible seven-digit telephone numbers you can create is a permutation problem. And the answer is huge (10^7) because you have ten possible values (the integers between 0 and 9) to fill each of the seven places.

REMEMBER

Order matters when you set up permutations. Even though two different phone numbers may have the same combination of numbers, such as 345-7872 and 543-7728, the numbers ring two different phones because you input them in a different order. Rely on factorials to figure out permutations.

Suppose a photographer wants to know how many different ways she can arrange five people in a single row for a wedding photo. The number of possible arrangements of the five-person wedding party is 5! or $5! = 5 \times 4 \times 3 \times 2 \times 1 = 120$.

As you can see, more possible arrangements exist as the number of objects in the arrangement increases.

Permutations get a little more challenging when you have a fixed number of objects, n, to fill a limited number of places, r, and you care about the order the objects are arranged in.

For example, consider the predicament of the big-league baseball coach of a 20-member team who needs to determine the number of different batting orders that these 20 ball players can fill in a nine-slot batting lineup. The coach could work this permutation out by writing all the factors from 20 back nine places (because 20 players can fill only nine slots in the batting order), like this:

$$20 \times 19 \times 18 \times 17 \times 16 \times 15 \times 14 \times 13 \times 12 = x$$

But this time-consuming process isn't practical in the middle of a game. Luckily, the coach can rely on the permutation formula for n objects taken r:

$$_nP_r = \frac{n!}{(n-r)!}$$

Apply the formula to figure out the possible number of batting orders:

$$_nP_r = \frac{n!}{(n-r)!}$$

$$_nP_r = \frac{20!}{(20-9)!}$$

$$_nP_r = \frac{20!}{11!}$$

That's all there is to it. Now you can apply the outcome formulas to a sample problem.

EXAMPLE

Alice received a bracelet with four distinct removable charms. How many different ways can she arrange the four charms on her new bracelet?

(F) 4
(G) 8
(H) 24
(J) 100

Because the bracelet has four charms, the number of arrangements or permutations is 4!: $4 \times 3 \times 2 \times 1$.

Then just multiply the numbers to get the number of possible arrangements (the order you multiply them in doesn't matter). Because $4 \times 3 \times 2 \times 1 = 24$, the correct answer is Choice (H).

Setting Up Sequences

A sequence is a set of ordered values. Every ACT Math Test is likely to contain at least one question that deals with sequences. Commonly tested sequences on the ACT can be one of two kinds:

> » **Arithmetic sequences are formed by adding a common value (called the common difference) to each term.** The following sequence has a common difference of 3: {0, 3, 6, 9}. This sequence has a common difference of –2: {8, 6, 4, 2, 0}. Both sequences are formed by adding the common difference to one term to get the next term.

> » **Geometric sequences are formed by multiplying each term by a common value (called the common ratio).** This geometric sequence has a common ratio of 3: {3, 9, 27, 81}. A geometric sequence with a common ratio of $\frac{1}{3}$ could look like this: {81, 27, 9, 3}.

ACT math questions may ask you to find specific terms in or the sum of a sequence of values. To answer these questions, keep in mind some important rules:

> » **To find the nth term of an arithmetic sequence, apply the following rule, where n represents the position of the term in the sequence, a_1 is the first term, and d is the common difference between the terms.**
>
> $a_n = a_1 + d(n-1)$

> » **To find the nth term of a geometric sequence, apply the following rule, where n represents the position of the term in the sequence, a_1 is the first term, and r is the common ratio.**
>
> $a_n = a_1 r^{(n-1)}$

> » **To find the sum of a sequence of numbers, apply the following rule, where n represents the number of terms in the sequence, a_1 is the first term, and d is the common difference between the terms.**
>
> $Sum = \frac{n}{2}[2a_1 + d(n-1)]$

You can solve most ACT series questions without memorizing all of these formulas. Just keep in mind that n stands for the position a value holds in the series and not the actual value itself. Here's a sample question to show you how.

The formula for a particular sequence is as follows: $S_n = S_{n-1} + n + 2$, where S_n is the value of the nth term. If $S_3 = 12$, what is the value of S_5?

EXAMPLE

(A) 7

(B) 12

(C) 18

(D) 25

CHAPTER 10 **Algebra and Other Sleeping Aids** 145

The trick to solving this question is to understand that n refers to the position number of the value in the sequence. So, S_5 refers to the fifth number in the sequence and $n = 5$. When you know the value of the third term, S_3, you can figure out the value of the fourth term, S_4, like this:

$$S_n = S_{n-1} + n + 2$$
$$S_4 = S_{4-1} + 4 + 2$$
$$S_4 = S_3 + 4 + 2$$
$$S_4 = 12 + 4 + 2$$
$$S_4 = 18$$

Notice that 18 is one of the answers, but the question doesn't ask for the fourth term. You need to apply the formula once more to figure out the value of the fifth term in the sequence:

$$S_n = S_{n-1} + n + 2$$
$$S_5 = S_4 + 5 + 2$$
$$S_5 = 18 + 5 + 2$$
$$S_5 = 25$$

The correct answer is Choice (D).

Managing Matrices

The ACT test makers will likely slip one matrix question into the Mathematics Test. If you see a question about a matrix, don't panic. They'll be easy to deal with once you review the following approach.

A matrix is simply an array of values. You can perform several operations with matrices. Adding them on the ACT is simple. Just add the number from the first matrix to the corresponding number in the same position in the second matrix, like this:

$$\begin{bmatrix} 8 & -4 \\ 10 & 2 \end{bmatrix} + \begin{bmatrix} 2 & 5 \\ 3 & -2 \end{bmatrix} = \begin{bmatrix} 10 & 1 \\ 13 & 0 \end{bmatrix}$$

The ACT may ask you to multiply matrices, though. Here are some considerations for finding a matrix product:

> » **When multiplying matrices, the number of columns in the first matrix must equal the number of rows in the second matrix as you move from left to right.** So, you can multiply a set of matrices if the first one has two columns of numbers and the second one has two rows, but you can't multiply a set where the first matrix has two columns of numbers and the second matrix has three rows, even if the second matrix also has two columns. This is usually the only information the ACT requires you to know.

> » **The resulting matrix product will always have the same number of columns as the number of rows in the first matrix and the same number of rows as there are columns in the second matrix.**

> » **When you multiply the values in a one-row matrix and a one-column matrix, you add the first number in the first matrix to the first number in the second matrix and then

add the product of the second value in the first and second matrices, to which you then add the product of the third values in each of the matrices:

$$\begin{vmatrix} 6 & 7 & 5 \end{vmatrix} \times \begin{vmatrix} 1 \\ 2 \\ 3 \end{vmatrix} = (6 \times 1) + (7 \times 2) + (5 \times 3) = 6 + 14 + 15 = 35$$

» For the rare ACT question that asks you to multiply matrices with more than one row and one column, you apply the same process but several times:

$$\begin{vmatrix} 6 & 7 & 5 \\ 3 & 2 & 1 \end{vmatrix} \times \begin{vmatrix} 1 & 4 \\ 2 & 3 \\ 3 & 2 \end{vmatrix} = \begin{vmatrix} 35 & 55 \\ 10 & 20 \end{vmatrix}$$

Here are the steps for arriving at the solution:

1. **Add the products of the first row of the first matrix and the first column of the second matrix, as we demonstrated here, to get the first value in the matrix product (35).**

2. **Add the products of the first row in the first matrix and the second column of the second matrix to find the second value in the matrix product (55):**

$$(6 \times 4) + (7 \times 3) + (5 \times 2) = 24 + 21 + 10 = 55$$

3. **Add the products of the second row of the first matrix and the first column of the second matrix to find the third value in the matrix product (10):**

$$(3 \times 1) + (2 \times 2) + (1 \times 3) = 3 + 4 + 3 = 10$$

4. **Add the products of the second row of the first matrix to the second column of the second matrix to find the fourth value in the matrix product (20):**

$$(3 \times 4) + (2 \times 3) + (1 \times 2) = 12 + 6 + 2 = 20$$

If the ACT asks you to find the determinant of a two-column, two-row matrix $\begin{vmatrix} a & b \\ c & d \end{vmatrix}$, apply the formula: $ad - bc$. The determinant of the matrix $\begin{bmatrix} 8 & 5 \\ 3 & 9 \end{bmatrix}$ is $(8)(9) - (5)(3)$, which is $72 - 15 = 57$.

Here is an example of the way the ACT commonly tests your knowledge of matrices.

EXAMPLE

For which of the following sets of matrices is the matrix product undefined?

(F) $\begin{bmatrix} a & b \\ c & d \end{bmatrix} \times \begin{bmatrix} e & f \\ g & h \end{bmatrix}$

(G) $\begin{bmatrix} a & b & c \\ d & e & f \end{bmatrix} \times \begin{bmatrix} h & r & j \\ k & l & m \\ n & o & p \end{bmatrix}$

(H) $\begin{bmatrix} a & b & c \\ d & e & f \end{bmatrix} \times \begin{bmatrix} g & h & r \\ j & k & l \end{bmatrix}$

(J) $\begin{bmatrix} a \\ b \\ c \end{bmatrix} \times \begin{bmatrix} d & e \end{bmatrix}$

CHAPTER 10 Algebra and Other Sleeping Aids   147

In plain English, an undefined matrix product means that you can't multiply the two matrices. So when you come across a set of matrices that *can* be multiplied, eliminate that answer. Don't get all befuddled by the fact that none of the answers contains actual numbers. It doesn't matter because the rule to remember is that the number of *columns* in the first matrix has to equal the number of *rows* in the second. Say the numbers to yourself as you check each answer choice.

The first matrix in Choice (F) has two columns. Say "two" to yourself. The second has two rows. Say "two" again. You could multiply these matrices, so eliminate this answer.

In Choice (G), the first matrix has three columns, and the second has three rows. This set follows the rule and can be multiplied. Eliminate this choice.

Take a look at Choice (H). At first, this set of matrices may look like a good candidate for a matrix product. After all, the two matrices have the same number of columns and rows. But that's not the rule. The first matrix has three columns, and the second has two rows. These matrices can't be multiplied, so this is the correct answer.

You can check the last choice to be sure. In Choice (J), the first matrix has one column; the second has one row. That means the correct answer is indeed Choice (H).

IN THIS CHAPTER

» Getting familiar with the format of the Math Test

» Taking a common-sense approach to the Math Test

» Speeding things up with some timing tips

» Knowing what to do — and what not to do — on the Math Test

Chapter 11
Numb and Number: Acing the Mathematics Test

Okay, you math whiz, here's a question for you. Quick, without your calculator, answer this question: How many seconds are there in a year? Answer: Exactly 12: January 2nd, February 2nd, March 2nd . . .

You can't escape the ACT Mathematics Test, no matter how hard you try. And, alas, its questions aren't quite as much fun as the ones we ask here. But don't worry. This chapter tells you what you need to know to ace the test.

What You See Is What You Get: The Format and Breakdown of the Math Test

No, the "breakdown" in the preceding heading doesn't refer to *your* (nervous) breakdown but rather to the breakdown of the number and types of problems in the Mathematics Test. This 50-minute test features 45 questions that fall into pretty standard categories.

The number of questions that test each concept varies from test to test. But it's not as if you have any control over the distribution of questions, right? (We can just see the letter: "Dear ACT: Please be sure that I have more geometry and fewer algebra problems — thanks . . . .")

The following is the short 'n' sweet version of the kinds of math questions you encounter in the dark alleyways of the ACT:

» **Pre-algebra:** (Normal people refer to this as *arithmetic*.) Quite a few questions cover basic arithmetic, including such concepts as fractions, decimals, and subtracting negative numbers.

- » **Elementary algebra:** You learn this type of material in your first semester or two of algebra. These questions test your ability to work with variables, set up algebraic formulas, solve linear equations, and do the occasional FOIL problem.

- » **Intermediate algebra/coordinate geometry:** Fewer than half of the questions cover more difficult quadratic problems, as well as inequalities, bases, exponents, radicals, basic graphing (finding points on an *x, y*–coordinate graph), and functions.

- » **Probability and statistics:** A few of the questions expect you to know how to solve problems involving average/mean, median, combinations, permutations, and probability.

- » **Plane geometry and trigonometry:** Many questions cover plane figures (what you think of as "just plain figures," like triangles, circles, quadrilaterals, and so on), and trigonometry. The trig questions make up no more than 10 percent of the test, so if you haven't had trig yet, don't despair. At least half of the trig questions are very basic, covering trig ratios and basic trigonometric identities. Confused? Don't worry about the exact number of questions. Just remember that you have 50 minutes to do 45 questions.

Absence Makes the Heart Grow Fonder: What Isn't on the Math Test

Instead of obsessing over how awful the ACT Mathematics Test is, focus on a few of its good points — namely, what isn't on the test:

- » **Calculus:** The ACT does not — we repeat, *does not* — test calculus. You don't even have to know how to pronounce *calculus* to get a good ACT Mathematics Test score. It helps to be familiar with foundational trigonometry concepts, and a little pre-calculus experience may help you work more quickly through one or two questions, but a good percentage of the math covers pre-algebra, geometry, and algebra 1.

- » **Traps:** Many standardized math exams are full of nasty old traps. The ACT is not. It's not out to get you like other tests. Here, the questions really test your math knowledge, not your patience. You don't have to be quite as paranoid on the ACT as you do on some other exams.

Getting into the Grind: The Approach

You've done multiple-choice math problems all your life. In fact, you probably don't have much more to learn about doing multiple-choice math questions. However, the following common-sense steps can help you stay focused as you move quickly through the Math Test:

1. **Identify the point of the question.**

    Yes, even the perplexing word problems have a point. Each question is trying to get you to supply a specific piece of information. It helps to read the end question first to determine what you're solving for. Does the question ask you to find the circumference or an area? Do you have to state the value of *x* or of 2*x*? Circle precisely what the question asks for. After you finish the problem, go back and double-check that your answer provides the circled information.

We just said that the ACT isn't out to trap you — but that doesn't mean you can't trap yourself. Among the answer choices are answers that you get by making careless errors. Suppose, for example, that the problem asks for the *product* of numbers, and you find the *sum*. Your answer will undoubtedly be there with the other wrong answers (and the one right one, of course). If the question asks for one-half of a quantity and you solve for twice the quantity, that answer will also likely be there. Because these types of answer choices are available to you, it's especially important that you identify what the problem *exactly* asks for and supply only that information.

To help you focus, especially on word problems, read the final lines of the question first. Knowing what you're solving for as you read the rest of the question saves time. As you read through the rest of the question, circle numbers and variables to help you focus on the information the question provides to figure out the answer.

2. **Budget your time and brain strain: Decide whether the problem is worth your time and effort.**

   You don't have to do every math problem in order, you know. Read the question and then predict how time-consuming it will be to solve. If you know you have to take several steps to answer the question, you may want to skip the problem, mark it, and go back to it later. If you're not even sure where to start the problem, don't sit there gnawing at your pencil as if it were an ear of corn (unless you're Pinocchio, wood really isn't brain food). Guess and go.

   Guess, guess, guess! The ACT has no penalty for wrong answers. You're going to (or already have) read that statement hundreds of times throughout this book. We say it every chance we get to remind you that you can guess without fear of reprisal. Whenever you skip a problem, choose an answer, any answer, mark it on your answer sheet, and hope that you get lucky. Put a big arrow in the margin of the test booklet next to the question (not on the answer sheet because it may mess up the computer grading) to remind yourself that you made a wild guess. But if you run out of time and don't get back to the question, at least you have a chance of guessing the answer right.

3. **Look before you leap: Preview the answer choices.**

   Look at the answer choices before you begin doing any pencil-pushing. Often, the choices are variations on a theme, like 0.5, 5, 50, and 500. If you see those answers, you know you don't have to worry about the digit, only the decimal. Maybe the answers are very far apart, like 1, 38, 275, and 495. You can probably make a wild estimate and get that answer correct. But if you see that the answers are close together (like 9, 10, 11, and 12), you know you have to invest a little more time and effort into being extra careful when solving the problem.

   We'd be wealthy if we had a nickel for every student who groaned and complained as they looked at the answer choices, "Man, I didn't really have to work that whole problem out. I could've just estimated from the answer choices." Absolutely true.

4. **Give yourself a second chance: Use your answer to check the question.**

   Think of this step as working forward and backward. First, work forward to come up with the answer to the question. Then plug the answer into the question and work backward to check it. For example, if the question asks you to solve for x, work through the equation until you get the answer. Then plug that answer back into the equation and make sure it works out. This last step takes less time than you may think and can save you a lot of points.

Not all the math questions on the ACT contain only one sentence or request that you simply "solve for x." In fact, many math questions require you to sift through a bunch of information to figure out what the real question is. These word problems, as they're called, require you to translate words into numbers and then arrange them in a way that makes mathematical sense. You know what we're talking about — those problems that tell you how fast Train A travels and what speed Train B moves at and then expect you to figure out exactly what hour the two trains will collide. Watch out!

Don't worry; we're here to help you make sense of all these words. Several words translate nicely into mathematical expressions, and many types of word problems lend themselves perfectly to specific formulas or strategies.

Translating English into Math

When you see a word problem on the Math Test, you may feel a little lost at first. Straightforward math equations seem so much more, well, straightforward. Even though word problems are written in English, they may seem like they're written in a foreign language. To help you with the translation, Table 11-1 provides you with some of the more common words you encounter in word problems and tells you what they mean (and look like!) in math terms.

TABLE 11-1 Common Words and Their Math Counterparts

Plain English	Math Equivalent
More than, increased by, added to, combined with, total of, sum of	Add (+)
Decreased by, diminished by, reduced by, difference between, taken away from, subtracted from, less than, fewer than	Subtract (−)
Of, times, product of	Multiply (×)
Ratio of, per, out of, quotient	Divide (÷ or /)
Percent	÷100
Is, are, was, were, becomes, results in	Equals (=)
How much, how many, what, what number	Variable (x, y)

REMEMBER

Subtraction phrases such as "taken away from," "subtracted from," "less than," and "fewer than" require you to switch the order of the quantities you're subtracting. For example, "Ten decreased by six" means 10 − 6 (which equals 4), but "Ten subtracted from six" means 6 − 10, or −4.

As you read through a word problem, analyze its language to determine what math operations it involves. Keep this general process in mind:

1. **Determine what you're supposed to solve for, specifically what the *x* is in the equation.**

2. **Analyze the rest of the information to figure out how to arrange the equation to solve for *x*.**

Many of the word problems on the ACT, like the following example, concern percentages.

152 PART 3 Don't Count Yourself Out: The Math Test

EXAMPLE

To pay for college expenses, Ms. Bond takes out a loan in the amount of $650 with a simple interest rate of 8%. What is the total amount of the loan with interest?

(A) $658

(B) $52

(C) $702

(D) $1,170

The problem asks for the total amount (that's the x) of Ms. Bond's loan with (which means +) interest, so you have to add what she owes in interest to the original amount of the loan. Before you add the interest amount, you must find out what the amount of interest is. The language of the problem tells you that Ms. Bond has to pay an interest rate of (meaning ×) 8% (which means you divide 8 by 100). Written with numbers rather than words, the problem looks something like this:

$$\frac{8}{100} \times 650 + 650$$

Perform the operation in parentheses first (as we explain in Chapter 8) to get 0.08. Next, multiply $650 by 0.08 to get $52. Ms. Bond pays $52 in interest. Add the interest amount to the loan amount to get your final answer: $650 + $52 = $702. The correct answer is Choice (C).

If you picked Choice (A), you added 8 to $650, which isn't the proper way to determine interest. Choice (B) is the correct interest amount but not the total amount of the loan plus the interest. If you opted for Choice (D), you incorrectly divided 8 by 10 rather than by 100 to come up with the interest amount.

TIP

Note that you can solve this percentage problem in one step. To find the resulting loan total after an increase of 8% from the original loan amount, just multiply the original value of $650 by 1 + the percentage, or 1.08: $650 × 1.08 = $702.

Time Flies When You're Having Fun: Timing Tips

A common complaint we hear from students about the Mathematics Test is, "There's just not enough time. If I had more time, I could probably ace every single question." True enough. Although having a little more than one minute per question sounds good, you'll be surprised how fast time goes by. We have a few suggestions to help you make the best use of your time.

Skim for your favorite questions

We think of this technique as eating dessert first (something we always do). Go for the chocolate cake first (the easy questions) to make sure time doesn't run out before you get to the good stuff. Leave the green beans (the harder problems) for the end. If you run out of time (which happens to many test-takers), at least you'll have finished the questions that you had the best chance of answering correctly.

CHAPTER 11 **Numb and Number: Acing the Mathematics Test** 153

In fact, consider approaching the last 10 questions in the Math Test (traditionally the hardest) in two passes. When you get to about question 35, follow these steps:

1. **Skim the problem to discover the answer to these two questions:**
   - Is the concept tested one I feel comfortable with?
   - Will it take me less than one minute to solve it?

2. **If the answer is yes to both questions, go for it!**
   Answer the question, mark your answer, and move on.

3. **If the answer to either question is no, skip it!**
   Draw a big X next to the question in your test booklet or flag it in the digital version, and check out the next question.

4. **Answer the remaining questions in the same way, never spending more than about 30 seconds on any one question and marking questions you skip.**
   If a question you first think will be easy turns out to be time-consuming, skip it, mark it, and move on.

5. **When you've seen all 60 questions, go back to the ones you've marked.**
   The point is to make it all the way through the section because some of the later questions in the section can be really easy. You would hate to miss them because you've spent too much time on one or two more difficult questions.

6. **Make sure you've marked answers for every question on your answer sheet.**

REMEMBER

If you decide to skip a question in any section on the ACT, make sure you mark an answer for it before you move on. You won't receive a penalty for wrong answers, so make sure you've selected an answer for every question in the section before the proctor calls time. You can always change the guess later and replace it with the answer you've selected.

Backsolve when the answers are actual values

On many problems, you can simply plug in the answer choices to see which one fits. This technique is call *backsolving*. If you find yourself thinking that there must be some sort of equation you can come up with to solve a complex problem, but you can't actually come up with that formula or you know what to do, but the computations will be super time-consuming, try plugging in the answers. This will only work if the answers contain no variables, of course, and will work best if the answers are all integers.

The ACT arranges answer choices from greatest to least or least to greatest, so unless there's some other compelling reason to start with another answer choice, begin with Choice (B) or (C), the middle values.

For example, suppose that the question is something like this:

EXAMPLE

Given the equation, $x + \frac{1}{2}x + \frac{1}{3}x = 110$, what is the value of x?

(A) 95
(B) 90
(C) 72
(D) 60

154 PART 3 Don't Count Yourself Out: The Math Test

Yes, you can use a common denominator and actually work through the problem to find x directly. But it may be quicker and easier to use your calculator to plug in the answer choices. Start with Choice (C). If $x = 72$, then $\frac{1}{2}x = 36$ and $\frac{1}{3}x = 24$. But $72 + 36 + 24 = 132$, not 110. Because the sum is too big, you know the number you plugged in is too big as well. Plug in the smaller number, Choice (D). Let $x = 60$: $60 + 30 + 20 = 110$. That works! (See Chapter 8 for more on working with common denominators and variables like x.)

Plug in values for variables

When you encounter a question that's mostly variables with possible answer choices that are expressions with mostly variables, this is a job for *plugging in*! Make up values to substitute for the variables to make solving these questions much easier. Here's how:

1. **Make up easy-to-work-with values for each of your variables.**

    Make sure your values follow the guidelines provided by the question. For instance, if the question tells you that x is an even integer, pick a simple even integer like 2 to substitute for x.

2. **Substitute the values for the variables in the problem to come up with an actual value the expression should equal.**

3. **Plug the values you've created into each of the answer choices to find which one results in the amount you come up with in Step 2.**

This simple example shows you what these steps look like in action.

EXAMPLE

The entrance fee for Great Mountains National Park is $10 for vans and $5 for cars. In one summer, the park collected x van fees and y car fees. Which of the following is an expression for the total amount in dollars that the park collected for the entire summer?

(A) $10x + 5y$

(B) $10x + 5x$

(C) $15(x + y)$

(D) $10(x + y) + 5(x + y)$

You may recognize the correct answer immediately, but bear with us and learn the approach so you'll be prepared for trickier questions later.

1. **Give your variables values.**

    Say $x = 2$ and $y = 4$. Don't worry that 2 van fees and 4 car fees in a whole summer don't make a lot of sense in real life. The goal is to keep your calculations quick and easy breezy.

2. **Substitute the values for the variables to figure out the total dollar amount that would be collected for 2 vans and 4 cars:**

    2 van fees at $10 is $20 and 4 car fees at $5 is $20. So the total amount collected is $40.

3. **Plug 10 for v and 5 for y in each answer choice to see which one results in $40.**

Check Choice (A). $10(2) + 5(4) = 40$. That's your answer! You could try the others just to be sure, but you'll see that no other answer results in $40.

CHAPTER 11 Numb and Number: Acing the Mathematics Test   155

Kindly refrain from showing off everything you know

Some of the ACT problems have extraneous information. For example, a geometry problem may list all sorts of numbers, including lengths of sides and measures of interior angles. If you read the question first and it asks you to find the area of a trapezoid, you know you need just the numbers for base and height. (Remember the formula? The area of a trapezoid is $A = \frac{1}{2}(\text{base}_1 + \text{base}_2)h$.) Extra red-herring info can make you waste a lot of time. We already know that you're brilliant (you bought this book, didn't you?); you don't need to prove it by doing more than you're asked during the test. If you convert every problem into two or three new problems, you'll never finish the Math Test on time.

Put aside two minutes to fill in the remaining ovals

The ACT assesses no penalty for guessing. We like to say that over and over and over again until you're so exasperated that you want to cut off our air supply. It's critical to remember that you don't lose points for wrong answers; always keep in mind that wild guesses are worth making. Nothing is worse than that sinking feeling you get when the proctor calls time, and you still have five problems you haven't even looked at. If you save a few minutes at the end, you can wildly fill in answers for those last ten problems. Choose the same answers for every guess. You have a good chance of getting at least two or three of the ten correct.

TIP

No guarantees, but we've found that the correct answers to the last several questions in the ACT math test tend to be the first or last answers on most tests. So if you run out of time on the last five or so math questions, you may increase your guessing percentage by choosing all A/Fs or D/Js. Just saying. . . .

REMEMBER

The proctor is *supposed* to tell you when you have only five minutes left in the test. Before the test actually begins, you may want to remind your proctor to do so. Also, be sure to wear a wristwatch for the paper test so you're in control of your own pacing. Don't own one? Buy one now and practice with it!

Do's, Don'ts, and Darns: What to Do and Not Do on the Math Test

Although the math questions are pretty straightforward, a few basic do's and don'ts are worth noting here.

Do get the lead out

Give your pencil a workout. If you have to solve a geometry problem, jot down the formula first and then just fill in the numbers. If you have the formula staring at you, you're not as likely to make a careless mistake as you would be if you tried to keep everything in your head. If the geometry problem has words, words, words, but no picture, draw the picture yourself. When you plug in the answer choices or make up your own numbers to substitute for variables, write down what you plugged in and tried. We see students redoing the same things over and over because they forgot what they'd already plugged in. Doodle away. You get scratch paper for the digital ACT, and plenty of white space in the paper test booklet.

Don't start working until you've read the entire problem

So you read the first part of a problem and start trying to solve for the area of the triangle or the circumference of the circle. But if you read further, you may find that the question asks only for a *ratio* of the areas of two figures, which you can figure out without actually finding the precise areas. Or you may solve a whole algebraic equation, only to realize that the question didn't ask for the variable you found but for something else entirely. Reading the question first can prevent this messiness. As we say in the "Getting into the Grind: The Approach" section earlier in this chapter, read the last line or two of the problem first and circle the part of the problem that specifies what you're solving for exactly.

Do reread the problem with your answer inserted

Very few students take this last critical step. Most test-takers are so concerned with finishing on time that they solve the problem and zoom on to the next question. Big tactical error. Rereading the question in light of your answer can show you some pretty dumb mistakes. For example, if the question asks you for the average of 5, 9, 12, 17, and 32, and your answer is 75, you can immediately realize that you found the sum but forgot to divide by the number of terms. (And, of course, 75 is one of the answer choices.) Maybe the question asks you to find one interior angle of a figure, and your answer is 190. If you look at the angle and see that it is *acute* (less than 90 degrees), you've made a mistake somewhere.

Don't strike out over a difficult question early on

Most standardized exams put their questions in order of difficulty, presenting the easy ones first, then the medium ones, and finally the hard ones. Things aren't as cut and dried on the ACT Mathematics Test. You may find a question that you consider pretty tough very early in the exam. Although *easy* and *hard* are subjective, many of our students over the years have been furious with themselves because they never looked at the last several questions — reasoning that if they couldn't get the earlier ones right, they obviously couldn't get the later ones at all. Wrong. We've seen some relatively simple questions, especially basic geometry questions, close to the end of the exam.

IN THIS CHAPTER

» Making your brain earn its keep with a handful of practice questions

» Testing your patience with the dreaded word problem

Chapter 12
More Fun than a Root Canal: Mathematics Practice Questions

You've had so much fun reviewing algebra, geometry, and trigonometry in the previous chapters that you simply can't wait to jump right in and practice what you know, right? Well, we don't want you to have to wait any longer to strut your stuff. Here's a set of a dozen math practice questions; give 'em your best shot!

Directions: Each of the following questions has four answer choices. Choose the best answer for each question.

1. $\dfrac{\left(a^4 \times a^3\right)^2}{a^4} =$

   (A) a^{36}

   (B) a^{10}

   (C) a^9

   (D) a^6

   First, do the operation inside the parentheses. When you multiply like bases, you add the exponents: $a^4 \times a^3 = a^7$. When you have a power outside the parentheses, you multiply the exponents: $\left(a^7\right)^2 = a^{14}$. Finally, when you divide by like bases, you subtract the exponents: $a^{14} \div a^4 = a^{14-4} = a^{10}$. The correct answer is Choice (B).

WARNING

If you picked Choice (D), you fell for a trap answer. If you said $a^4 \times a^3 = a^{12}$ and $a^{(12)(2)} = a^{24}$, you may have divided a^{24} by a^4 and gotten a^6. If you chose Choice (A), you fell for another trap. You may have reasoned that $a^4 \times a^3 = a^{12}$. Because 12 squared is 144, you may have thought that $a^{(12)^2} = a^{144}$ and that $a^{144} \div a^4 = a^{36}$.

All these trap answers are intentional, put there to test whether you know how to perform operations with exponents. If you're still confused about how to multiply and divide like bases, turn to Chapter 8.

2. The ratio of knives to forks to spoons in a silverware drawer is 3:4:5. Which of the following could be the total number of knives, forks, and spoons in the drawer?

(F) 60
(G) 62
(H) 64
(J) 65

The total number of utensils must be a multiple of the sum of the numbers of the ratios. In other words, add $3 + 4 + 5 = 12$. The total must be a multiple of 12. Only one answer choice, 60, divides evenly by 12, so you know the correct answer is Choice (F).

If you're confused about ratios (supposedly one of the easiest portions of the exam), check out Chapter 8.

3. An usher passes out 60 percent of his programs before the intermission and 40 percent of the remainder after the intermission. At the end of the evening, what percent of the original number of programs does the usher have left?

(A) 0
(B) 16
(C) 24
(D) 60

Whenever you have a percentage problem, plug in 100 for the original total. Assume that the usher begins with 100 programs. If he passes out 60 percent of them, he has passed out 60, leaving him with 40. Now comes the tricky part. After the intermission, the usher passes out 40 percent of the remaining programs: 40 percent of 40 is 16 ($0.4 \times 40 = 16$) and $40 - 16 = 24$. So the correct answer is Choice (C). You can also find the number of remaining programs in one step by multiplying 40 by 0.60 $(1 - 0.40)$: $40 \times 0.60 = 24$.

WARNING

Did you fall for the trap answer in Choice (A)? If you thought the usher first passed out 60 programs and then passed out the remaining 40, you believed that he had no programs left at the end of the evening. The word *remainder* is the key to this problem. The usher didn't pass out 40 percent of his original total, but 40 percent of the remaining programs.

If you chose Choice (B), you made a careless mistake. The number 16 represents the percentage of programs the usher passed out after the intermission. The question asks for the percent of programs the usher had left. We suggest that you circle the portion of the question that tells you what you're looking for. When you double-check your work, review this circled portion first.

4. A salesman makes a commission of $1.50 per shirt sold and $2.50 per pair of pants sold. In one pay period, he sold 10 more shirts than pairs of pants. If his total commission for the pay period was $215, what was the total number of shirts and pairs of pants he sold?

   (F) 40
   (G) 50
   (H) 60
   (J) 110

Let x be the number of pairs of pants the salesman sold. The number of shirts is $x+10$ (because the problem tells you that the salesman sold 10 more shirts than pairs of pants). Set up the following equation:

$$\$1.50(x+10)+\$2.50(x)=\$215$$

Now just follow these steps to solve for x:

1. **Multiply:** $1.50x+15+2.50x=215$
2. **Combine like terms:** $4.00x+15=215$
3. **Isolate the x on one side:** $4.00x=215-15$
4. **Subtract:** $4.00x=200$
5. **Divide:** $x=200\div4$, or $x=50$

WARNING

If you answered with Choice (G), you fell for the trap answer (after all that hard work)! Remember to go back and reread what the question is asking for. In this case, it wants to know the total number of pants and shirts sold. So you're not done working yet. If x (which equals 50) is the number of pairs of pants, then $x+10$ (which is 60) is the number of shirts sold. (Note that 60 is a trap answer as well.) Combine $50+60$ to get the right answer, 110. The correct answer is Choice (J).

5. Kim and Scott work together stuffing envelopes. Kim works twice as fast as Scott. Together they stuff 2,100 envelopes in four hours. How long would Kim, working alone, take to stuff 175 envelopes?

   (A) 20 minutes
   (B) 30 minutes
   (C) 1 hour
   (D) 3 hours

The ratio of Kim's work to Scott's work is 2:1. In other words, she does two out of every three envelopes. Scott does one out of every three envelopes, for a total of 700 envelopes $(2,100\div3)$. Scott stuffs 700 envelopes in four hours, and Kim stuffs 1,400 $(2,100-700=1,400)$ in four hours. Divide 1,400 by 4 to find that Kim produces 350 stuffed envelopes per hour; 175 is one-half of 350. Therefore, in one half-hour (or 30 minutes), Kim can stuff 175 envelopes. The correct answer is Choice (B).

TIP

When you encounter a word problem like this one, don't start thinking about equations immediately. Talking through the problem may help you more than creating a bunch of equations.

6. If *DC* = 6, point *O* is the center of the circle, and line *AD* is tangent to the circle, what is the area of the shaded portion of the figure?

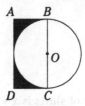

(F) $72 - 18\pi$

(G) $72 - 36\pi$

(H) 9π

(J) $36 - 18\pi$

The shaded area is the leftover portion of the figure. To find the area of the shaded portion, find the total area of the figure and subtract the area of the unshaded portion. In this figure, the shaded area is the total area of rectangle *ABCD* less the area of half the circle. If the side *DC* is 6 and the circle is tangent to *AD*, the radius of the circle is also 6.

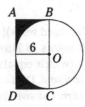

REMEMBER

The area of a circle is πr^2; therefore, the area of this circle is $\pi 6^2$ or 36π. Be careful to remember that you're working only with a semicircle. The shaded area subtracts only half the area of the circle, so you know you have to subtract 18π. That immediately narrows the answers to Choices (F) and (J).

Next, find the area of the rectangle. (The area of a rectangle equals length × width.) The width of *DC* is 6. Because the radius of the circle is 6, the diameter of the circle is 12. So *BC*, the diameter of the circle, is the same as the length of the rectangle. To find the area of the rectangle, simply multiply: $6 \times 12 = 72$. Finally, subtract: $72 - 18\pi$. The correct answer is Choice (F).

Shaded area questions should be one of the easiest types of questions to get correct. If you got confused on this problem, flip to Chapter 9.

7. When $5a^2 + (5a)^2 = 120$, what is the value of *a*?

(A) 2

(B) 3

(C) 4

(D) 5

162 PART 3 Don't Count Yourself Out: The Math Test

First, deal with the parentheses: $(5a)^2 = 5a \times 5a$, which is $25a^2$. Then add like terms: $25a^2 + 5a^2 = 30a^2$. Finally, solve the equation for a:

$$5a^2 + (5a)^2 = 120$$
$$30a^2 = 120$$
$$a^2 = 120 \div 30$$
$$a^2 = 4$$
$$a = 2$$

The correct answer is Choice (A).

WARNING

Choice (C) is the trap answer. If you divided 120 by 30 and got 4, you may have picked Choice (C), forgetting that 4 represented a^2, not a.

Of course, you also could simply plug in each answer choice and work backward to solve this problem. Start with one of the middle values in the answer choices. If $a = 4$, then

$$5(4)^2 + (5 \times 4)^2 =$$
$$5(16) + 20^2 =$$
$$+ 400 = 480$$
$$480 \neq 120$$

The value of Choice (C) is too great, so try Choices (A) and (B), which are smaller numbers.

8. Three times as much as $\frac{1}{3}$ less than $3x$ is how much in terms of x?

   (F) $9x$

   (G) $8x$

   (H) $6x$

   (J) x

   Working backward in this type of problem is usually the easiest way to solve it. One-third less than $3x$ is $2x$. You can calculate it this way: $3x - \frac{1}{3}(3x) = 3x - x = 2x$. Then just multiply by 3: $3 \times 2x = 6x$. The correct answer is Choice (H).

9. The following chart shows the weights of junior high school students. What is the sum of the mode and the median weights?

Weight in Pounds	Number of Students
110	4
120	2
130	3
140	2

   (A) 230 pounds
   (B) 235 pounds
   (C) 250 pounds
   (D) 255 pounds

CHAPTER 12 More Fun than a Root Canal: Mathematics Practice Questions   163

This question tests vocabulary as much as it tests math. The *mode* is the most frequently repeated number. In this case, 110 is repeated more often than any other term. The *median* is the middle term when the numbers are arranged in order. Here you have 110, 110, 110, 110, 120, 120, 130, 130, 130, 140, 140. Of these 11 numbers, the sixth one, 120, is the median. And $110 + 120 = 230$, so the correct answer is Choice (A).

TIP

Don't confuse *median* with *mean*. The *mean* is the average. You get the mean by adding all the terms and then dividing by the number of terms. If you confused median with mean, you'd really be in a quandary, because the sum of the mean and the mode is 232.73, and that answer isn't an option. If you picked Choice (B), you fell into a different trap. You found that 125 was the median by adding the first and last terms and dividing by 2. Sorry. To find the median, you have to write out all the terms from least to greatest (all four 110s, both 120s, and so on) and then locate the middle term.

10. Points *E*, *D*, and *A* are colinear. What is the ratio of the area of $\triangle EBD$ to $\triangle ABD$?

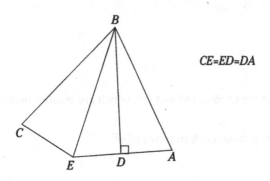

(F) 3:2

(G) 3:1

(H) 2:1

(J) 1:1

The area of a triangle is $\frac{1}{2}bh$. The base of *EBD* is *ED*. *ED* is equal to *AD*, which is the base of $\triangle ABD$. The bases of the two triangles are equal. The heights are equal, as well. By definition, the height of a triangle is a line from the tallest point perpendicular to the base. If the triangles have the same base and the same height, the ratio of their areas is 1:1. So the correct answer is Choice (J).

11. Given this equation $\dfrac{95c5}{+3cbc}$, solve for the sum of $a + b + c$.
    $\overline{ab3a2}$

(A) 14

(B) 13

(C) 12

(D) 11

TIP

If you're rushed for time, this problem is a good one to skip and come back to later. Mark a guess on your answer sheet, mark the question in your test booklet, and evaluate it after you've finished the last math question. Remember that the ACT doesn't assess a penalty for wrong answers. Never leave an answer blank. Even a wild guess is worthwhile. However, if you do a few of these practice problems, you'll be surprised at how quickly you can get them right.

164 PART 3 Don't Count Yourself Out: The Math Test

Don't panic. This problem is much easier than it appears. Start with the right-hand column, the ones or units column: $5 + c = a$ number that ends in 2. You know that the 2 must be a 12 instead of just a 2 because you can't add a positive number to 5 and get 2, which means $c = 7$. Jot down $c = 7$.

When you carry the 1 to the tens column, you get $1 + 7$, which is 8, and $8 + b = a$. You don't know a yet . . . or do you? Go to the far-left column (the thousands column). If the answer is $ab3\ a2$, the variable a must equal 1. You can't add two four-digit numbers and get 20,000-something. The most you can get is 10,000-something (for example, $9,999 + 9,999 = 19,998$). Now you know that a is 1. Jot down $a = 1$.

Go back to the tens column: $1 + 7 = 8$ and $8 + b = 11$ (it can't be 1; it must be 11). Therefore, $b = 3$. Carry the 1 to the hundreds column: $1 + 5 = 6$ and $6 + c$ (which is 7) = 13. Yes, this is true — a good check. Carry the 1 to the next column: $1 + 9 = 10$ and $10 + 3$ is 13, which is what we said ab was in the first place. Therefore, $c = 7$, $b = 3$, $a = 1$, and $7 + 3 + 1 = 11$. The correct answer is Choice (D).

REMEMBER

The most common mistake that students make on this type of problem is forgetting to carry the 1 to the next column. Double-check that you have done so.

12. $a\beta b = \frac{1}{a} + \frac{1}{b}$ What is the value of $\frac{2}{15} \beta \frac{2}{18}$?

(F) 14

(G) 14.5

(H) 15

(J) 16.5

This problem is a symbolism problem, one that you should think through in words and concepts instead of heading for an equation. The symbol β indicates that you add the reciprocals of the two numbers. For example, the reciprocal of a is $\frac{1}{a}$, and the reciprocal of b is $\frac{1}{b}$. Therefore, add the reciprocals of $\frac{2}{15}$ and $\frac{2}{18}$. $\frac{15}{2} + \frac{18}{2} = \frac{33}{2} = 16.5$. The correct answer is Choice (J).

REMEMBER

The β has this meaning for this problem only. The meanings of symbols vary from problem to problem; always read the problems carefully.

CHAPTER 12 **More Fun than a Root Canal: Mathematics Practice Questions** 165

4

Time to Read the Riot ACT: The Reading Test

IN THIS PART...

Discover the types of questions you encounter in the ACT Reading Test and the traps built into them.

Find out how to analyze answer choices to eliminate wrong options until you find the correct response.

Put the tips and techniques into action with a full-out practice chapter with four abbreviated passages and eight questions.

> **IN THIS CHAPTER**
> » Getting to know the Reading Test passages
> » Recognizing the different types of Reading Test questions
> » Getting familiar with typical Reading Test question formats
> » Eliminating illusion, delusion, and confusion with some tips

Chapter 13
This, Too, Shall Pass(age): Sailing through the Reading Test

After working through an ACT Reading Test, a student said, "If I'd known it would end up like this, I never would have let my first-grade teacher show me how to read!" Now, that's just silly. If they hadn't learned to read, they'd be lost on the ACT and other sources of fine entertainment. The first day you spent with your ABCs prepared the way for this chapter, which explains the approach to the third section of the ACT — the Reading Test.

In this chapter, you find out what types of passages to expect and what the questions look like. After you know the ins and outs of excelling on the Reading Test, you'll be glad you learned to read.

Facing 36 Questions: The Reading Test

The Reading Test consists of four passages and 36 questions. Each passage is supposed to be similar in difficulty to materials you encounter during your first year of college. The test contains one passage on each of the following topics:

» **Literary narrative:** The first passage in the section is a fiction passage from a novel or a short story. Some of the fiction passages are very fun to read. But don't expect that you'll have read them before. In all the years we've been preparing students for the ACT, we've had only one student tell us they remember having read the passage before in a novel. The ACT test makers obviously don't want to test you on what you're already familiar with (and maybe even have discussed in class); they want to test you on how well you evaluate a passage that's new to you.

- **Social studies:** The social studies passage comes after the prose fiction piece and covers sociology, anthropology, history, geography, psychology, political science, and economics. That's an incredibly wide range of topics when you think about it. The history passages are generally easier to understand; some of the psychology ones can be intense.

- **Humanities:** The third passage can be about music, dance, theater, art, architecture, language, ethics, literary criticism, and even philosophy. Most students tend to like the humanities passages because (believe it or not) they're actually interesting.

- **Natural sciences:** The last passage is what most people think about when they hear the word *science*. The natural sciences passage can cover chemistry, biology, physics, and other physical sciences.

  Are you panicking right now, screaming, "I haven't taken physics! No fair!"? Not to worry. The questions don't require you to know any particular subjects. Everything you need to answer the questions is right there in the passages, and you can go back to the passages as often as you like.

Timing

The Reading Test is 40 minutes long. Assuming you live to the average age of around 80, the Reading Test is only about 0.000000008 percent of your life. Now that doesn't seem so bad, does it? Because the test includes 36 questions, you need to spend just a little more than a minute per question, which includes reading the passage as well as working through the questions.

TIP

When you're finished with the first passage, glance at the clock. You should be no more than 10 minutes into the section. If you've taken significantly more time than that to finish the first passage, you need to work more wisely (and quickly!) on the remaining passages.

Scoring

Your reading score is based on your performance on all four passages and 36 questions. Colleges will also see a breakdown of how well you did in three categories of questions: key ideas and details, craft and structure, and integration of knowledge and ideas.

Getting Prepared: Reading Test Strategies

You've probably been reading since you were about 5 years old. It's a little late for us to teach you the basics. But we can tell you how to make the best use of your time in this test. To do your best on this 40-minute test, follow these guidelines.

Approach passages efficiently

The ACT Reading Test isn't particularly tricky, but time is short. Try these basic tips to help you move through the passages quickly and accurately:

- **Try leaping before you look.** For many students, the best way to save time and focus on what's important is to jump straight into the questions without even looking at the passage first. This strategy feels very uncomfortable at first, but with practice it can be a real time-saver. Here are the steps to follow to make the most of this approach:

1. **Read the short blurb at the beginning of the passage.**

   This short intro may give you a general idea of the passage's topic.

2. **Skim the questions to find the one that appears easiest to answer first.**

   Choose direct statement questions with line or paragraph references or those that contain elements such as dates, capitalized words, or proper names that are easy to skim for.

3. **As you read the passage parts to answer one question, initial, underline, or circle important info that may help you with subsequent questions.**

4. **When you've exhausted the question with easy references, tackle the big-picture question if there is one.**

   You may need to answer several questions before you have enough information to find the passage's main idea. Check the last paragraph for clues.

5. **Work on questions whose answer choices contain elements that are easy to find.**

6. **Save the inference questions for the end.**

To master this approach, be willing to leave a question if you spend more than 30 seconds searching for the answer. Eliminate obviously incorrect answers and take on another question in the set. Often, when you go back to the question, you can answer it based on work you've done on other questions.

» **You don't have to work in order.** Start with the passage you like best. If you're a science buff, answer questions in the last passage first. Then go to the other three passages. There's no good reason to leave your best chance for success for the end of the test when you're running out of time. Likewise, answer the questions in a set in the order that makes the most sense. Start with questions that refer you to particular parts of the passage or that ask you for definitions. Save more challenging questions for later when you've spent more time in the passage.

You can use the information you glean from answering some questions to help you answer other questions for the same passage.

What happens if your brain takes a little vacation on the paper-based test and you suddenly find you've filled in the bubbles all wrong? Maybe you started by reading Passage 2, with Questions 10–19, but you filled in the bubbles for Questions 1–9? Hey, you laugh now, but mixing up the bubbles is easy to do, especially when you skip around. The first reaction usually is panic; first, you erase all your answers, and then you try to remember what they were. Bad move. Here's how to handle this problem: As you answer a question, first circle the correct response in your booklet and then fill in the bubble for that response on the answer grid. That way, if you mess up and have to erase your answer grid, you can just glance at your answer booklet and find the right answers again.

» **Know how to eliminate wrong answers.** Using the process of elimination helps you weed out distracters and focus on the right answer. Sometimes you have to choose the best choice out of three pretty great choices. Other times, you must choose from four really crummy options. Common wrong answers to reading-comprehension questions include the following:

- **Choices that contain information that the passage doesn't cover:** Even if the information in these choices is true in real life, you can't pick them because the passage needs to be the source of the information. Eliminate these choices no matter how tempting they may be.

CHAPTER 13 **This, Too, Shall Pass(age): Sailing through the Reading Test** 171

- **Choices that contradict the passage's main point, author's tone, or specific details:** After you've read the passage, you should be able to quickly eliminate most of the choices that contradict what you know about the passage.

- **Choices that don't answer the question:** Paying careful attention to the wording of each question can help you narrow down your answer options. For example, a question may ask about a disadvantage of something discussed in the passage. If one of the answer choices lists an advantage rather than a disadvantage, you can eliminate that choice without thinking twice.

- **Choices that contain debatable words:** *Debatable words* are words that leave no room for exception, such as *all, always, completely, never, every, none,* and so on. The rest of the answer may look pretty good except for that unrelenting word.

  Don't automatically throw out every answer that has one of these words. But if your answer contains a debatable word, make absolutely sure that the information in the passage justifies the presence of that strong position.

REMEMBER

» **Don't read more into the passage than what's there.** Many questions are based on information that the passage specifically states. Other questions are based on information that the passage implies. Don't take matters to extremes or bring in background information that you happen to have. Suppose that the passage talks about the fall of communism in the Soviet Union and its satellite countries. You can't automatically assume the author also believes that communism will fail in China. Don't choose the answer that takes the reasoning too far.

Skim the passage effectively

If you feel uncomfortable jumping into the questions without an initial read of the passage, you can modify our suggested approach and still save time by skimming — but not reading — the ACT passages before you tackle the questions. When you practice reading questions, set a timer for 60 seconds on your phone. When the timer buzzes, stop reading and move to the questions. Here are some tips on how to accomplish that feat:

» **Know how paragraphs are organized.** Most writers (except writers of literature) pay attention to the maxim, "Tell 'em what you're gonna tell 'em; tell 'em; and tell 'em what you told 'em."

- **The first sentence of a paragraph presents its main topic.** Read the first several lines to get a glimpse of what the paragraph is about.

- **The middle sentences provide supporting evidence or examples for its main idea.** You can pretty much skip these lines on your first reading. Save reading this stuff for when you encounter a question that asks about supporting details.

» **Don't memorize.** We see some students stop reading, gaze out into the distance, and mutter to themselves, counting off on their fingers. These students are obviously trying to memorize facts from the passage: "Let's see, the three basic elements that make up Kleinschwab's Elixir are . . . ." Stop! You don't have to memorize anything; in fact, doing so can be counterproductive. Although you naturally want to remember some of what you read, you can (and should) go back to the passage as often as you want. When you go to the passage for information, you'll find it more quickly if you summarize (not memorize!) as you read.

» **Summarize.** As you read each paragraph's topic sentence, think about what you're reading and summarize it in your own words. Don't make things complicated. A simple "This paragraph is about the way the Greeks looked at nature, and the next paragraph covers the way the

Romans looked at nature" helps to focus your thoughts and keep track of where information occurs in the passage.

- *Question:* Should you highlight/underline or outline as you go?
- *Answer:* Other than a quick highlight of a paragraph topic, don't spend time underlining or outlining during your first read of the passage. When you go back into the passage to answer questions, you may want to keep track of information to help you answer other questions. Highlight key words (especially things like dates, proper names, unusual vocabulary, lists of examples, key transition words, and anything that really confuses you). Occasionally, jotting a note in the margin or your scratch paper to summarize a paragraph is particularly helpful. For example, next to Paragraph 1, you may write, "Need for elixir." Next to Paragraph 2, you may write, "Failed experiments." By Paragraph 3, you may write, "Success; uses of elixir." You get the idea.

» **Look for relationships and connections.** If the author contrasts two or more concepts, ask yourself what makes one idea different from the others. When a passage compares and contrasts theories, ideas, or techniques, keep track of which explanations apply to each and pay attention to which of the theories, ideas, or techniques the author seems to favor. Perhaps you're given thoughts in sequence. Try to keep track of what comes first, next, and last. For passages that talk about cause and effect, determine how one thing impacts another.

- *Question:* Should you read the questions before you read the passages?
- *Answer:* The large number of questions that accompany each ACT passage makes it tricky to get helpful information by skimming through the questions first.

Use these skimming tips to help you find information in the passage as you're answering questions, too

Skip a passage if necessary

Some students do well under time pressures and can finish all four passages and the questions in the allotted 40 minutes. Those students often don't have to read slowly and carefully, getting every little morsel the passages have to offer; instead, they can read quickly to get the overall idea. Other students get so totally nervous that if they have to rush, they mess up completely. If you're one of these students, a better strategy for you may be to concentrate on reading three of the passages carefully and answering all (or almost all) the questions correctly on them. Here are the steps to success if you apply what we call the *three-passage approach*:

1. **Pick the passage you like the least and mark guesses for all of its questions on your answer sheet.**

    Choose the same answer, all As/Fs, Bs/Gs, Cs/Hs, or Ds/Js, for all questions. It's highly likely that the correct answer for at least two of the questions will pop up in one column. Consider that passage answered and done.

2. **Gravitate to the passage type you like best.**

    Devote a little more than 13 minutes to answer its questions carefully. The key to success with this approach is to be super accurate. Mark your answers on the sheet.

3. **Do the same for your second favorite passage.**
4. **End with your third favorite.**
5. **If you have time remaining, return to the passage you began with and take on the questions that seem easiest to answer.**

    Make sure you mark answers for all 36 questions in the Reading Test.

Identifying Reading Question Types and Formats

The ACT Reading Test presents a variety of question types, but don't get too hung up on question types. Generally, you're simply examining the passage until it tells you the answers. Although you may encounter many different types of reading questions on the ACT, most fall into one of the following general types:

> » *Big-picture questions* ask you about the passage as a whole.
>
> » *Detail questions* ask you to regurgitate information straight from the passage.
>
> » *Inference questions* require you to make logical assumptions about the passage details.

The next sections break down each of these question types and explain how to answer them correctly.

Find key ideas and details

Questions that ask you for key points and details require a careful examination of the passage and its paragraphs.

Big-picture questions

Big-picture questions are almost always the first questions in the set of questions for a passage. A question may ask, "Which of the following is the main idea of the passage?" or "The primary purpose of Paragraph 3 is to do which of these?" You've likely tackled big-picture questions like these on other exams. As you answer them on the ACT, keep in mind these three characteristics of the overall idea:

> » **The big picture is broad and general.** It covers the entire passage (or the entire paragraph if the question asks about a paragraph). Be sure not to choose a "little" answer. The mere fact that a statement is true doesn't mean it's the main idea. Suppose you have a question that asks you for the main idea of a passage about high school education. One answer choice says, "The ACT gives students the heebie-jeebies." No one can argue with that statement, but it isn't the main idea of the passage.
>
> » **The answer to a big picture question may repeat the topic sentence or key words.** If the passage is about Asian philosophy, the correct answer may have the words *Asian philosophy* in it. Don't immediately choose any answer just because it has those words, but if you're debating between two answers, the one with the key words may be the better choice.
>
> » **The answer to a big picture question is always consistent with the tone of the passage and the attitude of the author.** If the passage is positive and the author is impressed by the philosophy, the main idea will be positive, not negative or neutral. If the author is criticizing something, the main idea will be negative.

REMEMBER

The best answer to a big picture question is general rather than specific. If an answer choice for a big picture question contains information that comes from just one part of the passage, it probably isn't the best answer. Here are some other ways to eliminate answer choices for main-idea questions:

> » **Avoid answer choices that contain information that comes only from the middle paragraphs of the passage.** These paragraphs probably deal with specific points rather than the main theme.
>
> » **Cross out any answer choices that contain information that the passage doesn't cover.** These choices are irrelevant.
>
> » **See whether you can eliminate answer choices based on just the first words.** For example, if you're trying to find the author's main point in a natural science passage with an objective tone, you can eliminate answers that begin with more subjective words, like *argue* or *criticize*.

Detail questions

The *detail question* covers one particular point, not the passage as a whole. This question is one of the easiest to get correct, especially when the detail question gives you a line reference (which doesn't happen too often). You use word clues from the wording of the question or its answer choices to determine where to go in the passage to find the information that will fairly obviously give you the specific answer.

Clues that you're dealing with detail questions with answers directly stated in the passage are in the verbs they contain. Questions that ask for information "according to the passage" or for what the author or passage *states*, *claims*, *indicates*, and so on, usually offer up answer choices that are word-for-word copies or really obvious paraphrases of information directly stated in the passage. Some sample questions include "According to the passage, James confronted Gary about the business when which of the following occurred?" or "The author states that the results of the experiments were considered unacceptable because. . . ."

The key to answering detail questions is knowing where the information is in the passage so you can get to it quickly. (Here's where summarizing the main point of each paragraph as you skim comes in handy; see the earlier section, "Skim the passage effectively" for more info.) Read the question carefully, and keep in mind that the right answer may paraphrase the passage instead of providing a word-for-word repeat.

If you're running short of time or your brain cells are about ready to surrender, look for this type of question and answer it first. You can often answer detail questions correctly even if you haven't read the entire passage. Find a key word in the question (such as, say, *elixir*) and skim the passage for that word.

The passage provides you with the correct answer to a direct statement question. Eliminate any answer choices that require you to make an assumption or inference that the passage doesn't specifically present. If you miss one of these questions, you've probably not read enough of the passage to locate the answer and have resorted to guessing based on what seems plausible rather than what's stated in the passage.

Most detail questions ask you to choose the one correct answer, but some questions are cleverly disguised to ask for the one answer that isn't true. We call these beauties *exception questions*. This question format used to appear much more frequently in the past than they do now, but they still pop up once in a while, so be prepared. You can recognize them by the presence of a negative word (usually *except* or *not*) in the question: "The passage lists all of the following as reasons that Gary objected to the new model EXCEPT:" When you see questions worded this way, you know you're looking for the one answer choice that isn't true.

Exception questions aren't that difficult if you approach them systematically. Determining which answer choice doesn't appear in the passage takes time because you may think you have to look in the passage for the choice and not find it. But we have a better way to find the right (or should we say wrong?) answer. Instead of determining whether an answer *isn't* true, just eliminate the three true answers. Doing so leaves you with the one false (and therefore correct) answer. Identifying choices that are true according to the passage is much easier than determining the one choice that isn't. Take your time, and you'll do exceptionally well on exception questions.

Determine craft and structure

Some questions ask you to evaluate word meanings, passage structure, and various points of view. The questions may ask you to choose a word that most effectively replaces an existing word in the passage. Or you may need to determine the general flow of the passage or distinguish different points of view within it. Don't overthink these questions. Like all other questions in the reading test, look for obvious clues to the right (and wrong) answers within the language of the passage.

Vocabulary in context

You may have to determine the meaning of a word by its use in context. These questions, creatively called *vocabulary-in-context questions*, are pretty easy to answer correctly because you can use the passage to figure out what the word in the question means. They give you a word or phrase (usually italicized or in quotations) and its line reference and ask you for another word that provides the same meaning, given what's going on in the passage.

The key to finding the best answer for a vocabulary-in-context question is to substitute the answer choices for the existing word in the passage. The answer choice that replaces the vocabulary word and makes sense within the context of the sentence and sentences around it is the right answer.

The only potentially tricky part about these questions is that they may test you on unfamiliar definitions of words that you know the meanings of. Sometimes, ACT passages use common words in uncommon ways. For example, the author may mention that "Lawrence was unable to cow Michael, despite his frequent threats." Although *cow* usually refers to a four-footed bovine, in this case, the word is used as a verb, meaning to intimidate or frighten. (Don't let the ACT cow you!)

If a set of questions has a vocabulary-in-context variety, answer it first. You don't have to know a lot about the passage to answer these babies, and the question tells you exactly where to go to answer it.

Passage structure questions

Sometimes a reading question asks you to examine the flow of information in the passage and how the author develops the main point. Answer options for these questions often contain two parts. Make sure you consider the entire answer choice as you move through the four options and eliminate any answer that is only half right.

For example, a question may ask you how the author organizes a passage about a particular artist. Say the author starts with a brief background of the artist's childhood and then shows how this history influenced the artist's paintings in adulthood. You'd have to eliminate this answer: "The author begins the passage with a biographical history of the artist and ends it with an examination of the artist's popularity." Although you may be tempted to choose this answer because it starts off so well, disregard the answer because it includes incorrect information about where the passage ends up.

Point of view questions

Occasionally, you may encounter questions that require you to analyze various perspectives provided in passages. A question may ask you whether the passage is told by a first-person narrator or from an omniscient third-person point of view. Usually, a simple examination of the pronouns reveals the answer. A first-person narrative will include references to "I," "me," and "my." An omniscient narrator refers to the people in the passage in the third-person as "him," "her," or "them."

A passage may also ask you to compare and contrast different perspectives on a similar topic. This question type occurs frequently in the set of comparative passages. Read the opinions carefully to note which points people agree on and which points set them on opposite sides. For more on comparative passages, see "Approaching Comparative Passages" later in this chapter.

Integrate knowledge and ideas

Questions that ask you to synthesize the points and details of the passage may require you to determine an author's implications. These questions may be worded slightly differently, but essentially they ask you to make inferences and examine intended meanings. They may even have you examine a graph or table.

Inference questions

Inference questions ask you about information that a passage implies rather than states directly. Specifically, they test your ability to draw conclusions from the information that's actually in the passage. You may have to read between the lines a little to find the answers to these questions. For instance, suppose you read a passage about hummingbirds. Information in one paragraph may state that hummingbirds fly south for the winter. Information in another paragraph may say that the Speckled Rufus is a kind of hummingbird. From this information, you can infer that the Speckled Rufus flies south in the winter.

You can usually spot inference questions because they contain words such as *infers*, *suggests*, or *implies*. An example could be this: "The passage suggests which of the following about Gary's response to John."

REMEMBER

When you face an inference question, look for the choice that extends the information in the passage *just a little bit*. Answer choices that make inferences that you can't support with what's stated in the passage are incorrect. Don't choose an answer that requires you to come up with information that isn't there. Sometimes knowing a lot about a passage's topic can throw you off because you may be tempted to answer questions based on your own knowledge rather than the passage.

Most nearly means

Occasionally, you see an ACT reading question worded this way: "When the author says that Gary was 'cleverly incommunicative,' she most nearly means that his response is which of these?" A question that asks for what a passage or an author most nearly means or suggests by quoted or italicized portions of a paragraph may be easily answered by simply examining the possible answer choices. Usually, the correct answer provides a definition or description of the quoted material and doesn't require you to check out the passage at all. For example, the answer to the question about Gary's response could be "Gary wisely chooses to refrain from responding to Jack's confrontation."

Approaching Comparative Passages

One of the passages in the Reading Test will consist of a set of comparative passages. You see two passages on the same general topic followed by nine questions. The set of passages may appear in any of the four passage types. The questions are grouped into three categories: those about the first passage, those about the second one, and those about both of them. So, you may see two shorter humanities passages instead of one long one. Some of the questions ask you about just one of the two passages. The others require you to compare ideas in the two passages.

When you see one of these comparison exercises on your test, treat the first two-thirds of the questions (the ones about each of the individual passages) the same way you do the one-passage format. Pay attention to the wording in the question to be sure you're answering it based on the appropriate passage.

The last several questions require you to compare two passages, asking you how they're different, on which points they agree, or how one author would respond to the opinion of the other author.

TIP

The trick to answering the comparison questions is to eliminate answer choices based on one passage at a time.

>> **For questions that ask you how passages are different, first eliminate answers that are untrue for one passage.** If any answers remain, eliminate those that are untrue for the other passage. The answers to these questions are usually worded like this: "Passage A focuses on Gary's side of the story while Passage B favors John's version." You know this answer is untrue if Passage A doesn't focus on Gary or if Passage B doesn't favor John. The minute you find one thing wrong with an answer, the entire answer has to be wrong.

>> **For questions that ask you for a point on which the authors would agree, eliminate answers that are untrue for either passage.** You can usually dismiss answers that clearly summarize one passage's position. Usually, the correct answer to these questions reflects a general point of agreement rather than a strong opinion held by one author or the other.

178 PART 4 Time to Read the Riot ACT: The Reading Test

IN THIS CHAPTER

» Celebrating diversity: Practicing the various passage types

» Distinguishing the time-worthy questions from the time-waster ones

Chapter **14**

Where Are SparkNotes When You Need Them? Reading Practice Questions

On the actual ACT, the Reading Test consists of four full-length passages, followed by nine questions. You have 40 minutes to read the four passages and answer all 36 questions. This abbreviated practice exam (we want to ease you into this stuff slowly) has four shorter passages and a total of eight questions. Use it to practice your approach to the reading questions. Don't worry about timing now. Think about what type of passage you're dealing with (literary narrative, social science, humanities, or natural science) and identify each question type. A short explanation of the answer follows each question. See Chapter 19 and the online review for complete tests, and check out Chapter 13 for everything you need to know about the Reading Test.

Directions: Answer each question based on what is stated or implied in the passage.

Passage 1 — Literary Narrative

This passage is adapted from the Robert Louis Stevenson novel *Kidnapped*.

Meanwhile such of the wounded as could move came clambering out of the fore-scuttle and began to help; while the rest that lay helpless in their bunks harrowed me with screaming and begging to be saved.

The captain took no part. It seemed he was struck stupid. He stood holding by the shrouds, talking to himself and groaning out aloud whenever the ship hammered on the rock. His brig was like wife and child to him; he had looked on, day by day, at the mishandling of poor Ransome; but when it came to the brig, he seemed to suffer along with her.

All the time of our working at the boat, I remember only one other thing; that I asked Alan, looking across at the shore, what country it was; and he answered, it was the worst possible for him, for it was a land of the Campbells.

We had one of the wounded men told off to keep a watch upon the seas and cry us warning. Well, we had the boat about ready to be launched, when this man sang out pretty shrill: "For God's sake, hold on!" We knew by his tone that it was something more than ordinary; and sure enough; there followed a sea so huge that it lifted the brig right up and canted her over on her beam. Whether the cry came too late or my hold was too weak, I know not; but at the sudden tilting of the ship I was cast clean over the bulwarks into the sea.

I went down, and drank my fill; and then came up, and got a blink of the moon; and then down again. They say a man sinks the third time for good. I cannot be made like other folk, then; for I would not like to write how often I went down or how often I came up again. All the while, I was being hurled along, and beaten upon and choked, and then swallowed whole, and the thing was so distracting to my wits, that I was neither sorry nor afraid.

Presently, I found I was holding to a spar, which helped me somewhat. And then all of a sudden I was in quiet water, and began to come to myself.

It was the spare yard I had got hold of, and I was amazed to see how far I had traveled from the brig. I hailed her indeed; but it was plain she was already out of cry. She was still holding together; but whether or not they had yet launched the boat, I was too far off and too low down to see.

While I was hailing the brig, I spied a tract of water lying between us, where no great waves came, but which yet boiled white all over, and bristled in the moon with rings and bubbles. Sometimes the whole tract swung to one side, like the tail of a live serpent; sometimes, for a glimpse, it all would disappear and then boil up again. What it was I had no guess, which for the time increased my fear of it; but I now know it must have been the roost or tide race, which carried me away so fast and tumbled me about so cruelly, and at last, as if tired of that play, had flung me and spare yard upon its landward margin.

1. The narrator compares the ship to the captain's wife and child to:

    (A) lament the captain's long separation from his family.
    (B) demonstrate the difficulty the captain has keeping focused on his job.
    (C) predict the captain's future madness.
    (D) show the depth of the connection the captain has to his ship.

The focus of the second paragraph is on how the captain is upset by the condition of his ship. To compare his ship to his wife and child is to show how much he loves the ship and, thus, to emphasize the deep attachment he has to the vessel. So the correct answer is Choice (D).

2. By saying that he "got a blink of the moon" in the fifth paragraph, the narrator most nearly means that:

    (F) he foresaw his own demise.
    (G) he saw the sky as he came up out of the water to get air.
    (H) he was hallucinating as he was drowning.
    (J) a barely perceptible quarter moon hung low in the sky.

The first line of the fifth paragraph describes the narrator's dunking and near drowning. He was bobbing up and down in the water, going under the sea and then coming up for air, at which point he saw the moon. Make sure you answer the question in the context in which you find the statement; don't use your own common sense. And if you picked Choice (J), you chose an answer that provided too many unjustifiable details to be right. The correct answer is Choice (G).

Passage 2 — Social Science

Multinational corporations frequently have difficulty explaining to politicians, human rights groups, and (perhaps most important) their consumer base why they do business with, and even seek closer business ties to, countries whose human rights records are considered very bad by United States standards. The CEOs say that in the business trenches, the issue of human rights must effectively be detached from the wider spectrum of free trade.

Discussion of the uneasy alliance between trade and human rights has trickled down from the boardrooms of large multinational corporations to the consumer on the street who, given the wide variety of products available to him, is eager to show support for human rights by boycotting the products of a company he feels does not do enough to help its overseas workers.

International human rights organizations also are pressuring the multinationals to push for more humane working conditions in other countries and to, in effect, develop a code of business conduct that must be adhered to if the American company is to continue working with the overseas partner.

The President, in drawing up a plan for what he calls the "economic architecture of our times," wants economists, business leaders, and human rights groups to work together to develop a set of principles that the foreign partners of United States corporations will voluntarily embrace. Human rights activists, angry at the unclear and indefinite plans for implementing such rules, charge that their agenda is being given low priority by the State Department. The President strongly denies their charges, arguing that each situation is approached on its merits without prejudice, and hopes that all the groups can work together to develop principles based on empirical research rather than political fiat, emphasizing that the businesses with experience in the field must initiate the process of developing such guidelines. Business leaders, while paying lip service to the concept of these principles, secretly fight against their formal endorsement as they fear such "voluntary" concepts may someday be given the force of law. Few business leaders have forgotten the Sullivan Principles, in which a set of voluntary rules regarding business conduct with South Africa (giving benefits to workers and banning apartheid in the companies that worked with U.S. partners) became legislation.

3. Which of the following best states the central idea of the passage?

   (A) Politicians are quixotic in their assessment of the priorities of the State Department.
   (B) Multinational corporations have little, if any, influence on the domestic policies of their overseas partners.
   (C) Disagreement exists between the desires of human rights activists to improve the working conditions of overseas workers and the practical approach taken by the corporations.
   (D) It is inappropriate to expect foreign corporations to adhere to American standards.

The main idea of the passage is usually stated in the first sentence or two. The first sentence of this passage discusses the difficulties that corporations have in explaining their business ties to politicians, human rights groups, and consumers in certain countries. From this statement, you may infer that those groups disagree with the policies of the corporations. So the correct answer is Choice (C).

TIP

Did you pick Choice (A) just because of the hard word, *quixotic*? It's human nature (we're all so insecure) to think that the hard word we don't know must be the right answer, but it isn't always so. Never choose an answer just because it has a word you can't define unless you're sure that all the answers with words you can define are wrong. *Quixotic* means idealistic, impractical (think of the fictional character Don Quixote tilting at windmills). The President's belief is not the main idea of the passage.

REMEMBER

Just because a statement is (or may be) true doesn't necessarily mean that it's the correct answer to a question. Many of the answer choices to a big-picture question in particular are often true or at least plausible. To answer a main-idea question, pretend that a friend of yours just came up behind you and said, "Hey, what'cha reading there?" Your first response is the main idea: "Oh, I read this passage about how corporations are getting grief from politicians and other groups because they do business with certain countries." Before you look at the answer choices, predict in your own words what the main idea is. You'll be pleasantly surprised how close your prediction is to the correct answer (and you won't be confused by all the other plausible-looking answer choices).

TIP

Choice (D) is a moral value, a judgment call. Who's to say what's appropriate and what's inappropriate? An answer that passes judgment, one that says something is morally right or morally wrong, is almost never the correct answer on the ACT.

4. Which of the following statements about the Sullivan Principles can best be inferred from the passage?

(F) They had a detrimental effect on the profits of those corporations doing business with South Africa.

(G) They represented an improper alliance between political and business groups.

(H) They placed the needs of the foreign workers over those of the domestic workers whose jobs would, therefore, be in jeopardy.

(J) They will have a chilling effect on the future adoption of voluntary guidelines.

Choice (F) is the major trap here. Perhaps you assumed that because the companies seem to dislike the Sullivan Principles, they hurt company profits. However, the passage doesn't say anything about profits. Maybe the companies still made good profits but objected to the Sullivan Principles on principle. The companies just may not have wanted such governmental intervention even if profits didn't decrease. If you picked Choice (F), you read too much into the question and probably didn't read the rest of the answer choices.

In Choice (J), the phrase "chilling effect" means a negative or discouraging effect. Think of something with a chilling effect as leaving you cold. Because few corporations have forgotten the Sullivan Principles, you may infer that these principles will discourage the companies from agreeing to voluntary principles in the future. Thus, the correct answer is (J).

TIP

To get this question correct, you really need to understand the whole passage. If you didn't know what was going on here, you'd be better off just to guess and move on. An inference question usually means you have to read between the lines; you can't just go back to one specific portion of the passage and get the answer quickly.

Passage 3 — Humanities

Many people believe that the existence of lawyers and lawsuits represents a relatively recent phenomenon. The opinion that many hold regarding lawyers, also known as attorneys, is that they are insincere and greedy. Lawyers are often referred to as "ambulance chasers" or by other pejorative expressions.

Despite this negativity, lawyers are also known for their fights for civil rights, due process of law, and equal protection. Lawyers were instrumental in desegregating the institutions in our society and in cleaning up the environment. Most legislators at the local, state, and federal levels of government are lawyers because they generally have a firm understanding of justice and the proper application of statutory and case law.

Lawyers are traditionally articulate public speakers or orators, too. One of the finest legal orators was Marcus Tullius Cicero, who was an intellectually distinguished, politically savvy, and incredibly successful Roman lawyer. Cicero lived from 143–106 B.C. and was one of only a few Roman intellectuals credited with the flowering of Latin literature that largely occurred during the last decades of the Roman Republic.

Cicero's compositions have been compared to the works of Julius Caesar. Their writings have customarily been included in the curriculum wherever Latin is studied. Cicero was a lifelong student of government and philosophy and a practicing politician. He was a successful lawyer whose voluminous speeches, letters, and essays tend to have the same quality that people usually associate with pleading a case. His arguments are well structured, eloquent, and clear. Cicero perfected the complex, balanced, and majestic sentence structure called "periodic," which was imitated by later writers from Plutarch in the Renaissance to Churchill in the 20th century.

5. *Pejorative*, as it appears in the last line of the first paragraph, most nearly means:

    (A) comic.
    (B) dishonest.
    (C) self-serving.
    (D) uncomplimentary.

Get clues for answering this question from the information around the word. The passage classifies "ambulance chaser" as a pejorative expression. In the next sentence, the author uses the phrase "this negativity" to refer to the act of using pejorative statements for attorneys. Therefore, *pejorative* must have a negative connotation. You can eliminate Choice (A) — even though the thought of an overweight attorney running after a screaming ambulance may make you laugh. Plug the remaining choices into the sentence to see which one makes the best substitute for *pejorative*. The obvious answer is *uncomplimentary*. So the correct answer is Choice (D).

If you picked Choice (B) or (C), you were probably thinking of words that describe the way that the author says many people think of attorneys. *Dishonest* is a synonym for *insincere*, and *self-serving* has a meaning that's similar to *greedy*. Trap answers like Choices (B) and (C) are why you must read your answers in the context of the sentence. By doing so, you see that *pejorative* describes the expressions that others give to attorneys, not the attorneys themselves.

6. Which of these, according to the author, is a way that lawyers have positively contributed to society?

    (F) They have fought legislation designed to clean up the environment.
    (G) They have proposed laws to make "ambulance chasing" illegal.
    (H) They have taught public speaking skills to disadvantaged youth.
    (J) They have advocated for the integration of public institutions.

The author covers the positive attributes of lawyers in the second paragraph, which mentions their contributions to cleaning up the environment and promoting integration. The passage doesn't say anything about the legalization of "ambulance chasing" or teaching public speaking, so you can eliminate Choices (G) and (H). Choice (F) is a little tricky if you don't read it carefully. Because Choice (F) says that attorneys have fought rather than promoted cleaning up the environment, it says just the opposite of what the passage states. So Choice (J) is the correct answer.

Passage 4 — Natural Science

Biomes are the major biological divisions of the earth. Biomes are characterized by an area's climate and the particular organisms that live there. The living organisms make up the "biotic" components of the biome, and everything else makes up the "abiotic" components. The density and diversity of a biome's biotic components is called its "carrying capacity." The most important abiotic aspects of a biome are the amount of rainfall it has and how much its temperatures vary. More rain and more stable temperatures mean more organisms can survive. Usually, the wetter a biome is, the less its temperature changes from day to night or from summer to winter. Biomes include deserts, rainforests, forests, savannas, tundras, freshwater environments, and oceans.

Deserts are areas that get less than 10 inches of rain per year. Most deserts are hot (like the Sahara), but some are actually cold (like parts of Antarctica). Therefore, the thing that distinguishes deserts is their extreme dryness. The organisms that live in a desert need to be able to survive drastic temperature swings along with dry conditions, so the desert's carrying capacity is extremely low. Desert animals include reptiles like lizards and snakes and some arachnids like spiders and scorpions.

Freshwater environments and oceans are also biomes. The freshwater biome includes elements like rivers, lakes, and ponds. These areas are affected by temperature swings, the amount of available oxygen, and the speed of water flowing through them. All of these are affected by the larger climate area the freshwater biome is in, which also affects the biotic components. Algae, fish, amphibians, and insects are found in freshwater biomes. Oceans cover about 70 percent of the earth's surface, so they comprise the biggest biome. Temperature swings aren't nearly as wide in the oceans as they are on land, and there's plenty of water to go around. Therefore, the carrying capacity of the oceans is huge. The density and diversity of organisms aren't quite as high as in the tropical rainforest, but the total number of organisms in the oceans is much bigger than all of the terrestrial biomes put together.

7. Which of the following best presents the organization of the passage?

(A) It first provides several terms related to biomes and then provides further illumination of the concepts by describing how they manifest in some biomes.

(B) It starts with general definitions of biotic and abiotic and then provides evidence that not all biomes demonstrate both categories.

(C) It begins with descriptions of several weather events and then shows examples of these events in a variety of biomes.

(D) It divides the earth into several biomes and then provides a thorough description of each of those biomes.

Apply the process of elimination. Look for the wrong elements in the answer choices. Choice (B) is untrue; the passage begins with definitions of biotic and abiotic, but it doesn't talk about biomes that don't contain both categories. The passage mentions weather types but doesn't describe them, so Choice (C) isn't right. The word "thorough" in Choice (D) is a red flag. The first paragraph lists several biomes, but the following paragraphs describe only a few of them, and the descriptions couldn't be classified as thorough. For example, they don't completely list the types of organisms that live in oceans.

The first paragraph provides general definitions of biomes, biotic, abiotic, and carrying capacity. The last two paragraphs provide more specific descriptions of the biotic and abiotic qualities of several biomes and how these qualities affect carrying capacity. Choice (A) is the best answer.

REMEMBER

It's usually easier to spot wrong answers than right ones, so focus on finding what's wrong with answers. Then the correct choice will arise above the others.

8. According to the passage, all of these elements affect the quality of a freshwater environment EXCEPT:

(F) oxygen levels.

(G) swings in temperature.

(H) the larger climate in which it exists.

(J) the policies of the country in which it exists.

The answer to this exception question comes straight from the passage. The third paragraph says that freshwater biomes are affected by temperature swings, the amount of available oxygen, and the speed of water flowing through them, so you can eliminate Choices (F), (G), and (H). The passage doesn't cover issues that are unrelated to the natural environment, so the correct answer is Choice (J).

TIP

The best way to answer exception questions is to turn the wording around a bit. For example, you can approach this question by asking yourself to choose the answer that states something that *doesn't* affect the quality of a freshwater environment.

5
Studying Brain Defects in Laboratory Rats: The (Optional) Science Test

IN THIS PART...

Get familiar with the types of passages you'll see on the optional ACT Science Test — what they look like, how to approach them, and when to ignore information in them altogether.

Discover the approach to the most common question types and practice that approach on a sample passage with a bunch of representative questions.

> **IN THIS CHAPTER**
> » Eliminating brain strain by figuring out what you do and don't need to know
> » Getting comfortable with data-interpretation and experimental procedure
> » Identifying the different types of questions as well as the traps built into them

Chapter 15
From Frankenstein to Einstein: Excelling on the Optional Science Test

Return your brain to the full upright and locked position. You don't have to use it as much as you may fear for the ACT Science Test. So relax, unclench your hands, and take a few deep breaths. You are not, repeat *not*, expected to be able to remember the entire periodic table or to know the difference between the substantia nigra and a Lorentz transformation. After all, your grades in science classes appear on your transcript for the admissions officers to read if they really want to assess your science knowledge. The point of the optional Science Test is to demonstrate that you have an important collegiate skill: the ability to approach novel information, sort it out, and draw conclusions from it. In other words, you don't have to know what a scientist knows, but you do need to be able to think as a scientist thinks.

Repeat: The Science Test is optional. Your science score appears on your ACT score report along with a separate STEM score (the average of your math and science scores), but the Science Test score isn't calculated in your ACT composite. However, some colleges may require or highly recommend taking it, especially if you're considering a STEM (science, technology, engineering, math) path. Therefore, it's probably a good idea to include the Science Test in at least one test day to keep your options open. Give it a try! It's not as scary as it looks.

REMEMBER

The fastest way to improve your science score is by repeating this mantra to yourself as you make your way through the test: Science questions are easier than they seem; almost everything I need to know to answer them is right in front of me.

Examining the Science Test's Format

The Science Test consists of 40 questions that are based on seven passages (five or six questions per passage). The passages cover all areas of science, and at least one will draw from engineering or technology. You have 40 minutes to answer the 40 questions, which means you have 5 or 6 minutes to spend per passage.

To save time and decrease distractions, *don't read the passage before you view the questions.* Jump into the questions right away. Most of the information you need comes right out of the charts and graphs (we cover how to evaluate those in the section "Analyzing Tables, Graphs, and Diagrams" later in this chapter), and the details in the paragraphs can be more confusing than enlightening. Get direction on where to look for the answers from the questions and answer choices. Only a few questions actually require you to do much reading from the text. You'll likely have to do some reading for questions based on passages with significantly more text than charts and graphs and for questions that ask you about experimental procedures.

Plan on allotting yourself 1 minute per question. Some of the questions will be so easy that you'll answer them in a heartbeat and build up a reservoir of time, which you can then spend on the harder questions. But, of course, some of the questions may seem so impossible that you'll want to sue your brain for non-support. We show you how to approach these brain-busters, but if you can't answer a question within a minute, take a guess and move on. Mark it because you may have a chance to tackle it later.

Classifying Passage Format

Although the passages tend to increase in difficulty as you move through the section, the change may not be super obvious. The questions may become a bit more challenging as you move through each individual passage, so the first question or two in a passage may be more easily and quickly answered than the last two. If you get hung up on the last question of a passage, mark your best guess and move on to the easier questions in the next passage.

The following sections discuss the three basic types of science passages that cover a variety of science topics, including:

> » **Data representation:** Of the six passages in a typical science test, two or three are this type.
>
> » **Research summaries:** Two or three are research summaries.
>
> » **Conflicting viewpoints:** One is this type.

Although these passage formats present information in slightly different ways, the general approach is the same regardless of the passage type:

> » Read through the answer choices before you read the questions to determine the question type and where to focus.
>
> » Match information in the questions and answers to corresponding information in the passage.

Data-representation passages

Passages that represent data tend to emphasize tables and graphs. They usually begin with a short paragraph that introduces the passage topic and defines terms, followed by one or more tables, graphs, or diagrams that are chock-full of result data. For these passages, you focus primarily on reading and evaluating the data in the tables and graphs (see the section "Analyzing Tables, Graphs, and Diagrams" later in this chapter) and only read the text if you need clarification of terms. Here's an example of a data-representation passage:

Using different quantities of microshels, scientists studied the prehistorical bird species known as *Braisia idioticus* to discover the effect that variations in paraloxin had on the rate in rics per second of samanity in the species as a whole. The results are summarized in Table 15-1:

TABLE 15-1: Effect of Paraloxin Variation on Samanity Rate in *Braisia Idioticus*

Paraloxin (microshels)	Samanity Rate (rics/sec)
0	14
1	18
2	23
3	25
4	27
5	89
6	90
7	34
8	29
9	24

Don't worry if you've never heard of paraloxin or samanity rate; we made them up! We examine how to handle this sample passage in the section "Considering Question Types" later in this chapter.

Research summaries

Research-summary passages usually also include one or more tables and/or diagrams, so they require the same data-interpretation skills. These passages include two or three separate experiments or studies to test one scientific topic. Each experiment or study has its own introductory text that conveys its specific setup. Make sure you focus on these paragraphs because these passages often contain questions that examine the relationship between two studies and compare and contrast their experimental design. We cover how to handle study comparison questions in the section, "Considering Question Types" later in this chapter. Here is an example of a simple research summary:

Researchers tested the travel distance of a rubber ball based on launch angle θ and launch velocity V. They designed a catapult that could be adjusted to propel the rubber ball at various angles and at various speeds, as shown in Figure 1. They then used the apparatus to conduct two experiments.

Experiment 1

The researchers set the catapult to propel the rubber ball at a constant velocity of 15 m/s and then launched it at several angle measures. For each launch, they measured the distance between the launching point of the catapult and the point at which the rubber ball landed on the ground. They recorded these distances in Figure 2 in meters (m).

Experiment 2

The researchers then set on the catapult and varied the velocity in m/s at which they launched the same rubber ball. They again measured the distance from the catapult to the point at which the rubber ball landed on the ground for each launch and recorded the results in Figure 3.

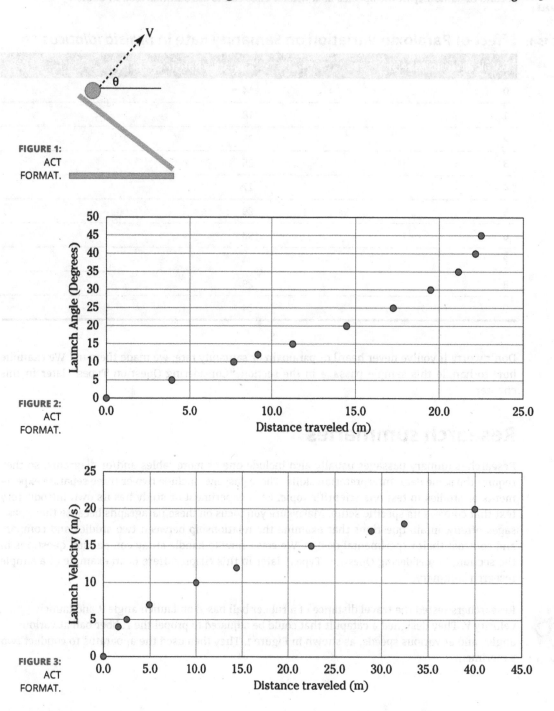

FIGURE 1: ACT FORMAT.

FIGURE 2: ACT FORMAT.

FIGURE 3: ACT FORMAT.

190 PART 5 Studying Brain Defects in Laboratory Rats: The (Optional) Science Test

Conflicting viewpoints

Each Science Test has one conflicting-viewpoints passage. The conflicting-viewpoints passage is easy to recognize because it usually begins with an introduction, followed by two, three, four, or more major portions of text with headings like "Student 1," "Student 2," and "Student 3" or "Scientist 1" and "Scientist 2." These headings designate different ways of interpreting the information presented in the introduction. Most frequently, the opinions come from inexperienced students and, therefore, may contain information that contradicts known scientific truths.

TIP

Although some conflicting-viewpoints passages may contain as many charts and graphs as the other two passage types, these passages are usually primarily text-based, and all the data is contained with the paragraphs.

Here is a plan of attack for approaching the traditional text-based conflicting-viewpoints passage.

1. **Jump right into answering the questions.**

   That way you only read those portions of the passage you need to answer each question.

2. **If you absolutely can't resist the temptation to read the passage before you answer the questions, don't spend more than about 30 seconds on your skimming.**

   Just note the highlights:

   - **Skim the introduction.** Glance long enough to determine what phenomenon the viewpoints are considering. Maybe several students discuss whether objects can travel faster than the speed of light, or a couple of scientists examine data to determine whether other planets in the solar system could support life.

   - **Read the first and maybe the last sentence of each viewpoint to get a rough idea of the students' main points and how they are the same and different.** These main ideas express the students' positions on the situation discussed in the passage's introduction. Read just enough to get the gist and note how the opinions are organized.

3. **Use clues from the questions and answer choices to direct you to the portions of the passage where you'll likely find the answers.**

   - **If the first question or so asks for an answer "according to the passage," search first in the introductory information that precedes the viewpoints.** The answers to these questions often involve the background information and aren't particular to any one opinion.

   - **Use the answers to help you focus.** Key words in the answers can direct you to the opinions that hold the answer. The ACT often organizes the opinions so that the same type of information appears in the same sentence for each opinion. So, if Student 1 describes in the first sentence what happens to Chemical 1 when it reacts with iron, Student 2's first sentence likely contains an opinion on the same reaction.

   - **Focus on data points in the questions and opinions.** If a question asks what happens when liquid reaches 102 degrees, search for degree information in the opinion paragraphs.

   - **If the question asks what's true for Scientist 1, concentrate on the section containing Scientist 1's viewpoint and find what's true for Scientist 2 in the Scientist 2 portion.** Doing so may seem obvious, but in the heat of the test moment, you may lose focus. When searching for the correct answer, concentrate primarily on the opinion's main idea — the stuff in the first and maybe last sentence.

TIP Don't get involved in the messy and often confusing middle-of-the-paragraph details unless a question makes you. When a question asks about a particular detail, such as the effect of gamma rays on man-in-the-moon marigolds, search both viewpoints specifically for language that relates to gamma rays or marigolds.

REMEMBER When you're dealing with a conflicting-viewpoints passage, your job is to follow the logic of each viewpoint. Don't try to decide which viewpoint is correct. No one cares — not the ACT, not the college admissions office, and certainly not you. In fact, the ACT sometimes presents a viewpoint that's clearly false. For example, one student may claim that evolution takes place as a result of the inheritance of *acquired* characteristics. You know that this viewpoint is wrong. Think about it: If you gnaw your fingernails down to the bone worrying about the ACT, it doesn't follow that someday your children will be born with no fingernails! Again, worry only about the logic of the viewpoint, not whether it's right or wrong.

Here is an example of a simple passage with conflicting viewpoints:

EXAMPLE A teacher presented three students with four test tubes containing four liquids: two clear and two caramel-colored. She explained that Liquid 1 was tap water, Liquid 2 was distilled water, Liquid 3 was coffee brewed with Liquid 1, and Liquid 4 was coffee brewed with Liquid 2. She then provided the students with four pH strips with results for the four liquids. Strip A indicated a pH of 7, Strip B indicated a pH of 6.5, Strip C indicated a pH of 4.9, and Strip D indicated a pH of 5.1. She asked each student to determine which pH result corresponded to each liquid and provide an explanation.

Student 1

Because Liquid 2 is distilled water, it has a neutral pH and must be associated with Strip A. Coffee is more acidic than water, so Liquid 3 and Liquid 4 must be associated with the strips with the lowest pH readings. Because Liquid 1 has a lower pH than Liquid 2, it must contain fewer bicarbonates than Liquid 2 and, therefore, must be more acidic than distilled water but not as acidic as coffee, so its pH must be the one indicated in Strip B. Therefore, Liquid 3 has to be more acidic than Liquid 4 because it was mixed with the more acidic water. Liquid 3 is associated with Strip C, and Liquid 4 is associated with Strip D.

Student 2

Student 2 is correct about the pH of distilled water, but because Liquid 1 has a lower pH than Liquid 2, it must contain more bicarbonates than Liquid 2. The combination of liquids and corresponding strips is as follows: Liquid 1 to Strip B, Liquid 2 to Strip A, Liquid 3 to Strip C, and Liquid 4 to Strip D.

Student 3

Because Liquid 2 is distilled water, it has a low pH and must be associated with Strip C. Coffee is more acidic than water, so Liquid 3 and Liquid 4 must be associated with the strips with the highest pH readings. Because Liquid 1 has a higher pH than Liquid 2, it must contain fewer bicarbonates than Liquid 2 and therefore, must be more acidic than distilled water but not as acidic as coffee, so its pH must be the one indicated in Strip D. Liquid 3 is associated with Strip B, and Liquid 4 is associated with Strip A.

Analyzing Tables, Graphs, and Diagrams

Most passages test your ability to read and extract information from tables, graphs, or diagrams. In fact, data analysis is a primary assessment of the Science Test. We start with general guidelines for analyzing data:

TIP

>> **Examine the table, diagram, or graph as a whole.** Identify what the graphic is displaying (for example, drug dosages, reaction times, kinetic energy, or astronomical distances). You may need to skim the text immediately preceding the table or figure to get a full understanding of what's going on.

>> **Pay attention to how the table or figure is labeled.**

>> **Note the units of measurement.** Tables and figures always present units of measurement very clearly. The axes on graphs are usually labeled, legends typically accompany diagrams, and column and row headings usually include the units.

>> **Look for trends in the data, noting any significant shifts.** The ACT Science Test frequently tests how data is related. Generally, a table or graph provides you with a clear picture of whether data is related directly, inversely, or not at all.

- **Direct or positive correlation:** When two pieces of data increase at the same time or decrease at the same time, they are related directly.

- **Inverse or negative correlation:** When one piece of data increases at the same time another decreases or decreases at the same time another increases, those data points have an inverse relationship.

- **No correlation:** Data have no relationship or correlation when they act independently of one another.

>> **Observe corresponding data across multiple tables and figures in the passage.** Sometimes science questions require you to use data from one graph or table to draw conclusions about a data piece on another table or graph. Look for matching wording in the labels (column headings in tables and axis labels in graphs) to find where data from different tables and graphs may intersect or overlap.

Tackling tables

Tables in passages may be simple (like Table 15-1) or complex with multiple columns and subcolumns. To examine even the most complex table most efficiently, focus on the column headings. As you read through the questions and their answer options, locate key words and terms that match the table's column designations. For example, if a question associated with Table 15-1 referenced microshels, you likely need to examine the first column of the table to answer the question.

To determine relationships in data provided in tables, isolate the columns that display the data in question and observe what happens to the data in one column as the other increases or decreases. For example, in Table 15-1, you see that as paraloxin increases, samanity rate gradually increases until paraloxin reaches 4 microshels. Then it hits a sharp peak when paraloxin rises to 5 and 6 microshels and then falls to levels comparable to those obtained when paraloxin was lower.

CHAPTER 15 **From Frankenstein to Einstein: Excelling on the Optional Science Test** 193

Grappling with graphs

Graphs on the ACT mostly contain lines or bars. They may be simple, displaying just two variables on the *x* and *y* axes, or they may be more complex, displaying multiple lines or bars or containing more than one variable on the vertical axes. More complex graphs are usually accompanied by a key. Figure 15-1 is a simple graph displaying plant height in *cm* as it relates to an amount of added growth factor in *mg*.

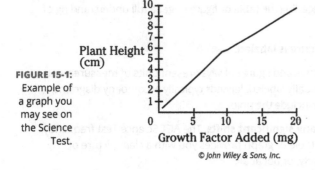

FIGURE 15-1: Example of a graph you may see on the Science Test.

© John Wiley & Sons, Inc.

To keep the data straight, concentrate on the labels:

» The horizontal and vertical axis designations and their increments

» The wording in the keys, if provided

» Any explanatory details offered at the bottom of the graph

Avoid making assumptions about the data. Read carefully, noting, for instance, whether the numbers on the vertical axis are expressed as totals or averages, in kilograms or grams, or whether the time designation on the horizontal axis is in days, hours, minutes, or seconds.

To evaluate data relationships on graphs, follow the trends usually indicated by lines or bars. When the value of one variable moves along a graph in the same direction as the value of another variable, those variables have a direct relationship, and the line on the graph has a positive slope. In the sample graph in Figure 15-1, plant height and the amount of growth factor added have a positive correlation; as one increases, the other increases also, and the line has a general positive slope. A positive correlation can also apply to decreasing values; as one decreases, the other variable also decreases. Variables with an inverse relationship (when one increases as the other decreases and vice versa) create a line with negative slope.

Dissecting diagrams

Passages may also contain pictures in addition to tables and graphs. These diagrams usually display a visual representation of an element of the experiment's setup. You likely won't need to refer to these pictures too often. In fact, you can ignore them when answering most science questions. For example, you likely don't need the picture of the catapult in the sample research summary (see the section "Research summaries" earlier in the chapter) to understand the overall experiment. Every now and again, however, diagrams are integral to understanding how an experiment is constructed and, therefore, successfully answering questions about it. To see what we mean, check out this introduction to a particular experiment and its accompanying diagram.

EXAMPLE

A student constructs a circuit using a battery, switches, resistors, and an electric motor. The current flows from the battery through one of the switches when the switch is closed. The current then proceeds through the resistor to the motor. See Figure 1.

To answer questions about this experiment, you need to examine the diagram to find out that the circuit involves four switches and five resistors and that the flow moves from the bottom right up through the switches and resistors to the motor at the bottom left. This picture provides you with a better understanding of how the student constructed the circuit than the explanatory paragraph alone does.

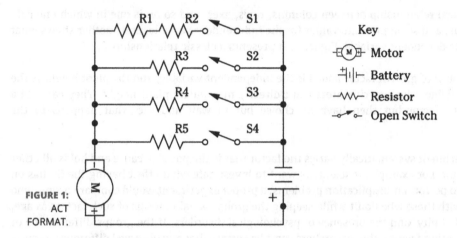

FIGURE 1: ACT FORMAT.

Examining Experimental Procedures

In addition to having a general understanding of how to analyze a passage's tables and figures, you also need to know a little about experimental procedures to excel in the science questions. Here are the basics:

REMEMBER

» **Purpose of the study:** Every experiment has a purpose. You may be very familiar with identifying the goal of the project or the purpose of the study, as you have probably done so on every lab write-up you've turned in since kindergarten. The ACT is kind enough to do your work for you by stating or implying the purpose in the introductory paragraph.

The ACT expects you to understand some key principles of why the researchers created the experiment in the first place. But don't worry! Identifying the purpose of the experiment takes only a few seconds. Usually, the purpose is to examine what effect x has on y. You can usually pick up on the purpose as you answer the questions and evaluate the charts.

» **Experimental design:** The passage tells you how the researchers have set up and controlled the experiment or study and provides information such as what apparatus they've used and which variables they've held constant.

» **Results:** Ultimately, an experiment or study needs to convey the collected data. These results are usually presented in a table or graph.

REMEMBER

You don't have time to analyze procedures in depth. Most of what you pick up about purpose and design results from answering the questions. Don't try to understand the research before you start examining the questions.

Independent and dependent variables

The Science Test assumes you know enough about experimental setup to distinguish independent variables and dependent variables.

An *independent variable* is the factor that the experimenter can change to a specific value, such as the amount of water added to a plant's soil. The *dependent variable* is the factor that isn't under the experimenter's direct control, such as the amount of energy released. In other words, the dependent variable is dependent on the independent variable.

The most typical relationship between columns, rows, axes, and so on is one in which one column, row, axis, and so on presents values for the independent variable, and another shows what happens to the dependent variable. Figure 15-1 presents a classic relationship.

Here, the amount of growth factor added is the independent variable, and the plant height is the dependent variable. The experimenters can't directly manipulate plant height. They can add a certain growth factor but then have no choice but to wait and see what happens to the plant height.

A proper experiment systematically varies the factor that is the possible cause and holds all other factors constant. For example, if scientists want to investigate what effect having the flu has on one's ability to perform multiplication problems, a proper experiment would compare people who have the flu with those who don't while keeping the groups equal in terms of such factors as age, mathematical ability, and the presence of psychological disorders. If the groups differ in one or more of these other factors, the researchers can't be certain that any observed difference in multiplication performance was a result of the flu. For instance, what would you think if the nonflu group, which consisted of 12-year-olds, did better on multiplication than the flu group, which consisted of 8-year-olds? You couldn't be certain whether age or the flu virus accounted for the difference.

The ability to distinguish the independent variable from the dependent variable is essential for answering many procedure questions. You may even get a question directly asking about this distinction.

The control

Most proper experiments have a *control*. Essentially, the control is an experimental element that is kept constant throughout the experiment to allow experimenters to compare results to what happens when the independent variable isn't applied. For example, the experimenters in the plant growth factor study, whose results are conveyed in Figure 15-1, would likely prepare a plant with no added growth factor to determine what happens to plant height in the absence of growth factor.

ACT science questions may ask you to come up with the experiment's control. Identify the independent variable and then find the elements of the experiment that test what occurs in the absence of that variable.

Defective experimental designs, in which experimenters don't include proper controls, produce limited results. By their very nature, some studies can't adhere to an ideal experimental design. For example, if a scientist suspected that 2-year-olds who had been vaccinated for measles got more colds than 2-year-olds who hadn't been vaccinated, a proper design would be to give one group the vaccine and to withhold it from another group. However, the experimenters can't just keep one group of kids unvaccinated (mothers tend to get cranky when you make their kids sick "in the best interests of science"). Instead, the experimenters would have to try to collect data on how frequently the children came down with colds before they were immunized (children aren't immunized against measles until they're at least 1 year old) and perhaps collect data about children who haven't been vaccinated from kids whose parents have voluntarily kept them from vaccinations because of religious beliefs or allergies.

Immersing Yourself in Answer Choices

The ACT science questions may include extraneous information designed to distract you and make you overthink the question. The trick is to focus on one bit of the question at a time rather than the whole enchilada. And one of the best ways to focus your approach is to consider the answer options.

The answer choices may give you more clues than the actual questions. The answers show you what you need to figure out and where to find it in the passage, so always read through the answers before you read the question. That way, you read only the parts of the question that are necessary to eliminate wrong answers. Usually, two answers are obviously incorrect. Look for those first so you can concentrate on the difference between the remaining two answers. Sometimes you can eliminate three answers easily without reading the questions at all.

Take a look at this somewhat silly sample question for a passage regarding plant experiments to see what we mean:

EXAMPLE

A new study is conducted under the same conditions as the original study on dandelion plants and Venus Flytrap plants, except that scientists applied Chemical B to the Venus Flytrap plants for six weeks instead of three weeks. Based on the original study data, is it likely that the Venus Flytrap plants in the new study will grow human hair after six weeks?

(A) Yes, because in the original study, dandelion plants exposed to Chemical B for more than three weeks showed evidence of human hair growth.

(B) Yes, because in the original study, Venus Flytrap plants exposed to Chemical B for more than three weeks showed evidence of human hair growth.

(C) No, because in the original study, dandelion plants exposed to Chemical B for more than three weeks showed no evidence after six weeks of human hair growth.

(D) No, because in the original study, Venus Flytrap plants exposed to Chemical B for more than three weeks showed no evidence of human hair growth.

Don't freak out because you're unfamiliar with the chemical components of Chemical B or because you failed the botany section of AP Biology. Knowing specifics about plants isn't required to answer an ACT science question. Before you begin to tear out your own hair, leap right into the answer choices. Notice the answers reveal that you have to evaluate only two pieces of data in the original study:

» Whether the original study shows that dandelion plants exposed to Chemical B for more than three weeks grew hair.

» Whether the original study shows that Venus Flytrap plants exposed to Chemical B for more than three weeks grew hair.

CHAPTER 15 **From Frankenstein to Einstein: Excelling on the Optional Science Test** 197

> ### WHY YOU SHOULD SAY "YES" TO *YES, YES, NO, NO* QUESTIONS
>
> If you're like most ACT test-takers, you may freak out a little when you see answers in what we call the *yes, yes, no, no* format. Don't! The groups of answer choices with two answers that begin alike and another two that begin alike may seem long and detailed, but they're usually some of the easiest science questions to answer correctly.
>
> Here's why: For two of the choices, the second part of the answer will often blatantly contradict information in the graphs and charts. Based on these falsehoods, you can quickly narrow your choices to just two. Plus, these answers usually point you to the one or two concepts you need to focus on to answer the questions. So not only do you have a 50 percent chance of answering the question right, you also know just what you need to consider when selecting the better of the two remaining options.
>
> The *yes, yes, no, no* format applies to any group of answer choices that have two answers start one way and two start with another (usually opposite) word. So you may see *even, even, odd, odd* questions, *cloudy, cloudy, clear, clear* questions, or perhaps even *clippity, clippity, clop, clop* questions for those rare passages that deal with equestrian science! After you realize how easy it is to answer questions presented in this format, you can be happy knowing that the same format appears in the English Test, too.

Eliminate answer choices that aren't true. If the original study showed no hair growth in dandelion plants after three weeks, you can cross out Choice (A) because it isn't true based on the data in the passage. If the original study showed hair growth in Venus Flytrap plants after three weeks, Choice (D) must be wrong because the data doesn't support it. Now the question is much easier. The answer has to be either Choice (B) or (C) and because Choice (C) deals with what didn't happen to dandelions instead of what did happen to Venus Flytraps, Choice (B) is likely the right answer.

REMEMBER

Follow the path of least resistance. Don't make the questions harder than they are. For more on answering questions with answers formatted like this one, see the nearby sidebar.

Considering Question Types

Ultimately, your Science Test score is based on the number of questions you answer correctly. In this section, we discuss the types of questions you can expect and how to answer them.

You may find yourself lamenting one of the following as you become embroiled in a science question:

» If only I had a calculator . . .

» If only I had paid more attention in biology, physics, chemistry, earth science, and so on . . .

When you entertain either one of these thoughts, you're overthinking the question. Relax and remind yourself to look for the obvious answer. The ACT can't test super-specific science knowledge because not all high school students follow the same science curriculum. Though several questions in each Science Test may check your knowledge of basic science concepts and vocabulary that aren't included in the passage content, this information is usually limited to foundational concepts you should have learned in middle school. We provide a set of flashcards in the online content for you to use to brush up on commonly tested science concepts and terms.

Science Test questions come in two general categories:

> » **Those that ask for results:** These questions ask you to interpret the results of a study or series of studies. For these, you focus strictly on reading data from charts and graphs, and you read text only when you need to define the information contained in the tables and figures.
>
> » **Those that ask about experimental procedures:** The second category of questions may ask you for the control, independent variable, or steps of an experiment or experiments. These questions require you to focus on the text rather than the charts and graphs. Look for the answers in the set-up paragraphs, even if the questions reference a particular figure.

The following sections take a closer look at these two categories and provide you with some examples.

Questions about results

Results questions appear in data-representation passages and research summaries and some conflicting-viewpoints passages that contain tables or graphs. The easiest way to spot results questions is to look for numbers in your answer choices, but other question formats test your ability to evaluate tables and graphs, too. The following sample questions show several ways the ACT may do that.

When you encounter a data-representation passage on the test, we suggest that you use the following approach to get through it quickly and painlessly:

1. **Ignore the passage at first and jump right to the first question.**

    No use wasting precious time reading or reviewing the passage details. There's plenty of time for careful examination of the passage as you answer the questions.

2. **Examine the question for clues to where in the passage you'll find the answer.**

    Sometimes the clues will be obvious: "According to Table 1, when is samanity rate greater?" Other times, you'll know which table or graph to check based on the specific data referenced in the question. For instance, if you encounter a question that asks for the relationship between microshels and ric/sec, you know that Table 15-1 is your chart.

3. **Read the table and chart carefully (see the section "Analyzing Tables, Graphs, and Diagrams" earlier in the chapter).**

Reading data

Many results questions simply require you to carefully read tables and graphs.

EXAMPLE

According to the information in Figure 15-1, what was the plant height when 5 mg of plant growth factor was applied?

(A) 1 cm

(B) 3 cm

(C) 7 cm

(D) 10 cm

Find 5 mg along the horizontal axis, and draw a vertical line at the 5 mg mark parallel to the y-axis. Note where the line you've drawn intersects the data on the graph. Check your answer options. The intersection point obviously isn't as high as 7 or 10 cm, so Choice (C) and (D) are

CHAPTER 15 From Frankenstein to Einstein: Excelling on the Optional Science Test   199 wrong. The point is closer to 3 cm than 1 cm, so the answer is Choice (B). Notice that you don't have to know anything about plants. You just have to look at what's in front of you.

EXAMPLE

According to the information in Figure 15-1, what range of added growth factor in mg resulted in the greatest change in plant height in cm?

(A) between 1 mg and 10 mg

(B) between 10 mg and 11 mg

(C) between 11 mg and 15 mg

(D) between 15 cm and 20 mg

Examine the data line on the graph. The line is steeper before plant height reaches about 6 cm, which corresponds to about 10 mg of growth factor. After that, the line's slope flattens a bit. Eliminate any answers that suggest that the greatest rate of height change occurs at a level of added growth factor of 10 mg. Choice (A) is the best answer.

EXAMPLE

According to the information in Table 15-1, as paraloxin in microshels increased, samanity rate:

(A) increased only

(B) decreased only

(C) increased then decreased

(D) decreased then increased

What? You don't know what paraloxin, samanity, rics, or microshels are? You've never heard of the ferocious flying *Braisia idioticus*? We're not surprised, considering that we just made them up. We're babbling here to make the point that you can get an idea of what the passage is discussing *without* having a clue about what all the terms mean. As you read the preceding table, say to yourself, "When this thing called paraloxin is changed, samanity rate, whatever it is, may also change. I need to take a closer look at the data to see what happens. The weird units simply measure paraloxin and samanity rate."

Check the column for Paraloxin. The data increases as you move from the top of the column to the bottom. As you move down the column for samanity rate, the numbers increase, so eliminate Choices (B) and (D). Don't stop, though. As Paraloxin increases from 6 to 9 microshels, the number for samanity rate goes down. Choice (C) is the best answer.

Use the example passage from the section "Research summaries" earlier in this chapter to answer the next two questions. The first one is an example of a question that displays answers in columns, and the second shows you that analyzing data in tables and graphs can help you eliminate more complicated answer choices, too.

Which of the following combinations of launch angle and launch velocity resulted in the greatest distance traveled?

EXAMPLE

	Angle in degrees	Velocity (m/s)
(A)	5	5
(B)	45	10
(C)	5	20
(D)	45	20

200 PART 5 Studying Brain Defects in Laboratory Rats: The (Optional) Science Test

Check the answer options and consider each column one at a time. The options for the first left column are 5 degrees and 45 degrees. Angle launch information is in Figure 2, and the question asks for the greatest distance, so you can eliminate Choices (A) and (C) because a 5-degree launch angle results in a shorter distance than a 45-degree launch angle does. You can also eliminate a velocity of 5 from consideration because Choice (A) is out. The remaining velocity choices in the right column are 10 and 20. Figure 3 indicates that a high-velocity results in a longer distance, so Choice (D) is correct.

According to the results of Experiment 1 in the catapult study, does a wider launch angle increase or decrease the distance the rubber ball traveled?

EXAMPLE

(A) Increase, because distance traveled (m) at 15 degrees was longer than distance traveled at 30 degrees

(B) Increase, because distance traveled (m) at 15 degrees was shorter than distance traveled at 30 degrees

(C) Decrease, because distance traveled (m) at 15 degrees was longer than distance traveled at 30 degrees

(D) Decrease, because distance traveled (m) at 15 degrees was shorter than distance traveled at 30 degrees

Often, you can eliminate at least two answers in these "yes, yes, no, no" question formats before you even read the question. Read the explanation in each answer choice and eliminate answers that contradict the data. To determine what happens to distance as a result of angle width, examine Figure 2 in the passage because it records the launch angle data.

The distance traveled at 15 degrees was a little more than 10 meters, and the distance the ball traveled at 30 degrees was about 20 meters. The explanations in Choices (A) and (C) contradict the data in Figure 2, so eliminate them. At this point, you can check the question to see whether the correct answer is "increase" or "decrease" based on the fact that a 30-degree angle resulted in a longer distance than the 15-degree angle. Because a 30-degree angle is wider than a 15-degree angle, the answer must be Choice (B).

Extending data through intrapolation and extrapolation

What if a question asks you about a point or value that isn't actually plotted (or given) on the graph or table? You can still answer the question. You *interpolate* by looking at the two closest values; in plain English, you just insert an intermediate term by estimating.

According to Table 15-1, the samanity rate when Paraloxin is 1.5 is most likely:

EXAMPLE

(A) less than 18 rics/sec.

(B) between 18 and 23 rics/sec.

(C) between 23 and 27 rics/sec.

(D) greater than 27 rics/sec.

Draw a horizontal line between 1 and 2 microshels of Paraloxin. Given that the samanity rates increase in this area of the table and because the samanity rate is 18 when Paraloxin is 1 and 23 when Paraloxin is 2, the samanity rate when paraloxin is 1.5 is probably between 18 and 23. Choice (B) is the correct answer. In addition to interpolation, you may have to deal with *extrapolation*. As the *extra* in its name implies, extrapolation asks you to come up with a value that's beyond the range depicted in the table or graph.

CHAPTER 15 From Frankenstein to Einstein: Excelling on the Optional Science Test   201

Suppose the researchers added a growth factor of 25 mg to a plant tested in the experiments whose data is reflected Figure 15-1. The plant height in cm for this plant will be closest to:

(A) 8 cm

(B) 10 cm

(C) 12 cm

(D) 15 cm

In the plant growth graph shown in Figure 15-1, you probably safely predict that the straight upward line will continue at a constant rate for a while as growth factor moves past 20 mg, the last number presented in the horizontal axis. Therefore, you can safely eliminate answers that are equal to or less than 10 mg. Choices (A) and (B) are wrong. Height increased 2 mg when the level of growth factor increased from 15 mg to 20 mg, so it's reasonable to extrapolate that plant height will increase another 2 cm when growth factor is increased another 5 mg. Even when the plant height increased at a higher rate for lesser growth factor amounts, the rate was never as high as 5 cm over a 5 mg increase in growth factor, so Choice (D) is justified. Choice (C) is the correct answer.

Another way the ACT may test your ability to extrapolate is by asking you how the results of one study may have an effect on another study. When you come up against a question like the next example that presents you with a new set of results from a different but related experiment, your job is to determine how these new results fit into what you already know.

Suppose the researchers in the catapult experiment in the section "Research summaries" earlier in this chapter conduct a third experiment in which they repeat Experiment 2 with a 30-degree launch angle. Compared to the rubber ball in Experiment 2, the rubber ball in Experiment 3 most likely traveled:

(A) a lesser height at each velocity tested

(B) a lesser distance at each velocity tested

(C) the same distance at each velocity tested

(D) a greater distance at each velocity tested

Experiment 2 was originally carried out at a 45-degree launch angle. You know from Experiment 1 that decreasing the launch angle decreases the distance traveled. From this information, you can logically deduce that the distance traveled will be less for each velocity tested. Choice (B) is the correct answer.

Questions that begin with "suppose" and answer options that have you choose among "less than a certain value," "between two values," "two other values," and "greater than a certain value" usually signal a question that asks you to extrapolate.

Questions about procedure

You can spot a procedure question because it asks about information that sets up or happens during the experiment rather than about what happened as a result of an experiment. Although you'll find some procedure questions in data-representation passages, they appear most often in research summaries. These questions can cover a variety of elements of experiment design.

You don't have time to analyze procedures in depth. Most of what you pick up about purpose and design results from answering the questions. Don't try to understand the research before you start examining the questions.

The questions test your ability to follow the logic of the experimental design itself. Why or how was the experiment designed? What was the purpose of choosing one variable or one control?

Experiment-design questions are some of the few question types for which you may need to read the text portion of a science passage. Usually, you find the answers to these questions in the introductory paragraph for each experiment. Often experiments build on each other, so the foundational setup for Experiment 3 may be in the introduction to Experiment 1. Read carefully to be sure you're setting up the right experiment.

Distinguishing between dependent and independent variables and identifying the control

The Science Test frequently tests your ability to identify the components of an experiment. Consider these two examples:

Which of the following is the dependent variable in Experiment 1 in the catapult passage introduced in the section "Research summaries" earlier in this chapter?

(A) Distance traveled

(B) Launch angle

(C) Velocity

(D) Catapult design

The dependent variable is the value that changes based on the independent variables set up by the researchers. The researchers control the velocity and launch angle, so they're independent variables instead of dependent variables. Choices (B) and (C) are wrong. Catapult design doesn't vary, so it's neither an independent nor a dependent variable. Choice (D) is wrong. The dependent variable (the variable being measured) was the distance traveled by the tennis ball. Choice (A) is the best answer. For more on the difference between independent and dependent variables, see the section "Independent and dependent variables" earlier in the chapter.

Students test the boiling points of three chemical substances when they are mixed with a solution. The students add the solution to each of four test tubes. They then add Chemical A to Tube 1, Chemical B to Tube 2, and Chemical C to Tube 3. The students then heat each tube and record the boiling point for each liquid in the test tubes. Which of the test tubes serves as the experimental control?

(A) Tube 1

(B) Tube 2

(C) Tube 3

(D) Tube 4

The way to identify the control is to note what the procedure description doesn't say. The students use four test tubes but only add chemicals to three of them. The tube without the chemical must be the control to determine the boiling point of the solution without the addition of one of the chemicals. Choice (D) is the answer. For more on the experiment control, see the section "The control" earlier in this chapter.

Comparing studies

Passages with more than one study may have a question that asks you to compare the setup of each. Save time on these questions by reading the setup for the second experiment. It's usually contained in the paragraph right before the results data (graph or table). That paragraph almost always tells you how the second experiment is the same as or different from the first.

CHAPTER 15 **From Frankenstein to Einstein: Excelling on the Optional Science Test**

These sample questions show a couple ways the ACT may compare the studies in the catapult passage that we introduce in the section "Research summaries" earlier in the chapter.

EXAMPLE

Which of the following expresses the difference between Experiment 1 and Experiment 2 in the catapult passage? In Experiment 2:

(A) the researchers varied launch angle and kept launch velocity constant while in Experiment 1, the researchers varied launch velocity and kept launch angle constant.

(B) the researchers varied both launch velocity and launch angle while in Experiment 1, the researchers varied launch velocity and kept launch angle constant.

(C) the researchers kept both launch angle and launch velocity constant while in Experiment 1, the researchers varied both launch angle and launch velocity.

(D) the researchers varied launch velocity and kept launch angle constant while in Experiment 1, the researchers varied launch angle and kept launch velocity constant.

The set-up paragraph for Experiment 2 clearly states that the researcher kept launch angle constant and varied launch velocity. Read just the first part of each answer choice, and eliminate any answers that state that researchers varied launch angle. Choices (A) and (B) both state that the researchers varied launch angle, so eliminate them. Choice (C) states that researchers in Experiment 2 kept launch velocity constant, so it's wrong. You didn't even need to read what the answers say about Experiment 1 to know that Choice (D) is the right answer.

EXAMPLE

Which of the following is a way in which the two experiments in the study were the same?

I. The studies propelled rubber balls from a catapult.
II. The catapult was set at an angle of 45 degrees.
III. The studies varied the speed of the rubber ball as it traveled from the catapult.

(A) I only
(B) III only
(C) I and II only
(D) I, II, and III

Both studies launched a rubber ball from the catapult, so the right answer has to contain I. Eliminate Choice (B). Experiment 1 didn't vary the velocity, so the answer won't include III; eliminate Choice (D). You just need to determine whether both studies set the angle at a 45-degree angle. Clearly, Experiment 2 did. The set-up paragraph tells you that. Check Experiment 1. There is a point on the graph associated with an angle degree measure of 45, so the researchers must have set the catapult at 45 degrees for that experiment, too. Choice (C) is correct.

TIP

Questions with Roman numerals are almost always procedure questions or questions that test your knowledge of basic science terms.

Testing your science knowledge

The ACT tests your knowledge of science with Roman numerals and in other ways. The ACT expects you to know just the fundamentals, information you likely learned in middle school science classes. This example is based on the catapult passage from the section "Research summaries" earlier in this chapter.

Which of the following expresses the difference between Experiment 1 and Experiment 2 in the catapult passage? In Experiment 2:

EXAMPLE

(A) the researchers varied launch angle and kept launch velocity constant while in Experiment 1, the researchers varied launch velocity and kept launch angle constant.

(B) the researchers varied both launch velocity and launch angle while in Experiment 1, the researchers varied launch velocity and kept launch angle constant.

(C) the researchers kept both launch angle and launch velocity constant while in Experiment 1, the researchers varied both launch angle and launch velocity.

(D) the researchers varied launch velocity and kept launch angle constant while in Experiment 1, the researchers varied launch angle and kept launch velocity constant.

The set-up paragraph for Experiment 2 clearly states that the researcher kept launch angle constant and varied launch velocity. Read just the first part of each answer choice, and eliminate any answers that state that researchers varied launch angle. Choices (A) and (B) both state that the researchers varied launch angle, so eliminate them. Choice (C) states that researchers in Experiment 2 kept launch velocity constant, so it's wrong. You didn't even need to read what the answers say about Experiment 1 to know that Choice (D) is the right answer.

Was the potential or kinetic of the rubber ball greater immediately before the ball was launched from the catapult?

EXAMPLE

(A) Potential energy, because the ball was not in motion immediately before it was launched from the catapult

(B) Potential energy, because the ball was already in motion immediately before it was launched from the catapult

(C) Kinetic energy, because the ball was not in motion immediately before it was launched from the catapult

(D) Potential energy, because the ball was already in motion immediately before it was launched from the catapult

You can answer this by focusing on the choice between potential and kinetic energy or by focusing on the truth of the explanation in each answer. Immediately before the ball was launched from the catapult, the ball wasn't in motion, so you can eliminate Choices (B) and (D). Kinetic energy is the energy an object has while it is in motion, so the ball in prelaunch stage must have more potential energy than kinetic energy. Choice (A) is correct.

You can use the online flash cards included with this edition of *ACT 2022 For Dummies* to drill the science information commonly tested in the Science Test.

TIP

Finding purpose

Another way the ACT may test experimental design is by asking you to identify the reason experimenters set up a study. Here's an example using the catapult passage from the section "Research summaries" earlier in the chapter.

The catapult study was designed to answer what question?

EXAMPLE

(A) Is it possible to launch a rubber ball from a catapult?

(B) What is the farthest distance a rubber ball can travel when it is launched from a catapult?

(C) What effect does the angle from which an object is propelled and the velocity with which it is propelled have on the distance an object travels?

(D) How long does it take a rubber ball to travel a distance of 45 meters when it is launched from a catapult at the greatest velocity and widest launching angle?

CHAPTER 15 **From Frankenstein to Einstein: Excelling on the Optional Science Test** 205

Find answers to eliminate. The study doesn't calculate time, so Choice (D) is unrelated. Although the study did reveal that a rubber ball could be launched from a catapult, that revelation wasn't the intended reason for the study, so Choice (A) is out. The study does test the distance the rubber ball traveled, but there's no indication that the study produced, or intended to produce, the farthest distance the ball could travel. Choice (B) isn't right, so Choice (C) is correct.

Questions about viewpoints

The questions in the conflicting-viewpoints passages are similar to those in the other two passage types. If the scientific viewpoints relate to charts and graphs, the questions will ask you to analyze them. If the viewpoints regard interpretations of a particular experiment, you'll see questions about the way the experiment is designed and be asked to evaluate the results from the perspective of a particular student or scientist. For more information about conflicting-viewpoints passages, see the section "Conflicting viewpoints" earlier in this chapter. The conflicting-viewpoints passage contains some question types that don't appear in the other passages, though. We cover the two most common ones in this section.

Comparing viewpoints

If a question asks you to compare and contrast viewpoints, focus on the main point of each opinion and eliminate answers based on one viewpoint at a time. Note the similarities and differences between viewpoints. The evidence used in the second viewpoint may be different from the evidence used in the first viewpoint, but it may also be the same. The key difference lies in how the second opinion interprets the evidence. Here is an example of a question that asks you to compare viewpoints based on the pH study passage from the section "Conflicting viewpoints" earlier in the chapter.

EXAMPLE

Which of the students would agree that the presence of bicarbonates in water lowers pH levels?

(A) Student 2 only
(B) Students 1 and 3
(C) Student 3 only
(D) Students 1, 2, and 3

Find where Student 1 discusses bicarbonates. Student 1 clearly states in the third sentence that lower pH indicates fewer bicarbonates. Therefore, Student 1 associates bicarbonates with a higher pH level. Eliminate Choices (B) and (D). Read the same sentence for Student 2. Student 2 states the opposite; low pH indicates more bicarbonates. Student 2 must be in the correct answer, so Choice (C) is out. The answer has to be Choice (A). If you check Student 3, you see that this student agrees with Student 1. Choice (A) is confirmed.

Supporting or weakening conclusions

Some questions ask you to support or weaken a particular viewpoint. The best way to strengthen a viewpoint is to come up with evidence that confirms that the opinion's assertions are valid. The best way to weaken a viewpoint is to present evidence that casts doubt on the assertions. For example, suppose a student claims that pandas are carnivores based on evidence that bears are carnivores. That pandas are carnivores because bears are carnivores is strengthened if pandas are bears. But it's weakened if pandas aren't bears.

WARNING

Keep in mind exactly which of the viewpoints you need to support or weaken for each question. Some of the wrong (trap!) answer choices deal with another viewpoint and, as a consequence, won't answer the question.

206 PART 5 Studying Brain Defects in Laboratory Rats: The (Optional) Science Test

The answer choices for a supporting or weakening question usually follow a predictable pattern. One choice, the correct answer, supports or weakens the correct viewpoint. One incorrect choice deals with the correct viewpoint but has the wrong effect on it (strengthens when you want to weaken, or vice versa). Another incorrect choice deals with the other viewpoint. Usually, this choice strengthens the other viewpoint, so it's there to test your ability to keep the viewpoints straight. Occasionally, this incorrect choice weakens the other viewpoint. Such a choice is tough to eliminate, but remember that weakening (or strengthening) one viewpoint doesn't automatically strengthen (or weaken) the other. The third incorrect choice likely presents irrelevant evidence.

Because supporting/weakening the conclusion questions may be unfamiliar to you, here's an example of how to work through the answer choices for one.

Suppose you have a passage about whether smoking cigarettes causes cancer. Scientist 1 says that it does, citing the fact that smokers have a higher incidence of cancer than nonsmokers do. Scientist 2 says that smoking cigarettes doesn't cause cancer, claiming that there's no proof that smoking causes the uncontrolled growth seen in cancer. Scientist 2 explains the association between smoking and cancer as a result of the fact that some people have a certain body chemistry that leads to both a smoking habit and cancer.

Which of the following strengthens Scientist 1's viewpoint?

(A) Nicotine, a major cigarette ingredient, has been shown to cause cancer in laboratory rats.

(B) Smokers invariably eat a lot of fatty foods, which have been shown to cause cancer.

(C) Injecting rats with Chemical ABC caused them to seek out tobacco and also produced cancer cells.

(D) Lack of exercise causes heart disease.

Choice (B) weakens Scientist 1's point of view by suggesting that another cause is at work. Choice (C) goes right along with Scientist 2's suggestion. Choice (D) is irrelevant. It discusses neither cigarettes nor cancer. The best answer is Choice (A); it supports Scientist 1's theory.

You don't care whether the answer choice's statement is actually true or false in the real world. For example, Choice (D), which claims that lack of exercise causes heart disease, may very well be true. So what? It has nothing to do with supporting Scientist 1's statement that smoking cigarettes causes cancer.

IN THIS CHAPTER

» Getting through a Science Test passage without blowing up your chemistry set

» Sorting through traps and tricks you may see on science questions

Chapter 16
Faking Atomic Ache Won't Get You out of This: Science Practice Questions

Question: What happened to the band director when he stuck his finger into an electrical outlet? Answer: Nothing. He was a bad conductor!

If your store of science knowledge is so low that you don't even understand this joke, don't worry. You don't need much specific science knowledge to do well on the Science Test. Nearly everything you need to answer the questions is stated or implied in the passages provided. (If you get the joke but don't laugh, maybe your standards are higher than our comedic ability!)

This chapter gives you a Science Test passage with about twice the usual number of questions. On the actual ACT, the passages have only 5 or 6 questions, not 12 as in this chapter. We give you double the usual number to give you practice in the various ways the ACT can test the same basic points. For now, don't worry about the format or the timing. Review the material in Chapter 15, then apply that material to the questions in this chapter.

Directions: Based on the following science passage, answer the 12 questions.

Don't forget to read all the explanations for the answers after you're done!

Passage

By using electrical recording devices, scientists have shown that many cells in the part of the brain involved with processing visual information respond only to lines of a certain orientation. For example, some brain cells fire when vertical lines are present but do not respond to horizontal lines. Animals that rely on vision must have an entire set of cells so that at least some part of their brains respond when lines of a given orientation are present in their environment.

Scientists conducted several studies on *R. norvegicus domestica* (a species of rat commonly used in laboratory experimentation) to explore how much brain organization is affected by the animal's environment and investigate the role that environment plays in the development of rat vision. Over a period of six weeks, scientists exposed rat pups of various ages to a variety of visual environments: continuous exposure to vertical lines, continuous exposure to horizontal lines, continuous exposure to lines of both horizontal and vertical orientations, and continuous exposure to complete darkness. They then observed the subjects' behavior in mazes with horizontal and vertical obstacles and monitored and measured electrical activity from the visual part of the subjects' brains. The rat pups that were 6 weeks and 6 months old at the beginning of the study had been raised in *normal* environments (environments with uncontrolled exposure to various stimuli and light and dark patterns) from birth until that time. The results of the series of studies are provided in Table 1, which shows the study number, age of *R. norvegicus domestica* at the beginning of the study, the type of environmental factors imposed during the study, the corresponding percentage of brain activity when the subjects were exposed to horizontal and vertical stimuli after the study, and the subjects' ability to navigate obstacles in mazes.

TABLE 1

Study	Age of *R. norvegicus domestica*	Horizontal Line Exposure	Vertical Line Exposure	Complete Darkness	Horizontal Stimuli Exposure	Vertical Stimuli Exposure	Collide with Horizontal Obstacles	Collide with Vertical Obstacles
1	Newborn	yes	Yes	no	50	50	No	no
2	6 weeks	yes	Yes	no	50	50	No	no
3	Newborn	No	No	yes	5	5	Yes	yes
4	Newborn	no	yes	no	0	75	Yes	no
5	Newborn	yes	No	no	75	0	No	yes
6	6 months	No	No	yes	50	50	No	no
7	6 months	No	Yes	no	50	50	No	no
8	6 months	yes	No	no	50	50	No	no

Column groups: Imposed Environmental Factor | % Brain Activity | Maze Navigation

Initial Analysis

This passage presents you with a short introduction and a single table that reports both procedure details and study results. You may be tempted to read through all that mess before you tackle the questions. Don't waste your time! All passages are best approached by skipping the passage and jumping right into answering the questions.

TIP

Use the information in the questions to direct you to the part of the passage you need to go to find the answers. If the question confuses you, get guidance from reading the answer choices. They can tell you what elements to focus on.

Questions

1. On the basis of Study 1, can newborn rat pups see vertical lines?

    (A) No, because the newborn rat pups did not collide with vertical obstacles.

    (B) No, because the newborn rat pups collided with horizontal obstacles.

    (C) Yes, because the newborn rat pups collided with horizontal obstacles.

    (D) Yes, because the newborn rat pups did not collide with vertical obstacles.

    This "yes, yes, no, no" question type concerns Study 1. A quick glance at the answer choices tells you that the only data you need to consider is whether the pups collided with vertical and horizontal obstacles. Focus your attention on Table 1's last columns. The table clearly shows that the pups avoided collisions with both horizontal and vertical obstacles. Examine your answer choices more thoroughly. You can immediately eliminate Choices (B) and (C) because they're not true. The pups in Study 1 avoided the horizontal obstacles.

    Now all you have to figure out is whether colliding with vertical obstacles indicates whether the pups can see vertical lines. Don't overthink this one. You don't have to worry that some ground-breaking study in Sweden may have revealed that the eye actually sees horizontal objects as vertical and vice versa. The pups avoided the vertical objects, so they likely saw them. The best answer is Choice (D).

REMEMBER

Take the path of least resistance. Pick the most logical answer given the data in the passage and your own knowledge of the world.

2. Scientists place a 3-week-old rat pup that had been raised in an environment with both horizontal and vertical visual stimuli in a maze of vertical and horizontal obstacles. Which of the following is the most likely result?

    (F) The rat pup collides with horizontal obstacles but avoids vertical obstacles.

    (G) The rat pup collides with vertical obstacles but avoids horizontal obstacles.

    (H) The rat pup collides with both vertical and horizontal obstacles.

    (J) The rat pup avoids both vertical and horizontal obstacles.

CHAPTER 16 Faking Atomic Ache Won't Get You out of This: Science Practice Questions   211

Suppose a newborn pup can get around the maze, and a pup raised in an environment with exposure to both horizontal and vertical stimuli for six weeks can get around the maze. In that case, you can logically conclude that a pup raised in a normal environment for three weeks would also be able to do so. Only Choice (J) has a pup that doesn't need a crash helmet, so it's your winner.

REMEMBER

Did you have Smart Students' Disease on this question and read more into the question? If you said, "Yeah, but what if . . ." and started imagining all sorts of horrible and unlikely possibilities ("Maybe the rat OD'd on cheese and staggered around . . ."), you made this problem much harder than it really was. Keep it simple, okay?

3. Scientists place a 6-month-old rat that had been raised in a normal environment in a maze of vertical and horizontal obstacles. Which of the following is the most likely result?

(A) The rat makes no attempt to get around the obstacles.

(B) The rat negotiates around both vertical and horizontal obstacles.

(C) The rat bumps into horizontal obstacles but gets around vertical obstacles.

(D) The rat bumps into vertical obstacles but gets around horizontal obstacles.

Did you try to answer this question based on Studies 1 and 2? Doing so worked for the previous question because it spoke of an age, 3 weeks, that was between newborn (Study 1) and 6 weeks (Study 2). Check the question for details. In this question, the rat is older than the oldest pup in Studies 1 and 2, meaning that you can't be sure that the present trend continues. (Common sense tells you that the trend probably will continue, but you must be able to distinguish between what will probably happen and what will necessarily happen.)

Skim the studies for ones that provide a more definitive answer. In Studies 6, 7, and 8, scientists took rats that had previously been exposed to a normal environment for six months and exposed them to a different environment for six weeks. Because the rat in this question didn't have to endure a different experience and the vision of the rats that were exposed to the different environments turned out okay, the rat that wasn't placed in such an environment should also be okay. So the correct answer is Choice (B).

TIP

If you were really lost on this problem, you could eliminate Choice (A) right away because it's much too extreme. Answers with words like *rarely* and *infrequently* are right much more often than their dramatic counterparts like *no* and *never*. Because nothing indicates a favoring of vertical over horizontal lines, or vice versa, you can eliminate Choices (C) and (D) as well.

4. Which of the following was not under the direct control of the experimenters?

(F) the length of time that the rat spent in a controlled environment

(G) the percentage of measured brain activity in response to exposure to horizontal lines

(H) the age at which the rat was tested for visual response

(J) the types of obstacles placed in a maze

212 PART 5 Studying Brain Defects in Laboratory Rats: The Science Test

This is an experiment set-up question, which means you may need to read a little of the introductory material to answer it. When an experimental factor, or *variable*, is under the direct control of the experimenters, the experimenters can decide exactly how much (or what type) of that factor to use without having to depend on any intervening process. Choice (F) is clearly under the control of the experimenters. The experimenters can let the rat out of the maze (the environment) any time they want. Choice (J) is just as clear. The experimenters can throw in more vertical or horizontal obstacles at will.

Choice (H) is a little tougher to eliminate. You may think that the rat's age is up to the rat (or at least up to its parents), but the experimenters can decide exactly how old the rats have to be in order to be used in a certain part of the experiment.

By process of elimination, Choice (G) is correct. The experimenters can try to affect brain activity by changing the environment, but exactly how many brain cells respond depends on physiological factors outside the experimenters' control.

TIP

The basic science info covered in Question 4 comes into play in many different passages. *Independent variables* — Choices (F), (H), and (J), in this case — are those that experimenters can manipulate independently of any other factor. For example, the experimenter can change the time spent in the dark environment from six weeks to five weeks without changing the type of obstacles in the maze. A *dependent variable* — Choice (G) in this case — depends on what else was done in the experiment.

5. What is the relationship between Study 6 and Study 3?

   (A) An examination of the results of Study 6 and Study 3 shows that the effects of six weeks in darkness may depend on the rat's age at the time scientists place the subjects in complete darkness.

   (B) The rats in Study 3 were exposed to a different experimental environment than those in Study 6.

   (C) Study 6 extends the findings of Study 3 by showing that longer periods of darkness also change brain-cell activity.

   (D) Study 6 contradicts the findings of Study 3 by showing that, when rats are placed in darkness for a longer period of time, the maze navigation results found in Study 3 are altered.

You can dump Choices (B), (C), and (D) because they aren't true. The two studies imposed the same environmental condition, complete darkness, so Choice (B) is wrong. The other two answers are wrong because Study 6 used older rats (ones that have been alive for a longer period of time), but these rats, as well as those of Study 3, were in darkness for only six weeks.

Often, three answer options for science questions are obviously wrong. The only answer left is Choice (A), which is correct.

6. Some humans who have suffered brain injuries have been able to recover a lost brain function by having the brain reorganize itself. On the basis of all the rat-vision studies, which of the following humans would be most likely to recover a lost function through brain reorganization?

   (F) a 50-year-old man who suffers a stroke (lack of oxygen to a certain region of the brain)
   (G) an 80-year-old woman who suffers a stroke
   (H) a 30-year-old combat soldier who suffers a bullet wound in the brain
   (J) a baby who has had part of the left side of his brain surgically removed, along with a tumor

Calm down, calm down — no one expects you to know exactly how each of these brain traumas affects brain functioning. Everything you need to answer this question is there in the passage. Plus, you can rely on what you know from your world experience to eliminate less logical answers to science questions. The key is to pick up on the ages. Which rats showed a change from the ordinary response pattern when the environment changed? The young rats. Similarly, a young human's brain is likely to be more flexible than that of an older human. Haven't you always pointed out to your parents not to be so narrow-minded and set in their ways? Choice (J), which features the youngest human, is the correct answer.

If you're almost having a stroke right now arguing with us, you probably didn't notice how carefully the question was worded: "Which of the following humans would be *most likely* to . . .?" True, you don't know for sure that the baby would have some lost brain function, but all you're asked is which of the answer choices is the most likely (and, no, "a student studying for the ACT" wasn't among them).

7. Scientists exposed a 1-year-old rat that was raised in a normal environment and had normal vision to only horizontal lines. Which of the following is the most reasonable prediction?

   (A) After three weeks, the cells in the visual part of the rat's brain fail to respond to vertical lines.
   (B) After six weeks, the cells in the visual part of the rat's brain fail to respond to vertical lines.
   (C) After six weeks, the cells in the visual part of the rat's brain respond to vertical lines.
   (D) After six months, the cells in the visual part of the rat's brain respond to vertical lines.

Study 8 shows that 6-month-old rats exposed to only horizontal lines for six months still have brain cells capable of responding to vertical lines. This info knocks out Choices (A) and (B). After six months, the wiring in the rat's visual part of the brain seems to be fixed, so you can assume that the 1-year-old rat's brain has fixed wiring.

Be careful of Choice (D). You can't say for sure what effects an exposure longer than six weeks will have. Choice (C) is a much safer (and correct!) choice.

TIP

Have you noticed throughout these answer explanations how often you can narrow the answers down to two choices very quickly? If you're in a hurry or if you're confused, make a quick guess. Remember that the ACT doesn't penalize you for wrong answers.

8. Suppose the researchers subjected *R. norvegicus domestica* that were 6 weeks old at the beginning of the study to six weeks of complete darkness. Based on information in the table, the level of brain activity in response to horizontal stimuli that the researchers measured in these subjects at the end of the study was most likely:

   (F) less than 5 percent
   (G) between 5 percent and 60 percent
   (H) between 60 percent and 75 percent
   (J) greater than 75 percent

   To answer this question, examine the results in the column that shows the brain response to horizontal stimuli for studies that exposed rats to complete darkness for six weeks, Study 3 and Study 6. The newborn rats in Study 3 displayed 5 percent activity when exposed to horizontal stimuli, and the 6-month-old rats in Study 6 displayed 50 percent activity when exposed to horizontal stimuli. This comparison indicates that rats that were older at the beginning of the study responded better to horizontal stimuli than the newborn subjects.

   Therefore, there is no reason to believe that rats that were 6 weeks old at the beginning of the study would show less brain activity than the newborns, so Choice (F) is incorrect. Nor does the table suggest any reason to believe that the younger rats would register a higher percentage of brain activity in response to horizontal activity than the older rats in Study 6. Therefore, Choices (H) and (J) must be wrong. The rats in the new study most likely had brain activity that measured above the 5 percent indicated for newborns, most likely closer to the 50 percent indicated for the older rats in Study 6. So the correct answer is Choice (G).

9. Which study best shows or studies best show that a particular environmental stimulus can lead to a change in the way the cells in the visual part of a rat's brain respond?

   (A) Study 4 only
   (B) Study 4 and Study 5 only
   (C) Study 5 and Study 8 only
   (D) Study 1, Study 5, and Study 8 only

   First, notice that the answer choices only concern Studies 1, 4, 5, and 8. Don't waste time evaluating Studies 2, 3, and 7.

   Study 1 was performed with newborn rat pups that received a variety of stimuli and weren't subjected to complete darkness. Because this study didn't isolate one particular controlled environmental stimulation, it doesn't best indicate how one environmental component affects the brain. You can eliminate Choice (D).

   Study 4 looks good. It isolates one controlled environmental stimulus. Exposure to only vertical lines caused a loss of cells able to respond to horizontal lines and a gain of cells able to respond to vertical lines. Because the correct answer must have Study 4 in it, eliminate Choice (C).

   Study 5 is very similar to Study 4 in that it tests what happens to the rats when exposed to just one controlled stimulus. Study 5 shows a loss of cells able to respond to vertical lines and a gain of cells able to respond to horizontal lines. So the correct answer is Choice (B).

Notice that by using the process of elimination, you can avoid examining Study 8 altogether. What a fantastic time-saver! If you want to be absolutely sure, go ahead and verify that Study 8 doesn't work. Study 8 shows that the controlled environment for 6-month-old rats didn't alter their brain activity or ability to navigate horizontal and vertical obstacles. Their results were the same as those for newborn and 6-week-old rats that received a variety of stimuli. This study, taken by itself, suggests little support for an environmental contribution.

10. If Study 4 is conducted but Studies 3 and 5 are not, can the scientists conclude that all cells in the visual part of a rat pup's brain require stimulation in order to function?

   (F) Yes, because Studies 3 and 5 test what happens when brain cells are not exposed to vertical lines.
   (G) Yes, because Study 4 tests both vertical and horizontal-responding cells.
   (H) No, because Study 4 only tests whether brain cells respond to vertical lines.
   (J) No, because Study 4 does not test whether vertical-responding cells require stimulation.

This "yes, yes, no, no" question tests whether you understand that experimental results are limited when only certain conditions are tested. Notice that the answer choices indicate that you're focusing on whether the studies tested responses to horizontal and vertical lines. Eliminate Choices (G) and (H) because they're not true. Study 4 didn't test responses to vertical lines.

Choices (F) and (J) provide true statements, but only Choice (J) pinpoints the limitations of Study 4 — that it doesn't test vertical-responding cells. Studies 3 and 5 did test the vertical factor and allow for a more general conclusion regarding brain cells and environmental input, so they're necessary to understand the role of all cells. So the answer has to be Choice (J). Study 4 is inadequate by itself.

11. On the basis of all the studies, which of the following best summarizes the role of the environment in the development of a rat's visual brain-cell responses?

   (A) The environment has no effect on the development of a rat's visual brain-cell responses.
   (B) Environmental input early in a rat's life contributes to the continuation of normal brain-cell responses to stimuli.
   (C) Environmental input can change the pattern of brain-cell responses throughout a rat's life.
   (D) The environment is the only factor that influences brain-cell responses.

If Choice (A) were true, the pups in Studies 3, 4, and 5 would have normal visual responses. Eliminate Choice (A). If Choice (C) were true, the rats in Studies 6, 7, and 8 would show a change in response patterns. Choice (D) is at odds with Study 1. If the environment is the only factor, why do newborn rats show responses to all types of stimuli? This reasoning leaves only Choice (B), which is correct.

TIP

Are you noticing and using the wording in the questions and choices to help you choose and eliminate answers? The conservative language ("contributes to the continuation" rather than "directly determines") reinforces Choice (B) as the answer. Notice how easily you can contradict Choice (A), which contains the word *no*, Choice (C), which says *throughout*, and Choice (D), which includes *only*.

12. Which of the following studies would probably add the most new information to the work done in this set of experiments?

    (F) A study identical to Study 3, except that the pups are in the dark environment for seven weeks.
    (G) A study identical to Study 6, except that the rats are in the dark environment for five weeks.
    (H) A study identical to Study 6, except that the study uses 1-year-old rats.
    (J) A study identical to Studies 4 and 5, except that the rats are exposed only to diagonal lines.

Study 3 shows that six weeks of darkness almost entirely wipes out the cells' ability to respond. Perhaps seven weeks would cause a complete cessation of responding, but the point made from Study 3 (namely, that lack of visual stimulation leads to impaired brain-cell responding) has already been established. Therefore, the study mentioned in Choice (F) won't add much.

Study 6 strongly suggests that the response patterns in the visual part of a rat's brain are fixed enough at six months so that six weeks of an abnormal environment have no noticeable effect. If six weeks have no noticeable effect, why would five weeks be any different? Eliminate Choice (G). If the brain-cell responses are fixed by the time a rat is 6 months old, you can reasonably expect that a 1-year-old rat would show the same responses. Eliminate Choice (H).

The study mentioned in Choice (J) would help because it would show what happens to cells that respond to lines that are oriented both vertically and horizontally. This study would add some information regarding how precise the brain cells are in regard to lines in the environment. For example, is a diagonal line close enough to a vertical line that the exposure only to diagonal lines still allows the rat to respond to vertical lines? The answer to this question may increase understanding of how the environment interacts with the visual part of a rat's brain.

6 Writing Rightly: The Optional Writing Test

IN THIS PART . . .

Receive a breakdown of the components of the ACT Writing Test prompt.

Evaluate the issue, examine the three provided perspectives, and choose your stance.

Earn a top writing score by learning the approach to crafting a clear, thorough essay that thoughtfully examines the issue in depth and provides convincing support for the thesis.

Create your own masterworks by responding to a couple sample essay prompts.

> **IN THIS CHAPTER**
> » Figuring out what the ACT is looking for in your essay
> » Breaking down the essay into manageable parts
> » Exploring the top five editing techniques

Chapter 17
Excelling on Your Essay: The Writing Test Review

The ACT provides an optional Writing Test in addition to the four multiple-choice sections. Its importance in the college application process is dwindling, and most colleges don't require or even recommend it. If you need to write an essay to enhance your application, make sure you present your best effort.

Writing a great essay is totally different from writing a really great ACT essay. A great essay is one you plan and think about for days, write for days, and edit for even more days. The whole process usually takes a considerable amount of time. But on the ACT, you have to cram all that planning, thinking, writing, and editing into only 40 minutes, and, trust us, that's not enough time to write something worthy of a literary award. But don't fret! All you need to do is figure out what the test makers are looking for; then you can give them exactly that.

What to Expect From the ACT Writing Test

If you want to write an ACT essay that pleases your readers, make sure you do all of the following:

> » **State and develop a perspective.** Establishing a perspective requires you to explain your thoughts using examples, reasons, and details.
>
> » **Evaluate and analyze the perspectives given.** Use them to help you form your thesis and add depth to your discussion, but don't think you need to analyze each perspective in your essay.
>
> » **Consider the relationship between your perspective and at least one other.** This analysis demonstrates that you thoroughly understand a complex issue.
>
> » **Maintain focus.** Staying focused requires you to stay on topic and make sure you don't add thoughts that aren't related to the prompt question.

> » **Back your ideas with detailed supporting information.** Rely on anecdotes and examples from your own experience.
>
> » **Organize ideas.** Organizing your thoughts and ideas requires you to present your ideas in a logical way, using transitional words and phrases and sequencing your ideas so that they build on each other.
>
> » **Communicate clearly.** Communicating clearly requires you to use a variety of sentence structures and vocabulary, spell correctly, and make sure your grammar and punctuation are correct.

To relieve your anxiety and help you manage the short amount of time you have to write the essay, we break down the essay into manageable chunks. If you follow the steps and advice we outline in this chapter, writing the essay will be much easier than you think.

Making the Grade: How the ACT Folks Score Your Essay

You'll be happy to know that you personally get not one, but two — yes, two — trained readers who score your essay. And if the first two don't agree, you get a third — yes, a third — reader all to yourself. Don't you feel special? The ACT folks sure think you are.

Here's the skinny on how you get your final Writing Test score: Two readers read your essay, and each one assigns it a numerical grade from 1 to 6. The sum of those ratings is your Writing Test subscore (2 to 12). When you choose to write the essay, the ACT people also report an English and Language Arts (ELA) score based on the results of your English Test and Writing Test performance. If you choose not to take the Writing Test, you get only the English Test score. The absence of the Writing Test score doesn't affect your ACT score in any other area, and neither your Writing Test nor your ELA score affects your ACT composite score in any way.

Examining the Prompt and Creating a Thesis

Responding to the ACT Writing Test prompt is somewhat like taking part in a debate. You'll read a consideration concerning a pertinent issue and then view three different perspectives. Your job is to get in on the action and form an opinion of your own.

The prompt may overwhelm you or bore you. It may include information that seems irrelevant. But no matter what, it poses a question worthy of careful consideration. Your first step is to review the information provided in the introduction and consider the three alternative positions that follow, and your second step is to form an opinion of your own. You don't really have to believe it yourself; you just need to write about it with confidence. The ACT people don't know you, and they certainly won't go to your house to ask you to explain yourself further. The key to starting a strong essay is taking a strong position right away. Here's what you need to do first:

1. **Read the question.**

    Here's the sample prompt (we refer to it throughout the rest of this chapter):

In some high schools, many teachers and parents have encouraged the school to require uniforms that students must wear to school. Some teachers and parents support school uniforms because they think their use will improve the school's learning environment. Other teachers and parents do not support requiring uniforms because they think it restricts individual freedom of expression. It is worth considering the impact created by introducing a school uniform requirement.

- **Perspective 1:** Schools should indeed require all students to wear school uniforms to improve the overall learning environment. Doing so will reduce distractions and problems that arise from students being judged by how they look and dress and will also make it harder for cliques to establish themselves.

- **Perspective 2:** Requiring uniforms in public schools is yet another way to muffle our students' freedom of expression. Uniforms also perpetuate the idea that in order to coexist, we must all conform to the same standard.

- **Perspective 3:** Requiring students to wear school uniforms helps level the playing field in terms of socioeconomic status. Kids will no longer be judged by how cheap or expensive their attire is, and families won't feel pressured to dress their school-age children in clothes they can't afford.

2. **Pay attention to the first paragraph.**

   Typically, the first sentence of the prompt describes the issue. The following two sentences provide the position of its proponents and the view of the opposition. Can you identify the issue in the prompt in Step 1? The first sentence tells you that the issue is whether uniforms should be required. The second sentence tells you the reasoning behind those who favor uniforms: improvement in the school's learning environment. The third sentence gives the case of the opposition: uniforms restrict freedom of expression. And the last sentence provides the consideration. Read this sentence carefully because it reveals the crux of the issue — in this prompt, the impact of requiring uniforms.

   The prompt's second paragraph requests the following:

   Write a unified, coherent essay in which you evaluate multiple perspectives as to whether high school students should be required to wear school uniforms. In your essay, be sure to do the following:

   - Clearly state your own perspective on the issue and analyze the relationship between your perspective and at least one other perspective.
   - Develop and support your ideas with reasoning and examples.
   - Organize your ideas clearly and logically.
   - Communicate your ideas effectively in standard written English.

3. **Develop your own perspective regarding the question being posed by the prompt.**

   Do you think schools need to have uniforms? Or do you think students should come to school naked (just needed to wake you up here — did it work?). Don't just start writing before you decide your position.

4. **Compare your perspective with those already provided.**

   Maybe your perspective is very similar to one of the three provided, or maybe it's entirely different. Your essay only has to contain elements of one perspective; you aren't required to analyze all three.

Putting Up Your Dukes: Defending Your Perspective

By now, you've read the prompt and all three perspectives, and you probably identify with one or two of them more than the others. Even if you don't, the time has come to write down your feelings about the issue on paper. Remember that the ACT folks don't care what you really feel; they just want an essay, and they want one pronto!

REMEMBER

Here are two "nevers" to remember as you begin your essay:

» Never tell the ACT folks the reasons why you agree or disagree with the prompt and perspectives in the first sentence.

» Never straddle both sides of an issue without coming out with a clear opinion.

Throwing a Good First Punch: The Hook

Now that you've considered all perspectives and taken a stance of your own, you need to expand your first paragraph. Getting the reader's attention is key to keeping it throughout your essay. You must *hook* (grab the attention of) your reader right from the beginning. Think of the first paragraph as a funnel going from large thoughts to smaller ones.

» **The first sentence needs to capture the overall debate of the prompt.** For example, if your prompt is about school uniforms, you may want to write something like this:

- The appropriateness of uniforms is the subject of widespread debate.

Although you haven't yet stated your position, you've let the reader know that the essay is going to be about uniforms. You haven't given up your hand yet, which makes the reader want to continue reading your essay. Good job!

» **The second sentence needs to express both sides of the argument.** Representing both sides is easier than you think because the original prompt gives you both sides of the debate. Reread the second and third sentences in the prompt. Reword them in your own voice and stick those thoughts right after your first sentence.

For example, you may write the following sentence about the uniform prompt:

- Although some people believe uniforms will improve the learning environment, others argue that uniforms may restrict individual freedom of expression.

Even though you may favor one view over another, you should mention both in your introduction to show that you recognize both sides of the argument. The ACT graders are sticklers for this point. Your score will be low if you fail to address the counterargument(s) at some point in your essay.

» **The third sentence establishes and expands on your position.** To establish your position, you merely have to state the points that you'll cover in your essay to support your side and then state your side. These points eventually turn into your essay's three body paragraphs (see the section "The Proof Is in the Pudding: Defending Yourself" for details on writing the body paragraphs.)

For example, you may write the following sentence to take the position for uniforms in high schools:

- Because certain types of clothing can distract students, lead to school violence, and interfere with a student's ability to fit in, I believe that high schools should require uniforms for students.

Alternatively, you could vary your sentence structure by presenting your thesis separately from the sentence that presents your three points that will become your three body paragraphs:

It's apparent to me that certain types of clothing can distract students, lead to school violence, and interfere with a student's ability to fit in. Therefore, I believe that high schools should require uniforms for students.

Your first paragraph is now complete:

> The appropriateness of dress codes is the subject of widespread debate. Although some people believe uniforms will improve the learning environment, others argue that uniforms may restrict individual freedom of expression. Because certain types of clothing can distract students, lead to school violence, and interfere with a student's ability to fit in, I believe requiring school uniforms will positively impact the high school experience.

TIP

The *thesis* should be the last sentence of your introduction paragraph. Don't give up your hand too early, and don't neglect to build the suspense.

Another way to hook your reader is to begin your essay with a story. If you're advocating for school uniforms, you may introduce your position by recounting the embarrassment your best friend experienced when a group of mean girls pointed out in the middle of chemistry class that her jeans clearly lacked a designer label.

The Proof Is in the Pudding: Defending Yourself

To create a great ACT essay, you must use specific examples, reasons, and details that prove your position on the prompt, and help refute counterarguments made by others. The ACT folks are looking for two things here, which we discuss in the following sections:

» Specific examples
» Variety of examples

Using specific examples

To get a handle on how specific your examples should be, consider the last time your parents questioned you about your Saturday night activities. We'll bet their questions included all the old stand-bys: Where did you go? Who was there? Why are you home so late? Who drove? How long has he had his license? You know that vague answers never cut it.

This skill that you've been practicing for years is going to come in handy when you take your ACT Writing Test, because you're already great at giving the specifics (or making them up). Really good examples discuss extremely specific details, events, dates, and occurrences. Your goal is to write in detail and to try not to be too broad and loose. For example, say that you're trying to find examples to support uniforms. You can conclude that allowing students to wear whatever they want leads to distraction among the students. Great, but you need to be more specific. You need to give an example from your life when you witnessed this distraction or cite a relevant article you've read. In other words, give dates, mention people, and rat on your friends! Just choose examples that you know a lot about so that you can get down to the nitty-gritty and be extremely specific.

Mixing things up with a variety of examples

Over the past few years, you may have had to come up with a variety of excuses for breaking curfew — the car broke down, traffic was horrendous, the movie ran late, you forgot the time, you fell asleep . . . you know the routine. Again, thank your parents for helping you with yet another skill you can apply to the ACT Writing Test. Coming up with specific examples about how you feel about uniforms just from your personal life is easy, but it's also boring.

Use a broad range of examples from different areas, such as literature, cultural experiences, your personal life, current events, business, or history. If you spend just a few moments thinking about the topic, you can come up with great examples from varied areas.

So, to answer the question, "Should schools require students to wear uniforms?" you may strengthen your own perspective by using examples like these:

> » **Personal life:** A scenario where you saw a girl wearing a short skirt and teeny top and noticed how it interfered with other student's ability to concentrate
>
> » **Current events:** An example from a magazine article you read about a high school shooting that explains how the boys who fired guns in their school were trying to hurt the kids who looked and dressed like jocks
>
> » **Cultural experience:** The concern regarding wearing gang-related colors and logos and the potential implications doing so may have regarding violence in the schools

A nice variety of examples like these definitely gets the attention of the ACT folks and helps you sound like the smart writer that you are.

Forming logical arguments

The ACT Writing Test provides you with an issue and three perspectives and expects you to examine the whole to create a logical thesis. Accomplishing this task is easier when you know a little about how to form arguments.

A logical argument consists of premises and a conclusion. The *premises* give the supporting evidence from which you can draw a conclusion. You can usually find the *conclusion* in the argument because it's the statement that you can preface with "therefore." The conclusion is often, but not always, the argument's last sentence. For example, take a look at this simple deduction:

> All gazelles are fast. That animal is a gazelle. Therefore, that animal is fast.

The premises in the argument are "All gazelles are fast" and "that animal is a gazelle." You know this because they provide the supporting evidence for the conclusion that that animal is fast. The perspectives in the Writing Test prompt are unlikely to be so obvious as to include a conclusion designated by a "therefore," but you can form your own "therefore" statement to determine the conclusion.

In *deductive reasoning*, you draw a specific conclusion from general premises, as we did for the earlier gazelle argument. With *inductive reasoning*, you do just the opposite; you develop a general conclusion from specific premises. Consider this example of an inductive argument:

Grace is a high school student and likes spaghetti. (Specific premise)

Javi is a high school student and likes spaghetti. (Specific premise)

Gidget is a high school student and likes spaghetti. (Specific premise)

Manny is a high school student and likes spaghetti. (Specific premise)

Therefore, it is likely that all high school students like spaghetti. (General conclusion)

Because an inductive argument derives general conclusions from specific examples, you can't come up with a statement that "must be true." The best you can say, even if all the premises are true, is that the conclusion can be or is likely to be true. The perspectives you see in the Writing Test will be based on inductive reasoning.

Inductive reasoning often relies on three main methods. Knowing these ways of reaching a conclusion can help you analyze perspectives and effectively draw your own conclusions:

>> **Cause-and-effect arguments:** This argument concludes that one event is the result of another. These types of arguments are strongest when the premises prove that an event's alleged cause is the most likely one and that there are no other probable causes. For example, after years of football watching, you may conclude the following: "Every time I wear my lucky shirt, my favorite team wins; therefore, wearing my lucky shirt causes the team to win." This example is weak because it doesn't take into consideration other, more probable reasons (like the team's talent) for the wins.

>> **Analogy arguments:** This argument tries to show that two or more concepts are similar so that what holds true for one is true for the other. The argument's strength depends on the degree of similarity between the persons, objects, or ideas being compared. For example, in drawing a conclusion about Beth's likes, you may compare her to Alex: "Alex is a student, and he likes rap music. Beth is also a student, so she probably likes rap music, too." Your argument would be stronger if you could show that Alex and Beth have other similar interests that apply to rap music, like hip-hop dancing or wearing bling. If, on the other hand, you show that Alex likes to go to dance clubs while Beth prefers practicing her violin at home, your original conclusion may be less likely.

>> **Statistical arguments:** These arguments rely on numbers to reach a conclusion. These types of arguments claim that what's true for the statistical majority is also true for the individual (or, alternately, that what's true of a member or members of a group also holds true for the larger group). But because these are inductive reasoning arguments, you can't prove that the conclusions are absolutely true. When you analyze statistical arguments, focus on how well the given statistics apply to the conclusion's circumstances. For instance, if you wanted people to buy clothing through your website, you may make this argument: "In a recent study of consumers' preferences, 80 percent of shoppers surveyed said they prefer to shop online; therefore, you'll probably prefer to buy clothes online." You'd support your conclusion if you could show that what's true for the majority is also true for an individual.

Hamburger Writing: Organizing Your Essay

Ever taken a bite of a big, juicy hamburger from a fast-food restaurant? Well, okay, we don't blame you for not wanting to see what's really lurking between the buns (even though it tastes darn good). But if you're feeling adventurous (and want to ace the essay part of the ACT), you may want to follow along as we dissect the classic fast-food burger and match each ingredient with a specific part of your essay. Yes, you heard right. Every great essay is organized like a big, juicy hamburger.

No matter your prompt's topic, the ACT graders want to see a specific format to your writing. In other words, they don't want all the ingredients thrown in any old way. By following the organization we outline in the next few sections, you can give the test graders a supersized essay worthy of a supersized score.

The top bun: Introduction

The top bun includes the funnel of information that leads to your thesis. We show you how to write it in the previous sections. Now you can move on to the essay's body paragraphs.

The three meats: Example paragraphs

Think of your supporting arguments in terms of three different kinds of meat — perhaps two beef patties and some bacon or a chicken club with turkey and bacon. Each meat represents a separate paragraph in your essay, the purpose of which is to add specific examples that help prove the position that you state in your top bun. (Are you getting hungry yet?)

Each meaty paragraph needs to include the following elements:

>> Three to five sentences

>> A solid topic sentence that relates directly to your position (remember, you already wrote your ideas in the top bun — your thesis)

>> A variety of reasons, details, and examples that illustrate that specific topic

In the thesis, we wrote about the uniform prompt, and we said that clothing can be distracting (see the section "Throwing a Good First Punch: The Hook" for more on this sample thesis). You can use that thought as the topic sentence for your first meat paragraph. For example, you may open your first body paragraph with something like this:

> Uniforms should be required because a variety of clothing choices can be very distracting in the learning environment.

Now you have to write a few sentences that prove that clothing can be distracting. Make sure that you use specific and clear examples from a variety of sources, including personal experience, history, culture, and literature. Don't stray off topic, or in this case, begin writing about anything other than the fact that clothing can be distracting. In other words, don't get distracted when writing about distraction!

Here's a sample meat paragraph that you (and the graders) can really sink your teeth into:

> Uniforms should be required because a variety of clothing choices can be very distracting in the learning environment. Social media and advertisements flash images of young girls wearing practically nothing, for example, a fashion that most teenagers try to emulate *(culture reference)*. However, wearing skimpy clothes and showing body parts can make some people look and react, which may interrupt an important part of class. That can be quite distracting when you're trying to learn the Pythagorean theorem *(personal experience reference)*. Furthermore, paying attention to the teacher is difficult when you hear people discussing another student's $150 Dolce and Gabbana jeans *(cultural reference)*. A uniform does away with these distractions by enforcing a more conservative style of clothing, allowing the focus in the classroom to remain on education rather than fashion.

Sounds good, right? Well, your essay isn't complete yet, even after a meaty paragraph like this one. You still have two more meats to gobble down! Lucky for you, you've already decided which topics you're going to discuss in the next two meaty paragraphs: You mentioned distractions, school violence, and fitting in as part of your essay's introduction (see the section "Throwing a Good First Punch: The Hook" for details). You just wrote about distractions in the first meat paragraph, so your second meat is about school violence, and your third is about fitting in. Don't get so caught up in your own argument that you forget the task at hand, though, and that includes careful consideration of the other perspectives provided. Pepper your paragraphs with nods to the opposition. Maybe you're refuting the points made by others, or maybe you're agreeing — but you do need to acknowledge them and consider their merits, if any.

To make things easier, structure the second and third examples by including the following elements:

» A solid topic sentence that defends your position

» A few sentences in which you give reasons, details, and examples that support the topic of this paragraph or refute a counterargument

» A variety of examples taken from different areas, such as literature, culture, personal experience, and history

You'll want to acknowledge arguments you don't agree with (the three perspectives provide examples, but you can come up with your own, too), and then show why they're not strong enough to change your position. For example, you could point out that the clothes you wear aren't the only form of personal expression and that the lack of distractions created by uniforms may actually make it easier to express yourself in other areas, such as art, music, and writing.

The lettuce, tomato, and special sauce: Transitions

Like the sandwich, your essay needs to taste good (that is, read well) as a whole. Transitions serve as the special sauce and other burger fixins that help smooth out the differences between your paragraphs. You must include transitions between your first and second, and second and third meat paragraphs. The most obvious way to do so is by using transitional words, such as *secondly, finally, another idea, another example, furthermore,* and *in addition,* just to name a few. If you use these obvious transitions, that will be good enough to earn a score of 5, but to achieve the perfect 6, your transitions will need to be more subtle. For example, you may transition from one paragraph to another by alluding in the second paragraph to a concept mentioned in the first one.

The bottom bun: Conclusion

No matter how full of this essay you are by the time you add your three meaty paragraphs and all the saucy transitions, you need to consume the bottom bun before you're done. Ideally, the bottom bun or conclusion of your essay should include the following two elements:

» A restatement of your position

» An expansion of your position that looks to the future

You can address both elements in three to four sentences. Just make sure you include your position, references to your meat topics, and one sentence that pulls everything together. Here's an example:

> Implementing a uniform policy would be beneficial *(restatement of your position)*. Requiring uniforms has the potential to limit distractions in the classroom, reduce school-related violence, and help students find more creative ways to fit in *(references to your meat topics)*. School uniforms would direct the appropriate focus back on education rather than keep it fixated on an adolescent fashion show *(looking toward the future)*.

Wielding the Red Pen: Editing and Proofing

With the finish line directly in front of you, all you have left to do is to make a quick sprint (or, should we say, edit?) to the end of your essay. You absolutely must make time to proof your masterpiece. If you don't, your essay score will reflect your hasty goodbye. You're not finished until you've double-checked (and corrected) your writing. This section gives you five quick editing and proofreading techniques that can keep you from tripping before you cross the finish line.

Chapter 5 reviews the basic rules of grammar and sentence structure and reminds you of simple things to watch for when you check your sentences. Being the wonderful student that you are, you've probably already studied that chapter and are now ready to launch straight into editing.

Using the touch method to look for spelling mistakes and ghost words

Your brain is smarter than you think it is. When you proofread, your brain may see your writing the way you intended it to be rather than the way it really is. Your sentences may be missing just a few little words here and there, but without them, your paragraphs and essay fail.

Use your pencil to touch every single word that you wrote quickly. Doing so helps you find words that you omitted, catch simple spelling errors, and locate places where you've repeated words or thoughts. The smallest errors are often the most costly. The three easiest mistakes to catch are misusing *there*, *their*, and *they're*, *your* and *you're*, and *it's* and *its*. Touching the words as you proofread helps you outsmart your brain and catch these simplest of mistakes.

Calling all action verbs: Be descriptive

You can't score your best if readers fall asleep in the middle of your essay. Wake them up by forcing them to read caffeine-filled words. In other words, use bold action verbs rather than mild-mannered, wimpy verbs. For example, instead of writing, "He ran to the store quickly,"

230 PART 6 **Writing Rightly: The Optional Writing Test**

replace *ran* with *bolted*, *sprinted*, or *flew*. These words express more action and give the sentence movement. *Ran* is boring. Replacing boring verbs with verbs that create vivid pictures definitely improves your essay.

Avoiding problems with punk-tu-a-tion: Punctuate properly

Rebellion against authority may be your motto on most days, but you can't rebel against grammar and punctuation rules on the ACT essay. They always win. Here are the questions you need to ask yourself when you edit your essay for punctuation and other common grammar mistakes:

> » Did I use the correct periods, exclamation points, and question marks?
> » Did I capitalize the first words of my sentences and proper nouns?
> » Do my subjects agree with my verbs?
> » Did I use commas correctly?
> » Are any of my sentences run-ons or fragments?
> » Are my words spelled correctly?

Handwriting check: Write legibly

You need to get into med school before you can start writing like a doctor. If the ACT graders can't read your essay, how will they know how brilliant it is? Illegible writing is an easy error to catch as you proofread your essay. If *you* can't read your writing, erase what you can't read and rewrite it. Pencils with good erasers — what a useful invention!

Writing Don'ts

Relax. You've been writing since the first grade; you have something to say, and this test is your way to prove it. All you need is a quick refresher on the basics of essay writing, which, lucky for you, we cover in the following sections. Avoid the pitfalls we describe here, and you'll be well on your way to a winning essay.

Writing before you think

If you have no destination, you're bound to get lost. The most important part of writing your essay is having a strong structure and a clear idea of where you're going. If you put your pen to the paper without knowing what the heck you're going to say, you can bet your bottom dollar that the ACT folks won't know what you're saying either.

REMEMBER

Make a quick plan before you start writing, and you'll avoid an essay that wanders aimlessly.

Panicking about time

Writer's block — when you simply can't think of anything to put down — often occurs in stressful situations and is frequently the result of a time crunch. You have 40 full minutes to complete the writing portion of the ACT. That's plenty of time to read the question, organize your thoughts, write your essay, and do a quick edit.

To get the most out of your 40 minutes, we suggest you break them down like this:

» 5 minutes to read the question and organize your thoughts
» 5 minutes to write your thesis and outline
» 25 minutes to write the bulk of your essay
» 5 minutes to edit and proofread

Notice that we don't include any time for panicking. Panicking takes 40 minutes just to get over, and by then, your time's up!

Referring to the perspectives by number

The ACT really doesn't want you to provide a thorough analysis of each of the perspectives. You need only contain an element of one of the perspectives in your essay. And you aren't expected to give the perspective titles or even reference them at all. Merely including an idea from one of them as you support your own opinion is enough to meet the goal of considering the perspectives.

Sticking to the status quo

The ACT Writing Test gives you a *prompt*, or topic, to write about. The prompt requires you to form an opinion on an issue and support it with compelling evidence from your own experience. You may think you're confined to a traditional five-paragraph expository exercise, but if you think you can pull it off, the ACT rewards a creative approach. If you're a good storyteller, you may want to use a personal anecdote that illustrates your position. You can use that story as a way of engaging the reader and making your point through imagery and action. If you're a financial whiz kid, you may want to dazzle the readers with a statistical analysis that shows the economic feasibility of your position or the financial impossibility of the opposition.

Of course, if you're more comfortable with the standard introductory paragraph, three supporting paragraphs, and conclusion, then, by all means, stick to the standard. Just make sure you produce an organized, well-thought-out essay that answers the question that they asked with the most specific, unique evidence you can think of.

Using words you don't know

Nobody can be Shakespeare, especially in 40 minutes — not even Bill himself. When writing your essay for the ACT, you don't have the thesaurus button on your word processor in front of you — which actually may be a good thing. One of the worst mistakes you can make is using words that you think sound good but aren't absolutely sure how to use. Instead of trying to use words that you don't know, impress the ACT readers with your thoughts and your ability to communicate clearly. Using words you don't know or understand completely may give the ACT graders a laugh, but you won't be laughing when you see your score.

Being overly critical of yourself

Nobody writes the perfect essay in 40 minutes. Nobody! The graders know that, and you need to, as well. Trying to be obsessively perfect does you more harm than good. If you spend too much time critiquing yourself, the ACT graders won't have anything to critique. Fortunately, you don't have to be perfect to get a high score. You can get a good score in 40 minutes if you follow the suggestions and format described in this book. Simply watch your time, stay organized, and express yourself clearly (and in your own words).

Writing like you speak

Everyone knows that speaking is much easier than writing. However, this test is neither the time nor the place to impress the test makers with your street vocabulary. Whatever you do, don't drop it like it's hot, don't think you're too cool for school, don't think you're kinda-like the, like, greatest, or like "ohmygod" this is so cool, or else it's your bad. In other words, you're not texting, you're not talking to your best friends, and you're not trying to communicate on the playground. You're writing for a bunch of old fogies who have no idea what the latest slang means. Stick to words that your grandparents understand.

Repeating yourself over and over again

One of the biggest mistakes that you can make on the ACT Writing Test is saying the same thing again and again in different words. Don't try to lengthen your essay by repeating yourself. The test graders get it the first time. If you find yourself repeating sentences for lack of things to say, then you didn't spend enough time planning the essay.

The way to avoid too much repetition is by organizing your thoughts and coming up with specific and different examples to prove your thesis before you start writing.

Failing to edit your essay

One of the most embarrassing things that can happen to you on a perfect first date is having toilet paper stuck to your shoe and having your date tell you about it! Date over. To counteract a potential faux pas like this one, make sure that you double-check your shoes before leaving the bathroom — a skill that you can also apply to finishing your ACT essay. (At last, a real-world skill you can finally use.)

Leave yourself time to proofread and check your essay for any obvious sentence structure errors, spelling mistakes, lack of clarity, missing or wrong punctuation, repetition, and illegible handwriting. By doing so, you eliminate any embarrassing toilet paper that's stuck to your writing before your date — or should we say your test grader — notices.

Reviewing Some Example Essays and Their Scores

The ACT essay receives a score from 1 to 6 from one of two readers in four areas: quality of analysis, strength of development, clarity of organization, and quality of writing. The lowest score you can receive from one reader in each area is — get this — a 1, and the highest score is a 6.

One of the best ways to avoid the common mistakes associated with receiving lower scores is to read examples of essays that have garnered different scores, which is where this section comes into play. Here we explain what you need to do to get the highest possible score on your essay by beginning with an example of an essay worthy of each score and then explaining why the sample deserves that particular score. Feel free to laugh at the ones with lower scores. We did. After reading these examples, you'll have a much better idea of what to avoid in your writing. To see the prompt for these essays, read the section "Examining the Prompt and Creating a Thesis" earlier in this chapter.

1 — 1 is the loneliest number: How not to be a 1

Like Perspective 1 says, kids should where uniforms. Then I wouldn't have to see all the gangsters walking around with there pants around there knees. But the girls should be able to where whatever they want, because no one minds when the show off there stomachs. Student and principles should both where uniforms. Its only fair.

Being number 1 may be great for high school football, but it isn't great on your ACT test. This writer chooses a side to some degree, but she doesn't support or back up her thesis. Not only does she fail to support her position, but she also wanders throughout the "essay." Her lack of focus, irreverent examples, and writing style merit a score of 1 in each area. Oh, and by the way, the number of spelling and word errors distracts the reader from her ideas and negatively influences the way the graders look at her essay.

2 — 2 little 2 late: Steering clear of coming in second

I don't agree with the teachers and parents in Perspectives 1 and 3 who think we should have uniforms. Our style of dress is what makes us individuals and sets us apart form each other.

At my school students who dress in certain ways find others who are like them. You always know who is interested in the same stuff as you by what they wear. Imposing a uniform doesn't allow us to make friendships with people you are like ourselves.

Uniforms would make people mad. Teachers would find it hard to control all their students because students would want to rebel. Kids wouldn't be able to find friends who are like them and this would cause them to rebel.

These are just a few reasons why we should not have a uniform at school. There are many more reasons then just these but these are the most important.

This writer takes a stance and shows that he can support his point of view, but his lack of organization leaves readers' heads spinning. He also appears to be agreeing with the second perspective but fails to mention the parallel between his own opinion and this perspective. The writer has paragraph structure in this essay, with an introductory paragraph and conclusion, but he's missing clear transitions between the two body paragraphs. His simple sentence structure and spelling errors let everyone know that his writing skills are not as sophisticated as they should be. A score of 2 may be better than a 1, but it isn't a score you should strive for.

3 — Still finding yourself on the wrong side of the tracks

In my opinion, kids should not have a uniform because it takes away freedoms that they should have. There are some clothing styles that teenagers wear that are not appropriate like tight revealing clothes. But to make students buy certain clothes like blue pants and white shirt infringes on their rights.

In America freedom of expression is very important and by forcing us to wear certain things schools are taking away one of our rights. If they start taking away this right, they might start taking away other ones too.

Uniforms are unfair because some families cannot afford them. Many kids would need a whole new wardrobe and their families would have a hard time buying this for them. Not only would they need clothes, but they also need clothes for outside of school. For poorer families this would be hard.

A uniform would take away some of our freedom of expression and it would be a financial strain for poorer families. I think that there should be no uniforms.

A score of 3 is almost a reason for celebration. Almost. This writer states her own perspective and advances her argument. The essay maintains a semblance of structure. She presents a clear point of view with two supporting points that address the language presented in the prompt. Her sentences are more complex than the ones written by most eighth-graders, and she presents a clear conclusion that sums up her points.

However, her overall writing style and propensity for rambling sentences leave something to be desired. When you add the average 3 scores from each reader, you get an overall score of 6. But a 7 is the lowest score you can receive and still be considered "college ready" in writing.

The ACT readers recognize her developing skill but she still has room for improvement. Her essay would be better if she discussed counterarguments and more fully developed her ideas. Her paragraphs aren't complete, and she doesn't include transitions to link her ideas and increase the essay's flow. Plus, she makes numerous punctuation mistakes. With a little work, this essay could make it to the right side of the tracks.

4 — Reaching 4 a better score

I believe that it would be a good idea for our schools to adopt uniforms. Some people argue that it would restrict student's freedom of expression, but I do not agree with this position. It is important that we have a right to express ourselves, but our society does not allow us to have unrestricted freedoms like this all the time. It is important to learn discipline, show respect for other's feelings and learn how to be successful operating in the real world. School uniforms create a better learning environment and also helps students prepare for their futures.

The most important benefit of imposing dress codes would be creating a better school environment. Students who are trying to concentrate and learn would be unfocused because of inappropriate clothing. Small clothing, tight tops, and sagging pants might be okay for after school but not appropriate for the classroom. Certain types of people might find profanity and obscene images offensive. Art and creative writing are better ways to express your creativity rather than on your clothing. Less distractions in the classroom would help a student to get a better education.

Another important benefit of having uniforms would teach students how to dress properly for different occasions. Clothes that you would wear to a party would not be appropriate for a dinner with your boyfriends parents. Likewise, you wouldn't wear your work clothes on a date. Some jobs in society require people to wear uniforms. Uniforms in schools help students to realize what the world is like and get ready to enter it.

Another important concern for students is trying to fit in. Uniforms take the emphasis off what you look like and put more emphasis on learning.

In conclusion, it is important for schools to require uniforms. Getting an education is the most important thing about school and uniforms take away distractions. Learning how to dress for the real world is also important. And it helps with the pressures of trying to fit in.

A score of 4 would make anyone want to run and frolic through green pastures because the ACT folks think you have writing skills that are adequate for college. You may not be the most eloquent writer, but at least you're clear and organized. Your respectable score reflects your ability. This writer takes a stance, backs it up using both points made in the prompts and some entirely new ones, and acknowledges counterarguments. He maintains focus throughout the essay, and he supports each idea in well-defined paragraphs with specific examples to make the graders happy. This writer demonstrates a simple organizational structure that works; the essay properly includes an introduction that sets up what the writer talks about in the body paragraphs and a conclusion that sums up his points without word-for-word repetition. This essay shows that the writer has learned adequate writing skills in school, even though he hasn't mastered perfect punctuation or impeccable word choice. (In the second paragraph, *less distractions* should be *fewer distractions*, and switching back and forth between third and second person isn't stylistically pleasing.)

5 — Shining brightly: A 5-star winner

There is a debate now amongst parents and teachers about whether a school uniform should be required. Mandating uniforms would positively impact the learning environment in our schools and significantly improve the excellence of our education. First, students would be able to focus on academics rather than the social facet of school. Second, the appearance of the school would improve. And third, students would be better prepared for the working world.

The most crucial benefit of requiring uniforms would be to significantly reduce the distractions in the classroom. For students to be successful in the future, it is important that we concentrate on the material being taught in the classroom. It is difficult to do this when you overhear students whispering about their newest Gucci purse or admiring their best friend's Prada shoes. Young people place such an emphasis on style and image rather than substance. In addition, students see school as a social venue rather than a learning environment.

Secondly, when students and faculty are well groomed, the aesthetic appeal of the school is improved. Formal attire is not necessary to achieve this. For example, requiring long pants and a collared shirt would be sufficient. Not only would the school look more professional, it would change the character of the school. Holding students to a higher standard would require them to do it for themselves. It would improve their maturity level as well.

Finally, sporting uniforms would prepare today's youth for the work of their future. A majority of jobs require uniforms or a standard dress code. I think it is important for schools to not only prepare students academically for their future, but also in proper conduct and grooming. Just because someone has impressive qualifications doesn't mean they'll be hired if they look like they just rolled in from the beach. Allowing students to dress however they choose might eventually be harmful to their future success.

The notion that uniforms would hinder a student's freedom of expression is valid, but I still think a dress code is a good idea. A dress code addresses the important issues at hand while at the same time allowing the student to find more appropriate ways of expression. You can express individuality through art, music, speech, and other means regardless of your clothing.

In conclusion, I strongly support the idea of enforcing a school uniform. Not only would uniforms improve our learning environment, but they would also improve the character of the school and ready its students for a successful future.

A score of 5 gets you a gold star on the blackboard! It isn't ACT perfection, but it's close. This writer is able to effectively state her position by clearly answering the question and addressing counterarguments. She presents a well-organized and fluid essay with a variety of specific examples drawn from both the prompts and her own perspective. She develops the ideas in each paragraph and uses them to support her argument. This writer explores a cultural component that shows advanced critical-thinking skills and displays a mastery of vocabulary and precise word choice. Some problems with sentence structure and changing from third to second person within the same sentence keep this essay from receiving a perfect score.

6 — Unlocking the code to a perfect score

The trend of inappropriate dress in our schools is causing alarm in our parents and educators. This population argues that wearing inappropriate clothes is distracting in the classroom and interferes with the learning environment. They believe that requiring uniforms would provide a reasonable solution to the problem. Although those opposed to uniforms believe that enforcing them would hinder the student's freedom of expression, I believe that the advantages far outweigh this potential disadvantage.

When freedom of expression begins to interfere with appropriate and meaningful education in the classroom, we must address this serious dilemma. The current lack of uniforms is not working. We are not breaking new ground when we suggest that the fashion that is spewed upon our youth in the mass media is riddled with sexual undertones. Examples can be seen in every teen magazine, youth-oriented television program, and in the most popular music videos. Further, clothing that advertisers would consider benign, stimulates and raises the hormone levels of every young male and promotes distractions in the classroom. The only solution to help create an environment where learning takes precedence is to adopt school uniforms. Obviously, a uniform policy would be easier to enforce a dress code and would bring many advantages to the entire academic population.

First and foremost, uniforms would help students to fight the materialistic world's values. Our society feels that designer labels, such as Joe's Jeans, Elizabeth and James, and Zoe Couture, create self-worth and that without these, a person is open to cruel comments and non-acceptance. Many students cannot afford to "buy" their self-worth and are required to rise above the standards our society and media feeds them. As a teenager, acceptance is the most crucial aspect of their daily lives, and school uniforms take away the financial burden that our society imposes upon them. Although uniforms must be purchased, this is a minimal financial burden compared to overly high-priced current designer wear that students ask for.

Uniforms could also help curb gang-related violence that occurs in many of our nation's schools. Specific colors, logos, and signs have been adopted into the lifestyle of gang members and each carries its own significance. What was once an ordinary red shirt could now be considered an intentional bullet fired in a gang battle. Uniforms decrease the division lines between gangs as well as protect students who are ignorant to the unwritten laws that govern gangs.

For myself, uniforms would dramatically decrease the amount of time I spend preparing for my day. No longer would I need to delve into the bottom of my closet to find an outfit that I haven't worn this week. I do not need to worry that my best friends might come to school in the same outfit as mine, because uniforms ensure that they will! Uniforms give me extra time to finish the homework I haven't done rather than spend time worrying about my wardrobe.

Some may argue that uniforms prevent creative expression, but those who agree with this opinion are limiting their notion of creativity to fashion. There are many other ways to express creativity. In fact, requiring uniforms may actually encourage freedom of expression. Without the distraction created by questionnable clothing, students may be better able to express themselves in art class, through scientific research, and with literary exploits. Uniforms help to ensure a learning environment that is free from distractions and fosters creative expression in areas that are important.

I highly value the worth of uniforms and feel they should be enforced throughout the entire school district. Solving problems in the entire district would help ensure a safer community, save money, encourage better learning, and give students a little extra time in the morning.

The secret to perfection on the ACT Writing Test is garnering a 6, and with an essay like this, you can likely earn it. The ACT graders are practically drooling over this writer's style because it recognizes the complexity of the issue, analyzes the provided perspectives, develops the author's own position, and then describes the relationships among all points. He supports the reasons for his position with specific, well-thought-out, and varied examples. His structure and organization are logical, and he includes smooth but subtle transitions between his paragraphs. His writing displays his own unique wit and personality, and he concludes his essay with a reference to an anecdote from a prior paragraph. Given the time limits, this essay is nearly perfect, and the occasional misplaced comma and the misspelling of *questionable* **won't concern the graders.**

IN THIS CHAPTER

» Using prompts to write practice essays

» Getting feedback from your parents and teachers

Chapter 18
Practicing Promptly with Practice Prompts: Essay Practice Questions

In Chapter 17, you do a lot of reading about writing. But you'll never get better at writing without actually writing — which is why you've turned to this chapter. Here, we give you two sample prompts to practice with, and we suggest that you time yourself so that you get a sense of what 40 minutes of writing feels like. Practicing like this helps you avoid panicking when you take the real test.

Directions: Follow the guidelines in Chapter 17 and create an essay on each of the following two prompts. You don't have enough space to write your essay in this chapter, so grab some extra pieces of paper. One to one and a half pages for each essay should do the trick. (Just make sure you don't peek at our writing tips that follow each prompt until after you're done writing!)

TIP

Be sure to give yourself a good, long break between essays. When you're done with each one, read through the tips we give you for writing each essay topic and assess your effort. Or, better yet, have your parents or English teacher read your essays for feedback.

Writing Prompt 1

Many successful people believe that a competitive environment fosters high achievement. In high schools, some parents and teachers think that competition among students encourages them to strive toward higher academic potential. Others think that academic competition negatively affects students' performance by causing undue stress and feelings of failure. Should high schools encourage or discourage a competitive academic atmosphere?

Read and carefully consider these perspectives. Each suggests a particular way of thinking about the benefits and drawbacks of a competitive school atmosphere.

> **Perspective 1:** For today's students, school is their training ground for real life. In real life, they will find themselves in constant competition. Whether for jobs, the affections of another, or a day on the golf course, students will not be able to avoid competition, so they may as well train for and get used to it in high school.
>
> **Perspective 2:** Today's high school students are under enough pressure without being faced with increased academic competition while at school. Peer pressure, pressure to excel in sports, and pressure to succeed in their parents' eyes is more than enough stress for students of high school age to deal with.
>
> **Perspective 3:** Academic competition among students should be encouraged to a point. Healthy competition gives our students a valuable opportunity to excel and gain self-esteem and gives all students a reasonable chance of winning. Unhealthy competition is that which either implicitly or explicitly rewards stronger students in a way that allows these students to exploit their perceived superiority over those students whose accomplishments have not been recognized.

Write a unified, coherent essay in which you evaluate multiple perspectives as to whether high schools should encourage competition. In your essay, be sure to do the following:

- Clearly state your own perspective on the issue and analyze the relationship between your perspective and at least one other perspective.
- Develop and support your ideas with reasoning and examples.
- Organize your ideas clearly and logically.
- Communicate your ideas effectively in standard written English.

Your perspective may be in full agreement with any of the others, in partial agreement, or wholly different.

In this prompt, you're tasked with assessing the strengths and weaknesses of a competitive high school environment. The question doesn't have a right or wrong answer; what's important is that you clearly evaluate the perspectives provided, state and develop one of your own, and explain how your own perspective relates to those given.

Say, for example, that you support the concept of competition. In that case, you may begin your essay with a thesis statement about how fostering a competitive learning environment at the high school level is necessary to provide students with a taste of what's to come when they enter the real world. Your introduction may point out that the real world is very competitive and that the purpose of high school is to provide students with a foundation for success, as stated by Perspective 1. Subsequent paragraphs may argue that many students thrive in a competitive environment and that measures like grading on a curve may encourage students to study more thoroughly and learn more in an effort not to fall behind. You must support your argument with examples, such as a quick summary of Darwin's Survival of the Fittest theory or the fact that the entire college admissions process is one big competition.

Be sure to consider the opposing side and the other perspectives provided. For example, you may explain how some people, like the author of Perspective 2, believe that an increasingly competitive environment in schools creates unnecessary stress at a time when students are still learning and becoming familiar with their own strengths and abilities and that high school is a time in students' lives when they should be able to hone their skills at their own pace, in whatever manner they learn most efficiently. To address this opposing side, point out that students who require extra time and attention may work with a tutor or log additional study hours in order not to be left behind . . . a luxury they're unlikely to see once they enter the far more cutthroat post-school job market.

Your closing paragraph is your last opportunity to make an impression on the reader. Use this paragraph to tie together the key points you made earlier in the essay. Present a succinct conclusion that brings the discussion full circle, perhaps by mentioning that more competitive high school students may become the leaders that help America compete with other nations worldwide.

Alternatively, you may choose to write against fostering a competitive environment at the high school level, as is done in Perspective 2, choosing instead to write about how the high school years are the last chance students have to focus on learning by whatever methods are most effective for them as individuals. The rest of life can be likened to a competition, and, as most high school students have yet to reach adulthood, many of them simply are not ready to excel in a highly competitive environment. You may argue that the adolescent and teen years are stressful and emotionally taxing enough without the added stress of competition in the classroom, something most people become more equipped to handle as they enter adulthood.

When you address the opposing arguments, you can say that while it's true that the future holds much competition, students will develop an ability to deal with that competition in college. You may note that students aren't required to apply for an education (although they may be in the case of private schools) until they reach the college level, and with good reason: They're simply not mentally and emotionally prepared for that level of competition in early adolescence.

REMEMBER

You don't need to (and likely shouldn't) refer to the provided perspectives in your essay; address the ideas in the opinions, but don't mention them by number. Whether you identify with a perspective already provided or have created a perspective of your own that's entirely different isn't as important as using solid examples and concise arguments to argue and support your case.

Writing Prompt 2

The prevailing attitude in many countries is that civic leaders must maintain the highest ethical and moral standards. Some people think that this attitude sets a good example for a country and its citizens. Others argue that leaders who show normal human flaws connect them with those they lead and thereby enable progress and growth. It is important to consider the role that ethical standards play in evaluating our leaders.

Read and carefully consider these perspectives. Each one suggests a particular way of thinking about the role of ethics in leadership.

Perspective 1: Why do we vote for our civic leaders if we want them to be just like everyone else? There are millions of people in this country, and we choose one to represent us all. Leaders should indeed be held to higher moral and ethical standards because all eyes, young and old, are on them at all times. We want the person in a position of power to be someone our children can look up to.

Perspective 2: People will be more likely to embrace and respect their political and civic leaders if they feel they are human and easy to identify with. Look at Bill Clinton — he clearly made errors and showed poor judgment, but he is still one of the most beloved ex-presidents in our nation's history.

Perspective 3: If we do not hold our political and civic leaders to a higher standard, how are we supposed to garner the respect of other countries? For many nations, our leaders are all they know of America. We want to gain their respect and admiration, and the best starting point for doing so is electing individuals of strong moral and ethical stature.

Write a unified, coherent essay in which you evaluate multiple perspectives as to whether leaders should be held to higher moral and ethical standards than the general population. In your essay, be sure to do the following:

> » Clearly state your own perspective on the issue and analyze the relationship between your perspective and at least one other perspective.
> » Develop and support your ideas with reasoning and examples.
> » Organize your ideas clearly and logically.
> » Communicate your ideas effectively in standard written English.

Your perspective may be in full agreement with any of the others, in partial agreement, or wholly different.

In this prompt, you may argue for or against holding leaders to a higher moral and ethical standard than the common citizen. Say that you agree with the author of Perspective 1 that leaders should be more accountable for their actions than the average person. Your thesis paragraph may state that leaders are leaders for a reason — because they embody the ideals of a given population and because anyone could be a leader if leaders shared the same flaws as everyone else.

Your subsequent arguments may cite examples of elected officials whose poor or lack of judgment resulted in problems for those they governed. For example, you may mention a politician who misused their power or access to government funds to help further their own agenda. You may note that a leader is inherently in a position to serve as a role model and should, therefore, be expected to act accordingly at all times while in the public eye.

You may choose to address the opposing side offered by the author of Perspective 2 by stating that, while it's true that all humans are flawed by nature, leaders become leaders because of something exemplary about them. People elect and choose them because they aren't just like everyone else. Therefore, it's acceptable to hold them to a higher standard.

To wrap things up, your closing paragraph needs to echo, not directly repeat, the key points you make in the essay to support your initial argument and whether you agree with the perspectives given.

Should you choose to support the opposing side, you may formulate your thesis around the idea that great leaders are a representation of the population they rule, flaws, and all. They were chosen for a leadership role based on their ability to relate and identify with the people they govern, and this ability enables them to make decisions in the best interests of their people effectively. Strengthen your argument with real-life examples, such as citing a politician whose moral character is undeniably questionable (like the Bill Clinton example provided in Perspective 2) and yet who is still revered as one of the best and most effective leaders of our time. Or offer a similar example of a leader whose questionable ethics didn't interfere with their ability to rule a given population effectively.

Providing inspirational examples of leaders who have been effective despite their character flaws has the added benefit of addressing the concerns of the opposition. You may point out that character flaws don't necessarily weaken a leader's accomplishments and may actually enhance the effectiveness of leaders who acknowledge their weaknesses. Perhaps leaders who are more representative of the common person may inspire others who work to overcome character flaws so that they, too, may one day land a position of power and decision-making. Plus, people are more likely to see flawed leaders as relatable, approachable figures who are more likely to have the general public's best interests at heart.

Conclude with a few lines that summarize the key arguments you make in your essay and draw a final conclusion as to why moral and ethical equals are the best choice for leadership roles.

7

Putting It All Together with a Full-Length Practice ACT

IN THIS PART . . .

Take a full-length ACT practice test in a quiet location with no interruptions to duplicate real conditions.

Find out why the right answers are right and the wrong answers are wrong.

Discover a lot of valuable information in each of the explanations.

Chapter 19
Practice Exam

Here's your chance to test what you know on an ACT sample test. The following exam consists of five tests: a 35-minute English Test, a 50-minute Mathematics Test, and a 40-minute Reading Test, plus an optional 40-minute Science Test and a 40-minute Writing Test.

To make sure you replicate the torturous climate of the real experience, take this test under the following normal exam conditions:

- Sit where you won't be interrupted or tempted to use your cellphone or binge multiple seasons of your favorite shows.
- Use the answer sheet provided to give you practice filling in the dots.
- Set your timer for the time limits indicated at the beginning of each test in this exam.
- Don't go on to the next test until the time allotted for the test you're taking is up.
- Check your work for that test only; don't look at more than one test at a time.
- Don't take a break during any test.

TIP

When you finish this practice exam, turn to Chapter 20. There, you can check your answers using an abbreviated answer key and read more detailed explanations of how to approach every question. Go through the answer explanations to all the questions, not just the ones you missed. Intertwined in the explanations are reviews of important concepts from the previous chapters and tips for improving the efficiency of your approach.

Note: The Science Test and Writing Test are optional. If you register to take the Science Test or Writing Test or both, you'll take them after you've completed the other three tests. For details about the optional Science Test, see Part 5. For Writing Test details, see Part 6.

REMEMBER

For additional practice exams, visit www.dummies.com/go/getaccess. Follow the prompts and you'll receive an email with your PIN and instructions.

Answer Sheet

Begin with Number 1 for each new test.

English Test

1. Ⓐ Ⓑ Ⓒ Ⓓ
2. Ⓕ Ⓖ Ⓗ Ⓙ
3. Ⓐ Ⓑ Ⓒ Ⓓ
4. Ⓕ Ⓖ Ⓗ Ⓙ
5. Ⓐ Ⓑ Ⓒ Ⓓ
6. Ⓕ Ⓖ Ⓗ Ⓙ
7. Ⓐ Ⓑ Ⓒ Ⓓ
8. Ⓕ Ⓖ Ⓗ Ⓙ
9. Ⓐ Ⓑ Ⓒ Ⓓ
10. Ⓕ Ⓖ Ⓗ Ⓙ
11. Ⓐ Ⓑ Ⓒ Ⓓ
12. Ⓕ Ⓖ Ⓗ Ⓙ
13. Ⓐ Ⓑ Ⓒ Ⓓ
14. Ⓕ Ⓖ Ⓗ Ⓙ
15. Ⓐ Ⓑ Ⓒ Ⓓ
16. Ⓕ Ⓖ Ⓗ Ⓙ
17. Ⓐ Ⓑ Ⓒ Ⓓ
18. Ⓕ Ⓖ Ⓗ Ⓙ
19. Ⓐ Ⓑ Ⓒ Ⓓ
20. Ⓕ Ⓖ Ⓗ Ⓙ
21. Ⓐ Ⓑ Ⓒ Ⓓ
22. Ⓕ Ⓖ Ⓗ Ⓙ
23. Ⓐ Ⓑ Ⓒ Ⓓ
24. Ⓕ Ⓖ Ⓗ Ⓙ
25. Ⓐ Ⓑ Ⓒ Ⓓ
26. Ⓕ Ⓖ Ⓗ Ⓙ
27. Ⓐ Ⓑ Ⓒ Ⓓ
28. Ⓕ Ⓖ Ⓗ Ⓙ
29. Ⓐ Ⓑ Ⓒ Ⓓ
30. Ⓕ Ⓖ Ⓗ Ⓙ
31. Ⓐ Ⓑ Ⓒ Ⓓ
32. Ⓕ Ⓖ Ⓗ Ⓙ
33. Ⓐ Ⓑ Ⓒ Ⓓ
34. Ⓕ Ⓖ Ⓗ Ⓙ
35. Ⓐ Ⓑ Ⓒ Ⓓ
36. Ⓕ Ⓖ Ⓗ Ⓙ
37. Ⓐ Ⓑ Ⓒ Ⓓ
38. Ⓕ Ⓖ Ⓗ Ⓙ
39. Ⓐ Ⓑ Ⓒ Ⓓ
40. Ⓕ Ⓖ Ⓗ Ⓙ
41. Ⓐ Ⓑ Ⓒ Ⓓ
42. Ⓕ Ⓖ Ⓗ Ⓙ
43. Ⓐ Ⓑ Ⓒ Ⓓ
44. Ⓕ Ⓖ Ⓗ Ⓙ
45. Ⓐ Ⓑ Ⓒ Ⓓ
46. Ⓕ Ⓖ Ⓗ Ⓙ
47. Ⓐ Ⓑ Ⓒ Ⓓ
48. Ⓕ Ⓖ Ⓗ Ⓙ
49. Ⓐ Ⓑ Ⓒ Ⓓ
50. Ⓕ Ⓖ Ⓗ Ⓙ
51. Ⓐ Ⓑ Ⓒ Ⓓ
52. Ⓕ Ⓖ Ⓗ Ⓙ
53. Ⓐ Ⓑ Ⓒ Ⓓ
54. Ⓕ Ⓖ Ⓗ Ⓙ
55. Ⓐ Ⓑ Ⓒ Ⓓ
56. Ⓕ Ⓖ Ⓗ Ⓙ
57. Ⓐ Ⓑ Ⓒ Ⓓ
58. Ⓕ Ⓖ Ⓗ Ⓙ
59. Ⓐ Ⓑ Ⓒ Ⓓ
60. Ⓕ Ⓖ Ⓗ Ⓙ
61. Ⓐ Ⓑ Ⓒ Ⓓ
62. Ⓕ Ⓖ Ⓗ Ⓙ
63. Ⓐ Ⓑ Ⓒ Ⓓ
64. Ⓕ Ⓖ Ⓗ Ⓙ
65. Ⓐ Ⓑ Ⓒ Ⓓ
66. Ⓕ Ⓖ Ⓗ Ⓙ
67. Ⓐ Ⓑ Ⓒ Ⓓ
68. Ⓕ Ⓖ Ⓗ Ⓙ
69. Ⓐ Ⓑ Ⓒ Ⓓ
70. Ⓕ Ⓖ Ⓗ Ⓙ
71. Ⓐ Ⓑ Ⓒ Ⓓ
72. Ⓕ Ⓖ Ⓗ Ⓙ
73. Ⓐ Ⓑ Ⓒ Ⓓ
74. Ⓕ Ⓖ Ⓗ Ⓙ
75. Ⓐ Ⓑ Ⓒ Ⓓ

Mathematics Test

1. Ⓐ Ⓑ Ⓒ Ⓓ Ⓔ
2. Ⓕ Ⓖ Ⓗ Ⓙ Ⓚ
3. Ⓐ Ⓑ Ⓒ Ⓓ Ⓔ
4. Ⓕ Ⓖ Ⓗ Ⓙ Ⓚ
5. Ⓐ Ⓑ Ⓒ Ⓓ Ⓔ
6. Ⓕ Ⓖ Ⓗ Ⓙ Ⓚ
7. Ⓐ Ⓑ Ⓒ Ⓓ Ⓔ
8. Ⓕ Ⓖ Ⓗ Ⓙ Ⓚ
9. Ⓐ Ⓑ Ⓒ Ⓓ Ⓔ
10. Ⓕ Ⓖ Ⓗ Ⓙ Ⓚ
11. Ⓐ Ⓑ Ⓒ Ⓓ Ⓔ
12. Ⓕ Ⓖ Ⓗ Ⓙ Ⓚ
13. Ⓐ Ⓑ Ⓒ Ⓓ Ⓔ
14. Ⓕ Ⓖ Ⓗ Ⓙ Ⓚ
15. Ⓐ Ⓑ Ⓒ Ⓓ Ⓔ
16. Ⓕ Ⓖ Ⓗ Ⓙ Ⓚ
17. Ⓐ Ⓑ Ⓒ Ⓓ Ⓔ
18. Ⓕ Ⓖ Ⓗ Ⓙ Ⓚ
19. Ⓐ Ⓑ Ⓒ Ⓓ Ⓔ
20. Ⓕ Ⓖ Ⓗ Ⓙ Ⓚ
21. Ⓐ Ⓑ Ⓒ Ⓓ Ⓔ
22. Ⓕ Ⓖ Ⓗ Ⓙ Ⓚ
23. Ⓐ Ⓑ Ⓒ Ⓓ Ⓔ
24. Ⓕ Ⓖ Ⓗ Ⓙ Ⓚ
25. Ⓐ Ⓑ Ⓒ Ⓓ Ⓔ
26. Ⓕ Ⓖ Ⓗ Ⓙ Ⓚ
27. Ⓐ Ⓑ Ⓒ Ⓓ Ⓔ
28. Ⓕ Ⓖ Ⓗ Ⓙ Ⓚ
29. Ⓐ Ⓑ Ⓒ Ⓓ Ⓔ
30. Ⓕ Ⓖ Ⓗ Ⓙ Ⓚ
31. Ⓐ Ⓑ Ⓒ Ⓓ Ⓔ
32. Ⓕ Ⓖ Ⓗ Ⓙ Ⓚ
33. Ⓐ Ⓑ Ⓒ Ⓓ Ⓔ
34. Ⓕ Ⓖ Ⓗ Ⓙ Ⓚ
35. Ⓐ Ⓑ Ⓒ Ⓓ Ⓔ
36. Ⓕ Ⓖ Ⓗ Ⓙ Ⓚ
37. Ⓐ Ⓑ Ⓒ Ⓓ Ⓔ
38. Ⓕ Ⓖ Ⓗ Ⓙ Ⓚ
39. Ⓐ Ⓑ Ⓒ Ⓓ Ⓔ
40. Ⓕ Ⓖ Ⓗ Ⓙ Ⓚ
41. Ⓐ Ⓑ Ⓒ Ⓓ Ⓔ
42. Ⓕ Ⓖ Ⓗ Ⓙ Ⓚ
43. Ⓐ Ⓑ Ⓒ Ⓓ Ⓔ
44. Ⓕ Ⓖ Ⓗ Ⓙ Ⓚ
45. Ⓐ Ⓑ Ⓒ Ⓓ Ⓔ
46. Ⓕ Ⓖ Ⓗ Ⓙ Ⓚ
47. Ⓐ Ⓑ Ⓒ Ⓓ Ⓔ
48. Ⓕ Ⓖ Ⓗ Ⓙ Ⓚ
49. Ⓐ Ⓑ Ⓒ Ⓓ Ⓔ
50. Ⓕ Ⓖ Ⓗ Ⓙ Ⓚ
51. Ⓐ Ⓑ Ⓒ Ⓓ Ⓔ
52. Ⓕ Ⓖ Ⓗ Ⓙ Ⓚ
53. Ⓐ Ⓑ Ⓒ Ⓓ Ⓔ
54. Ⓕ Ⓖ Ⓗ Ⓙ Ⓚ
55. Ⓐ Ⓑ Ⓒ Ⓓ Ⓔ
56. Ⓕ Ⓖ Ⓗ Ⓙ Ⓚ
57. Ⓐ Ⓑ Ⓒ Ⓓ Ⓔ
58. Ⓕ Ⓖ Ⓗ Ⓙ Ⓚ
59. Ⓐ Ⓑ Ⓒ Ⓓ Ⓔ
60. Ⓕ Ⓖ Ⓗ Ⓙ Ⓚ

Reading Test

1. Ⓐ Ⓑ Ⓒ Ⓓ
2. Ⓕ Ⓖ Ⓗ Ⓙ
3. Ⓐ Ⓑ Ⓒ Ⓓ
4. Ⓕ Ⓖ Ⓗ Ⓙ
5. Ⓐ Ⓑ Ⓒ Ⓓ
6. Ⓕ Ⓖ Ⓗ Ⓙ
7. Ⓐ Ⓑ Ⓒ Ⓓ
8. Ⓕ Ⓖ Ⓗ Ⓙ
9. Ⓐ Ⓑ Ⓒ Ⓓ
10. Ⓕ Ⓖ Ⓗ Ⓙ
11. Ⓐ Ⓑ Ⓒ Ⓓ
12. Ⓕ Ⓖ Ⓗ Ⓙ
13. Ⓐ Ⓑ Ⓒ Ⓓ
14. Ⓕ Ⓖ Ⓗ Ⓙ
15. Ⓐ Ⓑ Ⓒ Ⓓ
16. Ⓕ Ⓖ Ⓗ Ⓙ
17. Ⓐ Ⓑ Ⓒ Ⓓ
18. Ⓕ Ⓖ Ⓗ Ⓙ
19. Ⓐ Ⓑ Ⓒ Ⓓ
20. Ⓕ Ⓖ Ⓗ Ⓙ
21. Ⓐ Ⓑ Ⓒ Ⓓ
22. Ⓕ Ⓖ Ⓗ Ⓙ
23. Ⓐ Ⓑ Ⓒ Ⓓ
24. Ⓕ Ⓖ Ⓗ Ⓙ
25. Ⓐ Ⓑ Ⓒ Ⓓ
26. Ⓕ Ⓖ Ⓗ Ⓙ
27. Ⓐ Ⓑ Ⓒ Ⓓ
28. Ⓕ Ⓖ Ⓗ Ⓙ
29. Ⓐ Ⓑ Ⓒ Ⓓ
30. Ⓕ Ⓖ Ⓗ Ⓙ
31. Ⓐ Ⓑ Ⓒ Ⓓ
32. Ⓕ Ⓖ Ⓗ Ⓙ
33. Ⓐ Ⓑ Ⓒ Ⓓ
34. Ⓕ Ⓖ Ⓗ Ⓙ
35. Ⓐ Ⓑ Ⓒ Ⓓ
36. Ⓕ Ⓖ Ⓗ Ⓙ
37. Ⓐ Ⓑ Ⓒ Ⓓ
38. Ⓕ Ⓖ Ⓗ Ⓙ
39. Ⓐ Ⓑ Ⓒ Ⓓ
40. Ⓕ Ⓖ Ⓗ Ⓙ

Science Test

1. Ⓐ Ⓑ Ⓒ Ⓓ
2. Ⓕ Ⓖ Ⓗ Ⓙ
3. Ⓐ Ⓑ Ⓒ Ⓓ
4. Ⓕ Ⓖ Ⓗ Ⓙ
5. Ⓐ Ⓑ Ⓒ Ⓓ
6. Ⓕ Ⓖ Ⓗ Ⓙ
7. Ⓐ Ⓑ Ⓒ Ⓓ
8. Ⓕ Ⓖ Ⓗ Ⓙ
9. Ⓐ Ⓑ Ⓒ Ⓓ
10. Ⓕ Ⓖ Ⓗ Ⓙ
11. Ⓐ Ⓑ Ⓒ Ⓓ
12. Ⓕ Ⓖ Ⓗ Ⓙ
13. Ⓐ Ⓑ Ⓒ Ⓓ
14. Ⓕ Ⓖ Ⓗ Ⓙ
15. Ⓐ Ⓑ Ⓒ Ⓓ
16. Ⓕ Ⓖ Ⓗ Ⓙ
17. Ⓐ Ⓑ Ⓒ Ⓓ
18. Ⓕ Ⓖ Ⓗ Ⓙ
19. Ⓐ Ⓑ Ⓒ Ⓓ
20. Ⓕ Ⓖ Ⓗ Ⓙ
21. Ⓐ Ⓑ Ⓒ Ⓓ
22. Ⓕ Ⓖ Ⓗ Ⓙ
23. Ⓐ Ⓑ Ⓒ Ⓓ
24. Ⓕ Ⓖ Ⓗ Ⓙ
25. Ⓐ Ⓑ Ⓒ Ⓓ
26. Ⓕ Ⓖ Ⓗ Ⓙ
27. Ⓐ Ⓑ Ⓒ Ⓓ
28. Ⓕ Ⓖ Ⓗ Ⓙ
29. Ⓐ Ⓑ Ⓒ Ⓓ
30. Ⓕ Ⓖ Ⓗ Ⓙ
31. Ⓐ Ⓑ Ⓒ Ⓓ
32. Ⓕ Ⓖ Ⓗ Ⓙ
33. Ⓐ Ⓑ Ⓒ Ⓓ
34. Ⓕ Ⓖ Ⓗ Ⓙ
35. Ⓐ Ⓑ Ⓒ Ⓓ
36. Ⓕ Ⓖ Ⓗ Ⓙ
37. Ⓐ Ⓑ Ⓒ Ⓓ
38. Ⓕ Ⓖ Ⓗ Ⓙ
39. Ⓐ Ⓑ Ⓒ Ⓓ
40. Ⓕ Ⓖ Ⓗ Ⓙ

English Test

TIME: 45 minutes for 75 questions

DIRECTIONS: Following are five passages with underlined portions. Alternate ways of stating the underlined portions come after the passages. Choose the best alternative; if the original is the best way of stating the underlined portion, choose NO CHANGE.

The test also has questions that refer to the passages or ask you to reorder the sentences within the passages. These questions are identified by a number in a box. Choose the best answer and shade in the corresponding oval on your answer sheet.

Passage 1

Personal Trainers Help Drop Pounds

When it comes to losing weight fast; some methods are more effective than others. For those who are serious about slimming down in a short amount of time, one of the easiest ways is to hire a personal trainer.

Because there's no standard of licensure for the profession, it's critical that you do your homework prior to hiring one. [4] Seek out a certified fitness professional — ideally, someone who is able to communicate well and clearly. You also may want to pick someone whose physique mirrors one that you want for yourself. For example, if you're inspired by your trainer, you're more likely to stay on track and less likely to skip out on workout sessions.

It's also a good idea to select someone with whom you connect, at least to some extent, on a personal level. Not all personalities mesh well together. Some people thrive off positive reinforcement, others fare better when faced with constructive criticism.

To decide, whether a potential trainer will be a good fit, ask questions about training style and fitness philosophy. Weight loss and physical fitness starts with effective training methods, and a personal trainer can be the perfect person to get you on track toward a new and better you. [10]

1. Which choice makes the sentence most grammatically acceptable?
   - (A) NO CHANGE
   - (B) losing weight fast, some methods are
   - (C) losing weight fast: some methods are
   - (D) losing weight fast — some methods are

2. Which choice makes the sentence most grammatically acceptable?
   - (F) NO CHANGE
   - (G) profession, its critical
   - (H) profession, its' critical
   - (J) profession; it's critical

3. Which choice makes the sentence most grammatically acceptable?
   - (A) NO CHANGE
   - (B) them
   - (C) a coach
   - (D) it

4. At this point, the author is considering adding the following statement:

   This might include asking friends, family, or co-workers, or reading online reviews or testimonials.

   Should the writer make this addition here?

   (F) Yes, because it provides specific ways the reader may accomplish the prior suggestion offered in the passage.
   (G) Yes, because it further explains the benefits of using a personal trainer.
   (H) No, because it contains information that has been stated previously in the passage.
   (J) No, because it does not emphasize how easy it is to find a personal trainer.

5. Which choice is least redundant in context?

   (A) NO CHANGE
   (B) clearly
   (C) well and clear
   (D) in a clear manner

6. Which transition word or phrase is most logical in context?

   (F) NO CHANGE
   (G) However,
   (H) To illustrate,
   (J) Delete the underlined portion and capitalize if.

7. Which choice makes the sentence most grammatically acceptable?

   (A) NO CHANGE
   (B) reinforcement, others fare best
   (C) reinforcement, but others fare better
   (D) reinforcement, and, others fare best

8. Which choice makes the sentence most grammatically acceptable?

   (F) NO CHANGE
   (G) To decide whether a potential trainer will be a good fit,
   (H) To decide whether, a potential trainer, will be a good fit
   (J) To decide whether a potential trainer, will be a good fit,

9. Which choice makes the sentence most grammatically acceptable?

   (A) NO CHANGE
   (B) begins
   (C) starting
   (D) start

10. Suppose the author's intent was to create an essay that highlights some of the best ways to lose weight. Would this essay successfully achieve that goal?

    (F) Yes, because the essay shows that hiring a trainer is a helpful way to lose weight.
    (G) Yes, because the essay highlights the importance of creating and sticking to a workout regimen.
    (H) No, because the essay does not reveal that hiring a trainer may actually lead to weight gain from increased muscle mass.
    (J) No, because the essay focuses on only one method for losing weight.

Passage 2

The Pitching Machine

Known as America's pastime, baseball means much more to many. Hitting baseballs is a major part of many a childhood, and using a pitching machine can be a great resource for ball players at any level to fine-tune <u>their</u> skills behind the plate.
11

Among the more popular pitching machine models are circular-wheel machines and arm-action machines. If you're looking to buy one, look for a variety that closely <u>reenacts</u> the pitches you'll
12
experience during real game play. Machines that throw a variety of different pitches allow players to work on hitting while improving hand-eye coordination.

More advanced players who hit at more
                              ──────────────
                                    13
elevated levels may favor a fast-pitch machine.
Featuring many customizable options, a hitter can
                                     ────────────
adjust the amount of time that passes between the
──
                          14
release of each baseball and set the machines at
───
different heights.
──────────────────

   Baseball is a wonderful sport, and these pitching machines can prove tremendously effective for players of all skill levels. [15] The device is a home run for players who want to maximize their skills at the plate.

11. Which choice makes the sentence most grammatically acceptable?
    (A) NO CHANGE
    (B) they're
    (C) there
    (D) its

12. Which choice is clearest and most precise in context?
    (F) NO CHANGE
    (G) fakes
    (H) assimilates
    (J) replicates

13. Which choice is least redundant in context?
    (A) NO CHANGE
    (B) who hit at elevated levels
    (C) hitting at elevated levels
    (D) DELETE the underlined portion.

14. Which choice makes the sentence most grammatically acceptable?
    (F) NO CHANGE
    (G) adjustments may be made to the amount of time that passes between the release of each baseball and the machines' height settings.
    (H) time between baseballs may be adjusted and heights changed.
    (J) the machines may be adjusted to change their height and the amount of time that passes between the release of each baseball.

15. At this point at the end of the sentence, the writer is considering adding the following:

    but mostly for younger hitters

    Should the writer make this addition?
    (A) No, because it contradicts the author's point that pitching machines are equally effective for players of all skill levels.
    (B) No, because professional players likely benefit more from pitching machines than do little league players.
    (C) Yes, because it furthers the author's argument that young players benefit more from pitching machines than older ones.
    (D) Yes, because it builds upon the point made in the previous paragraph.

Passage 3

Teddy Roosevelt: A Political Maverick

   No figure better represents the Progressive Era than Theodore "Teddy" Roosevelt. Born into a wealthy New York family, Roosevelt has risen to
                                                ─────────
                                                    16
national prominence rather quickly. Early in his
         ──────────
             17
career, Roosevelt served as commissioner of the New York City Police Department before becoming the Assistant Secretary of the Navy. In the Spanish-American War, Roosevelt gained notoriety for leading his military volunteer unit, the "Rough
                                                ──────────
Riders" to victory in the Battle of San Juan Hill
───
                        18
in Cuba. In 1900, Roosevelt became Republican William McKinley's vice-presidential candidate. McKinley was assassinated in 1901. [19] At age 42, Roosevelt became the youngest to assume the presidency of the United States.

250   PART 7   Putting It All Together with a Full-Length Practice ACT

"TR," as he came to be known, exuded an active, vibrant personality. Roosevelt was intelligent, well read, and knowledgeable about the environment, history, and naval strategy. He demonstrated his love for sports and competition by participating in boxing, being a big-game hunter, and other outdoor pursuits. His dynamic lifestyle carried over into his presidency, which lasted from 1901 to 1909, and he became one of the most active presidents in the history of the United States. Among the topics he tackled were trusts, railroads, safety in the food industry, and the environment.

Roosevelt demonstrated his distaste for trusts during the coal strike crisis of 1902. No fewer than 50,000 coal miners went on strike, demanding better working conditions and higher pay. Roosevelt intervened, inviting the union representatives and mine owners to the White House to try to find a solution. Therefore, the owners refused to speak with the union representatives. Roosevelt was infuriated by this rebuff, and he threatened to send federal troops to operate the mines. At the urging of J.P. Morgan (the renowned financier who formed the U.S. Steel Corporation), the owners backed down and gave the miners shorter workdays (9 hours) and better wages (10% wage increases). 22

Railroad reform was another of Roosevelt's important contributions to the progressive cause. During the beginning of the 20th century, railroad companies controlled the prices of their services. Roosevelt believed that this system gave private companies too much power, which ultimately hurt consumers. For example, he supported the Hepburn Railroad Act, which gave the Interstate Commerce Commission the power to regulate the prices of railroad rates and audit railroad company's financial records. Congress passed the Hepburn Railroad Act, and Roosevelt signed it into law in 1906. Roosevelt proved that he would not hesitate to challenge the powers and abuses of big business.

16. Which choice makes the sentence most grammatically acceptable?
    (F) NO CHANGE
    (G) rises
    (H) rose
    (J) has rose

17. Which choice is clearest and most precise in context?
    (A) NO CHANGE
    (B) infamy
    (C) obscurity
    (D) anonymity

18. Which choice makes the sentence most grammatically acceptable?
    (F) NO CHANGE
    (G) the "Rough Riders," to victory in the Battle of San Juan Hill
    (H) the "Rough Riders" to victory, in the Battle of San Juan Hill
    (J) the "Rough Riders," to victory in the Battle of San Juan Hill,

CHAPTER 19 Practice Exam   251

19. The author is considering inserting a few lines about what led to McKinley's assassination and who was responsible. Would that insertion be appropriate here?

   (A) Yes, because it would clarify how Roosevelt came to assume the presidency.
   (B) Yes, because it contains important clarifying information about McKinley.
   (C) No, because the focus of the passage is Roosevelt, not McKinley.
   (D) No, because this information should appear earlier in the passage.

20. Which choice makes the sentence most grammatically acceptable?

   (F) NO CHANGE
   (G) was a big-game hunter
   (H) engaging in big-game hunting
   (J) big-game hunting

21. Which transition word or phrase is most logical in context?

   (A) NO CHANGE
   (B) However,
   (C) Finally,
   (D) As a result,

22. The author is considering deleting the preceding sentence. Without the sentence, the paragraph would primarily lose:

   (F) details that summarize one of Roosevelt's specific accomplishments.
   (G) interesting but irrelevant information.
   (H) foreshadowing of an event detailed in the next paragraph.
   (J) general observations about Roosevelt's achievements.

23. Which choice is clearest and most precise in context?

   (A) NO CHANGE
   (B) At
   (C) After
   (D) Through

24. Which transition word or phrase is most logical in context?

   (F) NO CHANGE
   (G) Nevertheless,
   (H) On the contrary,
   (J) Thus,

25. Which choice makes the sentence most grammatically acceptable?

   (A) NO CHANGE
   (B) companies
   (C) companies'
   (D) companys'

Passage 4

Remote Computer Repair

[1]

In today's fast-paced world, the multifaceted virtues of the internet enable our fingers to access virtually anything simply. While this facility has eased a good bit of how we do things in the modern working world, what it has failed to accomplish, is the prevention of a crisis when a computer suddenly crashes. So, remote computer repair provides a great resource for anyone that conducts a business in front of a computer screen.
                                26   27
                                                                                                28

[2]

If your computer experiences crashes, is prone to viruses, needs a tune-up, or requires hardware or software installation, remote computer repair can get you up and running again quickly. Rather than wait days or even weeks without your machine, consider having a trained professional perform repairs remotely so that you can avoid lost time or wages as a result from your damaged equipment.
                                      29
                                                                                    30

[3]

Remote computer repair is done by a professional logging into your computer using a highly secure Internet connection. Rather than paying you
31
an actual visit. It can be a great option for people who cannot be without they're computer for long or
32
for those who cannot get to a repair shop. Remote repair can get your laptop or PC in working order again in a matter of hours or even minutes, depending on the severity of the problem. 34
33

[4]

Whether you need to remove viruses, fix a frozen screen, or install a home or business office network, a remote computer repair person should be your first call to get your machine up and running. 35

26. Which choice makes the sentence most grammatically acceptable?

   (F) NO CHANGE
   (G) what, it has failed to accomplish
   (H) what it has failed, to accomplish
   (J) what it has failed to accomplish

27. Which transition word or phrase is most logical in context?

   (A) NO CHANGE
   (B) However,
   (C) On the other hand,
   (D) For instance,

28. Which choice makes the sentence most grammatically acceptable?

   (F) NO CHANGE
   (G) anyone, which conducts
   (H) anyone who conducts
   (J) anyone, who conducts

29. Which choice makes the sentence most grammatically acceptable?

   (A) NO CHANGE
   (B) wait days, or even weeks without your machine,
   (C) wait days or, even weeks, without your machine
   (D) wait days or even weeks, without your machine,

30. Which choice is clearest and most precise in context?

   (F) NO CHANGE
   (G) with
   (H) as
   (J) of

31. Which choice makes the sentence most grammatically acceptable?

   (A) NO CHANGE
   (B) connection rather
   (C) connection, and rather
   (D) connection; rather

32. Which choice makes the sentence most grammatically acceptable?

   (F) NO CHANGE
   (G) his or her
   (H) their
   (J) there

33. The author of the passage is considering deleting the underlined phrase from the sentence and ending it with a period. If the author were to delete this content, the sentence would primarily lose:

   (A) a minor detail about remote repair.
   (B) an example of the type of repair that can be accomplished remotely.
   (C) an explanation for a time difference.
   (D) a foreshadowing of the topic in the following paragraph.

CHAPTER 19 Practice Exam   253

34. Which of the following sentences most effectively concludes this paragraph?

   (F) More severe issues take longer than simple ones.
   (G) Remote computer repair can prove tremendously helpful for those who cannot be without their computers.
   (H) Calling a remote technician will also save you traveling time to and from the repair shop.
   (J) When computer issues arrive, your first call should be to a remote computer repair specialist.

35. To make this passage a coherent whole, Paragraph 4 should be:

   (A) placed where it is now.
   (B) placed before Paragraph 1.
   (C) placed after Paragraph 2.
   (D) deleted entirely.

Passage 5

Competition for Niches

[1]

Competing for a limited number of resources, such as nutrients, energy, and territory, results in the evolution of an organism's characteristics and behaviors to compensate. [2] Darwin's theory states that competition for resources are what
                                                         ──
                                                          36
drives evolution, so most characteristics and behaviors have evolved in order to improve its
                                                                                        ──
                                                                                        37
ability to compete and survive in the ecosystem. [3] Over the generations, each species in the ecosystem will settle into its own way of securing a living. [4] A niche includes the species' diet, its territory, its behaviors, its roles in the nutrient cycles, and anything else that helps define its lifestyle. [5] Another way to describe this is to say that each species establishes its own "niche" in the ecosystem. 38

[2]

Every niche has two types of components:
                                 ──────────
abiotic and biotic. "Abiotic" means nonliving. This
──────────────────
        39
category includes elements such as an area's physical terrain, average yearly rainfall, and average daily temperature. "Biotic" means living; this part of the niche includes all of the other species in the community — the predators, prey, parasites, competitors, and so on — with whom the particular
                                    ─────────
                                       40
species is likely to interact during its life.

Whenever the niche of a species overlap
────────   ───────
   41   42
with another, such as when two species occupy the same space or eat the same food, that species is automatically in competition with the other. Competition in the wild can take many forms and only occasionally involves direct combat. A species can win a competition by being faster, more efficient, smarter, or more colorful. In the end,
                                              ──────────
                                                  43
only three possible results of a competition exist: win, lose, or compromise. One species may win the competition and take over that part of the niche, it may lose and be forced to retreat from that part, or two species may find a way to divide that part of the niche so that they can coexist peacefully. 44

In addition to interspecific competition, competition between individuals of the same species, called *intraspecific competition*, also occurs. This competition can lead to the development of unusual qualities, such as, vibrant coloring.
        ─────────────────
              45
Sometimes only the prettiest, the smelliest, or the loudest are able to win the competition and pass on their lovely, stinky, or noisy genes.

254   PART 7   Putting It All Together with a Full-Length Practice ACT

36. Which choice makes the sentence most grammatically acceptable?

    (F) NO CHANGE
    (G) is
    (H) have been
    (J) were

37. Which choice makes the sentence most grammatically acceptable?

    (A) NO CHANGE
    (B) a life form's
    (C) it's
    (D) their

38. For the sake of logic and coherence in Paragraph 1, Sentence 5 should be placed:

    (F) where it is now.
    (G) before Sentence 2.
    (H) before Sentence 3.
    (J) before Sentence 4.

39. Which of the following substitutes for the underlined portion would NOT be grammatically acceptable?

    (A) components, and they are abiotic and biotic
    (B) components that are abiotic and biotic
    (C) components, abiotic and biotic
    (D) components — abiotic and biotic

40. Which choice makes the sentence most grammatically acceptable?

    (F) NO CHANGE
    (G) through whom
    (H) with which
    (J) that

41. Which choice is clearest and most precise in context?

    (A) NO CHANGE
    (B) Although
    (C) Whether
    (D) Often,

42. Which choice makes the sentence most grammatically acceptable?

    (F) NO CHANGE
    (G) overlaps,
    (H) are overlapping,
    (J) was overlapping,

43. Which transition word or phrase is most logical in context?

    (A) NO CHANGE
    (B) For example,
    (C) On the other hand,
    (D) Finally,

44. Which of the following additions here provides the best conclusion for this paragraph?

    (F) Otherwise, the species are more likely to engage in direct combat.
    (G) Competition between species is inevitable.
    (H) Those that fit the niche best are most likely to survive within it.
    (J) Each species generally occupies its exclusive niche.

45. Which choice makes the sentence most grammatically acceptable?

    (A) NO CHANGE
    (B) qualities such as:
    (C) qualities; such as
    (D) qualities such as

Passage 6

The Evolution of Greek Tragedy

Greek drama emerged in the fifth century B.C. from public performances of narrative lyrics. Three playwrights — Aeschylus, Sophocles, and Euripides — dominated the Athenian stage. 46 Actors, wearing masks and platform shoes, performed for large audiences, relying primarily on dialogue rather then action to tell there stories. These tragedies typically depicted a hero's downfall, often caused by a fatal character flaw. 48

CHAPTER 19 Practice Exam 255

A prime example is Sophocles' *Oedipus Tyrannus*, where Oedipus, despite his efforts, discovers he just can't get away from the prophecy that he would kill his father. Accepting his fate, he leaves the chorus to mourn the cruelty and inevitability of destiny. In contrast, Euripides a contemporary of Sophocles, portrayed characters with greater emotional depth, emphasizing human emotions over fate-driven tragedy. His play *Alcestis* highlights friendship's power to alter fate, diverging from the traditional tragic flaw narrative. 51. At this point in the paragraph, the author is considering adding this sentence:

46. Greek dramatists created great works in other centuries, too.

Would this addition be appropriate given the primary topic of the paragraph?

(F) Yes, because the paragraph is about Greek dramatists.

(G) Yes, because the sentence provides additional information about Greek dramatists that improves the readers understanding of how influential Greek drama was in early times.

(H) No, because the paragraph is about dramatists from all cultures and the sentence only mentions Greek dramatists.

(J) No, because the paragraph is specifically about fifth-century Greek drama.

47. Which choice makes the sentence most grammatically acceptable?

(A) NO CHANGE
(B) than action to tell there stories.
(C) than action to tell their stories.
(D) then action to tell their stories.

48. Given that all choices are accurate, which one provides the best transition from this paragraph to the following paragraph?

(F) The plays emphasized humanity's inability to escape fate, with any attempt to change destiny leading to greater suffering.

(G) Explorations of fate and personal struggle are themes that appear in many well-known plays.

(H) These plays were widely performed, and many people attended them.

(J) This is why Sophocles was an important playwright and why his plays are still studied in high school and college classrooms across the globe.

49. Which choice most effectively maintains the tone of the essay?

(A) NO CHANGE
(B) he cannot escape the prophecy
(C) it's an epic fail to try to outrun the prophecy
(D) he's stuck with the prophecy

50. Which choice makes the sentence most grammatically acceptable?

(F) NO CHANGE
(G) contrast Euripides, a contemporary of Sophocles
(H) contrast, Euripides — a contemporary of Sophocles —
(J) contrast, Euripides, a contemporary of Sophocles;

Mathematics Test

TIME: 50 minutes for 45 questions

DIRECTIONS: Each question has four answer choices. Choose the best answer for each question and shade the corresponding oval on your answer sheet.

1. What is the value of $y \times 2^x$ if $x = 3$ and $y = 2$?

    (A) 8
    (B) 16
    (C) 12
    (D) 64

2. The first four terms of a geometric sequence are .75, 1.5, 3, and 6. What is the fifth term?

    (F) 12
    (G) 9
    (H) 18
    (J) 11.25

3. In the following figure, A, B, and C are collinear. The measure of ∠ABD is three times that of ∠DBC. What is the measure of ∠ABD?

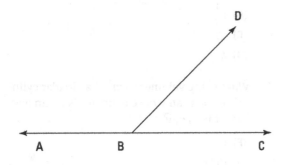

    (A) 135°
    (B) 120°
    (C) 67.5°
    (D) 60°

4. Which of the following is equivalent to $\dfrac{3}{\frac{3}{8}}$?

    (F) 3
    (G) 8
    (H) $\dfrac{9}{8}$
    (J) $\dfrac{1}{8}$

5. What is the measure of angle b in the following figure where lines C and D are parallel?

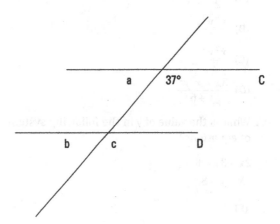

    (A) 37°
    (B) 53°
    (C) 127°
    (D) 143°

6. Ross has 2 black socks and 2 white socks lying in his drawer. If he mindlessly selects two socks from the drawer, what is the chance he will select the black pair?

    (F) $\dfrac{1}{6}$
    (G) $\dfrac{1}{4}$
    (H) $\dfrac{1}{2}$
    (J) $\dfrac{5}{6}$

7. A triangular ramp from the ground to the bed of a truck that stands 6 feet off the ground has a base of 8 feet. How long in feet is the length of the bottom of the ramp?

    (A) 5 feet
    (B) 5.29 feet
    (C) 8 feet
    (D) 10 feet

GO ON TO NEXT PAGE

CHAPTER 19 Practice Exam   257

8. At what point does $7x + 4y = 28$ intersect the y-axis in the standard (x, y) coordinate plane?

   (F) $(4, 0)$
   (G) $(7, 0)$
   (H) $(0, 4)$
   (J) $(0, 7)$

9. Simplify $\left(\dfrac{3x}{y}\right)\left(\dfrac{x^3 y^2}{6}\right)$.

   (A) $\dfrac{x^4 y}{2}$
   (B) $\dfrac{x^4 y^3}{2}$
   (C) $\dfrac{x^2 y^3}{2}$
   (D) $\dfrac{3x + x^3 y^2}{y + 6}$

10. What is the value of y in the following system of equations?

    $2x + 3y = 6$
    $x - y = 8$

    (F) 6
    (G) 2
    (H) 0
    (J) -2

11. Tickets to a movie cost $8 for adults and $5 for children. If 40 tickets are sold for a total of $251, how many adult tickets were sold?

    (A) 15
    (B) 17
    (C) 20
    (D) 23

12. Which of the following functions is represented on the standard (x, y) coordinate plane shown here?

    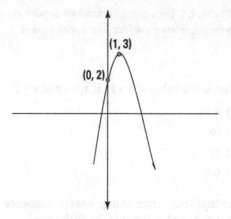

    (E) $y = -(x + 3)^2 + 1$
    (F) $y = -(x + 1)^2 + 3$
    (G) $y = (x - 1)^2 + 3$
    (H) $y = -(x - 1)^2 + 3$

13. Which of the following values for x makes $\log_6 9 + \log_6 x = 2$?

    (A) $\dfrac{1}{3}$
    (B) $1\dfrac{1}{3}$
    (C) 27
    (D) 4

14. What is the volume in cm^3 of a circular cylindrical soda can whose diameter is 10 cm and height is 15 cm?

    (F) 10π
    (G) 150π
    (H) 375π
    (J) 625π

15. If in the standard (x, y) coordinate plane the quadrilateral ABCD shown here was reflected over the line y = 2 to form quadrilateral $A_1B_1C_1D_1$, at what pair of coordinates would point A_1 lie?

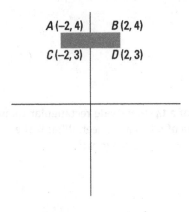

(A) (−2, 0)
(B) (6, 4)
(C) (2, 4)
(D) (−2, −4)

16. Klaus decided to give 20% of the money he got for his birthday to his favorite charity and put the rest in the bank. If he put $280 in the bank, how much money did he receive for his birthday?

(A) $56
(B) $70
(C) $350
(D) $336

17. In the right triangle shown here, what is cos C?

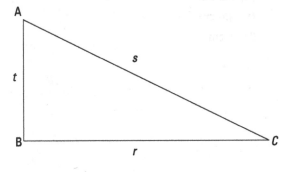

(A) $\frac{t}{r}$
(B) $\frac{s}{r}$
(C) $\frac{t}{s}$
(D) $\frac{r}{s}$

18. For all pairs of real numbers x and y where $x = 3y + 8$, what does y equal?

(F) $\frac{x}{3} - 8$
(G) $x - \frac{8}{3}$
(H) $3y + 8$
(J) $\frac{x - 8}{3}$

19. On the following number line, the distance between A and D is 28 units. The distance between A and C is 15 units. The distance between B and D is 18 units. What is the distance in units between B and C?

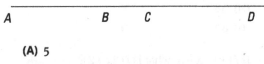

(A) 5
(B) 6
(C) 8
(D) 10

20. What is the perimeter of the following polygon whose angles each measure 90°?

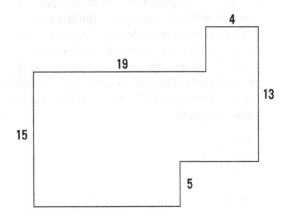

(F) 56
(G) 74
(H) 77
(I) 82

21. What is the circumference of a circle whose area is 16π?

(A) 8π
(B) 4
(C) 4π
(D) 8

22. The following stem-and-leaf plot shows all of the test scores Cydney received in her algebra course this year. Each test score reflects the number of points received out of a possible 100 points. What was Cydney's median math test score for the year?

Scores that Cydney Received on All Math Tests this Year	
7	899
8	23455677999
9	14669

   (F) 86
   (G) 87
   (H) 88
   (I) 89

23. If $f(x) = x - 3$, what is $f(2x+2)$?

   (A) $-x - 2$
   (B) $3x - 1$
   (C) $2x - 1$
   (D) $3x - 4$

24. A car's starting velocity is 10 meters per second as it enters a ramp to the freeway. The physics equation for velocity is $v = at + v_0$ where t stands for time and v_0 is the initial velocity. What is the car's acceleration (a) in meters per square second if it takes 10 seconds to reach 30 meters per second and it accelerates uniformly?

   (F) 3
   (G) 13
   (H) 7
   (J) 2

25. A license plate in the fictional state of Greenwood has two digits followed by two letters. How many different license plate combinations can Greenwood create if digits can be repeated but letters cannot?

   (A) 60,840
   (B) 65,000
   (C) 67,600
   (D) 71

26. On a recent math test, Caroline scored 99, Stephanie scored 97, Julie scored 92, and Amanda scored 88. Courtney was the only other person who took the test, and the average of the five scores was 91. What was Courtney's score?

   (F) 79
   (G) 88
   (H) 91
   (J) 94

27. The floor of a 14-foot-wide rectangular room has an area of 672 square feet. What is the length, in feet, of its diagonal?

   (A) 28
   (B) 45
   (C) 48
   (D) 50

28. For what values of x does $x^4 - 5x^2 + 4 = 0$?

   (F) 1 and 4 only
   (G) −1 and −2 only
   (H) 1, 4, −1, and −4 only
   (J) 1, 2, −1, and −2 only

29. Sam has 360 cubic centimeters of peanut butter to make nine sandwiches for her softball team. The bread measures 10 centimeters by 10 centimeters. If she spreads the peanut butter evenly over one piece of bread for each sandwich, how thick will the peanut butter layer measure on each sandwich?

   (A) 0.2 cm
   (B) 0.4 cm
   (C) 3.6 cm
   (D) 4 cm

30. What would be the slope of any line perpendicular to line m in the following figure?

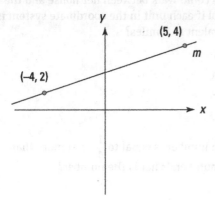

(F) $\frac{9}{2}$
(G) $\frac{2}{9}$
(H) $-\frac{2}{9}$
(J) $-\frac{9}{2}$

31. What is the measure in degrees of $\angle DBC$ in the following diagram if polygon ABCD is a trapezoid?

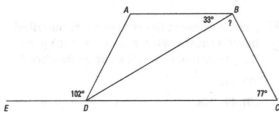

(A) 33
(B) 45
(C) 70
(D) 102

32. There is a straight 65-mile road between Denver and Boulder. If Jackson leaves Boulder at 3:15 PM traveling 40 mph and Emily leaves Denver at the same time traveling 60 mph, how many miles from Denver will the two pass each other?

(F) 20
(G) 26
(H) 32.5
(J) 39

33. The 337 cars on the lot at Madi's Auto Dealership come in a variety of colors. About $\frac{2}{3}$ of the cars on the lot are blue. Of those, about $\frac{1}{4}$ are royal blue and $\frac{3}{4}$ are navy blue. About how many cars are navy blue?

(A) 56
(B) 169
(C) 225
(D) 253

34. For all $x \neq 0$ and $y \neq 0$, $\frac{(3x^3y^2)^2}{3xy^{-3}} = ?$

(F) x^5y^7
(G) $3x^5y^7$
(H) $3x^5y$
(J) $3x^4y^7$

35. What is the largest possible sum of two integers that have a product that ranges between -8 and 0 exclusive?

(A) 4
(B) 5
(C) 6
(D) 8

36. Austin wants to open up a barbershop because there seems to be an insufficient number of them in the area. First, however, he needs to determine whether he will be running a profitable business. He has found a space to rent for $600 per month, and his monthly supplies will cost about $200. If he has to pay 10 barbers $12 per hour to cut hair, the barbers are working 120 hours per month, and he can sell 1,200 haircuts for $15 apiece, will his business make a profit after the first month?

(F) No, his business will lose $4,400 in the first month.
(G) No, his business will lose $2,800 in the first month.
(H) Yes, his business will make a profit of $2,800 in the first month.
(J) Yes, his business will make a profit of $4,400 in the first month.

Use the following information to answer questions 37–39.

The following figure maps in the standard (x, y) coordinate plane the locations that Becca frequents most often in her small town of Larkspur. Most weekday mornings, Becca walks from her house to school. After school, she stops at the library to study before she walks to the diner to begin her 3-hour shift as a server.

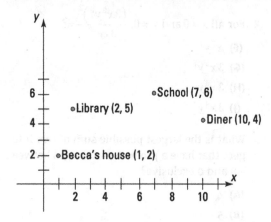

37. What is the slope of the straight line that marks the shortest distance Becca walks from the library to the diner?

(A) −8

(B) $-\frac{1}{8}$

(C) $\frac{1}{8}$

(D) 8

38. Which of the following represents the equation of a circle that is tangent to the x-axis and whose center is the point that marks Becca's house?

(F) $(x-2)^2 + (y-1)^2 = 1$

(G) $(x+2)^2 + (y+1)^2 = 4$

(H) $(x-1)^2 + (y-2)^2 = 4$

(J) $(x-1)^2 + (y-2)^2 = 2$

39. Which of the following is closest to the shortest distance, to the nearest mile, that Becca could walk between her house and the school if each unit in the coordinate system is equivalent to 2 miles?

(A) 5

(B) 11

(C) 14

(D) 17

40. $\frac{2}{5}$ of a number is equal to $\frac{1}{4}$ of 21 more than that number. What is the number?

(F) 28

(G) 35

(H) 42

(J) 140

41. If $y = 7x - h$ and $x = h + 7$, then what is the value of y expressed in terms of x?

(A) $y = 7xh + 49x - h$

(B) $y = 6x - 7$

(C) $y + h = 7x$

(D) $y = 6x + 7$

42. A circle whose radius is 7 cm is circumscribed inside a square. What is the area of the part of the square that is not taken up by the circle?

(F) 49π

(G) $49 - 14\pi$

(H) $196 - 14\pi$

(J) $196 - 49\pi$

43. What is the area in square units of the following rectangle?

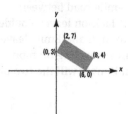

(F) 11.18

(G) 24

(H) 30

(J) 56.33

262   PART 7 Putting It All Together with a Full-Length Practice ACT

44. Which one of the following graphs best represents the inequality $y \leq \sin(x)+2$?

(F)
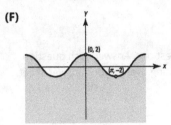

(G)
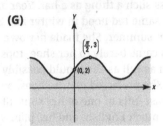

(H)
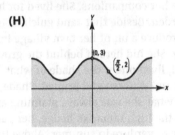

(J)
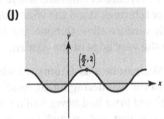

45. Jordyn has $600 in a savings account that earns 5% in interest compounded biannually, which means that she earns 5% of her existing money twice per year. The money she makes through interest is then added to the amount of money she already has in her savings account. After a year and a half, Jordyn moves $210 to a checking account that doesn't earn interest to buy a camera. How much money to the nearest cent does Jordyn have in her savings account after two years?

(A) $484.58
(B) $504
(C) $508.80
(D) $720.00

Reading Test

TIME: 40 minutes for 36 questions

DIRECTIONS: Each of the four passages in this section is followed by ten questions. Answer each question based on what is stated or implied in the passage and shade the corresponding oval on your answer sheet.

Passage I — Literary Narrative

This passage is adapted from the novel, *Song of the Lark*, by Willa Sibert Cather.

"And it was Summer, beautiful Summer!" Those were the words of Thea's favorite fairy tale, and she thought of them as she ran one Saturday morning in May, her music book under her arm. (05) She was going to the Kohlers' to take her lesson, but she was in no hurry.

It was in the summer that one really lived. Then all the little overcrowded houses were opened wide, and the wind blew through them with sweet, (10) earthy smells of garden-planting. People were out painting their fences. The cottonwood trees were a-flicker with sticky, yellow little leaves, and the feathery tamarisks were in pink bud. With the warm weather came freedom for everybody. The (15) very old people, whom one had not seen all winter, came out and sunned themselves in the yard. The double windows were taken off the houses, the tormenting flannels in which children had been encased all winter were put away in boxes, and the (20) youngsters felt a pleasure in the cool cotton things next their skin.

Thea had to walk more than a mile to reach the Kohlers' house. On a little rise of ground that faced the open sandy plain, was the Kohlers' (25) house, where Professor Wunsch lived. Fritz Kohler was the town tailor, one of the first settlers. He had moved there, built a little house and made a garden, when Moonstone was first marked down on the map. He had three sons, but they now (30) worked on the railroad and were stationed in distant cities. One of them had gone to work for the Santa Fe, and lived in New Mexico.

Mrs. Kohler seldom crossed the ravine and went into the town except at Christmastime, when (35) she had to buy presents to send to her old friends in Freeport, Illinois. As she did not go to church, she did not possess such a thing as a hat. Year after year she wore the same red hood in winter and a black sunbonnet in summer. She made her own dresses; the skirts came barely to her shoe-tops, (40) and were gathered as full as they could possibly be to the waistband. She preferred men's shoes, and usually wore the cast-offs of one of her sons. She had never learned much English, and her plants and shrubs were her companions. She lived for her (45) men and her garden. Beside that sand gulch, she had tried to reproduce a bit of her own village in the Rhine Valley. She hid herself behind the growth she had fostered, lived under the shade of what she had planted and watered and pruned. Shade, (50) shade; that was what she was always planning and making. Behind the high tamarisk hedge, her garden was a jungle of verdure in summer. Above the cherry trees and peach trees stood the windmill, which kept all this verdure alive. Outside, the sage- (55) brush grew up to the very edge of the garden.

Everyone in Moonstone was astonished when the Kohlers took in the wandering music-teacher. In seventeen years old Fritz had never had a crony, except the harness-maker and Spanish Johnny. (60) This Wunsch came from God knew where, and played in the dance orchestra, tuned pianos, and gave lessons. When Mrs. Kohler rescued him, he was sleeping in a dirty, unfurnished room over one of the saloons, and he had only two shirts in (65) the world. Once he was under her roof, the old woman went at him as she did at her garden. She sewed and washed and mended, and made him so clean and respectable that he was able to get a large class of pupils and rent a piano. As soon (70) as he had money, he sent to the Narrow Gauge lodging-house, in Denver, for a trunkful of music which had been held there for unpaid board. With tears in his eyes the old man — he was not over fifty, but sadly battered — told Mrs. Kohler that he (75) asked nothing better of God than to end his days with her, and to be buried in the garden, under her linden trees. They were not American basswood,

but the European linden, which has honey-colored
(80) blooms in summer, with a fragrance that surpasses
all trees and flowers and drives young people wild
with joy.

Thea was reflecting as she walked along that
had it not been for Professor Wunsch she might
(85) have lived on for years without ever knowing the
Kohlers, without ever seeing their garden or the
inside of their house.

Professor Wunsch went to the houses of his
other pupils to give them their lessons, but one
(90) morning he told Mrs. Kronborg that Thea had
talent. Mrs. Kronborg was a strange woman. That
word "talent," which no one else in Moonstone
would have understood, she comprehended
perfectly. To any other woman, it would have
(95) meant that a child must have her hair curled every
day and must play in public. Mrs. Kronborg knew it
meant that Thea must practice four hours a day. A
child with talent must be kept at the piano, just as
a child with measles must be kept under the
(100) blankets.

1. Which of the following examples best parallels
   the analogy that Mrs. Kronborg made in the
   final paragraph?
   (A) A student with good writing skills must
       work harder on math.
   (B) A young girl with beauty must be kept
       under close watch.
   (C) A person with outdoor allergies must be
       kept indoors.
   (D) A child with learning differences may
       benefit from tutoring.

2. The author associates all of the following with
   the onset of summer EXCEPT:
   (F) seeing new neighbors
   (G) the blossoming of cottonwood trees
   (H) home dwellers painting their fences
   (J) children wearing cool clothing instead
       of warm

3. The use of the word crony at line 58 most
   likely means:
   (A) elder.
   (B) buddy.
   (C) enemy.
   (D) teacher.

4. When the author says, "the old woman went
   at him like she did her garden" (lines 65-66),
   she most nearly means Mrs. Kohler:
   (F) determined to rid Professor Wunsch of
       his less desirable qualities.
   (G) tried in vain to improve his appearance.
   (H) spruced him up with care and attention.
   (J) tried to mold him into her idea of
       perfection.

5. The author makes all of the following asser-
   tions regarding Mrs. Kohler's personal style,
   EXCEPT:
   (A) she wore a black hood in the wintertime.
   (B) she wore a black sunbonnet in the
       summertime.
   (C) Mrs. Kohler preferred men's shoes over
       women's.
   (D) Mrs. Kohler made her own dresses.

6. The best way to describe the way Professor
   Wunsch feels toward Mrs. Kohler is:
   (F) indifferent.
   (G) amorous.
   (H) grateful.
   (J) bitter.

7. Mrs. Kohler's garden is best described as a:
   (A) haven where she hid, planned, and
       found purpose.
   (B) reminder of her homeland, filled with
       hedges, fruit trees, and sage-brush.
   (C) barren sand gulch that she fled to when
       she was lonely.
   (D) verdant paradise fed by Moonstone's
       frequent rainfall.

8. The author makes which of the following
   assertions about Mr. Kohler?
   (A) He played in the dance orchestra.
   (B) He had only three friends.
   (C) He had a son who lived in Santa Fe.
   (D) He was one of the first men to live in
       Moonstone.

CHAPTER 19 Practice Exam **265**

9. The author would most likely say that Thea differed from other children in that she:

(A) had few friends and attended few social gatherings.
(B) studied music with Professor Wunsch.
(C) was particularly fond of fairy tales.
(D) was musically gifted.

Passage II — Social Science

Passage A

This passage is adapted from *Posttraumatic Stress Disorder: Issues and Controversies*, edited by Gerald M. Rosen (2004).

Controversy has haunted the diagnosis of post-traumatic stress disorder (PTSD) ever since its first appearance in the third edition of the *Diagnostic and Statistical Manual of Mental Disorders* (05) (*DSM-III*). At the outset, psychiatrists opposed to the inclusion of the diagnosis in the *DSM-III* argued that the problems of trauma-exposed people were already covered by combinations of existing diagnoses.

(10) Ratifying PTSD would merely entail cobbling together selected symptoms in people suffering from multiple disorders (for example, phobias, depression, and personality disorders) and then attributing these familiar problems to a traumatic (15) event. Moreover, the very fact that the movement to include the diagnosis in the *DSM-III* arose from Vietnam veterans' advocacy groups working with antiwar psychiatrists prompted concerns that PTSD was more of a political or social construct (20) rather than a medical disease discovered in nature.

Although the aforementioned two concerns have again resurfaced in contemporary debates about PTSD, additional issues have arisen as well. For example, the concept of a traumatic stressor (25) has broadened to such an extent that, today, the vast majority of American adults have been exposed to PTSD-qualifying events. This state of affairs is drastically different from the late 1970s and early 1980s, when the concept of trauma was (30) confined to catastrophic events falling outside the perimeter of everyday experience. Early 21st-century scholars are raising fresh questions about the syndromic validity of PTSD.

Passage B

This passage is adapted from *Post-Traumatic Stress Disorder*, edited by Dan J. Stein MD, PhD, Matthew J. Friedman, MD, and Carlos Blanco, MD, PhD (2011).

Of the many diagnoses in the *Diagnostic and Statistical Manual of Mental Disorders* (*DSM-III*), very few invoke an aetiology in their diagnostic criteria: (i) organic mental disorders (caused, for example, by a neurological abnormality); (ii) substance-use (35) disorders (caused, for example, by psychoactive chemical agents); (iii) post-traumatic stress disorder (PTSD); (iv) acute stress disorder (ASD); and (v) adjustment disorders (ADs). The latter three are all caused by exposure to a stressful environmen- (40) tal event that exceeds the coping capacity of the affected individual. The presumed causal relationship between the stressor and PTSD, ASD, and AD is complicated and controversial. Controversy notwithstanding, acceptance of this causal relation- (45) ship has equipped practitioners and scientists with a conceptual tool that has profoundly influenced clinical practice over the past 30 years.

PTSD is primarily a disorder of reactivity rather than of an altered baseline state, as in (50) major depressive disorder or general anxiety disorder. Its psychopathology is characteristically expressed during interactions with the interpersonal or physical environment. People with PTSD are consumed by concerns about personal (55) safety. They persistently scan the environment for threatening stimuli. When in doubt, they are more likely to assume that danger is present and will react accordingly. Avoidance and hyper-arousal symptoms can be understood within this context. (60) The primacy of traumatic over other memories (for example, the re-experiencing symptoms) can also be understood as a pathological exaggeration of an adaptive human response to remember as much as possible about dangerous encounters in order to (65) avoid similar threats in the future.

10. According to Passage A, psychiatrists opposed to PTSD's inclusion in the *Diagnostic and Statistical Manual of Mental Disorders* (*DSM-III*) based their arguments on the following points, EXCEPT:

    (F) Today's definition of catastrophic trauma is a far cry from what it was in the late 1960s and early 70s.//
    (G) PTSD sufferers could already be grouped into one or more existing diagnosis categories.//
    (H) What qualifies as a "stressor" by today's definition has become far too broad.//
    (J) PTSD is more of a social and political construct than a legitimate affliction.

11. The author's attitude in Passage A can best be described as:

    (A) contemplative.//
    (B) indecisive.//
    (C) explanatory.//
    (D) argumentative.

12. The author of Passage A refers to the 1970s and 1980s in order to:

    (F) show how far American medicine has come over time.//
    (G) highlight a time that saw numerous catastrophic events.//
    (H) compare the number of PTSD sufferers between then and now.//
    (J) reveal how America's definition of "trauma" has changed over time.

13. Which of the following sentences best summarizes the main idea of Passage B?

    (A) PTSD is controversial, but it has had a profound impact on both sufferers and the medical profession as a whole over the years.//
    (B) PTSD is a legitimate, debilitating condition that deserves additional research and financial resources.//
    (C) PTSD was given a name largely because medical professionals needed a way to categorize veterans suffering from various mental conditions after returning from war.//
    (D) PTSD is no longer an accurate diagnosis, because the world has come to accept any number of situations as "stressors" that might set it off.

14. The author of Passage B makes all of the following assertions about PTSD EXCEPT:

    (F) that it is caused by exposure to a particularly stressful environmental factor that is more than the affected individual can handle.//
    (G) that PTSD is a disorder that results from an altered baseline state.//
    (H) that PTSD sufferers frequently search their surroundings for anything that might be viewed as a threat.//
    (J) that clinical practice over the years has been largely influenced by the acceptance of a causal relationship between a stressor and the onset of PTSD.

15. Which of the following best demonstrates the different perspectives between the psychiatrists and scholars mentioned in Passage A and the author of Passage B?

    (A) The psychiatrists in Passage A think that the definition of PTSD has become too broad, while the author of Passage B feels it is a legitimate condition that has played an important role in clinical practice.//
    (B) The psychiatrists and scholars in Passage A believe that PTSD is a genuinely debilitating condition, while the author of Passage B believes today's doctors are too quick to offer up a PTSD diagnosis.//
    (C) The psychiatrists and scholars in Passage A believe that PTSD is simply a combination of other existing conditions, while the author of Passage B feels that PTSD is a disorder of an altered baseline state.//
    (D) The psychiatrists and scholars in Passage A believe that social conditions led to the theory behind PTSD, while the author of Passage B believes it was politics.

16. The authors of both passages are most likely to agree on which of the following statements?

    (F) PTSD is a disorder of reactivity.//
    (G) The use of the PTSD diagnosis is highly political.//
    (H) PTSD sufferers are overly concerned with personal safety.//
    (J) PTSD is a highly controversial condition.

17. The authors of either Passage A or Passage B make all of the following assertions about the *Diagnostic and Statistical Manual of Mental Disorders* (*DSM-III*) EXCEPT:

(A) that few diagnoses listed also list causes.
(B) that psychiatrists initially did not want PTSD listed in the publication.
(C) that PTSD appeared in its third edition.
(D) that the information it contains about PTSD is wholly insufficient.

18. Which of the following statements is consistent with information contained in both passages?

(F) PTSD is caused by stressful factors that exceed one's ability to cope, and scientists and medical professionals are often too quick to make the proper diagnosis.
(G) PTSD is an increasingly prevalent problem in America, and years of research must be devoted to its causes and treatment.
(H) The PTSD diagnosis is a controversial one, and scientists and medical professionals have differing opinions on its causes and its inclusion in the *Diagnostic and Statistical Manual of Mental Disorders* (*DSM-III*).
(J) Scientists and medical professionals disagree over which stressors are sufficient to lead to PTSD.

Passage III — Humanities

Line
    Adapting literature for the screen can be daunting. To increase one's chances of creating a successful adaptation, Linda Seger suggests choosing original works with a good story. In her
(05) book, *The Art of Adaptation*, Seger goes on to clarify that a good story contains three elements: a goal, a problem or an issue, and a life-altering journey.

    Almost every aspect of life is touched by change. Outer physical change is readily apparent:
(10) Babies grow into adults, winter becomes spring, natural structures build up and erode. Less tangible but not less important are the inner changes that human beings experience. Just as a disruption of normal physical growth is unhealthy, so is a lack of
(15) inner growth. Although inner growth and change is healthy and exciting, it also requires courage and discernment. Journeying from a familiar state to a different one means sacrificing what is known and comfortable for something that is unknown and
(20) uncertain, and this transformation involves risk. Inner growth comes at a price, and humans face a fundamental dilemma: To change requires a sacrifice of the old and familiar, but to remain static is to sacrifice a chance at new life.

(25)   Experiencing myth and ritual in film may assist people with this universal dilemma. According to Joseph Campbell in his book *The Hero with a Thousand Faces*, the purpose and effect of myth and ritual ". . . was to conduct people across those
(30) difficult thresholds of transformation that demand a change in the patterns not only of conscious but also of unconscious life." Myth serves to draw people into and through the important transformation journey.

(35)   Through an examination of myths and rituals, Campbell distinguishes what he called the monomyth, a heroic quest for an immensely precious treasure at high personal cost. The hero of the monomyth endures a series of trials and even
(40) death or a death-like experience that liberates the hero from the past limitations of his old existence and renews life's possibilities. Mythology not only documents the transformation process of a mythic hero but also provides a means for other people to
(45) experience the hero's transformation.

    Campbell claims it is "the prime function of mythology and rite to supply the symbols that carry the human spirit forward, in counteraction to those other constant human fantasies that tend to
(50) tie it back." Myth may carry out this function by providing a vicarious heroic journey for the one who encounters myth in film adaptations of literary works. As viewers experience the transformations of film characters, they may gain insight
(55) into possibilities for their own heroic quests and, through contact with the stories of others, may embark on their own transformational journeys into more mature human beings.

19. The author's primary purpose in writing this passage is most likely to:

    (A) establish that to create a well-executed screen adaptation, one should choose a story modeled on a mythological journey.
    (B) show that positive change is not possible without taking risks.
    (C) warn that screenwriters should not attempt to adapt literary works that do not contain a mythic journey.
    (D) reveal that a good film adaptation contains a series of trials and a near-death experience.

20. The author of the passage suggests that inner growth requires:

    (F) an unhealthy forfeiture of established patterns of living and an acceptance of necessary risks.
    (G) viewing film adaptations of literary works.
    (H) courage to remain constant in changeable and unfamiliar environments.
    (J) sacrifice of one's comfortable fantasies and the exploration of uncharted territory.

21. Which of the following would the author of the passage be most likely to include in the list along with "... babies grow into" (line 11)?

    (A) Taste preferences change to include a wider appreciation of foods.
    (B) Young adults in their twenties make wiser decisions than adolescents.
    (C) Brown hair thins and turns to gray.
    (D) Best friends become strangers.

22. In saying "to change requires a sacrifice of the old and familiar, but to remain static is to sacrifice a chance at new life" (Line 25), the author most likely means that:

    (F) sacrifice is inevitable.
    (G) change of any kind is better than no change at all.
    (H) a life-altering journey is ultimately more fulfilling than the actual change one achieves as a result.
    (J) being resistant to change requires a more substantial risk than does facing the unknown.

23. The primary purpose of the second paragraph is to:

    (A) outline some of the ways humans may achieve inner growth.
    (B) offer a more detailed description of one of the components of a good story.
    (C) encourage the reader to risk inner growth by journeying from familiar to unfamiliar circumstances.
    (D) provide examples of some physical alterations humans may experience throughout their lives.

24. Each of the following is a characteristic of Campbell's monomyth EXCEPT:

    (F) liberation from past limitations.
    (G) great personal risk.
    (H) constant human fantasies.
    (J) a search for treasure.

25. According to Campbell, the purpose of ritual is to:

    (A) transform a person's unintentional patterns.
    (B) give people the tools to help others cross difficult thresholds in their lives.
    (C) force people to break bad habits.
    (D) promote a rich fantasy life.

26. When the author refers to "this universal dilemma" (line 27), she most likely means:

   (F) deciding whether to experience myth and ritual in films.
   (G) choosing between conscious and unconscious thoughts.
   (H) forgoing comfortable patterns to take on new challenges.
   (J) engaging in activities that promote physical growth.

27. Based on information in the passage, Linda Seger is most likely which of the following?

   (A) Mythic hero
   (B) Film script consultant
   (C) Book critic
   (D) Psychologist

Passage IV — Natural Science

This passage is adapted from *Reading the Weather*, by T. Morris Lonstreth.

Line
　　If there is anything that has been overlooked more than another it is our atmosphere. But it absolutely cannot be avoided, because if it were not for the atmosphere this earth of ours would be a
(05) wizened and sterile lump.

　　To be sure the earth does not loom very large in the eye of the sun. It receives a positively trifling fraction of the total output of sunheat. So negligible is this amount that it would not be worth
(10) our mentioning if we did not owe our existence to it. It is thanks to the atmosphere, however, that the earth attains this (borrowed) importance. It is thanks to this thin layer of gases that we are protected from that fraction of sunheat which,
(15) however insignificant when compared with the whole, would otherwise be sufficient to fry us all in a second. Without this gas wrapping, we would all freeze (if still unfried) immediately after sunset. The atmosphere keeps us in a sort of thermos
(20) globe, unmindful of the burning power of the great star, and of the uncalculated cold of outer space.

　　Yet, limitless as it seems to us, our invaluable atmosphere is a small thing after all. Half of its total bulk is compressed into the first three and a
(25) half miles upward. Only one sixty-fourth of it lies above the twenty-one mile limit. Compared with the thickness of the earth this makes a very thin envelope.

　　Light as air, we say, forgetting that this stuff that looks so inconsequential weighs fifteen (35) pounds to the square inch. The only reason that we don't crumble is because the gases press evenly in all directions, thereby supporting this crushing burden. A layer of water thirty-four feet thick weighs just about as much as this air-pack under (40) which we feel so buoyant. But if these gases get in motion we feel their pressure.

　　As it blows along the surface of the earth this wind is mostly nitrogen, oxygen, moisture, and dust. The nitrogen occupies nearly eight-tenths of (45) a given bulk of air, the oxygen two-tenths, and the moisture anything up to one-twentieth. Five other gases are present in small quantities. The dust and the water vapor occupy space independently of the rest. As one goes up mountains the water vapor (50) increases for a couple of thousand feet and then decreases to the seven mile limit after which it has almost completely vanished. The lightest gases have been detected as high up as two hundred miles and scientists think that hydrogen, the light- (55) est of all, may escape altogether from the restraint of gravity.

　　At first glance the extreme readiness of the atmosphere to carry dust and bacteria does not seem a point in its favor. In reality it is. Most bacteria (60) are really allies of the human race. They benefit us by producing fermentations and disintegrations of soils that prepare them for plant food. It is a pity that the few disease breeding types of bacteria should have given the family a bad name. Without (65) bacteria the sheltering atmosphere would have nothing but desert rock to protect.

　　Further, rain is accounted for only by the dust. Of course this sounds very near the world's record in absurdities. But it is a half-truth at least, for (70) moisture cannot condense on nothing. Every drop of rain, every globule of mist must have a nucleus. Consequently each wind that blows, each volcano that erupts is laying up dust for a rainy day. Apparently the atmosphere is empty. Actually it is (75) full enough of dust-nuclei to outfit a full-grown fog if the dew point should be favorable. If there were no dust in the air all shadows would be intensest black, the sunlight blinding.

(80) But the dust particles fulfill their greatest mission as heat collectors — they and the particles of water vapor which have embraced them. It is in reality owing to these water globules and not to the atmosphere that supports them that we are
(85) enabled to live in such comfortable temperatures.

So it comes about that the heavy moist air near the earth is the warmest of all. So high altitudes and low temperatures are found together. But after the limit of moisture content has been reached the
(90) temperature gets no lower according to reliable investigations. Instead a monotony of 459° below zero eternally prevails –459° is called the absolute zero of space.

The vertical heating arrangements of the
(95) atmosphere appear somewhat irregular. But horizontally it is in a much worse way. The surface of the globe is three quarters water and one quarter land and irregularly arranged at that. The shiny water surfaces reflect a good deal of the heat which
(100) they receive, they use up the heat in evaporation and what they do absorb penetrates far. The land surfaces, on the contrary, absorb most of the heat received, but it does not penetrate to any depth. As a consequence of these differences, land warms up
(105) about four times as quickly as water and cools off about four times as fast. Therefore, the temperature of air over continents is liable to much more rapid and extreme changes than the air over the oceans.

28. The primary purpose of the passage is to:

  (F) explain why the earth's temperatures rise and fall.
  (G) highlight the role of dust particles in determining the weather.
  (H) explore the many roles of bacteria.
  (J) describe the role of the earth's atmosphere.

29. The author makes all of the following assertions about dust EXCEPT:

  (A) dust plays a larger role in producing warm temperatures than the atmosphere.
  (B) dust accounts for only rain.
  (C) particles of dust form the nucleus of rain droplets.
  (D) volcanic eruptions and blowing winds are some of the sources of dust layers.

30. According to the author, the wind, as it blows along the surface of the earth, is comprised of all the following EXCEPT:

  (F) dust particles.
  (G) nitrogen gas.
  (H) bacteria.
  (J) hydrogen.

31. According to the passage, what does the author consider dust's most important role?

  (A) Serving as a heat collector.
  (B) Forming the basis of rain.
  (C) Minimizing the sun's glare.
  (D) Providing a thick layer of protection around the earth.

32. Which of the following does the author consider one of the world's absurdities?

  (F) Without dust, sunlight would be blinding.
  (G) The irregularly configured surface of the earth is made up of three quarters water and one quarter land.
  (H) Air temperatures over vast expanses of land are prone to much more rapid and extreme changes than the temperatures over oceans.
  (J) No other factors but dust account for the presence of rain.

33. The main point of the last paragraph is that:

  (A) air over water and air over land are subject to different heating and cooling patterns.
  (B) the earth's vertical heating arrangements are better than its horizontal heating arrangements.
  (C) land surfaces absorb most of the heat received by the sun.
  (D) deficiencies in the earth's atmosphere create dangerously extreme variances in temperature.

34. According to the author, the element that prevents humans from burning under the sun's heat is:

   (F) a small fraction of sunheat.
   (G) the uncalculated cold of outer space.
   (H) a thin layer of gases weighing just about fifteen pounds to the square inch.
   (J) a thick layer of gases that forms a sort of thermos globe.

35. The word *trifling* in line 7 most likely means

   (A) shallow.
   (B) insignificant.
   (C) silly.
   (D) novel.

36. When the author claims that "dust and water vapor occupy space independently of the rest" (lines 43–45), he most likely means:

   (F) gases become lighter as one climbs higher into the atmosphere.
   (G) dust and water make up more of the air's atmosphere than nitrogen does.
   (H) moisture and dust exert more atmospheric pressure than gases.
   (J) the properties of dust and water vapor are not determined by the other components of the atmosphere.

Science Test (Optional)

TIME: 40 minutes for 40 questions

DIRECTIONS: Following are seven passages and then questions that refer to each passage. Choose the best answer and shade in the corresponding oval on your answer sheet.

Passage I

A conductivity meter measures the electrical conductivity in a solution and is used to measure the number of impurities in freshwater. One way to purify water is to remove ions. A solution with a higher ion content has a higher conductivity than a solution with fewer ions. A group of scientists studied water solution samples from 3 different sites from which they took 3 separate measurements — temperature in degrees Celsius, conductivity ($\mu S/m$), and species richness (number of invertebrate species found) — 10 different times. Site 1 was located 5 kilometers upstream of the city center, Site 2 was located in the city center, and Site 3 was 5 kilometers downstream of the city center. Temperature and conductivity were measured with a conductivity meter. Species richness was collected, and invertebrates were placed in 98% ethanol to preserve the specimens. The collection was taken to the lab and dissecting microscopes were used to count and identify the invertebrate species. The results are shown in Table 1.

1. Based on Table 1, in Site 1, as the temperature of the solution increased, conductivity:

   (A) increased only.
   (B) decreased only.
   (C) stayed the same.
   (D) varied with no general trend.

2. The scientists' research suggests that the collection site or sites whose water solution contains the greatest number of impurities is/are:

   (F) Site 1
   (G) Site 2
   (H) Site 3
   (J) Site 1 and Site 3

TABLE 1

Site 1: Upstream			Site 2: City Center			Site 3: Downstream		
Temperature (Celsius)	Conductivity ($\mu S/m$)	Species Richness	Temperature (Celsius)	Conductivity ($\mu S/m$)	Species Richness	Temperature (Celsius)	Conductivity ($\mu S/m$)	Species Richness
23	200	10	25	900	1	22	655	5
23	155	12	24	800	2	23.5	599	4
24	220	11	23	821	1	22.5	621	6
23.5	185	9	23	906	3	25	632	4
24	188	10	24	855	2	25	588	5
22.5	190	11	22	899	1	24	612	7
25	203	14	23	865	4	23	641	6
24	253	12	24	845	1	23	625	5
23	211	10	22	933	2	23.5	598	4
25	177	8	23	865	2	24	600	3
23.7	198.2	10.7	23.3	868.9	1.9	23.6	617.1	4.9

GO ON TO NEXT PAGE

CHAPTER 19 Practice Exam   273

3. The conductivity of typical drinking water ranges between 50 and 500 $\mu S/m$. Based on the results of the scientists' research, which of the three sites contain(s) water solutions that may be safe to drink?

   (A) Site 1 only
   (B) Site 3 only
   (C) Site 1 and Site 2
   (D) Site 2 and Site 3

4. Suppose an additional study was conducted in the same manner at a site located in rural pastureland several miles upstream from Site 1. The average conductivity of this site was measured to be 500 $\mu S/m$. The average species richness of this new site would most likely be:

   (F) less than 1.9.
   (G) between 1.9 and 4.9.
   (H) between 4.9 and 10.7.
   (J) greater than 10.7.

5. The scientists most likely used which of the following to collect the data necessary to determine species richness?

   (A) Balance
   (B) pH meter
   (C) Nets
   (D) Thermometer

Passage II

Convict cichlids are highly aggressive freshwater fish that are found in streams and rivers in Central America. Their aggression allows them to protect their breeding territory from intruders that enter and consume their offspring. Both males and females are aggressive, and aggressiveness is also related to size.

Experiment 1

Researchers collected 30 males and 30 females and separated them into 3 categories based on size: small (50–69 mm), medium (70–89 mm), and large (90–109 mm). They allowed one fish (the focal fish) to claim a territory in an aquarium tank for 5 days. On day 6, they placed an intruder of equal size to and of the same sex as the focal fish into the aquarium and watched the aggressive behaviors for 30 minutes. Aggressive behaviors viewed were lateral displays, frontal displays, biting, mouth wrestling, and chasing. All behaviors were lumped together, and the total time spent in these behaviors was averaged for each group. Table 1 records the findings of average number of minutes within 30-minute time periods that the convict cichlid fish exhibited acts of aggression based on size and sex.

TABLE 1

	Small (50–69 mm) Focal Fish & Intruder	Medium (70–89 mm) Focal Fish & Intruder	Large (90–109 mm) Focal Fish & Intruder
Males	12	18	23
Females	6	10	14

Experiment 2

Researchers repeated Experiment 1 but varied the size of the intruder they introduced into the tank on day 6. In the study, 10 females and 10 males received an intruder that was 20 mm smaller than the focal fish, 10 females and 10 males received an equal-sized intruder, and 10 males and 10 females received an intruder that was 20 mm larger than the focal fish. All intruders were the same sex as the focal fish. The same types of aggressive behaviors as those in Experiment 1 were observed for 30 minutes and recorded.

Behaviors were grouped together, and the total time spent in these behaviors was averaged for each group. Table 2 records average number of minutes of aggression within a 30-minute time period in convict cichlid fish based on intruder size and sex.

TABLE 2

	Intruder 20 mm Smaller than Focal Fish	Equal-Sized Intruder	Intruder 20 mm Larger than Focal Fish
Males	12	20	11
Females	6	11	5

6. The two experiments were likely designed to answer which of these questions?

   (F) Are highly aggressive fish more likely to exist in fresh or saltwater?

   (G) What are the most common types of aggressive behaviors exhibited by convict cichlids?

   (H) Is size or gender a better indicator of the potential for aggression in convict cichlids?

   (J) How does the relative size of an intruder fish affect the number of aggressive behaviors exhibited by a focal fish?

7. According to Experiment 1, which of the following is the correct order of cichlids from highest to lowest aggression?

   (A) Large female, large male, medium female, small male.

   (B) Large male, large female, medium male, small female.

   (C) Large male, medium male, large female, small male.

   (D) Large male, medium male, small male, large female.

8. Based on Experiment 1 and Experiment 2, male cichlids exhibited:

   (F) about half as much aggression as female cichlids.

   (G) about twice as much aggression as female cichlids.

   (H) about the same amount of aggression as female cichlids.

   (J) about half as much aggression as female cichlids in Experiment 2 and about twice as much aggression as female cichlids in Experiment 1.

9. Experiment 1 and Experiment 2 differed in that Experiment 2 varied which independent variable?

   (A) Gender of the intruder.

   (B) Relative size of the intruder to focal fish.

   (C) Level of aggression in the intruder.

   (D) Number of days provided for the focal fish to establish its territory.

10. The scientists who conducted the research wanted to use the lab data to determine which combination of two cichlids would be the best protectors of their offspring. Based on the results of the two experiments, which of the following pairs was the one the scientists likely concluded was the best?

    (F) Medium male paired with a large female.

    (G) Large male paired with a small female.

    (H) Medium male paired with a medium female.

    (J) Small male paired with a small female.

11. Where dark gray bars represent male cichlids and light gray bars represent female cichlids, which of the following graphs provides the most accurate representation of the results of Experiment 2?

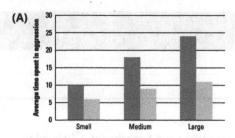
(A)

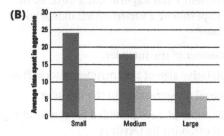
(B)

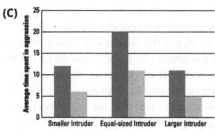
(C)

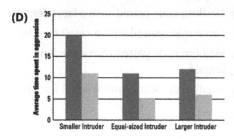
(D)

Passage III

Genetically modified organisms (GMOs) are any organisms that are modified with respect to their genetics. A wide range of methods exist for producing GMOs, from procedures as simple as selective breeding (which has been conducted for thousands of years) to the more recent technology of inserting genes of one organism into those of another organism. GMOs have been used to produce medical advances such as creating insulin for people with diabetes. However, more recently there have been debates over the role GMOs should play in foods.

Two researchers present their opinions.

Researcher 1

GMO foods were first designed in an attempt to control pests without using pesticides. Traditional pesticides can be harmful to the environment, so reducing pesticides would provide significant environmental benefits. In addition, GMO foods are thought to increase crop yields. Given that our world population continues to grow exponentially, food may become a limited resource and using genetically modified foods may assist in the sustenance of an exploding global population. GMOs have been a part of food production for several decades, and no scientific evidence exists to support the view that the nutritional value of GMOs is less than that of food that has not been genetically modified. Nor does evidence suggest that GMOs cause harm to the organisms that consume them. Some studies have reported minor increases in food allergies associated with GMOs, but that information is likely correlational, not causational.

Researcher 2

Genetically modified foods may have been first implemented to replace pesticides, but recent data shows that pests become resistant to the GMO plants more quickly than to plants that have not been genetically modified and are treated with pesticides. Reducing pesticides benefits the environment, but this reduction can be achieved without resorting to producing GMOs. Planting a variety of species instead of monocultures and using natural pest repellants (e.g., lady bugs) would reduce pesticide use in a better way than GMOs. Not all GMOs yield higher crops, and other options to combat limited food production, such as home and community gardening, exist. Placing the burden of food production on individuals would reduce the strain on big corporations. Recent efforts in urban areas include converting spaces on rooftops to community farms. Although current studies show no direct correlation between GMOs and health problems in humans, GMOs have not been studied long enough to rule out the possibility of long-term effects. The nutritional value of GMOs may be similar to that of organically grown food, but the taste and overall quality are not. Anyone who has eaten both organic foods and GMOs will attest to the former's superiority. The last problem with GMOs is that cross contamination can occur. Plant pollen can travel long distances and GMO plants can hybridize with organic crops.

12. According to Researcher 1, what are the benefits of GMOs?

   (F) They reduce pesticide use and increase crop yields.
   (G) They increase pesticide use and decrease crop yields.
   (H) They increase the nutritional value of food and do not cause harm to organisms.
   (J) Researcher 1 sees no benefits of GMOs.

13. According to the passage, with which of the following statements would both researchers agree?

   (A) Increasing pesticide use would be good for the environment.
   (B) There is no direct correlation between GMOs and health problems in humans.
   (C) GMO foods have improved taste and quality.
   (D) GMO foods increase food allergies in many of the humans who consume them.

14. According to Researcher 2, a major disadvantage of GMOs is that:

   (F) their pollen can travel long distances.
   (G) their use decreases the number of naturally occurring pest reducers.
   (H) their use increases the prevalence of harmful pesticides.
   (J) they are directly correlated with health problems in humans.

15. According to Researcher 1, a harmful effect that may be correlated to GMO foods is:

   (A) pesticide resistance.
   (B) production of tumors in consumers.
   (C) decreased nutritional value.
   (D) increased food allergies in consumers.

16. According to Researcher 2, the use of pesticides may be reduced by all of the following EXCEPT:

   (F) replacing only some organically grown crops with GMOs.
   (G) planting a variety of species instead of monocultures.
   (H) using ladybugs as repellants.
   (J) increasing the number of community farms.

17. According to Researcher 2, GMOs have been linked to which of the following?

    (A) An increase in the number of pesticides.
    (B) An increase in the number of home and community gardens.
    (C) Inferior food quality.
    (D) A larger burden placed on food-producing corporations.

18. Which of the following graphs is consistent with Researcher 1's view but not Researcher 2's?

(A)
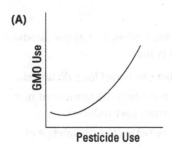

(B)
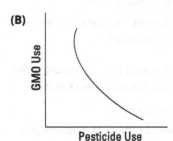

(C)
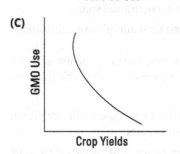

(D)
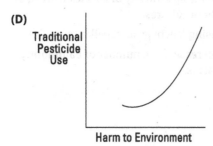

Passage IV

Plants need several elements to grow, such as light, water, and nutrients. The most important nutrients are nitrogen (N), phosphorus (P), and potassium (K). These inorganic nutrients are converted from organic nutrients during the process of decomposition. Certain organisms, called *decomposers*, help speed up the process of decomposition. Researchers wanted to test whether applying decomposers in the form of compost or synthetic fertilizers were better for growing plants. In addition, the researchers wanted to determine the optimal light conditions for plant growth. The researchers conducted the following two experiments, where the amount of water applied in each case was kept at a constant.

Experiment 1

The three researchers set up three treatment groups. In each contained environment, the researcher planted 20 pea seeds. The first treatment group contained sandy soil with nothing else added. The second treatment group contained sandy soil to which was added a compost mixture by earthworm decomposers. The third group contained potting soil that was enriched with synthetic fertilizers. Once planted, the seeds received 12 hours of sunlight per day and were watered once a day for eight weeks. After eight weeks, each plant stem was measured from the top of the soil to the top of the main stem. The researchers recorded the measurements in Figure 1.

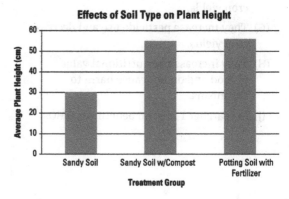

FIGURE 1

278   PART 7   Putting It All Together with a Full-Length Practice ACT

Experiment 2

The same experiment was conducted using only the sandy soil mixed with earthworm-generated compost for all 60 plants. Each treatment group received different amounts of daily exposure to sunlight. One group received 6 hours, another 10 hours, and the other 14 hours of sunlight. Each group received 20 seeds that were planted at the same time and were watered once a day for 8 weeks. After 8 weeks, each plant stem was measured from the top of the soil to the top of the main stem. The results are displayed in Table 1.

TABLE 1

Hours of Daily Sunlight	Plant Height (cm)
6	40
10	50
14	59

19. Which of the following is an independent variable in the two experiments?

    I. Type of soil
    II. Plant height
    III. Hours of sunlight

    (A) I only
    (B) II only
    (C) I and III only
    (D) I, II, and III

20. According to the results of the two experiments, the environment that would produce the greatest amount of plant growth would be:

    (F) sandy soil and at least 12 hours of daily sunlight.
    (G) sandy soil with compost and at least 10 hours of daily sunlight.
    (H) Potting soil and at least 6 hours of daily sunlight.
    (J) Potting soil and at least 14 hours of daily sunlight.

21. Which of the following best describes the difference between the two experiments?

    (A) In Experiment 1, light length per day was varied; in Experiment 2, the soil type was varied.
    (B) In Experiment 1, light length per day was constant; in Experiment 2, the soil type was varied.
    (C) In Experiment 1, the soil type was varied; in Experiment 2, light length per day was varied.
    (D) In Experiment 1, the soil type was varied; in Experiment 2, the amount of daily water was varied.

22. If the researchers set up a third experiment similar to Experiment 2 where they tested the effect of the amount of daily sunlight on seeds grown in the potting soil, then based on the results of Experiments 1 and 2, they could reasonably predict which of the following about the average height of the resulting plants in Experiment 3?

    (F) For all hours of sunlight exposure, plant height after eight weeks in Experiment 3 would be taller than plant height after eight weeks in Experiment 2.
    (G) For all hours of sunlight exposure, plant height after eight weeks in Experiment 3 would be shorter than plant height after eight weeks in Experiment 2.
    (H) For all hours of sunlight exposure, plant height after eight weeks in Experiment 3 would be similar to plant height after eight weeks in Experiment 2.
    (J) Plant height for seeds exposed to ten hours of daily sunlight after eight weeks in Experiment 3 would be shorter than plant height of those grown in only sandy soil after eight weeks in Experiment 1.

GO ON TO NEXT PAGE

23. After conducting Experiments 1 and 2, researchers drew the conclusion that if pea seeds grown in sandy soil with compost were provided 16 hours of daily sunlight under the same conditions as the prior two experiments, their plant height after 8 weeks would measure no more than 65 cm. Is this conclusion reasonable based on the results of the two experiments?

    (A) Yes, because the ratio of plant height to number of daily hours of sunlight decreased as the researchers increased the amount of daily sunlight exposure.
    (B) Yes, because the ratio of plant height to number of daily hours of sunlight increased as the researchers increased the amount of daily sunlight exposure.
    (C) No, because the ratio of plant height to number of daily hours of sunlight decreased as the researchers increased the amount of daily sunlight exposure.
    (D) No, because the ratio of plant height to number of daily hours of sunlight increased as the researchers increased the amount of daily sunlight exposure.

24. Which of the following conclusions about plant growth is justified based on the two experiments?

    (F) Plant height is increased when seeds receive a combination of increased nutrients, greater exposure to sunlight, and large amounts of water.
    (G) Exposure to sunlight has a greater effect on plant height than soil type.
    (H) Soil type influences plant height more significantly than either exposure to sunlight or water.
    (J) Nutrients in the form of compost and synthetic fertilizers affect plant height similarly.

Passage V

On a scale of 0 to 14, pH measures how acidic or alkaline a solution is. Most living aquatic organisms live at or near pH 7. Scientists from the United States Geological Survey (USGS) confirmed reports of increasing numbers of dead fish in small lakes and ponds within a 3,500 square km area of land over a six-month period, and no known pollutants had entered the affected area. The scientists checked the water quality of the ponds to determine the cause of the mass fish kills.

Experiment 1

The scientists took samples from 10 of the ponds that had experienced increased fish deaths (contaminated ponds) and another 10 ponds in the same area where increased numbers of deaths were not evident (healthy ponds).

Water samples were extracted from each of the 20 ponds for three consecutive mornings at the same time each day. Each sample was tested for temperature and pH levels. The results of the two measurements for the three samples were averaged for each site. The results for the 10 contaminated ponds were then averaged, and separate averages were calculated for the 10 healthy ponds. The averages for both were represented in Figures 1 and 2.

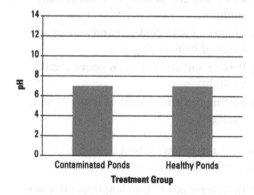

FIGURE 1

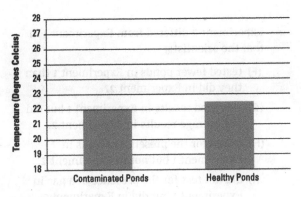

FIGURE 2

Experiment 2

High levels of nitrogen and phosphorus from fertilizer runoff can cause algae blooms, which may indicate increased decomposition and resultant decreases in oxygen (O_2). The scientists conducted a second experiment in which they tested water samples from the same 20 ponds for nitrates (NO_2) and dissolved oxygen (O_2). As in Experiment 1, the measures were averaged and the results were recorded in Figure 3.

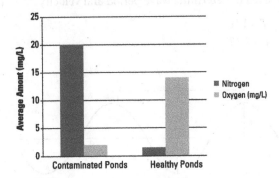

FIGURE 3

25. In Experiment 1, which of the following was true about the contaminated ponds as compared to the healthy ponds?

(A) The pH of the contaminated ponds was higher.

(B) The temperature of the contaminated ponds was higher.

(C) Both pH and temperature were higher in the contaminated ponds.

(D) Neither pH nor temperature was higher in the contaminated ponds.

26. Based on the two experiments, which of the following best expresses the relationship between pH levels and O_2 levels in the two types of ponds?

(F) Pond water with low levels of O_2 had high levels of pH.

(G) Pond water with low levels of O_2 had low levels of pH.

(H) Pond water with high levels of O_2 had pH levels that were more alkaline than acidic.

(J) There is no apparent relationship between pH levels and O_2 levels in the two types of ponds.

27. Based on the information in the passage, which of the pond types likely had more algae blooms?

(A) The contaminated ponds, because their water samples had a higher average ratio of nitrogen to oxygen.

(B) The contaminated ponds, because their average water temperature was higher than that of the healthy ponds.

(C) The healthy ponds, because their water samples had a higher average ratio of nitrogen to oxygen.

(D) The healthy ponds, because their average water temperature was higher than that of the contaminated ponds.

28. Granite contains very few bases. Limestone contains bases. Natural bases can neutralize acids present in the rain, snow, or soil. If the acids are neutralized by the natural bases, the pH of the lake will remain about the same. If the scientists determined that runoff from snowmelt that feeds the ponds in the area has a pH lower than 7, based on information in the passage, which of the following is most likely regarding the composition of the rocks in the two types of ponds?

   (F) The contaminated ponds contain more granite-based rock, and the healthy ponds contain more limestone-based rock.
   (G) Both types of ponds contain limestone-based rock.
   (H) Both types of ponds contain mostly granite-based rock.
   (J) The contaminated ponds contain more limestone-based rock, and the healthy ponds contain more granite-based rock.

29. Rapidly moving water tends to contain more dissolved oxygen than do more stagnant bodies of water. Based on this information, which of the following was most likely?

   (A) Water in the contaminated ponds moved more slowly than the water in the healthy ponds.
   (B) Water in the healthy ponds moved more slowly than the water in the contaminated ponds.
   (C) Water in the two pond types moved at about the same speed.
   (D) The water depth of the contaminated ponds was greater than the water depth of the healthy ponds.

30. Experiment 2 differed from Experiment 1 in that the scientists:

   (F) tested fewer ponds in Experiment 1 than they did in Experiment 2.
   (G) averaged results in Experiment 1 but did not average results in Experiment 2.
   (H) tested for the presence of a gas in Experiment 1 but not in Experiment 2.
   (J) did not test for the presence of a gas in Experiment 1 but did in Experiment 2.

Passage VI

A wave is an oscillation that occurs through matter or space. A wave consists of many characteristics that define it. The wavelength (λ) is the distance between two crests or two troughs as shown in Figure 1. The period (T) is the time it takes a wave to complete one oscillation. The frequency (v) is the number of periods per unit time, measured in hertz (Hz). The wave velocity (c) is the distance traveled in a period per unit time. The period of the wave completely defines its frequency, and vice versa. The following equations are used to determine wave period and velocity.

$$T = 1/v$$
$$c = \lambda / T$$

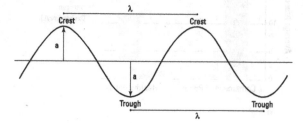

FIGURE 1

Oceanographers took 265 days' worth of data for deep-water waves in three bodies of water off the coast of the United States: the Atlantic Ocean, Pacific Ocean, and Gulf of Mexico. Table 1 charts the average wavelength and velocity for each body of water.

TABLE 1

	Velocity (c) in m/s	Wavelength (λ) in m	Frequency (v) in Hz
Atlantic Ocean	0.95	425	0.0022
Pacific Ocean	0.95	625	0.0015
Gulf of Mexico	0.86	650	0.0013

31. Compared to the average period (T) for a wave in the Pacific Ocean, the average period (T) for a wave in the Atlantic Ocean would likely be:

   (A) the same, because the average velocity of waves in the Atlantic Ocean is the same as the average velocity of waves in the Pacific Ocean and the average wavelengths in both oceans are different.

   (B) the same, because the average wavelength of waves in the Atlantic Ocean is the same as the average wavelength of waves in the Pacific Ocean and the average velocities of waves in both oceans are different.

   (C) different, because the average wavelength of waves in the Atlantic Ocean is different from the average wavelength of waves in the Pacific Ocean and the average velocities of waves in both oceans is the same.

   (D) different, because the average velocity of waves in the Atlantic Ocean is different from the average velocity of waves in the Pacific Ocean

32. According to information in the passage, which of the studied bodies of water most likely has the greatest average wave period (T)?

   (F) The Atlantic Ocean has the greatest average period.

   (G) The Pacific Ocean has the greatest average period.

   (H) The Gulf of Mexico has the greatest average period.

   (J) Both the Atlantic and Pacific Oceans have greater average periods than the Gulf of Mexico.

33. The frequency of a wave cycle in the deeper waters of another large body of water was found to be 0.0075 m/s. Based on information in the passage, its wavelength is most likely:

   (A) less than 425 m.
   (B) between 425 and 625 m.
   (C) between 625 and 650 m.
   (D) greater than 650 m.

34. The amplitude (a) is the distance from the wave's centerline to its crest or trough. Based on information in the passage, which of the three bodies of water had the greatest average wave amplitude?

   (F) Atlantic Ocean
   (G) Pacific Ocean
   (H) Gulf of Mexico
   (J) The passage does not provide sufficient information to determine the greatest average wave amplitude.

35. For all tested bodies of water, as wavelength increased, frequency:

   (A) decreased only.
   (B) increased only.
   (C) generally stayed the same.
   (D) decreased then increased.

Passage VII

Specific genes are responsible for producing particular traits in an organism. In complex organisms, offspring inherit a combination of genes from two distinct parents. Offspring receive two alleles for each trait — one from one parent and one from the other.

The genetic makeup of an individual, determined by the two alleles they inherit for a given trait, is known as their genotype. The way these traits are physically expressed is referred to as the phenotype. In many cases, one allele is dominant over another recessive allele. This means that the dominant allele's trait is the one that appears in the phenotype, even though the individual also carries the recessive allele. However, in instances of incomplete dominance, the combination of alleles leads to a phenotype that is distinct from either of the individual allele traits.

In a certain population of humans, there are two alleles that determine hair texture. The C allele codes for curly hair, while the S allele codes for straight hair. In this case, the trait for hair type follows a pattern of incomplete dominance. Individuals who inherit two C alleles (CC) have curly hair, while those with two S alleles (SS) have straight hair. The figure below illustrates a family tree that outlines some of the observed genotypes and phenotypes, with lines indicating the relationships between parents and their offspring.

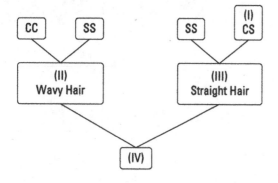

36. The hair texture of Individual I must be:
    (F) curly.
    (G) straight.
    (H) the same as that for Individual IV.
    (J) wavy.

37. What are the percent chances that Individual IV will have the same hair texture as Individual I?
    (A) 0
    (B) 25
    (C) 50
    (D) 100

38. The genotype of offspring of Individual III and an individual with curly hair could be:
    (F) CS only.
    (G) either CC, CS, or SS.
    (H) wavy only.
    (J) either curly or straight.

39. What percent of the offspring of Individual III and an individual with the same genotype would have curly hair?
    (A) 0
    (B) 25
    (C) 50
    (D) 100

40. Individual III and an individual with the genotype CC produce six offspring. How many of their offspring will possess a different hair texture from that of their parents?
    (A) 0
    (B) 2
    (C) 4
    (D) 6

DO NOT TURN THE PAGE UNTIL TOLD TO DO SO STOP **DO NOT RETURN TO A PREVIOUS TEST**

Writing Test

TIME: 40 minutes

DIRECTIONS: Respond to the following prompt with a well-organized essay that follows the rules of Standard English. Write your essay on a separate sheet of lined paper.

Some people believe that the elderly population should be required to reapply for a driver's license and retake a driving test after they reach a particular age. As the Baby Boomer generation ages, more and more elderly drivers are taking to the roadways, and with the aging process comes a variety of issues that can lead to problems behind the wheel. Hearing loss, diminished vision, and longer reaction times are just a few of these possible concerns. Is it fair to force an entire population to reapply for something they have already earned and been using for decades? Given the increasing number of elderly drivers on the road, this is an important issue worthy of careful consideration.

Read and carefully consider these perspectives. Each suggests a particular way of thinking about whether elderly drivers should have to reapply for a driver's license once they reach a certain age.

Perspective 1: Elderly drivers should have to retake their driving tests once they reach a particular age for both their own safety and that of all others out on the roadways. Certain abilities decrease with age, and many of those abilities that do decrease are critical for maintaining safe driving practices.

Perspective 2: Forcing elderly drivers to retake their driving tests based on age rather than a demonstrated lack of ability behind the wheel is essentially a form of age discrimination and should not be put into practice.

Perspective 3: Requiring all elderly drivers to reapply for driver's licenses after they reach a given age puts an unnecessary strain on already limited resources in our DMVs and driving schools, and it would take attention away from the inexperienced teen population that is learning the rules of the road for the first time.

Essay Task

Write a unified, coherent essay in which you evaluate multiple perspectives as to whether elderly drivers should be forced to reapply for a driver's license once they reach a given age. In your essay, be sure to:

- Clearly state your own perspective on the issue and analyze the relationship between your perspective and at least one other perspective.
- Develop and support your ideas with reasoning and examples.
- Organize your ideas clearly and logically.
- Communicate your ideas effectively in standard written English.

Your perspective may be in full agreement with any of the others, in partial agreement, or wholly different.

Chapter 20
Practice Exam: Answers and Explanations

So you've completed the Practice Exam in Chapter 19, and now you want to check your answers and find out your score. Well, you've come to the right place!

In this chapter, we provide detailed answer explanations for each problem on the test to help you understand why one answer is correct, and the others aren't. Along the way, you find zillions of tips, traps, and other valuable information you can use when you face the actual exam on test day. So be sure to read all the explanations carefully — yes, even the ones you got right!

After the explanations, you find the scoring guide that helps you determine what score you would've received if this practice test were real. If you're short on time, skip to the end of this chapter, where we provide an abbreviated answer key.

English Test

1. **B.** The underlined part contains a semicolon, so you're likely dealing with proper punctuation. For the semicolon to be proper, the words before it and after it must express a complete thought. The words after the semicolon make up an independent clause; they have a subject *methods* and a verb *are* and don't begin with a subordinating conjunction. But the words before the semicolon begin with the subordinating conjunction *when*, so even though they have the subject and verb *it comes*, they don't form a complete thought. The semicolon is wrong, and so are the colon and dash. The proper way to separate a beginning dependent clause from the rest of the sentence is with a comma. Choice (B) is correct. To review punctuation rules, flip to Chapter 5.

2. **F.** Quickly eliminate Choice (H). The form *its'* doesn't exist. Then check the pronoun *it* in the underlined portion. You know the contraction form (*it's*) is okay because you substitute *it is* for *it's*, and the sentence sounds just fine. Eliminate Choice (G) because it contains the possessive form of *it*. Choice (J) has the proper form of *it*, but it improperly separates the beginning dependent clause from the rest of the sentence with a semicolon instead of a comma. Choice (F) is best.

3. **C.** The underlined word is ambiguous — *one* what? The pronouns offered by Choices (B) and (D) don't provide clarity, so the best answer is the clearly-stated noun in Choice (C).

4. **F.** The predominate question you ask yourself for an addition question is whether the proposed addition's topic is relevant to the substance of the paragraph. The paragraph is about finding a personal trainer, and the new sentence relates to that topic. So you can eliminate Choices (H) and (J). Of the two remaining answers, Choice (F) is best because the sentence offers ways to find a personal trainer rather than the benefits of using one.

5. **B.** To communicate well and communicate clearly mean roughly the same thing, so Choice (A) is redundant. Choice (C) is redundant and improper because it uses the adjective *clear* to describe the verb *communicate*. Both Choices (B) and (D) eliminate the redundancy, but Choice (B) does so more precisely (think fewest words).

6. **J.** The underlined part is a transition. To pick the best transition, check the sentence or sentences before it and the sentence that contains it. The answer that brings the two thoughts together best is the correct transition. The idea before the transition is that you may wish to choose a trainer with a similar physique. Staying on track isn't an example of choosing someone with a similar body shape, so Choice (F) doesn't work. Choice (H) provides the same transition, so it must be wrong. Choice (G) shows contrast, and the ideas aren't opposite. The best solution is to eliminate the transition altogether.

TIP

If the answer choices contain two similar transition words, eliminate both. You can't have two right answers, so they must both be wrong.

7. **C.** The underlined part creates a comma splice. The words before and after the comma both express complete thoughts. So Choice (A) is out. Choice (B) doesn't correct the punctuation problem. Rule out Choice (D) because a comma after an *and* that joins two complete thoughts is rarely proper. The answer has to be Choice (C). It fixes the comma splice by inserting a conjunction between the two independent clauses and doesn't create another punctuation error.

8. **G.** The answer choices are the same but for the commas. The underlined part is a beginning prepositional phrase, so it should be separated from the rest of the sentence with a comma at the end. Choice (H) is out because it doesn't have a comma at the end of the phrase. Choice (J) sticks a comma between a subject *trainer* and its *verb will be*, so it can't be right. The comma between *decide* and *whether* in Choice (F) serves no purpose. The best answer is Choice (G); it places the comma at the end of the phrase and contains no unnecessary additional punctuation.

9. **D.** When you see an underlined verb, first check for subject/verb agreement. The subject of the sentence is compound: *weight loss and physical fitness*. Compound subjects take plural verbs. Don't be fooled by the ending *s*; the verb *starts* is singular. *Begins* is also singular. Choices (A) and (B) are wrong. Choice (C) tries to replace the verb with an *ing* word that can't work as a verb on its own. The answer is the plural verb *start* in Choice (D).

10. **J.** This big-picture question actually asks you about the passage's main purpose. Focus on the exact language of the question and ask yourself whether the essay highlights some of the best ways to lose weight. It talks about one way to lose weight, but it doesn't go into any others. The correct answer likely begins with *No*. When you check Choices (H) and (J), you see that Choice (J) is the better answer. The essay only highlights one weight loss method, so it wouldn't provide much information about more than one way to lose weight.

11. **A.** Check the underlined possessive pronoun for proper form. *Their* renames *players*, so the plural format is proper and Choice (D) can't be right. The next step is to decide whether you need the possessive form. Because *skills* is a noun, the possessive form is necessary.

REMEMBER

Whenever a noun immediately follows a pronoun or other noun, the first noun should be in possessive form.

12. **J.** Within the context of the sentence, you're looking for an answer that clarifies that the machines simulate actual pitches. Check for obviously incorrect answers. Choice (G) is clearly incorrect. The definition of *fakes* implies that the pitches would be false, which isn't the same as the similarity suggested by the context. *Assimilates* sounds a lot like simulate, but its meaning of adapting to a new environment isn't correct in the sentence. Choice (H) is wrong. *Reenacts* is used specifically to refer to the simulation of an event rather than an object, so Choice (F) is wrong. The best word to indicate the machine simulates real pitches is Choice (J), *replicates*.

13. **D.** *Advanced* and *elevated* have the same meaning, so it's redundant to use both. Eliminate Choices (A), (B), and (C) because they're repetitive and awkward. The solution is to eliminate the clause as suggested by Choice (D).

14. **J.** The lengthy underlined part appears in a sentence with a beginning participle (verb part) phrase. A beginning participle phrase *always* describes the subject of the sentence, so check the subject to see whether it makes sense that it would feature many customizable options. A *hitter*, *adjustments*, and *time* don't feature customizable options. Only *machines* can have customizable options. So Choice (J) is the only logical answer.

TIP

Whenever you see a lengthy underlined portion in a sentence with a participle phrase at the beginning, check for *dangling particles* — a phrase that doesn't logically describe the subject of the sentence.

15. **A.** If you can't quickly determine whether the proposed addition is relevant, check what comes after *because* in each answer to eliminate choices that aren't true. Choice (C) is a definite *no* because nowhere in the essay does the author stress that young players are more likely to benefit from pitching machines than older ones are. Eliminate Choice (B) because the author never claims that older players are more likely to experience the benefits of a pitching machine. Similarly, Choice (D) isn't true; the prior paragraph doesn't contain a point that the suggested addition would build upon. Choice (A) is the best answer. The addition would contradict the author's statement in the first paragraph that pitching machines are a great resource for players at all levels.

16. **H.** The underlined verb doesn't have a subject/verb agreement problem, so check the tense. The verb is in present perfect tense, which would indicate that Roosevelt's rising may still continue. Later you see that Roosevelt was around in 1900, so it's unlikely that he's still living, let alone rising. The correct tense is the simple past *rose*, Choice (H). Choice (J) is clearly incorrect because *has rose* isn't a proper verb construction, and Choice (G) can't be right because the other past actions in the paragraph are expressed in past tense.

CHAPTER 20 Practice Exam: Answers and Explanations   289

17. **A.** To answer this question correctly, you need to know the meaning of *prominence*. *Prominence* is defined as "the state of being important or famous." While *infamy*, Choice (B), does mean "widely known," its connotation is negative, which doesn't match the tone of the passage or the author's overall impression of Teddy Roosevelt. Choices (C) and (D) are both antonyms of *prominence*, indicating that Teddy Roosevelt was not, in fact, very well-known at all. The passage implies that Roosevelt was very well known, so stick with Choice (A) and leave the underlined portion as is.

18. **G.** Note that a comma exists before the underlined part, which means that *unit* is followed by a nonessential descriptive phrase. The element that describes *unit* is "the 'Rough Riders.'" So choose the answer that puts commas on both sides of that noun phrase. Choices (G) and (J) complete the task, but Choice (J) adds an incorrect comma after *Hill*. Choice (G) is best.

19. **C.** Inserting information about how and why McKinley was assassinated may be relevant to a passage about McKinley, but the passage is about Roosevelt, and McKinley is not mentioned again. And how Roosevelt came to assume the presidency is not nearly as important as what he did once he had the job, so the proposed addition is irrelevant, and Choices (A) and (B) are out. The passage doesn't mention McKinley elsewhere, so Choice (D) is wrong. Choice (C) is correct.

20. **J.** Note that the underlined part is an element of a series of activities Roosevelt participated in. To keep the series parallel, pick the activity expressed in Choice (J). Were you tempted by Choice (H)? Continuing the series with *engaging* seems to fit with the *–ing* construction of *participating*, but the third element doesn't begin with a gerund, so Choice (H) can't be correct.

REMEMBER

Every element of a series should begin with the same grammatical format to maximize parallel structure.

21. **B.** The underlined part provides a transition, so read the sentence before it and the sentence it's a part of to see how the ideas in each sentence relate. The preceding sentence states that Roosevelt invited union members and mine owners to work out a solution. The next sentence states that the owners refused to speak with the union. The two ideas suggest contrast: Roosevelt invited them, *but* the owners refused. The best answer is *however* in Choice (B). For Choice (C) to be correct, the idea that the owners refused would have to be the final step in a series, but the events continue after the sentence with the underlined words. Choices (A) and (C) create a cause-and-effect relationship, but Roosevelt's invitation didn't cause the owners to refuse. Choice (B) is best.

TIP

Questions about transition words often contain two answers that provide the same transition. Once you determine that two answers are similar, you can eliminate both. Because they can't both be right, they must both be wrong.

22. **F.** Consider the message in the proposed deletion. The sentence concludes with a detailed example of one of Roosevelt's accomplishments. Choice (F) states this purpose clearly. Choice (J) is wrong because the sentence contains specific information rather than general observations. Choice (H) is also incorrect. The next paragraph is about railroads rather than mines, so you know that the sentence doesn't foreshadow a subsequent point. Without the last sentence, the reader wouldn't know the outcome of the incident, so Choice (G) can't be correct.

TIP

The correct answer to a deletion question is rarely that the deleted material is irrelevant or unnecessary. If you choose such an answer, make sure the deleted portion has nothing to do with the topic of the paragraph.

23. **B.** The underlined word and answer choices are prepositions. Choose the one that fits the meaning of the sentence. Notice that the main verb *controlled* is in simple past tense. So the event happened at one point in time. Later in the paragraph, you discover that the law designed to deal with railroad control was finalized in 1906. The railroads couldn't have controlled prices after the beginning of the 20th century, so Choice (C) is wrong. Choices (A) and (D) suggest continuation over a long period rather than a specific point in time, so they don't work. The best answer is Choice (B), which properly conveys that the control existed specifically in the first years of the 20th century.

24. **J.** The underlined part provides a transition between the statement that Roosevelt believed that the system gave companies too much power and hurt consumers with the information that he supported an act that regulated the railroad. Eliminate Choices (G) and (H) because they provide the same transition. They can't both be right. The remaining choices suggest an example or a cause and effect. Supporting the act isn't an example of Roosevelt's belief. Instead, his belief is the *reason* for his support of the act. The best answer is Choice (J) because this shows cause and effect.

25. **C.** The apostrophes in the answer choices should clue you into checking for possessive form. The underlined word is a noun followed by the noun phrase "financial records." A noun followed by another noun or noun phrase almost always indicates possessive form. So your answer will contain an apostrophe and you can eliminate Choice (B). Choice (D) is wrong because the plural of *company* is *companies*. The remaining choices require you to determine whether the noun is plural or singular. It must be plural because if it were singular, it would be preceded by an article such as *the* or *a*. The way to make *companies* possessive is to end the word with an apostrophe. Choice (C) is correct.

TIP

When you see possessive form in the ACT English test answers, the correct answer will almost always be possessive. If you pick an answer that isn't possessive, double-check to make sure you haven't missed something.

26. **J.** Believe it or not, the subject of this sentence is the noun clause "what it has failed to accomplish." The comma after *accomplish* in Choice (F) separates the subject from the verb *is*, and a single comma is never correct when it lies between the subject and the verb. Choices (G) and (H) place a comma in the middle of the noun clause, so they can't be right. The correct punctuation is Choice (J) with no commas at all.

27. **A.** The underlined part provides a transition between the statement that computers crash and remote repair provides a great resource. The ideas aren't contrasting, so eliminate Choices (B) and (C). Repair isn't an example of a computer crash, so Choice (D) is wrong. The best solution is to leave the sentence as is; computers crash so computer repair is great. Choice (A) is correct.

28. **H.** Eliminate Choices (F) and (G) because *anyone* refers to a person and *who* is the pronoun that refers to people. The difference between the remaining answers is the comma after *anyone*. The comma indicates that the clause that begins with *who* isn't essential to the meaning of the sentence, but without it, the sentence would suggest that remote computer repair is great for *anyone* instead of *anyone who owns a business*. Choice (H) without the comma is better.

29. **A.** Examine the added commas in the answer choices. Those in Choice (B) suggest that "or even weeks without your machine" is nonessential information that you can easily remove without changing the meaning of the sentence. Without the words, though, you don't know what you're waiting for. Choice (D) creates the same confusion by indicating that "without

your machine" isn't essential. If you extracted "even weeks" from the sentence as suggested by Choice (C), the last part would read "wait days or without your machine," which makes no sense. It also eliminates the necessary comma after *machine* that separates the beginning phrase from the main idea of the sentence. Because Choices (B), (C), and (D) aren't correct, you know Choice (A) must be right. It suggests that you don't have to wait days or weeks if you seek remote repair.

30. **J.** To answer this question correctly, pick the preposition that goes with result. English speakers say "as a result of" rather than "as a result from," "as a result with," or "as a result as." Choice (J) is best.

TIP

An underlined preposition means you need to read the sentence very carefully to make sure you choose the answer that provides the intended meaning.

31. **B.** "Rather than paying you an actual visit" isn't a complete sentence, so it needs to be part of the sentence that comes before it. Eliminate Choice (A). Choices (C) and (D) present other ways of punctuating two complete thoughts in the same sentence, so they also can't be right. The best answer is Choice (B), which correctly completes the rest of the first sentence of this paragraph with the remainder of the description of remote computer repair. There's no need for any punctuation.

32. **H.** *They're* is the contraction of "they are" and doesn't show possession. You need possessive form because you have a pronoun *they* followed by a noun. Choice (F) is incorrect. Choice (G) is awkward and incorrect because "his or her" is singular and the renamed noun is *people*, which is plural. *There* indicates place not possession, so Choice (J) is wrong. The possessive form of *they* is *their*, so pick Choice (H).

33. **C.** Check the purpose of the underlined part. It provided additional information about the factor that determines whether a repair will take hours or minutes. That function is best described by Choice (C). The phrase isn't a detail about or example of remote repair, so Choices (A) and (B) can't be right. The next paragraph summarizes the passage, so the phrase doesn't provide foreshadowing as indicated by Choice (D).

34. **H.** Eliminate Choices (F), (G), and (J) because they're redundant. The paragraph already makes the points in Choices (F) and (G), and the idea in Choice (J) is indicated in previous paragraph statements. Choice (H) completes the description of the time benefits of remote repair, so it's the best answer.

35. **A.** To answer this question correctly, you first need to determine whether the fourth paragraph appears out of place. Given that it's the concluding paragraph and nicely summarizes the information contained in the previous paragraphs without introducing any new information, it's likely fine where it is. To be sure, check the other options. The first paragraph provides a clear introduction to the passage, so eliminate Choice (B). Choice (C) isn't logical because you wouldn't state the benefits of remote repair before you define it. Choice (A) is correct.

36. **G.** The underlined word is a verb, so check for subject/verb agreement. The subject is the singular *competition* and not the plural *resources*, so the verb must be singular. The only singular option is Choice (G).

37. **B.** The underlined pronoun has no clear reference. The nouns that precede the pronoun are *competition, resources, evolution, characteristics,* and *behaviors*. None of these nouns logically name something that can improve its ability to compete. Because you can't point to the particular noun the pronoun renames, you don't know whether the proper form is *it* or *they*. The only possible answer is Choice (B) because it clarifies exactly what has the ability to compete.

Whenever you encounter an underlined pronoun, look for the noun it renames. If you can't point to the specific noun in the preceding sentence or two, the issue is an unclear pronoun reference. Look for the answer that replaces the pronoun with a specific noun.

38. **J.** Search the fifth sentence for ideas that need prior reference. The sentence refers to "this" (meaning "this statement"), so it needs to follow the sentence that contains that particular statement. The sentence in the paragraph that's most like saying that each species establishes its own niche is the third. Moving the fifth sentence after Sentence 3 also defines *niche* before it's further described in the fourth sentence. Choice (J) is best.

39. **B.** The original sentence sets up the two components of a niche using a colon. You know that a dash may replace a colon, so Choice (D) works and should be eliminated. Choice (C) properly uses a comma to designate the two types, so cross out that option. Choice (A) is okay; it creates two independent clauses and punctuates them properly with a comma and conjunction. The problem answer is Choice (B). It implies that niches have two components that are both abiotic and biotic. Because it distorts the message, Choice (B) is the least appropriate substitute and therefore, the most appropriate answer.

40. **H.** The pronoun *whom* refers only to people, so Choices (F) and (G) are wrong. Choice (J) omits the preposition that goes with *interact* and states that a species interacts predators, prey, and so on rather than interacts *with* them. The best answer is Choice (H) because it contains the proper pronoun and includes the necessary preposition.

41. **A.** Evaluating this sentence may be easier if you simplify it: Species compete whenever their niches overlap. It sounds right the way it is, but check the other possibilities to be sure. Choice (B) is incorrect; the species don't compete *although* their niches overlap. It doesn't make sense that species compete *whether* their niches overlap, so Choice (C) is wrong. Choice (D) changes the beginning dependent clause to an independent clause, so it can't be right. The best answer is Choice (A).

42. **G.** The underlined verb doesn't agree with the number of its subject. The subject *niche* is singular, so it needs the singular verb *overlaps*. All of the other options suggest plural verbs. Pick Choice (G).

43. **A.** The underlined transition joins together a sentence that presents the ways a species can win a competition with a sentence that lists the three possible results of a competition. The second sentence isn't an example of winning, nor does it present an opposite position. So Choices (B) and (C) can't be right. At first, Choices (A) and (D) may seem to provide the same transition, but *finally* suggests the final element or step in a chronological list. Choice (A) provides the more precise transition by suggesting a conclusion rather than a chronological end.

44. **H.** Even if you don't remember that Darwin was a firm believer in "survival of the fittest," you can probably still see why Choice (H) is the best option. Choices (F) and (J) contradict the earlier statements that competition only occasionally involves direct combat and that species may occupy the same niche, so they can't be right. Choice (G) repeats an earlier point, so it isn't the best choice. Stick with Choice (H).

45. **D.** The easiest answers to eliminate are Choices (B) and (C). The words that follow *qualities* don't create a complete thought, so the semicolon in Choice (C) is wrong. The words that precede the colon in Choice (B) don't form a complete thought, so that option is punctuated improperly. The first comma in Choice (A) may be okay, but the comma following "such as" is never proper. By process of elimination, Choice (D) is best.

46. **J.** Check for relevance. The paragraph is primarily about fifth-century Greek drama. It gives a little of its history, specifies three of its major dramatists, describes the way that the actors dressed, and mentions the chorus. The dramatists of the time make up just one element of the paragraph. Therefore, inserting a sentence that's about Greek dramatists from other times is inappropriate. Choice (J) is the best answer.

    The paragraph isn't primarily about Greek dramatists, the influence of Greek drama, or dramatists in general, so Choices (F), (G), and (H) have to be wrong.

47. **C.** When looking at the answer choices, check for the most obvious mistakes first. A good place to start is *their* versus *there*. Choices (B) and (A) are wrong because *there* refers to a place, not possession. That leaves Choices (C) and (D).

    Now, check *then* versus *than*. A good trick is to remember that *then* rhymes with *when*, so it refers to time, while *than* is used for comparisons. Because the sentence is comparing dialogue to action, *than* is the right word. Choice (D) is incorrect, which leaves Choice (C) as the best answer.

48. **F.** The easiest answer to rule out is Choice (H) because talking about how popular these plays were doesn't connect well to the next paragraph about *Oedipus Tyrannus*. Choice (J) is also wrong because it focuses on Sophocles' importance today instead of smoothly leading into a discussion of his play. Choice (G) is a little better because it mentions fate and struggle, but it's too general and doesn't set up the idea that trying to fight fate only makes things worse. That's why Choice (F) is the best option — it clearly connects Greek tragedy's big theme to the example of *Oedipus Tyrannus*.

49. **B.** Eliminate Choice (C) because "epic fail" is slang, making it too informal for an academic essay. Choice (D) is also too casual — "he's stuck with the prophecy" sounds like everyday speech rather than formal writing. Choice (A) is incorrect because "he just can't get away from" is too conversational and doesn't match the serious, analytical tone of the passage. Choice (B) is the best choice because it maintains a formal and academic tone while clearly conveying the idea that Oedipus is unable to avoid his fate.

50. **H.** Check the semicolon in Choice (J) first because semicolons are easy to evaluate. Semicolons separate two independent clauses (complete sentences). Choice (J) is incorrect because it places a semicolon before a phrase that isn't a complete sentence.

    Next, check the commas. Choice (G) is incorrect because it's missing a comma after *contrast*, which is needed to separate the introductory phrase from the rest of the sentence. Choice (F) is also wrong because it doesn't include a comma after "Euripides" to properly set off the descriptive appositive "a contemporary of Sophocles."

    That leaves Choice (H) as the best choice. The dashes correctly set off "a contemporary of Sophocles."

Mathematics Test

1. **B.** According to the order of operations, exponential parts of the equation must always be solved before multiplication parts of the equation. Because $x = 3$, $2^x = 8$ because $2 \times 2 \times 2 = 8$. Next, that value must be multiplied by the value of y, which is 2, giving you the final answer of 16, which is Choice (B).

   Beware of Choice (D), which mixes up the order of operations by multiplying 2 and y and then raising the resulting value of 4 to the power of x.

2. **F.** A geometric series is a series of numbers in which each number is multiplied by a common value to determine the number that comes after it. In this particular geometric series, the first number is multiplied by 2 to find the second number, which is then multiplied by 2 to find the third number, and so on, because $0.75 \times 2 = 1.5$ and $1.5 \times 2 = 3$. Find the 5th term, then, by multiplying the 4th term (6) by 2 to get Choice (F), 12.

3. **A.** To find the measure of $\angle ABD$, you can set up an equation calling the measure of $\angle ABD = 3x$ and $\angle DBC = x$. $\angle ABD$ and $\angle DBC$ combine to measure 180° because A, B, and C are collinear. In this case, $3x + x = 180$. Simplify this equation to $4x = 180$. When you divide both sides by 4, you get $x = 45$. Don't stop there and pick Choice (E), though. That's the measure of $\angle DBC$. Multiply 45 by 3 to get 135°, which is the measure of $\angle ABD$.

   If you picked Choice (C), you incorrectly presumed that A, B, and C form a right angle.

4. **G.** Divide by multiplying 3 by $\frac{8}{3}$. The 3s cancel, so the answer is 8.

   Don't get caught picking Choice (J), which simplifies the 3 in the numerator and the 3 in the numerator of the denominator to equal 1. That's not the way to divide a fraction.

   REMEMBER

   When you divide by a fraction, you solve by simply multiplying by the reciprocal of the second fraction.

5. **D.** Angle a and the 37° are supplementary, which means their sum measures 180°. So the measure of angle a is $180 - 37$ or 143°. Because lines C and D are parallel and crossed by a transversal, angle a corresponds with angle b, which means they have the same degree measure. So angle b also measures 143°.

6. **F.** Before you find the chance that Ross will pick two black socks, you first have to find the chance that the first sock he picks will be black. That chance is $\frac{2}{4}$ or $\frac{1}{2}$ because 2 out of 4 socks are black. Then, you have to multiply that fraction by the probability that the second sock will be black. Be careful, because the second probability isn't also $\frac{1}{2}$ because Ross has already picked a black sock from the drawer. After the first sock, only 3 socks remain in the drawer and only 1 is black. So the chance that the second sock he picks will be black is actually $\frac{1}{3}$. The chance that both socks Ross picks will be black can then be found by multiplying $\frac{1}{2}$ by $\frac{1}{3}$, which is $\frac{1}{6}$. Pick Choice (F).

CHAPTER 20 Practice Exam: Answers and Explanations   295

7. **D.** This question concerns a simple right triangle. The following figure shows the values of the leg lengths.

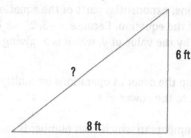

The ramp length is the hypotenuse. Memorize the 3-4-5 Pythagorean triple; ACT math questions incorporate it frequently. The lengths of the sides of this triangle are just those of the traditional 3-4-5 triangle times 2, so the missing side is 10 feet.

If you don't remember Pythagorean triples, you can find the length of the ramp, which is the hypotenuse in this case, by plugging values into the Pythagorean theorem ($a^2 + b^2 = c^2$) and solving for c, but it's much faster to rely on common side ratios of right triangles.

8. **J.** Make answering this question quick and simple by noticing first that the point on the x-axis that also lies on the y-axis has an x-coordinate of 0. The x-coordinate is the first number in the ordered pair. Eliminate Choices (F), (G), and (K) because they don't have x-coordinates of 0. You know the answer is either Choice (H) or (J). Substitute 0 for x in the equation and solve for y. That gives you $0 + 4y = 28$ so $y = 7$. The point that $7x + 4y = 28$ intersects the y-axis is (0, 7), Choice (J).

You can also approach this problem by solving the original equation for y to put it in the format of the equation of a line: $y = mx + b$, where b is the y-intercept. When you solve for y, you get $y = -\frac{7}{4}x + 7$. So you know the y-intercept is 7. The only answer with a y-coordinate of 7 is Choice (J).

9. **A.** When simplifying expressions that involve only multiplication, you can simply combine like variables. First, multiply the numerators to get $3x^4 y^2$. Then multiply the denominators to get $6y$. Divide the y terms: $\frac{y^2}{y} = y$. The coefficients reduce to $\frac{1}{2}$ to make the final answer $\frac{x^4 y}{2}$.

When you multiply the same variable raised to powers, you combine the terms by simply adding the powers. To divide the same variable raised to powers, subtract the exponents.

10. **J.** To solve a series of equations, you must cancel out one of the variables. Because the question asks that you find y, it makes sense to cancel out x in order to isolate y. To do this, multiply the bottom equation by -2 and stack the two equations like this:

$$2x + 3y = 6$$
$$-6x + 2y = -16$$

When you add the equations, the x terms cancel, the y terms add to $5y$, and the sum of the right side of the equation is -10: $5y = -10$. When you solve for y, you get -2.

You can also solve systems of equations by plugging the two equations into your Desmos or other graphing calculator and finding the point where the two lines intersect. The y value of this point is the solution.

11. **B.** To find the number of adult tickets sold, create a system of equations that models the given information. The equation for the total of 40 tickets sold could be $a + c = 40$, where a is the number of adult tickets sold, and c is the number of children's tickets sold. The other equation is $\$8a + \$5c = \$251$ because the price of adult tickets times the number of adult tickets sold plus the price of children's tickets times the number of children's tickets sold equals the total cost of tickets sold. Because you want to find the number of adult tickets sold, it makes sense to cancel out the c variable and solve for a. First, multiply the first equation by -5 to get $-5a - 5c = -200$. Add that equation to $8a + 5c = 251$:

$$8a + 5c = 251$$
$$-2a - 5c = -200$$

Adding up these two equations, you find that $3a = 51$. When you divide both sides by 3, you find that $a = 17$.

12. **J.** First of all, you can tell from the graph that the parabola faces downward, so the x^2 term has to be negative. Right away, you can eliminate Choice (H). You can also tell that the graph has a vertical displacement of 3. Vertical displacement is indicated by the term that is added to or subtracted from the x^2 term. This means that you can get rid of Choice (F). You're down to Choices (G) and (J). The difference is that Choice (G) adds the 1 in parentheses and Choice (J) subtracts the 1. When the parabola moves in a positive direction horizontally, the number is subtracted from, not added to, x inside the parentheses. This means that the final answer is Choice (J).

You can check your answer by testing the vertex point in your equation to make sure it is valid. In this case, that point is (1, 3). When you plug the point into the equation in the answers, you get $3 = -(1-1)^2 + 3$ or $3 = 3$, which is true.

13. **D.** When you add logs with the same base, you multiply the number being logged. So rewrite the question as $\log_6(9x) = 2$. Plug in your answer options for x. Choice (D) is correct because the product of 9 and 4 is 36, which is the value you get when you multiply 6 by itself two times.

TIP

The easiest way to solve logs is to know that the log base raised to the power of the answer equals the number being logged. In this problem, $6^2 = 9x$, so $x = 4$. Be careful not to get caught picking Choice (C), which adds rather than multiplies the numbers being logged.

14. **H.** Plug the values you know into the equation for volume of a circular cylinder: $V_c = \pi r^2 h$. To solve for V, you need the radius of the base and the height of the cylinder. The diameter is 10 cm, so the radius is half that, 5 cm. The height is 15 cm. The resulting solution is this:

$$V_c = (5\,cm)^2 (15\,cm)\pi$$
$$V_c = (25\,cm)(15\,cm)\pi$$
$$V_c = 375\pi$$

TIP

After you memorize simple geometry formulas, questions that ask you to find the value of a shape's dimension will be some of the easiest and quickest to solve in the ACT Math section.

15. **A.** The original point A lies at $(-2, 4)$. Because the whole quadrilateral is reflected over the horizontal line $y = 2$, to find the reflected point A, you only need to reflect point A over the line $y = 2$. The x-coordinate of the point does not change because $y = 2$ is a horizontal line. You can eliminate Choices (B) and (C) because they don't contain x-coordinates of -2.

CHAPTER 20 Practice Exam: Answers and Explanations   **297**

The original y value of point A is 4, which is 2 units above the line y = 2, so reflected point A is 2 units below the line y = 2. This makes the y value of reflected point A equal to 0 and the point (−2, 0), which is Choice (A).

If you picked Choice (D), you reflected point A over the x-axis instead of the line y = 2.

16. H. First, eliminate Choices (F) and (G). If Klaus gave money away, he started out with more than $280. Then set up an equation. If Klaus gave 20% of his money and ended up with $280, that $280 is 80% of what he originally received. You can write 80% as 0.8 and *of* means multiply, so the equation is $0.8x = \$280$. To solve, divide each side by 0.8: $x = 350$. Choice (H) is correct.

Be sure not to just take 20% of the $280. Remember, the $280 already has been reduced by 20%, so 20% of that value is actually less than the amount that Klaus put in the bank.

17. D. The equation you use to find cosine is $\cos = \frac{\text{adjacent}}{\text{hypotenuse}}$. When you look at the figure, the side adjacent to angle C is a and the hypotenuse of triangle ABC is side b. So $\cos C = \frac{a}{b}$.

REMEMBER

You'll for sure encounter at least a couple trig questions that require you to apply the trig identities, so memorize the acronym SOH CAH TOA. Know it cold for test day.

18. J. To solve the equation for y, you must get y on its own side of the equation. First, subtract each side by 8 to get $x - 8 = 3y$. Then just divide both sides of the equation by 3 to get $\frac{x-8}{3} = y$, which is Choice (J).

If you forgot to also divide 8 by 3, you would have mistakenly selected Choice (A).

19. A. Label the whole line (from A to D) with a distance of 28, from A to C with 15, and from B to D with 18. It's easy to see that the distance from B to C is the overlapping portion of what you just labeled. Add the distance from A to C and the distance from B to D to get 33. Subtract 28 from 33 to get the distance of the overlap; the length between B and C is 5. Choice (A) is the answer.

TIP

Another way to solve this problem is to set up an equation. Call the distance between B and C x because that's the unknown. So the distance between A and B is $15 - x$ and the distance between C and D is $18 - x$. Set the sum of the three shorter segments equal to the longer length between A and D: $(15 - x) + x + (18 - x) = 28$. Simplify to get $33 - x = 28$ and you can see that x (the distance between B and C) equals 5.

20. J. The fastest way to approach this problem is to notice that the measure of the perimeter is the same as the perimeter of a 23-by-18 rectangle. The length is $19 + 4$ or 23, and the width is $13 + 5$ or 18. So the perimeter is $(2)(23) + (2)(18)$, which is $46 + 36$ or 82. The answer is Choice (J).

21. A. To find the circumference of a circle, you need to know its radius. The question doesn't give you the radius of the circle, but you do know its area. Can you find the radius from the area? Sure! Apply the area formula: $16\pi = \pi r^2$. Divide both sides by π to get $16 = r^2$. Find the square root of both sides to determine that the radius is 4. Then you can plug the value of the radius in the formula for circumference:

$$C = 2\pi 4$$
$$C = 8\pi$$

The answer is Choice (A).

TIP

Memorize the equations for area and circumference of a circle; you'll use them a bunch on the ACT. To refresh your memory, here they are: $A = \pi r^2$ and $C = 2\pi r$.

22. **G.** The median value of Cydney's math test scores is the middle score. First, put the scores in ascending order. Then determine the total number of test scores; there are 19. Because the total number of test scores is odd, the median is the one value in the middle. If the total number were even, the median would be the average of the two middle values. You can then find the median by crossing off the smallest and biggest numbers on either end of the set, one by one, until you get to the middle. Or you can divide 19 by 2 to get 9.5. That tells you that there are 9 values to the left of the median and 9 to the right. Either way, the middle value is 87.

23. **C.** The first expression gives you the equation for the output, and the second tells you what value (the input) to substitute for x in the first. To find $f(2x+2)$, you plug in $2x+2$ for x in $x-3$. So the output when the input is $2x+1$ is $(2x+2)-3$, which simplifies to $2x-1$. The answer is Choice (C).

TIP

When you see a function question on the ACT, get excited. These are simple substitution problems, so they're really easy!

24. **J.** The ACT Math test will likely have at least one question that gives you an equation in a word problem and asks you to solve for one of the variables. All you have to do is plug in the proper values for the other variables and solve.

    You are given the equation $v = at + v_0$ and are asked to find the acceleration (a). Reformat the equation so you're solving for a. Subtract v_0 from both sides and then divide both sides by t. The equation to solve for acceleration is $a = \frac{v - v_0}{t}$. Now find the values for the other variables. You know that initially the car travels 10 meters per second, so plug in 10 for v_0 to get $a = \frac{v - 10}{t}$. Next, note that the time that the car accelerates is 10 seconds, so plug in 10 for t: $a = \frac{v - 10}{10}$. You're told that the final velocity is 30 meters per second, so substitute 30 for v and solve:

    $$a = \frac{30 - 10}{10}$$
    $$a = \frac{20}{10}$$
    $$a = 2$$

    The answer is Choice (J).

25. **B.** Digits can be repeated, and there are 10 different digits from 0 to 9. Letters cannot be repeated, and there are 26 possibilities in the alphabet. Apply the multiplication principle by multiplying the total possibilities for each element of the license plate. There are 10 for the first position, 10 for the second, 26 for the third, and 25 for the fourth because you can't repeat the letter in the third position. The product of 10, 10, 26, and 25 is 65,000.

    If you picked Choice (A), you calculated the problem as though the digits could not be repeated, but letters could be. Choice (C) presumes that both digits and letters can be repeated.

26. **F.** Set up the average equation and plug in what you know. The average of the 5 scores is a 91. The sum of the scores is $99 + 97 + 92 + 88 + x$ where x represents Courtney's score. The number of scores is 5. The equation is as follows:

    $$91 = \frac{99 + 97 + 92 + 88 + x}{5}$$

CHAPTER 20 **Practice Exam: Answers and Explanations** 299

If you multiply both sides of the equation by 5, you end up with $455 = 376 + x$. When you solve the equation, x is 79, which is Courtney's score. The answer is Choice (F).

REMEMBER

The ACT Math section will likely have a few average questions. Make sure you know the formula like the back of your hand (but don't write it there!). By definition, an *average* equals the sum of all the scores divided by the number of scores:

$$\text{Average} = \frac{\text{Sum of scores}}{\text{Number of scores}}$$

You'll often have to find one of the numbers that makes up the sum in the numerator, so be prepared.

27. **D.** The diagonal is the length that extends from one vertex across the rectangle to the opposite vertex. It cuts the rectangle into two right triangles. When you know the side lengths of the rectangle, you can use what you know about right triangles to find the hypotenuse, which is also the diagonal of the rectangle.

The question gives you the rectangle's area as 672 square feet and its width as 14 feet. To find the value of the length, apply the area formula: $A = lw$. So $672 = 14l$ and $48 = l$. The sides of the right triangle with a hypotenuse that is the diagonal of the rectangle are 48 and 14. You could apply the Pythagorean theorem, but first check for a Pythagorean triple. A common factor of 48 and 14 is 2. The triangle is a 7-24-25 right triangle times 2. Multiply 25 by 2 to discover that the hypotenuse and therefore the diagonal of the room is 50 feet, which is Choice (D).

28. **J.** Factor the quadratic. Find the square root of the first term. Then consider the last term, 4, and ask yourself what the factors of +4 are that have a sum of −5. Those two factors are −4 and −1, so the binomial factors of the quadratic are $(x^2 - 4)(x^2 - 1)$. If you want, you can apply FOIL to your factors to make sure you factored correctly. At this point, you may be tempted to pick Choice (F), but you aren't through; the terms can be factored further. Notice that the binomial factors are the differences of perfect squares. Finding their factors is easy. The two factors are the sum and difference of the square roots of each perfect square in the expression. So when you factor $(x^2 - 4)$, you get $(x+2)(x-2)$. When you factor $(x^2 - 1)$, you get $(x+1)(x-1)$. The fully factored quadratic is $(x+1)(x-1)(x+2)(x-2) = 0$. The expression in its entirety equals 0 when any one of these factors equals 0. Set each equal to 0, and you see that the full set of values for x that solve the equation are 1, 2, −1, and −2, which is Choice (J).

TIP

When you see a quadratic equation, your first thought should be to find its binomial factors. Once you factor, you'll likely discover the next step.

29. **B.** First, find the area that requires peanut butter. If one piece of bread measures 10 centimeters by 10 centimeters, the area of each piece is 100 square centimeters. So 9 pieces of bread will have a total area of 900 square centimeters because 100 square centimeters 9 times is 900 square centimeters. Because Sam has a total of 360 cubic centimeters of peanut butter and the total area of the sandwiches that she'll spread peanut butter on is 900 square centimeters, she needs to spread peanut butter reaching a height of 0.4 centimeters on each sandwich because 360 divided by 900 is 0.4. The correct answer is Choice (B).

30. **J.** To find the slope of any line perpendicular to a given line, first find the slope of the given line. The graph shows that the given line travels through the points (−4, 2) and (5, 4). The slope is the rise over the run or $m = \frac{y_2 - y_1}{x_2 - x_1}$. Plug values into the slope equation to solve:

$$m = \frac{4-2}{5-(-4)}$$
$$m = \frac{2}{9}$$

The slope of a perpendicular line is the opposite reciprocal of the slope of the line it intersects. So switch the sign to negative and flip the numerator and denominator to find the slope of any perpendicular line: $-\frac{9}{2}$. Choice (K) is right.

If you picked Choice (F), you forgot to switch the sign. Choice (G) results if you switched the sign and forgot to find the reciprocal.

31. **C.** A trapezoid has parallel bases, so line *BD* is a transversal that crosses parallel lines. So angle *BDC* and angle *DBA* are corresponding angles. Both equal 33 degrees. All you have to do to determine the measure of angle *DBC* is to add 33 and 77 and subtract the sum from 180 because the angles of a triangle total 180 degrees: 180 − (33 + 77) = 70. Angle *DBC* measures 70 degrees and the answer is Choice (C).

32. **J.** On this question, units are the most important and tricky aspect to manage. To solve this question, set up an equation that allows you to cancel the units. Divide Jackson's distance travelled by his speed and Emily's distance travelled by her speed so that hours = hours. Assign the distance Emily travels to be *x* because that signifies the distance from Denver. The distance Jackson travels is 65 − *x* because the total distance is 65 miles. Your equation looks like this: $\frac{x}{60} = \frac{65-x}{40}$. Cross-multiply and solve:

$$40x = 60(65-x)$$
$$40x = 3{,}900 - 60x$$
$$100x = 3{,}900$$
$$x = 39$$

Because *x* is the distance measured from Denver, the answer is 39 miles, which is Choice (D).

If you simply multiplied Jackson's distance times his speed and Emily's distance times her speed and solved the equation, you would have gotten Choice (B). Not only is this wrong mathematically, but it also doesn't make sense. If Emily is driving from Denver and drives faster than Jackson, they will pass each other more than halfway between Boulder and Denver, and the point 26 miles from Denver is closer to Denver than Boulder.

33. **B.** To find the blue cars on Madi's lot, take $\frac{2}{3}$ of the 337 total. *Of* means multiply and $\frac{2}{3} \times 337$ is 225 blue cars. If $\frac{3}{4}$ of those are navy blue, multiply $\frac{3}{4} \times 225$ to find that 169 cars are navy blue. You can also solve this problem in one step by multiplying $\frac{2}{3} \times \frac{3}{4} \times 337$ to get 169.

Either way, the answer is Choice (B).

34. G. This is just a simplification question. Answer it by canceling terms. Because the whole numerator is squared, you need to square every component of the numerator before you do anything else. First, determine that 3 squared is 9. Next, find the value of $(x^3)^2$ and $(y^2)^2$ by multiplying the exponents: $(x^3)^2 = x^6$ and $(y^2)^2 = y^4$. The new expression is $\frac{9x^6y^4}{3xy^{-3}}$. Divide the coefficients to get 3 and eliminate any answer that doesn't have a coefficient of 3. Then divide the variables by subtracting the exponents: $\frac{x^6}{x} = x^5$ and $\frac{y^4}{y^{-3}} = y^7$. Combine all of these components to get your final answer of $3x^5y^7$. The answer is Choice (G).

Remember to subtract the negative exponent by adding 4 and 3; otherwise, you'll mistakenly pick Choice (H). If you just add rather than multiply the exponents in the first step, you'll incorrectly pick Choice (J).

35. C. Approach this problem by trying answer choices. The question asks for the largest sum, so start with the greatest answer. Consider Choice (D). Possible integers that add up to 8 are 9 and −1, but their product is −9, which doesn't fit within the given range. Try 6. The integers −7 and −1 have a sum of 6, and their product, −7, fits within the range. Once you know 6 works, pick Choice (C) and move on. Even if the other answers work, they aren't the largest options.

36. H. To determine whether Austin will make a profit, you need to find Austin's costs in the first month and subtract that amount from the total he will earn in the first month: Income − Expenses = Profit. Calculate his costs. The question states that Austin's rent and supplies will cost a flat $800 per month. Add to that the amount of money he will pay the barbers. If he pays each barber $12 per hour and they each work 120 hours per month, he will pay each barber $1,440 per month. Because there are 10 barbers, he will pay all barbers a total of $14,400 in the first month. His total monthly cost will be $14,400 + 800$ or $15,200 in the first month. Now, to find Austin's profits, multiply the number of haircuts he will sell by the price of each haircut. The problem tells you that he will sell 1,200 haircuts for $15 apiece, so his total revenue will be $18,000. The revenue will be more than the costs, so you can eliminate the *No* answers, Choices (F) and (G). When you subtract his costs from his revenue, you see his overall profit in the first month will be $2,800: $18,000 − $15,200 = $2,800$. The answer is Choice (H).

37. B. The equation to find slope is $m = \frac{y_1 - y_2}{x_1 - x_2}$. Simply plug in values to answer this question. The library is at point (2, 5) and the diner is at point (10, 4). When you plug those values into the slope equation and solve, you get this:

$$m = \frac{5-4}{2-10}$$
$$m = -\frac{1}{8}$$

The answer is Choice (B).

38. H. For this problem, apply the general equation for a circle: $(x-h)^2 + (y-k)^2 = r^2$, where h and k are the x- and y-coordinates of the center of the circle and r is its radius. The radius of the circle is 2, so the correct answer has to be an equation that is equal to 2 squared or 4. Eliminate Choices (F) and (J), and you're done. Choice (H) is obviously correct because Choice (G) adds rather than subtracts within the parentheses. If you picked Choice (J), you forgot to square the radius.

There is an "equation of a circle" question on almost every ACT, so you must know the general equation.

REMEMBER

39. **C.** Apply the distance formula or create a right triangle with Becca's walk as the hypotenuse:

$$d = \sqrt{(y_2 - y_1)^2 + (x_2 - x_1)^2}$$
$$d = \sqrt{(6-2)^2 + (7-1)^2}$$
$$d = \sqrt{(4)^2 + (6)^2}$$
$$d = \sqrt{16 + 36}$$
$$d = \sqrt{52}$$

Multiply the distance in units by 2 to get the approximate number of miles Becca walks:

$$2\sqrt{52} = \text{miles}$$
$$2\sqrt{4 \times 13} = \text{miles}$$
$$4\sqrt{13} = \text{miles}$$

The square root of 13 is between the square root of 9 and the square root of 16, or somewhere between 3 and 4. The product of 4 and 3 is 12; the product of 4 and 4 is 16. The only answer that falls between 12 and 16 is Choice (C). If you use the square root key on your calculator, you find that the distance is approximately 14.42 miles.

40. **G.** For this question, set up an equation that models the word problem. Use x to represent the number you're trying to find. In English/math translation, *of* means multiply, *is* means equals, and "more than" means add, so your equation is $\frac{2}{5}x = \frac{1}{4}(x+21)$. Be careful to notice that you multiply the second fraction by the sum of x and 21; otherwise, you may incorrectly pick Choice (J).

To solve the equation, get rid of the fractions by multiplying the whole equation by 4 to come up with $(4)\frac{2}{5}x = (x+21)$ and then again by 5. Your new equation is $8x = 5(x+21)$. Expand the right side of the equation to get $8x = 5x + 105$. Subtract $5x$ from both sides to get $3x = 105$. When you divide both sides by 3, you know the number is 35, Choice (G).

You can also approach your answer by backsolving. Plug in the answers until you find the one that fits. $\frac{2}{5}$ of 35 is 14 and $\frac{1}{4}$ of 56 is also 14, so Choice (G) works.

TIP

41. **D.** To eliminate h, rearrange and stack the equations:

$$y = 7x - h$$
$$-7 = -x + h$$
$$y - 7 = 6x$$

Add 7 to both sides and you see the answer is Choice (D).

The key to this question is to know that "y expressed in terms of x" means that the only two variables in your answer should be x and y, and y should be alone on one side of the equation.

REMEMBER

42. **J.** Approach this question like you would a shaded area question. It may help to draw a picture. Draw a square with a circle that touches all sides in the center. Draw a radius of the circle and label it 7 cm. It's easy to see that the diameter of the circle is 14 cm and that the sides of the square are equal to the diameter of the circle. Label the sides of the square as 14 cm, like this:

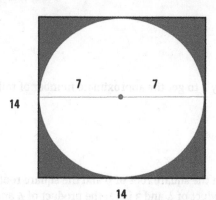

Eliminate Choice (H) because its value is negative, and the shaded area can't be negative. Find the area of the square by squaring the side length: $14^2 = 196$, so you can automatically narrow your options to Choice (H) or (J).

Apply the formula for area of a circle ($A = \pi r^2$) by substituting 7 for r. The circle's area is 49π. The answer that presents the difference between the two areas is Choice (J).

If you picked Choice (H), you applied the circumference formula rather than the area formula.

TIP

The best way to solve a shaded area problem is by finding the total area and the unshaded area and then calculating the difference between those two areas.

43. **C.** Use the distance formula to find the side lengths of the rectangle. Plug in the values of one of the longer lines in the rectangle and solve:

$$d = \sqrt{(y_2 - y_1)^2 + (x_2 - x_1)^2}$$
$$d = \sqrt{(0-3)^2 + (6-0)^2}$$
$$d = \sqrt{(-3)^2 + 6^2}$$
$$d = \sqrt{9 + 36}$$
$$d = \sqrt{45}$$

When you apply the formula to the shorter side of the rectangle, you get this:

$$d = \sqrt{(y_2 - y_1)^2 + (x_2 - x_1)^2}$$
$$d = \sqrt{(7-3)^2 + (2-0)^2}$$
$$d = \sqrt{4^2 + 2^2}$$
$$d = \sqrt{16 + 4}$$
$$d = \sqrt{20}$$

To find the area of the rectangle, multiply the length of the shorter side by the length of the longer side. $\sqrt{45} \times \sqrt{20} = \sqrt{900}$, which is 30. Choice (C) is correct.

44. **G.** Consider the equation in the question: $\sin x + 2$ is the regular $\sin x$ graph moved up 2. You can eliminate all answer choices except Choices (G) and () because all of the other choices have no vertical translation (they don't show a vertical movement of the $\sin x + 2$ graph). Plug in values to $\sin x + 2$ to determine which of the remaining answers is true. Try 0: $\sin 0 - 0$ So on the correct graph, when $x = 0$, the y value will be 2. This is only true for Choice (G).

45. **C.** Jordyn starts with $600, and every six months, she makes 5% on her existing money. So after 6 months, Jordyn has 1.05 times the $600 she started with, which is $630. But you don't just add $30 every month because Jordyn makes 5% on what she already has in the bank account. So after one year, she makes 5% of $630, not $600. Take 1.05 times $630 to find her balance of $661.50 after one year. At a year and a half, Jordyn has 1.05 times $661.50, or $694.58. At this point, she moves $210 to a checking account, so she has a balance of $484.58.

    This isn't your final answer, though! You have to compound this value one more time because the question asks how much money she has after two full years. After two years, Jordyn has 1.05 times what she had after a year and a half, which is $484.58, so she has a final balance of $508.80. Choice (C) is correct.

Reading Test

1. **C.** First, go to the last paragraph to find Mrs. Kronborg's analogy. It appears in the last sentence right after the statement that Mrs. Kronborg knew talent meant practicing. She compares the need for a talented child to practice in the way that a child with measles needs to sleep. So a talented child *should* practice, and a child with measles *should* sleep. The answer that provides a similar *should* statement is Choice (C). A person with outdoor allergies *should* stay indoors.

    Choice (A) is unlike the analogy because it mentions two separate skills — math and writing. For Choice (B), while it's obvious why a child with measles must be kept under blankets, it is decidedly less obvious why a beautiful child should be kept under close watch. So, that's probably not the best choice, either. Choice (D) uses *may* instead of *must*. *Must*, like *should*, is an absolution, while *may* is hypothetical. You can feel confident in selecting Choice (C).

TIP

    You're supposed to choose the best answer out of the four options. To determine which is the best, use that secret weapon known as *POE*, or the process of elimination. By eliminating answers you know can't be right, you help isolate the answer that fits the best.

2. **F.** The second paragraph begins, "It was in the summer that one really lived," so check there first. The author mentions fence painting in the third sentence, cottonwood trees in the fourth sentence, and the shedding of warm clothes for cotton at the end. So eliminate Choices (G), (H) and (J). By process of elimination, check Choice (F). The paragraph suggests that people see their neighbors, but it doesn't specifically say the neighbors are *new*. Choice (F) is correct.

3. **B.** This vocabulary-in-context question is best answered by substituting each answer for *crony* in the fifth paragraph. Not only does it not make sense to say that Fritz had never had an elder, but the paragraph also doesn't say whether the music teacher was older than Fritz. Eliminate Choice (A). Choice (D) doesn't seem right. The author later says Fritz hasn't

had a crony since "the harness-maker and Spanish Johnny." There is nothing in the passage that suggests that either of these individuals ever taught him anything. Because the passage directly states that the Kohlers took this person in to live with them, you can reasonably assume that they don't view him as an enemy — so eliminate Choice (C). If you replace *crony* with *friend*, the paragraph makes sense. Choice (B) is best.

4. **H.** Eliminate Choice (F), because the statement compares the way Mrs. Kohler treated Professor Wunsch to the way she treated her garden, and nothing in the passage suggests that there was anything undesirable about her garden. Eliminate Choice (G) because the paragraph goes on to discuss how Mrs. Kohler was successful in making the professor particularly clean and respectable — so she certainly wasn't trying in vain. Now, you're left with either Choice (H) or (J). Of the two, Choice (H) is better. The paragraph indicates that Mrs. Kohler helped get the professor in tip-top shape, but it doesn't provide clues to what would make up her idea of perfection. Stick with Choice (H).

5. **A.** Answering this question correctly requires careful attention to detail. A close reading of the fourth paragraph and its description of Mrs. Kohler's typical attire reveals the answer. The black bonnet in summer appears in the third sentence, the handmade dresses in the fourth, and the men's shoes in the fifth. Choices (B), (C), and (D) are mentioned and therefore, wrong. If you read the paragraph carefully, you notice that the hood Mrs. Kohler wore in the winter was red, not black, so Choice (A) is the correct answer.

6. **H.** The fact that Professor Wunsch says that his greatest desire was to spend the rest of his days with Mrs. Kohler and then be buried in her garden lets you know that his feelings toward her must be positive, so you can confidently eliminate Choices (F) and (J), since they are negative. Now, you're down to either Choice (G) or Choice (H). Nothing in the passage suggests he felt amorous or romantic toward her, so examine Choice (H) more closely. Does it make sense that the professor would be particularly grateful to the woman that took him in, cleaned him up, and helped him find work? Indeed it does. Choice (H) is your answer.

7. **A.** Eliminate answers that contain elements that don't fit. Although the passage describes the garden as verdant, it doesn't suggest that it's the frequent rainfall that makes it green. Notice that the third paragraph describes the Kohler property as an open, sandy plain; it's unlikely that Moonstone receives frequent rainfall, so eliminate Choice (D). You can also easily get rid of Choice (C). The garden is a jungle of verdure, so it isn't best described as a barren sand gulch. Examine the remaining two choices for clues that would help you eliminate one. Choice (B) is true all the way up to the last word. Mrs. Kohler hasn't cultivated sage-brush in her garden, so the best answer must be Choice (A). The passage states that she hid and planned in her garden, and it's reasonable to assume that she found purpose in creating shade there.

TIP

Usually you can easily eliminate two answer choices. Then focus on the remaining two to find the one answer that contains an element that can't be justified by the passage. Eliminate that answer to discover the correct option.

8. **J.** The passage doesn't devote a lot of attention to Mr. Kohler; he's only mentioned in the third and fifth paragraphs. You can get rid of Choice (A). Professor Wunsch is the musician, not Fritz Kohler. The fifth paragraph states that Mr. Kohler was friends with the harness-maker and Spanish Johnny but doesn't mention a third crony, so Choice (G) is wrong. Examine Choice (H) carefully. The passage says that one of Mr. Kohler's sons had gone to work for the Santa Fe in New Mexico, but it means the railroad. You know that the son lived in New Mexico, but you don't know that he specifically lived in Santa Fe. Thus, Choice (H) is also wrong, and so the best answer is Choice (J). Because the passage states that Mr. Kohler was one of the first settlers in Moonstone, you can logically conclude that he was one of the first to live there. Pick Choice (J).

9. **D.** The final paragraph of the passage discusses Thea's musical talent, and since *gifted* is a synonym for *talented*, Choice (D) is likely your answer. To be sure, though, take a look at the other possibilities. While the passage suggests Mrs. Kohler doesn't get out much, it doesn't indicate the same about Thea. You can't justify Choice (A). The first paragraph states that Thea has a favorite fairy tale, but it doesn't say she was particularly fond of fairy tales in general. Choice (C) is too much of a stretch. Choice (B) is true. Thea did study music with Professor Wunsch, but so did other children. Although Choice (B) is true, it doesn't show a way that Thea differed from other children. Stick with Choice (D).

REMEMBER

Just because something in an answer choice is true doesn't necessarily mean it answers the question correctly.

10. **F.** The last sentence of the first paragraph refers to those opposed to the inclusion of PTSD in the manual and claims that the diagnosis is already covered. Choice (G) is a reason and not an exception, so eliminate it. You can find information about the broadened concept of stressors, so Choice (H) is a reason and therefore, wrong. The last sentence of the second paragraph contains the reason in Choice (J). The only answer that doesn't appear in the passage is Choice (F).

TIP

An EXCEPT question requires you to find correct answers and then eliminate them. So, before you examine the answer choices, remind yourself to cross out "right" answers and choose the remaining "wrong" answer.

11. **C.** The opinions in Passage A are those of early 21st-century scholars and not necessarily the author. The author presents others' viewpoints without comment, so the primary tone is objective and explanatory. The best answer is Choice (C).

12. **J.** The "state of affairs" referred to in the author's mention of the 1970s and 80s is to the broadening scope of what constitutes trauma and not medicine or the increasing number of PTSD sufferers since those decades. You can eliminate Choices (F) and (H). Although the paragraph talks about the catastrophic events of the time, it does so to highlight that those events were extraordinary rather than numerous. Choice (G) is wrong. The main reason the author mentions the 70s and 80s is to point out that the definition of traumatic events then was different than it is currently. Choice (J) is the best answer.

13. **A.** You can easily eliminate Choices (C) and (D) because they contain points made in Passage A and not Passage B. At first glance, Choice (B) looks promising: the author of Passage B does seem to clarify that PTSD is legitimate and debilitating. But the rest of the answer doesn't work. The passage makes no mention of further research or funding for PTSD. The whole answer has to work for it to be correct. Choice (A) is better: the first paragraph indicates that the diagnosis is controversial but that its acceptance has helped practitioners, and the second paragraph focuses on how PTSD impacts its sufferers. The best answer is Choice (A).

14. **G.** Read through the answer choices to find out where the passage may discuss each one. You can find choices (F) and (J) in the first paragraph. Choice (F) paraphrases the second sentence of that paragraph, and Choice (J) states the information in the last sentence. The fourth sentence of the second paragraph provides nearly the same wording as Choice (H). Because these three answer choices express information directly stated by the passage, they must not be the exception and must be wrong. The passage refers to an "altered baseline state" in the second paragraph, but the reference is designed to show what PTSD is not rather than what it is. Choice (G) is the exception and, thus, the right answer.

15. A. To help you focus, analyze each answer one passage at a time. The psychiatrists mentioned in Passage A don't recognize a PTSD diagnosis and therefore, wouldn't consider it to be a debilitating condition. Eliminate Choice (B). The rest of the answers seem to work for Passage A, so consider the author of Passage B. The author doesn't feel that PTSD is a disorder of an altered baseline state, nor does the author mention politics, so Choices (C) and (D) don't work. The answer that fits both passages is Choice (A).

16. J. Consider one passage at a time. Passage B doesn't talk about the politics of a PTSD diagnosis and wouldn't agree with Choice (G). Passage A doesn't refer to PTSD as a disorder of reactivity, nor does it state that sufferers are overly concerned with their safety. Choices (F) and (H) are wrong. Both passages state that PTSD is a controversial diagnosis. The best answer is Choice (J).

17. D. The author of Passage A claims that psychiatrists initially objected to the PTSD diagnosis in the third edition of the manual, so neither Choice (B) nor (C) is the exception. Passage B claims that few diagnoses in the manual listed causation, so Choice (A) is present and not an exception. Neither passage states that the manual is insufficient; the best answer is Choice (D).

18. J. Neither passage recommends additional research into PTSD, so Choice (G) is unlikely. Passage B isn't concerned with the speed of some professionals' PTSD diagnoses, so Choice (F) is wrong. Although both passages indicate that PTSD diagnosis is controversial, Passage B isn't concerned with its inclusion in the *DSM-III*; Choice (H) is out. Passage B states that "the presumed causal relationship between the stressor and PTSD . . . is complicated." Passage A suggests in the last paragraph that the types of stressors that could cause PTSD have broadened to a point where some medical professionals question the validity of the diagnosis. Therefore, both passages consider the exact relationship between stressors and PTSD to be controversial. Choose Choice (J).

When answering questions about the similarities and differences between two passages, examine the answer choices one passage at a time to help you focus and eliminate wrong answers more efficiently.

19. A. To answer this big idea question, apply the process of elimination. Rule out choices with information that is too specific. The passage discusses the idea in Choice (D) only in the fourth paragraph, so it's wrong. You should also get rid of answers that contain ideas that are too broad. Choice (B) focuses on the concept of positive change in general rather than what makes for a good screenplay. Rule out Choice (C) because it's not true. The passage contains no warnings. The best answer has to be Choice (A). It ties the initial theme of what makes for a good film adaptation to the explanation of the life-changing mythological journey included throughout the rest of the passage.

For questions that ask you for the purpose or tone of an entire passage, choose answers that apply to the whole passage, not just part of it. Eliminate ideas that appear in only one or two of the paragraphs or that concern concepts that are more general than the passage's topic.

20. J. This question asks for the author's suggestion, which tells you that the correct answer is implied rather than directly stated. In the second paragraph, the author makes a primary observation about inner growth and change — that it means letting go of the familiar and risking the unknown. The answer that paraphrases this idea best is Choice (J). The author states that inner growth is healthy, so you can eliminate Choice (F) based on its first two words. Even though the rest of this first answer choice seems pretty good, don't ignore its implication that inner growth is unhealthy. Read Choice (H) carefully; it actually contradicts the notion that inner growth requires change. The second paragraph says that inner

308 PART 7 Putting It All Together with a Full-Length Practice ACT

growth requires courage but not the courage to stay the same. The last line of the paragraph conveys that remaining static isn't a requirement for inner growth but instead an obstacle to achieving it. Choice (G) may seem correct at first, but the passage only says that experiencing myth in film may assist with the dilemma of whether to risk change. It doesn't say inner growth requires viewing films. The answer must be Choice (J). The second paragraph states that inner growth requires sacrificing the old and familiar and risking the unknown and uncertain. The last paragraph quotes Campbell's claim that human fantasies tend to tie back to the human spirit, so you can reasonably conclude that comfortable fantasies are included in the "old and familiar," and uncharted territory is another way of alluding to the unknown.

21. **C.** The referenced list provides examples of situations where outer physical change is readily apparent. Choose the answer that provides another instance of outer physical change. Choices (B) and (D) don't express physical changes. Choice (A) is physical, but it isn't outwardly apparent. The only answer choice that expresses an outer physical change you can see is Choice (C).

22. **J.** The statement points out that even though making a change involves sacrifice or risk, the risk of not taking that risk is missing out on a chance at a new life. The rest of the passage clarifies the author's view that embracing this new life is better than missing it by holding on to old ways. Therefore, the best synopsis of the quote is Choice (J). Choice (F) may seem tempting, but the statement suggests the inevitability of sacrifice only as it relates to the transformation journey and not to the inevitability of sacrifice in general. The quote specifically addresses the change that comes with risk rather than change in general, so Choice (G) is wrong. Choice (H) can't be right because nowhere does the passage suggest that the journey is more fulfilling than the resulting change. Stick with Choice (J).

TIP

Sometimes you can answer questions that ask what a quote or phrase most likely means by focusing on which answer best paraphrases the quote. If you like, you can then go back into the passage to make sure it justifies your answer.

23. **B.** Answer this question by asking yourself why the author included the second paragraph in the essay. The paragraph focuses on what it means to undergo a life-altering journey, which is one of the elements of a good story mentioned in the first paragraph. Choice (B) offers a neat paraphrase of this objective. The essay is more explanatory than encouraging, so it's unlikely that the author specifically includes the second paragraph to persuade readers to change their lives. Cross out Choice (C). Although the paragraph does offer up some examples of physical change, this inclusion merely serves to contrast inner change and outer change and isn't the main reason for the paragraph. Choice (D) isn't correct. Because the paragraph discusses only one real way to achieve inner growth instead of several, Choice (A) isn't a better option than Choice (B). Stick with Choice (B).

24. **H.** Focus on the fourth paragraph and eliminate answers that appear in the passage. The second sentence states that the hero experiences a liberation from past limitations, so eliminate Choice (F). The idea of great personal risk and quest for treasure are suggested by the reference at the end of the first sentence to a treasure quest that results in personal cost. Choices (G) and (J) are out. By process of elimination, the answer is Choice (H).

25. **A.** The passage references Joseph Campbell in the third paragraph, so start there. It states that the purpose of ritual is to provide transformation that demands changes in conscious and unconscious patterns. That sounds most like Choice (A). Choice (B) references difficult thresholds in general, but the reference is specifically to thresholds of transformation. The paragraph doesn't suggest that ritual forces anything, nor does it mention fantasy. So Choices (C) and (D) are wrong, and the best answer is Choice (A).

CHAPTER 20 Practice Exam: Answers and Explanations   309

26. **H.** The sentence refers to *this* universal dilemma, so look in the prior paragraph for clues. The last sentence mentions two sacrifices: one that results from changing and one that results from not changing. Find the answer that states this dilemma best. Choice (J) is out because the growth is inner, not physical. Choice (F) is wrong because the dilemma isn't relevant to just the film experience. Of the remaining answers, Choice (H) defines the dilemma better. It's about choosing to change rather than choosing between types of thoughts. Pick Choice (H).

27. **B.** From the first paragraph, you know that Seger is an author of a book about adaptation and that the adaptation is likely from literature to film. Therefore, she's most likely a film script consultant. Pick Choice (B).

28. **J.** While the roles of bacteria, or Choice (H), are indeed discussed, this discussion appears in only a small part of the passage and not until about halfway through. If bacteria were the main purpose of the passage, one could expect that they would be mentioned in the very first paragraph — so eliminate Choice (H). Similarly, while some attention is given to the earth's changing temperatures, or Choice (F), there isn't nearly enough to have temperature change be the passage's central or primary focus. So, you're down to either Choice (G) or (J). Of the two, Choice (J) is broader and more all-encompassing and better summarizes the passage in its entirety. While the author notes that "If there is anything that has been overlooked more than another it is our atmosphere," he really only devotes the first couple paragraphs to discussing why the atmosphere is overlooked. When you examine the passage in its entirety, Choice (B) is the strongest choice.

29. **B.** The correct answer is Choice (B). The passage claims that rain is "accounted for only by the dust," which means that the rain exists because the dust exists. You can't conclude, however, that this statement means that rain is the only element dust accounts for. Choices (C), and (D) are all mentioned by the author in Paragraph 7, and Choice (A) is mentioned in Paragraph 8.

30. **H.** The author begins the fifth paragraph with a discussion of the wind, where he plainly states that it is "mostly nitrogen, oxygen, moisture, and dust." So you can eliminate Choices (F) and (G). He also mentions five other gases. At the end of the paragraph, you learn that hydrogen is one of these gases, so get rid of Choice (J). He doesn't specifically say that bacteria are part of wind, so the answer is Choice (H).

TIP

There's no rule that you have to answer the questions in order. If you have trouble figuring out the answer to a question that involves much of the passage, skip it and go back after you've answered other questions. Often, something you read for one question will help you answer another.

31. **A.** While both Choice (B) and Choice (C) are ways in which dust affects the earth, neither is discussed in such a way that would suggest the author considers them dust's greatest role. So, your answer is either Choice (A) or (D). Choice (D) sounds like something the author might say about atmosphere rather than dust, and furthermore, the author essentially paraphrases Choice A) at the start of Paragraph 8. Choice (A) is correct.

32. **J.** While Choice (A) is an assertion made by the author, he doesn't appear to consider this fact an absurdity, so go ahead and knock that one out of contention. Eliminate Choice (B) for the same reason. Take a closer look at the remaining choices. Choice (C) is indeed noted by the author in the passage's final paragraph, but it is done in a matter-of-fact manner, suggesting that the author doesn't consider it an absurdity. Only in his discussion of rain and dust does he use the word *absurdities*, so you may confidently select Choice (D).

33. **A.** Not only are Choices (B) and (C) incorrect — land surfaces absorb most of the heat received, and water surfaces reflect most of it — but even if they were written correctly, these responses would be supporting points made in the final paragraph, not the *main* point. So the answer is either Choice (A) or (D). Choice (D) is actually an assertion made in the second-to-last paragraph, so give Choice (A) a closer look. Does it adequately summarize the information in the final paragraph? It does, so you may feel confident that Choice (A) is correct.

34. **H.** The author asserts in the second paragraph that it is the atmosphere that protects us from "that fraction of sunheat which, however trifling when compared with the whole, would otherwise be sufficient to fry us all in a second." Choice (F) makes no sense. The fraction of sunheat wouldn't protect humans from the sun's heat. Choice (G) isn't discussed until the end of the paragraph, long after the discussion of humans' protection from the sun's heat — so it can't be right. As for Choice (J), the author mentions that the atmosphere keeps us in a sort of thermos globe; however, the gas layer is thin rather than thick. So Choice (H) is the strongest option.

35. **B.** To answer this question correctly, look for clues in the context. The line in question states, "It is thanks to this thin layer of gases that we are protected from that fraction of sunheat which, however trifling when compared with the whole, would otherwise be sufficient to fry us all in a second." So you're likely looking for a word that means something close to "a small part." Thus, *insignificant* is the strongest answer. To be sure, though, take a look at the others. Choice (A), *shallow*, certainly doesn't mean a small part, so knock that one out of contention. Eliminate Choice (D) because *novel* means new, not small. As for Choice (C), *trifling* could mean silly, but try substituting the word *trifling* in the paragraph with *silly*. Does it make sense to say the earth receives a silly fraction of sunheat? No, so Choice (B) is correct.

36. **J.** Read the answers to see which one best paraphrases the quoted material. The *rest* refers to the other components of wind, so Choice (J) seems most logical. The passage doesn't say that dust and water are heavier or appear in greater quantities than the others. If you chose Choice (G) or (H), you made assumptions not justified by the passage. Choice (F) is about gases rather than dust and wind, so it isn't correct. Choice (J) is best.

Science Test

1. **D.** The question points you to the data for Site 1 on the table. It asks you to determine the relationship, if any, between temperature and conductivity. Don't assume that the temperatures increase as you move down the chart. Note that the first two temperatures are both 23 but the conductivity for both entries is very different. So there isn't an obvious relationship between the two and Choice (D) is the best answer.

TIP

The answer that states there's no apparent relationship or that data is insufficient is often the last answer and may be correct. So don't be afraid to pick it. Don't assume there must be a relationship.

2. **F.** The table doesn't have a category for number of impurities, so you need to read a bit of the text to determine which column gives you the information you need to assess purity. The first sentences indicate that removing ions is a way to purify water and that conductivity and ion content are directly related — the more ions a solution has, the higher its conductivity. So use the conductivity column on the table to assess the sites' relative purity. The site with the lowest conductivity is Site 1. Its average conductivity is around 200 as compared to 870 at Site 2 and 620 at Site 3. Pick Choice (F).

CHAPTER 20 Practice Exam: Answers and Explanations   311

You know that Choice (J) can't be right because the conductivity averages for Sites 1 and 3 are very different.

3. **A.** This question provides new information — that drinking water's conductivity usually ranges between 50 and 500. Use it to evaluate the table. The only site with conductivity levels between 50 and 500 is Site 1. The answer has to be Choice (A).

This question was very similar to the second question. Don't be thrown off if you think the ACT Science questions test you more than once on the same general concept. They do it all the time.

4. **H.** To extrapolate for this question, use the table to find the average conductivity that's closest to 500. Site 2's average at about 620 is higher than 500, and Site 1's average at about 200 is much lower. The average species richness for Site 1 is 10.7 and for Site 2 is 4.9. The answer has to lie between those two values. So pick Choice (H).

5. **C.** The passage indicates that species richness was collected from freshwater sites. It then explains that based on the collection, invertebrate specimens were counted and identified. The logical means of collecting invertebrates is nets, Choice (C). The passage doesn't associate temperature, pH, or weight with species richness, so the other answers must be wrong.

6. **J.** The passage doesn't test the behaviors of saltwater fish, so Choice (F) is incorrect. The setup for Experiment 1 lists the types of aggressive behaviors the scientists viewed as a fact rather than a question to answer through experimentation; eliminate Choice (G). The two experiments include gender and size considerations in their setup, but the main difference between them is the relative size of the intruder fish and the focal fish. Experiment 1 established the number of aggressive behaviors presented when one intruder and focal fish are of similar size. The second experiment provides information the scientists can use to determine whether the number of aggressive behaviors changes when they vary the comparative size of intruders and focal fish for a larger number of fish. The scientists do not mix the sexes of the intruders and focal fish, so Choice (H) isn't correct. The scientists must be primarily concerned with how the relative size of the intruder affects the number of aggressive behaviors in the focal fish. Choice (J) is best.

7. **C.** The question directs you to Experiment 1, so focus on the data in Table 1. Before you do, however, take a look at the answer choices. All but the first begin with large male as the one with the highest aggression. Notice that in the column for large fish, the males have more aggressive behaviors than the females, so eliminate Choice (A). The second entry in the remaining choices is either large female or medium male. Check Table 1 to see which has more aggressive behaviors. The large female has 11 and the medium male has 18, so the male is more aggressive and Choice (B) is wrong. Choice (C) and (D) differ in the order of the last two fish. The large female has one more aggressive behavior than the small male, so based on the table, the answer has to be Choice (C).

8. **G.** Use information from both tables to answer this question. You know from answering Question 6 about Experiment 1 that male fish are generally more aggressive than female fish, so eliminate Choices (F) and (H). Check Table 2 to see whether the findings change in the second experiment. The males are generally more aggressive in the second experiment, too, so the answer has to be Choice (G).

9. **B.** To answer this question, you determine how the experiments differed based on what's true for Experiment 2. First, run through the answer choices to eliminate options that aren't true about the independent variables in Experiment 2. The number of days didn't vary in Experiment 2, so eliminate Choice (D). The researchers were testing for aggression,

so Choice (C) wasn't an independent variable and must be wrong. The gender and relative size of the intruders varied in Experiment 2. The difference between the two experiments, though, was that Experiment 2 varied the comparable sizes of intruders to focal fish. This variation didn't occur in Experiment 1, so the best answer is Choice (B).

10. **F.** Read the introductory text to discover that aggression allows the fish to protect their young. In both experiments, bigger fish meant more aggression for both genders. So the best answer is one that pairs the fish with the most aggressive behaviors. From Table 1, you learn that the medium male and large female would have about 32 aggressive behaviors between them. The large male and small female would have about 29 aggressive behaviors. So get rid of Choice (G). The other answers contain smaller males than Choice (G), so you can eliminate them as well. The answer is Choice (F).

REMEMBER

Don't overthink this question. You're choosing the best answer and are given only the number of aggressive behaviors and time spent in aggressive behaviors to evaluate. Between the two experiments, you see that the number of aggressive behaviors correlates directly with the number of minutes engaged in those behaviors. So the combination that produces the most aggressive behaviors has to be better than any other answer with a smaller number of behaviors.

11. **C.** Translate the data in the table for Experiment 2 to a bar graph. Table 1 shows the number of minutes spent in aggression. Bigger focal fish (smaller intruder fish) spent about the same amount of time as smaller focal fish (larger intruder fish) and less time than that for equal-sized focal fish and intruders, so pick the graph that best reflects this trend. The bottom labels on Choice (A) and (B) correspond with Table 1 instead of Table 2, so they have to be wrong.

Choice (D) is wrong because it shows lower bars for equal-sized intruders, which contradicts Table 2. The answer has to be Choice (C).

12. **F.** The question directs you to Researcher 1, so start there. Researcher 1's overall opinion on GMOs is positive, so Choice (J) is unlikely. Choice (G) doesn't describe benefits, so eliminate it. Choices (F) and (H) are benefits, but the researcher never says that GMOs increase nutritional values. The statement is that they haven't been shown to have fewer nutrients than organics, but that's not the same as having more nutritional value. Choice (F) is the best answer.

13. **B.** The first researcher is generally positive about GMOs and the second is generally negative, so they are unlikely to agree on much. Eliminate Choice (A) because both researchers say the opposite — decreasing pesticides is good for the environment. Researcher 2 states that the taste and quality of GMOs are inferior to organics, so Choice (C) is out. Researcher 1 mentions allergies, but Researcher 2 doesn't, so Choice (D) is wrong. Both researchers state that no correlation exists between health problems and GMOs, so the best answer is Choice (B).

14. **F.** Researcher 2 states directly that no correlation exists between health problems and GMOs, so Choice (J) is out. The first sentence of Researcher 2's paragraph states that pests become resistant to GMOs, but that doesn't necessarily mean that their use decreases naturally occurring pest reducers or increases the use of harmful pesticides. So Choices (G) and (H) are out, and by process of elimination, Choice (F) is correct. The last disadvantage mentioned by Researcher 2 is that plant pollen travels large distances, which means organic foods are contaminated by GMOs.

15. **D.** Choice (A) is mentioned by Researcher 2 but not Researcher 1. Choice (B) is mentioned by neither. And Researcher 1 specifically states that GMOs do not have reduced nutritional value. Eliminate Choices (A), (B), and (C). The first researcher mentions the possibility of increased allergies in the last sentence of the opinion. So the answer has to be Choice (D).

16. **F.** The second researcher mentions planting a variety of species, using natural repellants such as ladybugs, and increasing community farms as ways of reducing pesticides. Eliminate all answers but Choice (F). This researcher warns that GMOs can pollinate organic crops, so it's unlikely that he would advocate for growing some GMOs.

17. **C.** A link suggests a cause-and-effect relationship. Researcher 2 discusses the rise of community gardens as a possible way to reduce pesticide use and put less strain on food-producing corporations. Neither is necessarily linked to GMO use. Although the researcher states that pests become resistant to GMOs more quickly, he doesn't state that pesticide use increases as a result. The researcher isn't impressed with the food quality of GMOs, so the best answer is Choice (C).

18. **G.** Scan the options. The graphs show several relationships concerning GMOs and pesticide use, and you're supposed to choose the one that represents what Researcher 1 thinks. The first few sentences of Researcher 1's opinion indicate an inverse relationship between GMOs and pesticide use. As GMOs increase, pesticides decrease. So you can eliminate Choice (F). Choice (H) is out because Researcher 1 states that increased use of GMOs increases crop yields. Researcher 1 agrees that increased pesticide use creates increased harm to the environment, but so does Researcher 2, so Choice (J) is consistent with the opinions of both researchers. The best answer is Choice (G). Researcher 2 isn't convinced that GMOs directly cause a decrease in pesticide use because pests become resistant to GMO plants, which suggests that pesticides would eventually be necessary with GMOs as well.

19. **C.** An independent variable is an element that the experimenters change in the setup and execution of the experiment. The researchers tested both sandy and potting soil, so the type of soil is an independent variable. Eliminate Choice (B) because it doesn't contain I. Table 1 reveals that the researchers varied the number of hours of daily sunlight the plants received, so hours of sunlight is also an independent variable, so Choice (A) must be wrong. Plant height varied based on the design of the experiment, so it was a dependent variable. Choice (D) can't be right. The answer is Choice (C).

20. **J.** More daylight creates greater plant height, and potting soil or sandy soil with compost produces taller plants than sandy soil alone. The answer with potting soil and the most sunlight is Choice (J).

21. **C.** Look at the table and figure. The table records results from Experiment 2. The column headings are hours of sunlight, so you know that the light varied in that experiment. Eliminate Choices (A), (B), and (D). Choice (C) is the only answer that states the light was varied in Experiment 2.

22. **H.** The second experiment used sandy soil with compost. Experiment 1 indicates that potting soil and sandy soil with compost have similar results, so what's true for Experiment 2 will likely also be true for Experiment 3. The answer that says this best is Choice (H).

23. **A.** Read the information that follows the Yes and No in each answer. It's true that the ratio of pant height to daily number of hours decreased as researchers increased the number of hours, so keep Choice (A) in the running. But eliminate Choice (B) because the ratio decreased as the number of hours increased. For the same reason, keep Choice (C) and eliminate Choice (D). Now go back and read the question to determine whether the answer is *yes* or *no*. The conclusion is reasonable because the plant height would likely be close to 65 cm. The ratio of plant height to number of hours is decreasing as the number of hours increases. Pick Choice (A).

TIP

Approach "Yes, Yes, No, No" questions by evaluating the answers before you read the question. Usually you can eliminate answers before you even read the question. And reading the answers first shows you which information to focus on when you answer the question.

24. **J.** No experiment tested the relative effects of sunlight, soil type, or water on plant height, so you don't know which had a more significant effect. Therefore, Choices (G) and (H) are wrong. Choice (F) may appear correct, but the experiments didn't test water, so you don't know what amounts of water result in the greatest plant growth. Choice (J) is best because it is justified by the information in Figure 1 — plants grown in potting soil and sandy soil with compost grew to similar heights.

25. **D.** Focus on Figures 1 and 2 because they record results for Experiment 1. Figure 1 shows that the pH of the two types of ponds was similar, so Choices (A) and (C) are wrong. Figure 2 shows that healthy ponds had slightly higher temperatures, so Choice (B) is out. The answer is Choice (D).

26. **J.** The pH levels in the ponds were very similar, but the oxygen level in the healthy ponds was significantly higher. So there's no relationship between pH levels and oxygen levels. Pick Choice (J).

27. **A.** The introduction to Experiment 2 states that algae blooms may be caused by high levels of nitrogen. Based on Figure 3, the contaminated ponds had higher nitrogen levels, so they likely had more algae blooms. Choice (A) is best. Algae blooms aren't associated with water temperature, so Choices (B) and (D) can't be right, and Choice (C) isn't true. The healthy ponds had lower levels of nitrogen.

28. **G.** The pH of both types of ponds is the same, so the types of rocks are likely the same for both of them. Therefore, you can eliminate Choices (F) and (J). If the runoff has a pH lower than 7 but Figure 1 shows the pond water to have a pH around 7, the rocks in the pond may be neutralizing the acidity of the runoff. The question tells you that limestone contains bases and bases can neutralize acids, so the ponds are more likely to contain limestone-based rock. The granite wouldn't affect the pH. Choice (G) is a better answer than Choice (H).

29. **A.** The question doesn't concern water depth, so eliminate Choice (D). The contaminated ponds have less dissolved oxygen than the healthy ponds, so it's more likely their water is moving more slowly and the healthy pond water is moving more quickly. Choice (A) says it best.

30. **J.** The set-up information for Experiment 2 clearly states that the ponds tested in Experiment 2 were the same as those in Experiment 1 and that the measures were averages as in Experiment 1, so Choices (F) and (G) must be wrong. Only Experiment 2 tested for the amount of oxygen in the ponds, and oxygen is a gas, so the correct answer is Choice (J).

CHAPTER 20 Practice Exam: Answers and Explanations   315

31. C. Eliminate Choices (B) and (D) because their explanations are wrong. The average velocities of waves in the two oceans are the same, and the wavelengths of waves in the two oceans are different. Choice (A)'s explanation is correct: the Atlantic and Pacific Oceans have waves with similar average velocities and different average wavelengths, but similar velocities and different wavelengths wouldn't produce similar periods. The passage expresses the relationship between velocity (c) and period (T) as $c = \lambda / T$, so for the T to be the same for waves in both oceans, their wavelengths would also have to be the same. The correct answer is Choice (C).

32. H. Table 1 provides information on the tables, but no column provides the data for wave period. Above the table is an equation that solves for T: $T = 1/\nu$ and ν is frequency. The greatest wave period is the one with the lowest value in the denominator, so the answer is Choice (H). According to the table, the Gulf of Mexico has the shortest frequency and therefore, the greatest average wave period.

33. A. The table indicates an inverse relationship between wavelength values and frequency values: as wavelength increases, frequency decreases. A frequency of 0.0075 m/s is greater than the other frequencies, so the wavelength for this body of water must be less than 425 m. Pick Choice (A).

34. J. You know that amplitude is the distance from the centerline to the crest, but you don't know how to calculate amplitude from the data in the passage. Don't be afraid to pick Choice (J) and move on.

35. A. Because the relationship between wavelength and frequency is inverse, as wavelength increased, frequency decreased. Pick Choice (A).

36. J. Individual I's genotype is CS. Though the figure doesn't show the genotype CS for any individual, you can figure out that Individual II must also be CS. Their only option is to receive the C allele from one parent and the S allele from the other. Therefore, under incomplete dominance, they must have the same hair texture as Individual II. Individual II has wavy hair, so Individual I must also have wavy hair. Choose (J).

37. C. Because their parents have the genotypes CS and SS, Individual IV can be either CS or SS. Individual II is CS. Therefore, there's a 50% chance that Individual IV will have the same hair texture as Individual II. Choice (C) is correct.

38. F. You can eliminate Choices (H) and (J) because they're phenotypes rather than genotypes. All of the offspring of a curly haired individual (CC) and an individual with straight hair such as Individual III (SS) would have the genotype CS. Every child would get a C from the curly haired parent and an S from the parent with straight hair. Choose (F).

39. A. Individual III has the genotype of SS and therefore, doesn't carry the gene for curly hair. If Individual III has children with another individual who doesn't carry the gene for curly hair, there is a 0% chance their offspring will have curly hair, which is Choice (A).

40. J. Individual III has straight hair and therefore, has a genotype of SS. All offspring of individuals with the genotypes SS and CC have the genotype CS. Therefore, all six will have hair texture that is different than their parents'. Pick Choice (J)

Writing Test

If you wrote the optional essay for this test, check it over and make sure your essay contains these necessary features:

> **A clear position:** Did you take a stand and stick to it? Remember that which side you take isn't a big deal. How well you support your position makes or breaks your essay. You should take only a few seconds to choose which side to argue before you start writing.

> **A clear understanding of the complexity of the issue:** Top essays include a careful analysis of possible positions to weigh the pros and cons of all and arrive at the best possible solution.

> **A strong thesis:** Did you create a thesis that answers the question posed by the prompt and sets up your essay? Try to slip in some of the wording from the prompt. Make sure your thesis introduces the two or three main points you use to back up your stand on the issue.

> **A steady focus:** Every element of your essay should be about your thesis. Make sure you didn't stray off topic.

> **Good organization:** We know it sounds boring, but your essay must have an introduction, body, and conclusion. Make sure you devote each paragraph in the body to a discussion of one of your two or three main supporting points. Check out the hamburger organization plan that we outline in Chapter 17 to help you evaluate the organization of your essay.

> **Excellent examples:** Professional essay readers really love to see creative, descriptive examples that strengthen your points. Vivid details draw readers in and endear them to your writing prowess.

> **Clear and interesting writing:** Check your essay for sentence structure variety, precise word choice, and impeccable spelling, grammar, and punctuation.

Sample response

The issue of whether elderly drivers should be forced to retake driver's tests once they reach a certain age is indeed polarizing. Studies show that a driver's ability to drive safely diminishes once they reach a particular age, but some believe that forcing drivers to reapply is offensive and a form of age discrimination. Despite the potential for offense, requiring that drivers test after a certain age is necessary to maintain public safety.

Diminished vision and decreased reaction time are common effects of the aging process, and they are also common consequences of drinking and driving. No one argues that drinking and driving are dangerous, so why would we accept the same dangerous behaviors in our elderly population? Laws are enacted to ensure public safety. People shouldn't be able to drive while impaired, whether that impairment is from taking substances or advanced age.

Given the increased safety that mandatory testing would ensure, issues of age discrimination don't hold up. Simply put, some things require more attention as we age. Take a mammogram, for example. Most young women don't have them performed regularly because they aren't as likely to develop breast cancer as older women, but the procedure is a necessary step to ensure safety as women age. Discrimination is justified when the circumstances result in benefits. If forcing older populations to retest once they reach a certain age is age discrimination against the elderly, then allowing those over age 62 to receive social security benefits is discriminatory against those under 62. Allowing those over 21 to consume alcohol is not discriminatory to those who have yet to reach the age of 21. Some age discrimination is necessary when taking into consideration the different circumstances for different age groups.

People change as a result of the aging process. Creating laws that are appropriate for these changes to maintain safety is logical and justifies issues of age discrimination. Having elderly drivers reapply for driver's licenses is necessary to maximize safety and allow the greatest number of people to enjoy full, long, and healthy lives.

Score One for Your Side: Evaluating Your Test Results

The ACT scoring may be weird (Why is 36 the high score? Why not a 21 or a 49 or a 73?), but it's very straightforward. Follow these simple directions to evaluate your practice exam results:

1. **Count the number of correct responses in each of the practice tests — English, Mathematics, Reading, and Science (see the answer key at the end of the chapter).**

   Do NOT subtract any points for questions you missed or questions you didn't answer. Your score is based only on the number of questions you answered correctly. That number is called your *raw score*.

2. **The ACT then converts the raw score to a scaled score.**

   Each ACT has its own scale, but you can get a general idea of your scores for this practice test by finding the percentage of questions you answer correctly. As a reminder, you do that by dividing your raw score by the total number of questions in each section and multiplying by 100, as such:

   - For 95 percent and above, your scaled score will likely be in the 34–36 range.
   - For 90–95 percent, your scaled score will likely range between 31 and 34.
   - For 85–90 percent, your scaled score will likely range between 28 and 31.
   - For 75–85 percent, your scaled score will likely range between 23 and 28.
   - For 55–75 percent, your scaled score will likely range between 20 and 23.
   - For 55 percent and below, your scaled score will likely be 19 and below.

3. **To find your *composite score*, add your English, math, and reading scale scores and divide that sum by 3.**

   Fractional averages follow standard rules for rounding up or down to the nearest integer.

   For example, say that your scale scores were 24, 31, and 28; your composite score would be 83 ÷ 3 = 27.67 or 28.

English Test

1.	B	14.	J	27.	A	40.	H
2.	F	15.	A	28.	H	41.	A
3.	C	16.	H	29.	A	42.	G
4.	F	17.	A	30.	J	43.	A
5.	B	18.	G	31.	B	44.	H
6.	J	19.	C	32.	H	45.	D
7.	C	20.	J	33.	C	46.	J
8.	G	21.	B	34.	H	47.	C
9.	D	22.	F	35.	A	48.	F
10.	J	23.	B	36.	G	49.	B
11.	A	24.	J	37.	B	50.	H
12.	J	25.	C	38.	J		
13.	D	26.	J	39.	B		

Mathematics Test

1.	B	14.	H	27.	D	40.	G
2.	F	15.	A	28.	J	41.	D
3.	A	16.	H	29.	B	42.	J
4.	G	17.	D	30.	J	43.	C
5.	D	18.	J	31.	C	44.	G
6.	F	19.	A	32.	J	45.	C
7.	D	20.	J	33.	B		
8.	J	21.	A	34.	G		
9.	A	22.	G	35.	C		
10.	J	23.	C	36.	H		
11.	B	24.	J	37.	B		
12.	J	25.	B	38.	H		
13.	D	26.	F	39.	C		

CHAPTER 20 Practice Exam: Answers and Explanations

Reading Test

1.	C	10.	F	19.	A	28.	J
2.	F	11.	C	20.	J	29.	B
3.	B	12.	J	21.	C	30.	H
4.	H	13.	A	22.	J	31.	A
5.	A	14.	G	23.	B	32.	J
6.	H	15.	A	24.	H	33.	A
7.	A	16.	J	25.	A	34.	H
8.	J	17.	D	26.	H	35.	B
9.	D	18.	J	27.	B	36.	J

Science Test

1.	D	11.	C	21.	C	31.	C
2.	F	12.	F	22.	H	32.	H
3.	A	13.	B	23.	A	33.	A
4.	H	14.	F	24.	J	34.	J
5.	C	15.	D	25.	D	35.	A
6.	J	16.	F	26.	J	36.	J
7.	C	17.	C	27.	A	37.	C
8.	G	18.	G	28.	G	38.	F
9.	B	19.	C	29.	A	39.	A
10.	F	20.	J	30.	J	40.	J

The Part of Tens

IN THIS PART . . .

Bust ten common myths about the ACT.

Involve your parents with ten ways they can help you succeed on the ACT.

> **IN THIS CHAPTER**
> » Recognizing that not everything you hear is true
> » Finding out what's true and what isn't

Chapter 21
Ten Wrong Rumors about the ACT

They're whispered in the bathrooms and written in notes passed in the classroom. What are they? They're the vile and vicious rumors about the ACT — rumors that seem to grow with each telling. One of our jobs as test-preparation instructors is to reassure students and their parents that the latest rumors they've heard about the ACT are likely false. Here, we address ten of the rumors you may have heard. Quick hint: They're all wrong!

You Can't Study for the ACT

If you really believed this rumor, you wouldn't have bought this book (and we're really glad you did!). Of course, you can study for the ACT!

The ACT tests grammar; you can certainly refresh your memory of the grammar rules. The ACT tests algebra, geometry, and arithmetic; you can definitely study formulas and rules in those areas. In addition, a little preparation can make you very comfortable with the format and timing of the test, which reduces your test-taking anxiety and ultimately improves your score. This book, in particular, discusses tricks and traps that the test-takers build into the exam; by knowing what they are ahead of time, you can avoid falling into them on test day.

Different States Have Different ACTs

This rumor is based on the fact that the score sheet compares your performance to that of other students who have taken the ACT in your state. When you receive your ACT score, you find out your percentile rank nationally and within your state. However, all students in all states take the exact same ACT on any one test date. (Of course, the ACT changes from one date to the next;

otherwise, you could keep retaking the same test. You'd be surprised how many students don't realize this little nuance and merrily say to us, "Oh, I remember the questions from last time, so I'll do great next time.") If you take the ACT internationally, you do have different test questions from those on paper tests — and a different format. International tests are offered online, but most U.S. students take paper tests.

The ACT Has a Passing Score

The ACT has no such thing as a passing or failing score. By looking at the college websites of the schools you're interested in attending, you can get a pretty good idea of the score you need to get based on your GPA. If you have a high GPA, your ACT score can be lower than if you have a low GPA. In fact, you may be pleasantly surprised how low your ACT score can be. Scoring on the ACT isn't like scoring on high school exams, for which the 65th percentile is failing. If your score is in the 65th percentile on the ACT, you've actually done above average, better than 65 percent of the others who've taken the test.

The ACT Tests IQ

The ACT is a college entrance exam. It tests your potential for doing well in college. If you're the type who normally studies hard for an exam, you'll probably study hard for the ACT and do well on it, and then study hard for college exams and do well on them, too. The key is in the preparation. You have the same opportunity to do well on the ACT regardless of whether you're a Super-Brain or as cerebrally challenged as the rest of us. With this book, you find out how to improve your ACT scores with all sorts of tricks, tips, and techniques — something that's much harder to do on IQ exams.

You Should Never Guess on the ACT

Wrong, wrong, wrong. You should always guess on the ACT. This exam has no penalty for guessing. Never leave an answer blank. Fill in something, anything, on the chance that you may get lucky and get the question correct.

Random guessing on the ACT can only help you.

The ACT Is Adaptive Like the SAT

Although beginning in April 2025, the ACT shortened the test; the ACT didn't adopt a format that gives you different questions depending on how you respond to earlier questions. Every tester answers the same questions for each test administration regardless of how they perform on prior questions.

The ACT Is Easier Than the SAT

Maybe. Maybe not. The exams test similar subjects. Both have grammar, reading, and math questions. The ACT reading passages — both in the Reading Test and in the English Test — tend to be at a slightly easier reading level than the reading, writing, and language passages on the SAT. The math questions on the ACT are straightforward and all multiple-choice, with none of the grid-in questions featured on the SAT. However, the ACT does feature a few advanced math concepts that may not appear on the SAT.

TIP

The SAT and ACT present questions in slightly different ways, so we suggest that you practice taking both tests to see which one fits you better.

Selective Colleges Prefer the SAT to the ACT

All colleges accept both the ACT and SAT. It may be true that decades ago, the SAT was more popular on the two coasts, and the ACT flourished in the middle of the country, but the ACT has grown in popularity to the point that the number of students who take the ACT is about equal to those who take the SAT.

You Have to Write an Essay

Wrong. You don't have to write an essay during the ACT. It's optional, and the number of colleges that want to see an essay score has been decreasing over the years. Even so, to be sure your bases are covered, taking this portion of the test is a good idea, even though you probably don't want to.

You Have to Know A Lot about Science for the ACT

As of April 2025, the ACT Science Test is optional. You don't have to answer science questions to receive an ACT composite score. That being said, the ACT Science Test doesn't really test your science knowledge. It's primarily a test of how well you evaluate science charts and tables and how familiar you are with the scientific method. And you should always check with the colleges you're applying to. Just because the ACT doesn't make you take the Science Test doesn't mean that colleges won't require a science score from you. Additionally, if you're planning to pursue a STEM (science, technology, engineering, and mathematics) major, you should show off your abilities with a Science Test score.

IN THIS CHAPTER

» Discovering constructive ways to help your student prepare

» Pointing out your role the day of the test

Chapter 22
Ten (or So) Ways You Can Help Your Child Succeed on the ACT

As a parent, you may wonder what you can do to help your student study for the ACT. Well, wonder no longer! This chapter has ten specific steps for helping your child do their best.

Give Awesome Test-Prep Materials

If you bought this book, you did your child a huge favor. Reading this book and taking the full-length practice test in Chapter 19, as well as the tests online, give your child an edge over other juniors and seniors who haven't prepared. Nicely done!

Encourage Studying

Help your child work out a study schedule and give incentives to stick to it, such as picking out the family's dinner menu for one week or allotting more screen time.

Supply a Good Study Environment

Make sure your child has a quiet study area where they can concentrate without being disturbed by siblings, pets, friends, TV, cell phones, or the computer. Quality study time is time spent without distractions.

CHAPTER 22 Ten (or So) Ways You Can Help Your Child Succeed on the ACT   327

Take Practice Tests Together

You'll be better able to discuss the questions and answers with your child if you take the practice tests, too. Read through the answer explanation chapter (Chapter 20) together and discover which question types they may need to improve on. Then, look up those particular topics in earlier chapters for a refresher on the rules that govern them.

Model Good Grammar

Help your children recognize mistakes in English usage questions by speaking properly with them and *gently* correcting grammar mistakes in your conversations. Before you know it, they'll be correcting you!

Help Memorize Math Formulas

The online Cheat Sheet for this book has a list of tips your student needs to know for the math test; check it out at www.dummies.com and search for the ACT Cheat Sheet. Quiz them to make sure they remember them.

Encourage Reading

One of the best ways to improve reading scores is to actually read. Incorporate reading into your family's schedule and set up times to read short passages together and discuss their meanings.

Explore Colleges Together

Your child's ACT scores become more important to them when they realize what's at stake. Taking them to college fairs and campus visits can foster enthusiasm for college and make taking the ACT more relevant.

Arrive at the Test Site on Time

If the test site is unfamiliar to you, take a test drive before the exam date to make sure you don't get lost or encounter unexpected roadwork on the morning of the test. That day, make sure the alarm is properly set so they rise with plenty of time to get dressed, eat a healthy breakfast, and confirm they have the items they need to take with them to the exam.

Index

A

abbreviations, 42
absolute value, 73
ACT. *See also specific topics*
  about, 9–10
  compared with SAT, 324–325
  digital, 10
  guessing, 12, 324
  mistakes to avoid, 18–20
  repeating, 14–15
  scoring, 12–13
  special circumstances, 11–12
  subjects, 13–14, 38–39
  success on, 17–20
  test download, 1
  website, 22
  what not to take, 11
  what to take, 10–11
ACT Math Prep For Dummies (Zegarelli), 5
action verbs, 36, 230–231
acute angles, 96–97
adding, 75, 78–79, 88, 126–127
addition questions, 55
adjectives, 37
admission ticket, 10
admissions process, college, 325, 328
adverb phrases, 37–38
adverbs, 37–38
affect/effect, 58
algebra
  adding expressions, 88
  complex numbers, 125–126
  coordinate plane, 119–121, 130–139
  dividing expressions, 88–89
  evaluating graphs of functions, 137–139
  example questions, 133, 136–137
  extracting by factoring, 90–91
  FOIL method, 89–90
  functions, 129–130
  logarithms, 128–129
  matrices, 146–148
  multiplying expressions, 88–89
  outcomes, 142–145
  percent increase/decrease, 139–140
  permutations, 144–145
  probability, 140–142
  radicals, 126–128
  roots, 126–128
  sequences, 145–146
  solving for x in equations, 87–88
  solving simultaneous equations, 91–93
  subtracting expressions, 88
  variables, 86–87
Algebra I For Dummies (Sterling), 5
Algebra II For Dummies (Sterling), 5
algebraic expressions, 87
among/between, 58
amount/number, 58
amplitude, 120
analogy arguments, 227
angles, analyzing, 96–99
answer grid, making mistakes on, 19
answer keys, Practice Exam, 319–320
answer sheet, Practice Exam, 246–247
answers and explanations
  English Test, Practice Exam, 287–294
  Mathematics Test, Practice Exam 1, 295–305
  Reading Test, Practice Exam, 305–311
  Science Test, Practice Exam, 311–316
  Writing Test, Practice Exam, 317–318
apostrophes, 43
appositives, 42
approach, deciding on for Reading Test, 170–172
arc, of circles, 111
area, 101, 110
as...as, 58
asides, 42
as/like, 59
asymptote lines, 120, 136
averages, 84–85
axis of symmetry, 134

B

backsolving, 154–155
base, 82
better/best, 58
between/among, 58
big picture questions, 57, 174–175
books, at test-site, 11
breakdown, of Math Test, 149–150

C

calculator, 11
calculus, 10
Cartesian coordinate plane. *See* coordinate plane
categories, on English Test, 29–30
cause and effect, 56
cause-and-effect arguments, 227
cellphone, 11
central angle, of circles, 110
Cheat Sheet (website), 3
cheating, 20
chord, of circles, 110
circles, 109–114, 134
circumference, of circles, 110
classifying triangles, 99
clauses, 39, 41, 42
clothing, for test, 10
coefficient, 87
college admissions process, 325, 328
colons, 40, 47
commas, 40–42, 47–48
common difference, 145
common ratio, 145
common side ratios, 102–103
comparative passages, 178
comparing viewpoints, 203–204, 206
complementary angles, 97
complex numbers, 72, 125–126
composite numbers, 73–74
composite score, 12
compound inequality, 124
concentration, losing, 19
conclusions, 206–207, 230
conflicting viewpoints, 191–192
conflicting-viewpoints passages, 191–192
conjugated verb, 36
conjunctions, 38
constants, 86
contrast, 56
control, 196–197, 203
Conventions of Standard English (CSE), as category of English Test, 29
conversions, 76–77
coordinate geometry questions, 10
coordinate planes, 119–121, 130–133
coordinating conjunctions, 38
correlative conjunctions, 38
corresponding angles, 97–98
cosecant (csc), 116
cosine (cos), 116, 118
cotangent (cot), 116
counting principle, 143
creating smooth transitions, 56
csc (cosecant), 116
cube, volume of, 108
cylinder, volume of, 108

D

dashes, 42, 47
data-representation passages, 188–189
data-representation questions, 188–189
dates, 42
decimals, converting, 76–77
defending your perspective, 224
degree, of functions, 138
DELETE option, 32
deletion questions, 55
demonstrative pronouns, 37, 49
denominator, 77
dependent clauses, 39, 52
dependent variable, 196, 203
diagrams, reading, 194–195
diameter, of circles, 109–110
diction questions, 58–59
difference, 75
different from, 58
digital test, 10
direct statement questions, 175–176
directions, 10
distance formula, 132
distinctions, 42
distributive property, 75
dividing, 75, 77–78, 88–89, 127–128
domain, of functions, 137
double-checking, importance of, 20
Dummies (website), 3

E

editing, in Writing Test, 230–231
effect, cause and, 56
effect/affect, 58
either/or, 58
electronic devices, at test-site, 11
elementary algebra questions, 10
eliminating superfluous words, 54
ellipse, 134
encouraging reading, 328
English, 13
English Grammar For Dummies (Woods), 5
English Grammar Workbook For Dummies (Woods), 5
English Language Arts (ELA) Score, 13
English Test

    categories on, 29–30
    example questions, 31–32
    format, 30–32
    Practice Exam answer key, 319
    Practice Exam answers and explanations, 287–294
    Practice Exam questions, 248–256
    practice questions, 61–67
    traps on, 32–33
environment, for studying, 328
equation of a circle, 134
equation of a line, 132–133
equations, solving for x in, 87–88
equilateral triangle, 99
er/est, 58
errors, commonly tested, 45–58
essays, 222, 228–230, 239–242, 325
est/er, 5
even numbers, 75–76
example coordinate planes, 120–121
example essays, Writing Test, 233–238
Example icon, 3
example paragraphs, in essays, 228–229
example questions
    algebra, 133, 136–137, 144–145
    angles, 98–99
    backsolving, 154–155
    basic operations, 76
    circles, 112–114
    data-representation questions, 189
    English Test, 31–32
    equation of a line, 133
    exponents, 83
    extracting by factoring, 91
    functions, 129
    inequalities, 124–125
    Law of Cosines, 122
    Law of Sines, 122
    logarithms, 129
    percent increase/decrease, 140
    percentages, 80
    polygons, 109
    possessives, 50
    prime numbers and factorization, 74
    probability, 141–142
    proportions, 82
    punctuation, 46, 48
    quadrilaterals, 107
    radicals, 127–128
    ranges, 86
    Science Test, 189–190, 192, 195, 197–198, 199–202, 203–207
    solving for x in equations, 88
    solving simultaneous equations, 93
    triangles, 104
    trigonometric functions, 117, 122
    variables, 155
    word problems, 153
exception questions, 175–176
exponents, 82–83
expressions, 87, 88
exterior angle measure, of polygons, 107
extracting by factoring, 90–91
extrapolation, 201–202
extremum, 138
eyeglasses, at test-site, 11

F

factorial function, 143
factoring, extracting by, 90–91
factorization, 73–74
factors, 90
farther/further, 59
faulty reference, 49
fewer/less, 59
foci, 134
FOIL method, 89–90
formats, 30–32, 149–150, 176–177, 188–192
formulas, 131–133, 328
fractions, 76–79
functions, 115–117, 129–130, 137–139
further/farther, 59
future tense, 36

G

general form, 134
geometry
    angles, 96–99
    circles, 109–114
    line terms, 95–96
    polygons, 107
    quadrilaterals, 104–107
    triangles, 99–104
    volume, 108–109
Geometry For Dummies (Ryan), 5
good/well, 59
grammar and usage, 35–43, 328
graphing, 119–121, 133–135
graphs, reading, 194
greater than (>), 124
greater than or equal to (>=), 124
greatest common factor, 77
guessing, 12, 324

H

handwriting, in essays, 231
hook, in Writing Test, 224–225
horizontal line, 96
humanities, in Reading Test, 170
hyperbola, 136–137
hypotenuse, 102, 115

I

icons, explained, 3
if/whether, 59
imaginary numbers, 72, 125–126
imply/infer, 59
improper fraction, 79
independent clauses, 39
independent variable, 196, 203
inequalities, 123–125, 133–135
inference questions, 177
infer/imply, 59
infinitive, 36
inhaling deeply, as stress-buster, 17
initial analysis, in Science Test, 211
inscribed angle, of circles, 110–111
integers, 72
interior angle measure, of polygons, 107
intermediate algebra questions, 10
interpolation, 201–202
intersect, 96
introduction, in essays, 228
IQ, rumors about, 324
irrational numbers, 72
isosceles triangle, 99, 102–103

K

Knowledge of Language (KLA)
  addition questions, 55
  'big picture' questions, 57
  as category of English Test, 29
  deletion questions, 55
  eliminating superfluous words, 54
  mission questions, 54–55
  positioning questions, 57
  standard expressions, 57–59
  transitions, 56

L

Law of Cosines, 121–122
Law of Sines, 121–122
learning differences, 11–12
least/less, 59

least/not, 59
less than (<), 124
less than or equal to (<=), 124
less/fewer, 59
less/least, 59
like terms, 87
like/as, 59
line segments, 95
linear inequalities, graphing, 133–135
lines, 95–96, 132–133
linking verb, 36
literary narrative, in Reading Test, 169
local maximums, 138
local minimums, 138
logarithms, 128–129
losing concentration, 19

M

major axis, 134
many/much, 59
map, 10
mathematics, 13
Mathematics Test
  about, 71
  absolute value, 73
  algebra. *See* algebra
  approaching the, 150–152
  average, 84–85
  basic operations, 75–76
  breakdown, 149–150
  composite numbers, 73–74
  decimals, 76–77
  Do's and Don'ts, 156–157
  exponents, 82–83
  format, 149–150
  fractions, 77–79
  geometry. *See* geometry
  median, 85
  mode, 85
  number line, 73
  number types, 71–74
  order of operations, 83–84
  percentages, 76–77, 79–80
  Practice Exam answer key, 319
  Practice Exam answers and explanations, 295–305
  Practice Exam questions, 257–263
  practice questions, 159–165
  prime numbers, 73–74
  proportions, 81–82
  range, 86
  ratios, 80–81

timing tips, 153–156
trigonometry. *See* trigonometry
weighted averages, 85
what isn't on it, 10
word problems, 152–153
matrices, 146–148
medians, 85
memorizing math formulas, 328
midpoint, 95, 109
midpoint formula, 131–132
military duty, 12
minor axis, 134
misplaced modifiers, evaluating, 52–53
mission questions, 54–55
mistakes to avoid, 18–20
mixed numbers, 79
modes, 85
modifiers, 52–53
more/most, 59
most/more, 59
much/many, 59
multiplying, 75, 77–78, 88–89, 127–128

N

natural numbers, 72
natural sciences, in Reading Test, 170
'nearly means,' 177
negative integers, 72
negative numbers, 75–76
neither/nor, 58
NO CHANGE option, 32, 56
nonrestrictive clauses, 42
not equal to (≠), 124
notes, 11
not/least, 59
nouns, 37
number line, 73
number/amount, 58
numbers, 71–74. *See also* Mathematics Test
numerator, 77
numerical coefficient, 83

O

objective pronouns, 37
obtuse angles, 96–97
odd numbers, 75–76
operations, 75–76, 83–84
order of operations, 83–84
ordered pair, 131
organizing your essay, 228–230

origin, 131
outcomes, calculating, 142–145

P

panicking over time, 19
parabola, 134, 135
parallel line, 96
parallelism, evaluating, 52
parallelogram, 105
participle, 36
parts of speech, 36–38
passage structure questions, 176
passing score, rumors about, 324
past perfect tense, 36
past tense, 36
PEMDAS mnemonic, 83–84
pencils, 10
percent increase/decrease, 139–140
percentages, 76–77, 79–80
percentile score, 13
perimeter, 101, 107
period, 39, 46–47, 120
periodic functions, 117
permutations, 144–145
perpendicular line, 96
personal pronouns, 37, 49
photo ID, at test-site, 10
phrases, 38, 39
physical disabilities, 12
piecewise function, 138–139
place names, 42
plane geometry questions, 10
point of view questions, 177
polygons, 108–109
polynomials, 89
positioning questions, 57
positive integers, 72
positive numbers, 75–76
possessive pronouns, 37
possessives, 50
possible total, 80–81
Power of Writing (POW)
    addition questions, 55
    'big picture' questions, 57
    as category of English Test, 29
    deletion questions, 55
    eliminating superfluous words, 54
    mission questions, 54–55
    positioning questions, 57
    standard expressions, 57–59
    transitions, 56

Index   333

Practice Exam
　about, 245
　answer key, 319–320
　answer sheet, 246–247
　English Test, 248–256, 287–294, 319
　Mathematics Test, 257–263, 295–305, 319
　Reading Test, 264–272, 305–311, 320
　Science Test, 273–284, 311–316, 320
　scoring guide, 318
　Writing Test, 285, 317–318
practice questions
　English Test, 61–67
　Math Test, 159–165
　Reading Test, 179–184
　Science Test, 209–217
practice tests, importance of, 328
pre-algebra questions, 149
predicates, 38
prepositions, 38
present perfect tense, 36
present tense, 36
previewing passages, 170–171
prime factorization, 73–74
prime numbers, 73–74
probability, 140–142
probability questions, 150
procedure questions, 202–206
process of elimination (POE), practicing as stress-buster, 18
product, 75
Progress Toward Career Readiness Indicator, 13
prompt, in Writing Test, 222–223
pronouns, 37, 49–50
proofing, in Writing Test, 230–231
proportions, 81–82
proving yourself, 225–227
punctuation
　apostrophes, 43
　colons, 40
　commas, 40–42
　dashes, 42
　in essay, 231
　example questions, 46, 48
　periods, 39
　placement of, 45–48
　question marks, 39
　semicolons, 40
Pythagorean theorem, 102–104
Pythagorean triples, 102–103

Q

quadrant, 131
quadratic equations, graphing, 134
quadrilaterals, 104–107
question marks, 39
questions. *See also* example questions; practice questions
　addition, 55
　big picture, 57, 174–175
　coordinate geometry, 10
　data-representation, 188–189
　deletion, 55
　diction, 58–59
　direct statement, 175–176
　elementary algebra, 10
　English Test, Practice Exam, 248–256
　exception, 175–176
　inference, 177
　intermediate algebra, 10
　Mathematics Test, Practice Exam, 257–263
　mission, 54–55
　passage structure, 176
　plane geometry, 10
　point of view, 177
　positioning, 57
　pre-algebra, 149
　probability, 150
　procedure, 202–206
　Reading Test, Practice Exam, 264–272
　research-summary, 189–190
　result, 199–202
　Science Test, Practice Exam, 273–284
　on Science Test, 198–207, 211–217
　skimming, 153–154
　statistics, 150
　trigonometry, 10
　types of, 30–32, 169–170
　viewpoint, 206–207
　vocabulary-in-context, 176
　Writing Test, Practice Exam, 285
　"yes, yes, no, no," 31–32, 198
quotients, 75

R

radians, measuring in, 118–119
radicals, 126–128
radius, of circles, 109
ranges, 86, 138
ratio 3:4:5, 102
ratio 5:12:13, 102
rational numbers, 72

334　ACT Prep 2026/2027 For Dummies

ratios, 80–81, 102–103
reading, 13, 193–195, 328
Reading Test
    comparative passages, 178
    identifying question types, 174–177
    Practice Exam answer key, 320
    Practice Exam answers and explanations, 305–311
    Practice Exam questions, 264–272
    practice questions, 179–184
    question formats, 176–177
    question types, 169–170
    scoring, 170
    strategies for, 170–173
    timing, 170
real numbers, 72
reciprocal, 78
rectangle, 105
rectangular solid, volume of, 108
reflex angles, 97
reflexive pronouns, 37, 49
regular polygon, 107
relative pronouns, 37, 49–50
relieving stress, 17–18
religious obligations, 12
Remember icon, 3
repeating ACT, 14–15
replacing and with a comma, 41
research summaries, 189–190
research-summary questions, 189–190
restrictive clauses, 42
result questions, 199–202
rhombus, 105
right angles, 96–97
rise over run, 132
roots, 126–128, 138
rubbernecking, 19
rumors, 323–324
run-on sentence, 41
Ryan, Mark (author), 5

S

SAT, 1, 324–325
SAT Math Prep For Dummies (Zegarelli), 5
scaled score, 12
scalene triangle, 99
science, 14
Science Test
    about, 187, 325
    conflicting-viewpoints passages, 191–192
    data-representation questions, 188–189
    example questions, 189–190, 192, 195, 197–198, 199–202, 203–207

format, 188–192
Practice Exam answer key, 320
Practice Exam answers and explanations, 311–316
Practice Exam questions, 273–284
practice questions, 209–217
research-summary passages, 189–190
scoring, 12–13, 170, 222
scoring guide, Practice Exam, 318
scratch paper, 11
secant (sec), 116
sector, of circles, 111–112
semicolons, 40, 46–47
sentences, 38–39, 52–59
separation of clauses, using commas for, 41
sequences, 145–146
series, using commas for a, 41
similar triangles, 100–101
similarity, 56
simplifying fractions, 77
simultaneous equations, solving, 91–93
sine (sin), 115, 118
skimming, 153–154, 172–173
slope, 132
slope-intercept form, 132–133
social studies, in Reading Test, 170
solving
    polygons for volume, 108–109
    simultaneous equations, 91–93
    for x in equations, 87–88
special circumstances, 11–12
square, 104–105
square root, 126–128
standard expressions, 57–59
states, rumors about, 323–324
statistical arguments, 227
statistics questions, 150
STEM score, 12–13
Sterling, Mary Jane (author), 5
straight angles, 96–97
strategies, for Reading Test, 170–173
stress, relieving, 17–18
stretching, as stress-buster, 18
study plan, 21–25
studying, 5–6, 323, 327–328
subjective pronouns, 37
subjects, 13–14, 38
subordinating conjunctions, 38
subtracting, 75, 78–79, 88, 126–127
success, 17–20, 327–328
superfluous words, eliminating, 54
superscoring, 15, 21
supplementary angles, 97

Index 335

supporting conclusions, 206–207
symbols, 123–125, 129–130
symmetry, axis of, 134
system of equations. *See* simultaneous equations

T

tables, reading, 193
tangent (tan), 116
tenses, verb, 36, 51
term, 87
test site, arriving on time, 328
test-prep materials, 327
Thales's theorem, 111
thesis, in Writing Test, 222–223
thinking positive thoughts, as stress-buster, 18
time and timing, 19, 33, 153–156, 170
time-consuming questions, 33
Tip icon, 3
tips for success, 327–328
titles, 42
touch method, 230
transitions, 56, 229
transversal, 99
trapezoid, 106
traps, on Math Test, 10
triangles, 99–104
trigonometric functions, 117, 119–121
trigonometry
  coordinate planes, 119–121
  functions, 115–117
  Law of Cosines, 121–122
  Law of Sines, 121–122
  radians, 118–119
  unit circle, 117–118
trigonometry questions, 10

U

unclear reference, 49
underlined words, analyzing, 30–31
Understanding Complex Tests Indicator, 13
unit circle, 117–118
usage errors. *See* errors

V

variables, 86–87, 155, 196, 203
verbs, 36, 51, 230–231
vertex, 134
vertical angles, 97–98
vertical line, 96
viewpoint questions, 206–207

viewpoints, 191–192, 203–24, 206
vocabulary-in-context questions, 176
volume, solving polygons for, 108–109

W

Warning icon, 3
wasting time, 33
watch, 11
weakening conclusions, 206–207
weighted averages, 85
well/good, 59
whether/if, 59
whole numbers, 72
Woods, Geraldine (author), 5
word problems, 152–153
worrying, 20
worse/worst, 58
writing, 14
Writing Test
  about, 221
  defending your perspective, 224
  don'ts, 231–233
  editing, 230–231
  essay practice questions, 239–242
  example essays, 233–238
  hook, 224–225
  organizing your essay, 228–230
  Practice Exam answers and explanations, 317–318
  Practice Exam questions, 285
  prompt, 222–223
  proofing in, 230–231
  proving yourself, 225–227
  scoring essays, 222
  thesis, 222–223
  tips for, 221–238
Writing Test score, 13

X

x, solving for in equations, 87–88
x-axis, 131

Y

y-axis, 131
"yes, yes, no, no" questions, 31–32, 198
yourself, proving, 225–227

Z

Zegarelli, Mark (author), 5

About the Authors

Lisa Zimmer Hatch, MA, has helped teens and adults excel on standardized tests, gain admission to colleges of their choice, and secure rewarding professional careers since 1987. Along with her late husband, Scott A. Hatch, JD, she co-founded and administered award-winning standardized test-preparation and professional career courses for live college lectures, online forums, and other formats through more than 300 universities worldwide.

Lisa and Scott worked together to teach students internationally through live lectures, online forums, and independent study opportunities. They developed curricula for multiple formats, and their books have been translated for international markets. Together, they authored numerous law and standardized test-prep texts, including *GMAT For Dummies, LSAT For Dummies, 1,001 Practice Problems For Dummies, SAT II U.S. History For Dummies, SAT II Biology For Dummies, Catholic High School Entrance Exams For Dummies,* and *Paralegal Career For Dummies* (John Wiley & Sons, Inc.).

Lisa is currently an independent educational consultant and the president of College Primers, where she applies her expertise to guiding high school and college students through the testing, admissions, and financial aid processes. She is dedicated to helping students gain admission to the colleges or programs that best fit their goals, personalities, and finances. She graduated with honors in English from the University of Puget Sound, earned a master's degree in humanities with a literature emphasis from California State University, and completed the UCLA College Counseling Certificate Program. She is a member of the Higher Education Consultants Association (HECA), where she serves on the Professional Development Committee, and a member of the College Consultants of Colorado, where she served as president from 2024 to 2025.

Scott A. Hatch, JD (1952–2023), was a dedicated educator and author who helped thousands of students prepare for standardized tests and professional careers. He earned his undergraduate degree from the University of Colorado and his Juris Doctor from Southwestern University School of Law. He was listed in *Who's Who in California* and *Who's Who Among Students in American Colleges and Universities* and was named one of the *Outstanding Young Men of America* by the United States Junior Chamber (Jaycees). He also served as a contributing editor for the *Judicial Profiler* and *Colorado Law Annotated* and was the editor of several national award-winning publications. In addition to his test-prep work, Scott authored *A Legal Guide to Probate and Estate Planning* and *A Legal Guide to Family Law,* the inaugural texts in B & B Publications' *Learn the Law* series.

Dedication

We dedicate *ACT Prep 2026/2027 For Dummies with Online Practice* to our children and their families, whose patience, understanding, and support have meant the world to us. Lisa is also honored to dedicate this edition to Scott A. Hatch, whose passion for education, dedication to his students, and love of learning continue to inspire us.

Authors' Acknowledgments

This book wouldn't be possible without the contributions of Julia Brabant, Dr. Alison Hatch, Zachary Hatch, Zoe Hatch, Jennifer Seeley, Jackson Springer, Julia Brabant, and Hank Zimmer, who provided practice test material and helpful input. We also acknowledge the input of the thousands of students who've completed our test-preparation courses and tutorials over the last

40 years. The classroom and online contributions offered by these eager learners have provided us with lots of information about what areas require the greatest amount of preparation.

Our project organization and attempts at wit were greatly facilitated by the editing professionals at Wiley. Our thanks go out to Elizabeth Stillwell and Chad Sievers for their patience and guidance throughout the process and to technical editors Amy Nicklin and Ana Teodorescu for their helpful suggestions during the editing process.

Finally, we wish to thank our literary agent, Margo Maley Hutchinson, at Waterside Productions in Cardiff for her support and assistance and for introducing us to the innovative *For Dummies* series.

Publisher's Acknowledgments

Acquisitions Editor: Elizabeth Stillwell
Project Editor: Chad Sievers
Technical Editor: Amy Nicklin and Ana Teodorescu

Production Editor: Magesh Elangovan
Cover Image: © Camille Tokerud/Getty Images